Studia Fennica
Historica 17

The Finnish Literature Society was founded in 1831 and has from the very beginning engaged in publishing. It nowadays publishes literature in the fields of ethnology and folkloristics, linguistics, literary research and cultural history.

The first volume of Studia Fennica series appeared in 1933.

Since 1992 the series has been divided into three thematic subseries: Ethnologica, Folkloristica and Linguistica. Two additional subseries were formed in 2002, Historica and Litteraria. Subseries Anthropologica was formed in 2007.

In addition to its publishing activities the Finnish Literature Society maintains a folklore archive, a literature archive and a library.

Rhetorics of Nordic Democracy

Edited by Jussi Kurunmäki & Johan Strang

Finnish Literature Society • Helsinki

Studia Fennica Historica 17

The publication has undergone a peer review.

VERTAISARVIOITU
KOLLEGIALT GRANSKAD
PEER-REVIEWED
www.tsv.fi/tunnus

The open access publication of this volume has received part funding via
Helsinki University Library.

A digital edition of a printed book first published in 2010 by the Finnish Literature Society.
Cover Design: Timo Numminen
EPUB Conversion: eLibris Media Oy

ISBN 978-952-222-228-2 (Print)
ISBN 978-952-222-786-7 (PDF)
ISBN 978-952-222-785-0 (EPUB)

ISSN 0085-6835 (Studia Fennica)
ISSN 1458-526X (Studia Fennica Historica)

DOI: http://dx.doi.org/10.21435/sfh.17

Contents

Acknowledgements

This book has come a long way. In the early 2000s, when we conducted the joint project on the democratisation and welfare state in Finland and Sweden (funded by the Kone foundation), we noticed that it was, actually, quite difficult to write about Nordic democracy in general terms, if we wanted to be faithful to our methodological view that political concepts, not least democracy, gain their specific meanings in their particular contexts of use. It seemed to us that Nordic democracy could mean almost any positively evaluated thing associated with the Nordic countries and, at the same time, it meant almost nothing, precisely because it was used for so many things. Moreover, we also noticed that what had been discussed in terms of Nordic democracy was usually dealt with as a sum of societal practises and the functioning of political institutions in the Nordic countries, rather than as a question whether there was a particular *Nordic* understanding, or meaning, of democracy. What we wanted to do was to get away from such 'consequentalism' and get into an analysis of the way in which these concepts have been used.

Luckily, we were not alone with such an ambition. Nobert Götz and Peter Hallberg immediately shared our concern and helped us to formulate the framework of the enterprise that has now resulted in this book. We were also happy to be able to recruit people who had the special knowledge on topics that we thought were crucial to the task at hands and who, most importantly, shared our overall perspective on the history of politics. Thank you, dear friends, for your enduring interest and patience!

Yet, good intentions and skills seldom do the work alone. At the same time as we thank all our contributors for having 'delivered the goods' (Myrdal 1939) we also express our deep gratitude for the support that we have gained from the Centre for Nordic Studies (CENS) and the Nordic Centre of Excellence: 'The Nordic Welfare State – Historical Foundations and Future Challenges' (NordWel) at the University of Helsinki, as well as from our other university affiliations, the Department of Political Science at Stockholm University, and the Stein Rokkan Centre for Social Studies in Bergen. We want to thank especially Pauli Kettunen and Henrik Stenius for their inspiration during these years, and Kari Palonen and Drude Dahlerup as well as many other colleagues for their valuable comments. We also want to thank Tiina Saxman for her research in an initial phase of the project. Not least, we want to express our gratitude to the Finnish Literature Society for publishing this volume, and especially Aino Rajala for her invaluable copy-editing effort.

The book was planned and written under a period when we, the editors, have worked within projects financed by the Kone Foundation, NordForsk (NordWel), CENS, the Academy of Finland, and the Swedish Research Council.

Finally, we thank our families.

Stockholm and Bergen, 15 October, 2010

Jussi Kurunmäki & Johan Strang

JUSSI KURUNMÄKI AND JOHAN STRANG[1]

Introduction: 'Nordic Democracy' in a World of Tensions

Even the most universalistically oriented philosophical or theoretical accounts of democracy often discuss a number of paradigmatic cases. We are accustomed to learn that, while the Athenian democracy is the ancient birthplace, democracy has had a number of places and cultural contexts that have provided a range of different democratic models, perhaps also equally applicable in other places and times. There is French revolutionary democracy, the direct democracy of the Swiss cantons, American democracy as famously described by Tocqueville, and British parliamentarism. During the Cold War, the West and the East were coordinates of competing conceptions of democracy. Today, democracy is often discussed in terms of the challenges that globalisation and multiculturalism pose to it, the bottom line being that 'democracy' has become a general identity marker of the West. Much has been written about socio-economic and cultural backgrounds of democratic regimes as well as their institutional settings. By contrast, not much is known about the political manoeuvres and speech acts by which 'democracy' has been tied to particular regions and cultures in concrete historical situations. This book is about such manoeuvres. It explores a series of efforts to rhetorically produce and reproduce a particular Nordic version of democracy as an exemplary model.

In this book the conceptualisation of democracy in the Nordic countries is examined by focusing on the uses of the particular term 'Nordic democracy'. In other words, we study the different meanings that different historical actors have given to it in various circumstances. Our aim is to point out the specific debates and contexts in which the notion 'Nordic democracy' has been taken in use. We are particularly focused on rhetorical re-descriptions of the past, i.e. on the ways in which historical actors describe the past in a new manner, for example by redefining certain key concepts in order for them to serve certain particular political aims.[2] We regard this focus on rhetoric

---

1 Norbert Götz significantly contributed to the making of this chapter by discussing its several draft versions. His role was also important in the framing of the whole project. We wish to express our gratitude for his generosity.
2 See Skinner, Quentin (1996) *Reason and rhetoric in the philosophy of Hobbes*. Cambridge: Cambridge University Press, 139–145; Skinner, Quentin (2002) *Visions of Politics. Volume I: Regarding Method*. Cambridge: Cambridge University Press, 153, 182–187.

as compatible to the main ideas of conceptual history (*Begriffsgeschichte*), according to which the meaning of a concept is always potentially contested and likely to change when it is used in different contexts by actors with diverging political intentions.[3] The aim of this book is not to judge whether there actually exists a particular Nordic democratic tradition or a special Nordic form of democracy that could be said to characterise the histories and traditions of all the five different Nordic countries.[4] We are interested in the instrumentality and political function of the claim that there is such a thing as Nordic democracy.

This volume will show that the rhetorical figure 'Nordic democracy' was in the first place a product of the age of totalitarianism and the Cold War. It was used as an identity marker in 'a world of tensions'.[5] It was launched in the 1930s and used as an antidote against both ideological and geopolitical threats, which, naturally, often have been quite difficult to separate from each other. It has been used in order to demarcate Scandinavia and the Nordic countries as an island of democratic order and peaceful compromise in contrast to totalitarian and militaristic ideologies and regimes. However, the geopolitical considerations do not alone suffice to explain the emergence of this particular rhetoric and its identity-building role in the Nordic countries. More correct is to claim that the rhetoric of 'Nordic democracy' emerged as a result of the interplay between geopolitics and domestic political developments in the Nordic countries – the class compromises, the coalitions between the Social Democrats and the Agrarians, and the Social Democrats' turn from class-based rhetoric to a political language that increasingly drew on the concept of nation during the 1930s. It is no coincidence that the same mix of values that is characteristic of 'Nordic democracy' is also associated with the notion of the 'Nordic welfare state' (or the 'Nordic model'). Yet, while 'Nordic democracy' addresses an ideological level of political culture and political identity, the 'Nordic welfare state' is more likely to trigger a discussion of institutional solutions. Somewhat paradoxically therefore,

3 For an early programmatic outline of conceptual history, see Koselleck, Reinhart (1972) 'Einleitung'. In Otto Brunner, Werner Conze & Reinhart Koselleck (eds) *Geschichtliche Grundbegriffe. Historisches Lexikon zur politisch-sozialen Sprache in Deutschland,* vol. 1, Stuttgart: Ernst Klett, XIII–XXVII; see also Koselleck, Reinhart (2002) *The Practice of Conceptual History: Timing History, Spacing Concepts.* Stanford: Stanford University Press, 20–37. For a history of the concept of democracy in general, in particular in a German context, see Maier, Christian et al. (1972) 'Demokratie'. In Otto Brunner, Werner Conze and Reinhart Koselleck 1972, 821–899. On similarities between and compatible characters of a conceptual history analysis and rhetorical analysis, see Palonen, Kari (1999) 'Rhetorical and Temporal Perspectives on Conceptual Change'. *Finnish Yearbook of Political Thought,* Vol. 3, 41–59; see also Skinner 2002, 175–187.
4 As Pauli Kettunen notes, 'Nordic democracy', 'Nordic model' as well as 'Nordic society' all refer to five separate national institutions despite the attribute 'Nordic'. Kettunen, Pauli (2005) 'The Power of International Comparison – A Perspective on the Making and Challenging of the Nordic Welfare State'. In Niels Finn Christiansen, Klaus Petersen, Nils Edling, Per Haave (eds) *The Nordic Model of Welfare – a Historical Reappraisal,* Copenhagen: Museum Tusculanum Press, 52.
5 This phrase is borrowed from: McKeon, Richard & Rokkan, Stein (eds) (1951) *Democracy in a World of Tensions. A Symposium prepared by UNESCO.* Paris: UNESCO.

the 'Nordic welfare state' gained much attention abroad, while 'Nordic democracy', despite frequent attempts of international promotion, remained a domestic or intra-Nordic concept with little international resonance.[6] But without the idea of Nordic democracy the Nordic welfare states would look quite different from what they have become. This book will provide an important means of acknowledging the ideological and geopolitical context in which the 'Nordic welfare state' was conceptualised and canonised, a context that is often overlooked in studies preoccupied with domestic policy measures. It will also show the ways in which 'Nordic democracy' was used to provide the welfare politics with cultural and historical legitimacy and foundations.

$$* \quad * \quad *$$

The structure of the book is the following: In this introductory chapter, we will present the literature in which the very expression 'Nordic democracy' has been explicitly highlighted, i.e. a number of publications which can be taken as cornerstones in the promotion of the idea of Nordic democracy from the mid-1930s to the early 21st century. The first chapter thus aims at giving an analysis of its own while adding to it some remarks concerning the findings of the more in-depth investigations of this volume.

The case studies start off in the context of the crisis of democracy in the 1930s and 1940s. In the second chapter JUSSI KURUNMÄKI focuses on the first wave of the rhetoric of Nordic democracy in Sweden and Finland, which is analysed against the background of a changed geopolitical situation in Europe and as a part of political struggles concerning the concept of democracy. The chapter recapitulates with a discussion on national aspects of the rhetoric of Nordic democracy and the significance of this rhetoric for the general acceptability of democracy in the middle of the thirties. In the third chapter JOHAN STRANG widens the political and historical anchorage of the rhetoric of Nordic democracy by adding a philosophical one to it. Strang relates the emergent use of 'Nordic democracy' in the 1930s and 1940s to the theoretical defence of democracy that a number of central Scandinavian

---

6   Robert A. Dahl's works on democracy may be an exception in this regard. We discuss his view of democracy in the Nordic countries later in this chapter. However, for example, David Held makes no notion of Nordic democracy. Instead, the Swedish system is shortly discussed in terms of 'broad corporatist arrangements' and 'tripartite relations'. See Held, David (1996) *Models of Democracy. Second Edition.* Cambridge: Polity Press, 230. In Arend Lijphart's well-known classification, the main categories are 'the Westminster model of democracy' and 'the consensual model of democracy'. In this typology, Sweden and Norway are placed in-between the majority and consensual models, and Denmark, Finland and Iceland in the group of consensual systems. See Lijphart, Arend (1984) *Democracies: Patterns of Majoritarian and Consensus Government in Twenty-One Countries.* New Haven and London: Yale University Press, 215–222. In his theory of state formation and nation-building, Stein Rokkan often discussed the Scandinavian counties as forming a separate category. Nevertheless, he did not make any notion of 'Nordic democracy'. See Peter Flora with Stein Kuhnle and Derek Urwin (eds) (1999) *State Formation, Nation-Building, and Mass Politics in Europe: The Theory of Stein Rokkan. Based on his collected works.* Oxford: Oxford University Press, passim.

intellectuals and philosophers committed themselves to during the crisis of democracy, arguing that ultimately the defence often relied upon cultural arguments, and thus these intellectuals contributed to and utilised the rhetoric of Nordic democracy.

In chapter four, CARL MARKLUND turns the attention from how the idea of Nordic democracy was shaped in the Nordic countries to an outside perspective by examining the interest shown by American scholars and politicians for the Nordic experiment in the 1930s. Seen from the perspective of the American crisis of democracy, Marklund argues, the Nordic countries, and in particular Sweden, were viewed not so much as exceptional in their commitment to political democracy but, rather, in their practice of 'industrial democracy' and 'economic democracy'. Now, if the Second World War figured behind some of the discussions on crisis analysed by Strang and Marklund, chapter five is very much centred upon the wartime rhetoric of Nordic democracy. In this chapter, JAN HECKER-STAMPEHL looks at how the Nordic Associations (*Föreningarna Norden*) built their rhetoric to a considerable degree on references made to the Nordic tradition of freedom and democracy in order to keep up the Nordic democratic morale during the Second World War. 'Nordic democracy' served both as a moral bulwark against the foreign threats but also as a basis on which the post-war cooperation between the countries could be built.

The book will then proceed with three chapters that probe deeper into the historical dimensions of 'Nordic democracy'. In chapter six JEPPE NEVERS looks at how the Danish socialists in the period from the late nineteenth century until the 1930s overcame their disinclination and gradually embraced democracy and turned it into one of their favourite key concepts. In chapter seven, RUTH HEMSTAD analyses how the failure of nineteenth century Scandinavianism was repressed or selectively remembered when the labour movement launched the ideas of 'labour Scandinavianism' and 'Nordic democracy' during the 1930s. Hemstad also pays attention to the narrative of Nordic cooperation as pictured in the main literature of Nordic democracy, showing, for example, how the union conflict between Sweden and Norway in 1905 has been overlooked. Turning again our attention to an outside perspective, PETER STADIUS shows in chapter eight how the Nordic countries already at the turn of the nineteenth century were portrayed in Spain as a democratic heaven, but also as something of a modernistic threat. His analysis also pays attention to the role that the equal voting rights that were granted for women in Finland in 1906 played in the formation of the image of democratic culture in the North.

Chapter nine takes an insight into political language during an era that has been referred to in support of the idea that there is a specific Nordic – or Swedish – tradition of democracy. In his examination of the radical rhetoric of the Swedish Age of Liberty (1719–1792) PETER HALLBERG shows how history was consciously reinterpreted in ways which served particular political purposes in the context of the struggle over the estate privileges between the Nobility and the non-Noble estates. Hallberg points out that, while it remains true that 'Nordic democracy' was not used in the material analysed in the chapter, there was nevertheless a notion of a particular 'democratic spirit' in the reformist rhetoric that was closely connected to values like transparency, popular participation, and above all to liberty as non-domination, which were regarded as basing on an ancient tradition that was unique to the Nordic countries.

The closing chapters will then examine how the historical and cultural dimensions attached to 'Nordic democracy' were used in the Cold War context during the latter half of the twentieth century. In chapter ten PETRI KOIKKALAINEN analyses how Finnish politicians and intellectuals tried to navigate in a polarised world by making effective use of Finland's Nordic democratic heritage. 'Nordic democracy' signified not only a neutral island between the blocks, but also a third way between capitalism and socialism. This brings Koikkalainen to the so-called convergence-theories, popular in Finland during the 1960s, according to which the opposing ideologies of communism and capitalism would slowly become de-ideologised and eventually converge into each other. In chapter eleven, NORBERT GÖTZ considers the role that the democratic self-image of Nordic countries had in the discussions on the practise of sending parliamentary representatives to the General Assembly of the United Nations.[7] He shows how this practise was seen, mostly by the Nordics themselves, not only as a characteristic, historically and culturally anchored feature of the Nordic democracies, but also as a model for other countries to follow. However, his analysis also shows that the very figure 'Nordic democracy' was used quite occasionally in the researched material. When explicit in use, 'Nordic democracy' was most often involved in critical situations of political or diplomatic crisis.

* * *

'After the Nazi takeover, the Nordic democracy [*det nordiske folkestyre*] has discovered what it is like to have a Dictatorship as a neighbour.' This is how the Danish social democratic intellectual Hartvig Frisch opened his book *Pest over Europa – Bolschevisme, Fascisme og Nazisme* (Plague over Europe – Bolshevism, Fascism and Nazism) (1933).[8] According to Frisch, it was time for the Nordics to show that there is strength in the Nordic democracy (*det nordiske Demokrati*). For him, the political democracy and parliamentarism created by the Nordic peasants was the foundation on which the labour movement had been able to build a '*social democracy*'.[9]

This link between the legacy of peasant freedom, existing parliamentary institutions, and the current social democratic agenda of the labour movement in the context of the rise of totalitarianism was also characteristic of the most notable event in the promotion of the concept of 'Nordic democracy':

---

7 See e.g. Götz, Norbert (2008) '"Blue-eyed Angels"' at the League of Nations: The Genevese Construction of Norden'. In Norbert Götz and Heidi Haggrén (eds) *Regional Cooperation and International Organizations: The Nordic Model in Transnational Alignment*. London: Routledge, 25–46.

8 Frisch, Hartvig (1933) *Pest over Europa – Bolschevisme, Fascisme og Nazisme*. Copenhagen: Henrik Koppels Forlag, 5.

9 Frisch 1933, 9 (emphasis in original).

the celebration of the 'Day of Nordic Democracy' in Malmö in August 1935 by the Swedish Social Democratic Youth and the Socialist Youth International.[10] Although our findings indicate that the rhetoric of 'Nordic democracy' was not exclusively an invention of the Social Democrats' party headquarters, as discussed by KURUNMÄKI in chapter two, there is no doubt that there was a clear intention to make 'Nordic democracy' a party brand.[11] Per Albin Hansson, the Swedish Prime Minister and leader of the Labour Party (the Social Democrats) boldly argued that Norden should become a mighty agitator against dictatorship and a model for other countries.[12] The rhetoric of Nordic democracy was more than just a principled statement against totalitarianisms, for it was also a tool by which the Social Democrats established themselves as a party that was a respectful bearer of national and Nordic cultural and historical heritage. The promotion of 'Nordic democracy' can be seen as one of the rhetorical 'moves'[13] by which social democracy de-radicalised its own societal vision while simultaneously aiming at improving the prevailing bourgeois conception of democracy by adding an egalitarian societal and economic dimension to it.

These re-profiling efforts of the Social Democrats gained positive attention abroad. The single most important person from outside *Norden* to promote the idea of Nordic democracy was the American journalist Marquis W. Childs. To be sure, Childs picked up the very formula 'Nordic democracy' only once, in an article in which he claimed having found 'evidence of the underlying vitality of this "Northern democracy"' in Sweden.[14] However, in the 1930s he published a series of works presenting a highly favourable picture of Scandinavian political and social life, including the condition of democracy in the North. The foundation was laid in Childs' 1934 booklet *Sweden: Where Capitalism Is Controlled*, which was a eulogy of the virtuous consequences of consumer cooperatives, social democratic reform policy and planned economy.[15] The book *Sweden: The Middle Way* was published

10 Four speeches held on the occasion by leading social democratic politicians from Denmark, Finland, Norway and Sweden (H. P. Hansen, Väinö Tanner, Johan Nygaardsvold, and Per Albin Hansson) were published in *Fyra tal om Nordisk Demokrati* (1935). Stockholm: Frihets förlag.

11 There were other occasions that were named 'the Day of Nordic Democracy' after the festival in Malmö, of which one was held in Turku, Finland, in 1938. See Majander, Mikko (2004) *Pohjoismaa vai kansandemokratia? Sosiaalidemokraatit, kommunistit ja Suomen kansainvälinen asema 1944–51*. Helsinki: Suomalaisen Kirjallisuuden Seura, 56–57. Moreover, the Nordic Cooperation Committee of the Labour Movement granted, in 1939, the Nordic social democratic youth organisations the right to decide which events could be called 'the Day of Nordic Democracy'. See Wahlbäck, Krister and Blidberg, Kersti (1986) *Samråd i kristid: Protokoll från den Nordiska Arbetarrörelsens Samarbetskommitté 1932–1946*. Stockholm: Kungl. Samfundet för utgivandet av handskrifter rörande Skandinaviens historia, 188.

12 *Fyra tal om nordisk demokrati* 1935, 5, 11.

13 On rhetorical moves in argument, see Skinner 2002, 115.

14 Childs, Marquis W. (1937/38) 'Sweden Revisited'. *Yale Review* N.S. 27/1, 30–44, at 35. It should be noted that 'Northern' was a common translation to English of the Scandinavian term 'nordisk' in the 1930s.

15 Childs, Marquis W. (1934) *Sweden: Where Capitalism Is Controlled*. New York: The John Day Company.

in 1936 and portrayed the Swedish labour movement as willing and able to compromise and to make gradual reforms, rendering the political culture of the country immune to the extremes of fascism, communism, and liberal capitalism. Childs credited the Social Democrats for having strengthened the basis on which democratic government rested in the country.[16] Two years later, he spelled out the message even further in the book *This Is Democracy: Collective Bargaining in Scandinavia*.[17] As the straightforward title suggests, there was an evident model-building intention behind it, although, as MARKLUND shows in this volume, the exemplary character of these countries dealt more with 'industrial democracy' than with 'political democracy'.

Childs was by no means the only person outside of the Nordic countries to acknowledge and promote the new orientation of the Scandinavian labour movement. A favourable presentation of Swedish (and to some extent Scandinavian) politics can also be found, for example, in the volume *Democratic Sweden,* produced by The New Fabian Research Bureau in 1938. The book was aimed at a British labour audience and it pictured Swedish politics in bright light, despite pointing out its class character. Although there was clearly sympathy for a revolutionary change in this account, the book described Sweden as a country in which the prospects of peaceful transition to socialism were favourable.[18] It was stated, by quoting P. A. Hansson, that 'Socialism and Bourgeois Democracy in the Northern countries of Europe have never come into hopeless opposition to each other; the Bourgeois democrats have not allowed themselves to be driven by fear of socialism from their democratic ideal and the Social Democrats have not, for fear of contamination, fled from bourgeois democracy. Instead the former were able to unite on the solution of the democratic tasks which are common to them'.[19]

The social democratic compromise politics as well as inherited cultural conditions were credited also in Ernest Darwin Simon's book *The Smaller Democracies* (1939), in which the British liberal politician discussed the 'Scandinavian achievement'. According to him, the Scandinavian countries were the only countries in Europe which became steadily more democratic and more prosperous after the World War. The social democratic governments had shown good leadership, moderation and good sense.[20] Simon also pointed out the recent good shape of Scandinavian democracy

16 Childs, Marquis W. (1936) *Sweden: The Middle Way*. New Haven: Yale University Press, 119, 164–165.
17 Childs, Marquis W. (1938) *This Is Democracy: Collective Bargaining in Scandinavia*. New Haven: Yale University Press.
18 Greaves, H. R. G. and C. P. Mayhew (1938) 'Constitution'. In Cole, Margaret and Charles Smith (eds) *Democratic Sweden: A Volume of Studies prepared by Members of the New Fabian Research Bureau*. London: Routledge, 25.
19 Greaves and Mayhew 1938, 24–25. The quotation was fetched from the speech Hansson had given on Nordic democracy in Copenhagen in 1935. See Hansson, P. Albin (1935) *Demokrati*. Stockholm: Tidens Förlag, 219-220.
20 Simon, Ernest Darwin (1939) *The Smaller Democracies*. London: Victor Gollancz, 174–175.

by emphasising its *longue durée*. Thus, he held that '[p]eace and security and a tradition of local independence have certainly contributed much to laying the foundations of Scandinavian democracy'.[21]

The social democratic middle way position was received in progressive quarters as compatible with the intentions of the 'American way' as it was understood in the New Deal period.[22] Gunnar Myrdal, the Swedish economist and social scientist, who at the time was in the United States writing his *An American Dilemma* which gave him international reputation, contributed to this opinion building by presenting the case of successful defence of democracy in the Nordic countries in two articles published in the progressive American journal *Survey Graphic* in 1939. Myrdal explained to the Americans that the Nordic countries were too small to maintain an external defence which would make them safe in a military sense, and that the only way they could defend democracy was by making the population immune to communist and Nazi propaganda. This, in turn, was something that the social democratic governments of the Nordic countries had accomplished through a skilful economic and social policy that 'delivered the goods', Myrdal argued.[23]

Myrdal was to some extent drawing on another Swedish scholar whose name was also to become internationally known. The political scientist Herbert Tingsten, the foremost specialist on political ideologies in Sweden and known outside his home country due to a path-breaking study on political behaviour,[24] had in 1938 published an article, titled plainly 'Nordisk demokrati', that can be regarded as the first explicit scholarly contribution to the rhetoric of Nordic democracy. As JAN HECKER-STAMPEHL shows in this volume, Tingsten argued that the reason why it was meaningful to speak about Nordic democracy was that there was a Nordic community that shared the same democratic values, which had their origin in the heritage of rule of law and primordial Scandinavianism. According to Tingsten, the Nordic countries formed the finest example of how a successful democratic order was possible to achieve and sustain. In other words, these countries witnessed of the efficiency and adaptability of a democratic system.[25] As a matter of fact, Tingsten was recycling the idea he had formulated in his *Demokratins seger och kris* (Democracy's Victory and Crisis) in 1933, according to which the crisis of democracy was a consequence of the decline of shared values.[26]

21 Simon 1939, 184–185.

22 Ruth, Arne (1984) 'The Second New Nation: The Mythology of Modern Sweden'. *Daedalus*, Vol. 113, No. 2, 53–96, at 56.

23 Myrdal, Gunnar (1939) *Maintaining Democracy in Sweden, I. With Dictators as Neighbors, II. The Defences of Democracy*. A Bonnier reprint from *Survey Graphic – Magazine of Social Interpretation*, May–June, 4.

24 Tingsten, Herbert (1937) *Political Behaviour – Studies in Election Statistics*. London: P. S. King & Son.

25 Tingsten, Herbert (1938) 'Nordisk demokrati'. *Nordens kalender*, Vol. 9, 41–50.

26 Tingsten, Herbert (1933) *Demokratins seger och kris. Vår egen tids historia 1880–1930*. Utgiven av Yngve Lorents. Stockholm: Albert Bonniers Förlag, 22, 60–61.

In the aftermath of the Second World War, the concept of democracy was intensively discussed everywhere. A couple of decades after its celebrated breakthrough, democracy had managed to outlive its most severe crisis. As it was commonly held, democracy had established itself as the most powerful political system, both morally and militarily. Democracy was univocally supported, and sometimes interpreted as an 'over-ideology', underneath which a variety of practical implementations were feasible. This is what Tingsten suggested in his book *Demokratiens problem* (The Problem of Democracy) in 1945.[27] Tingsten's attempt at de-ideologising democracy by placing it above everyday politics was one of many rhetorical moves in the political struggle over the meaning of the concept of democracy during the immediate post-war era. As it was, the victorious powers of the Second World War were divided into two camps, both claiming to represent true democracy and denying the legitimacy of the other. The UNESCO report *Democracy in a World of Tensions* (1951) profoundly illustrates both the ambitions and the impossibility of finding a common ground for understanding democracy.[28]

It is in such a context of a 'world of tensions' that the second wave of literature on Nordic democracy or Scandinavian democracy, emerging in the 1940s and 1950s, should be understood. The notion of Nordic democracy not only survived the transformation of the international context, the emerging polarisation of the Cold War actually provided it with increased weight, particularly regarding the middle way associations. Simultaneously, the partisan social democratic use of 'Nordic democracy' of the mid-thirties was largely deserted, and the concept was now used beyond party lines in order to signify features of the Nordic countries as wholes. It is possible to view this as a sign of the augmented and transformed position of the Social Democrats in the Nordic countries. In other words, the Social Democrats had succeeded in establishing the party and the labour movement as respectful bearers of the national heritage, and the Nordic countries – save Finland and Iceland – had been social democratised to a considerable degree. Moreover, the new international context made it possible for the Social Democrats to more strongly than before present their partisan standpoint as a national destiny.

In the preface to the volume *Nordisk Demokrati* (1949) the two Danish editors Hal Koch and Alf Ross noted that '[t]he war was barely over before it stood overwhelmingly clear that there existed no common understanding of the meaning of democracy'.[29] The explicitly stated purpose of the

---

27 Tingsten, Herbert (1945) *Demokratiens problem*. Stockholm: Norstedts.
28 The enterprise was an ambitious study of the idea of democracy, based on an enquiry that was sent to more than five hundred experts in the fields of philosophy, law, history, political science, sociology, economics, communications analysis, and logic. The turnover was about one fourth of the total. The questionnaire was conducted and analysed by two Norwegian scholars, Arne Næss and Stein Rokkan, who gained international reputation in the study of democracy during the Cold War era. See McKeon & Rokkan 1951.
29 Koch, Hal & Ross, Alf (eds) (1949) *Nordisk demokrati*. Oslo: Halvorsen & Larsen, Stockholm: Natur och Kultur, København: Westermann, XIV (our translation).

book was to show to the world that somewhere between New York and Moscow there was a Nordic area where a superior and more harmonious form of political and social life had grown out of the experiences of the peoples themselves. In his own contribution to the book Ross followed Tingsten in his attempt to de-politicise democracy and to stress its formal and procedural aspects. According to Ross, who had established himself as a democracy theoretician through his book *Hvorfor Demokrati?* (Why Democracy?) in 1946, democracy was characterised primarily by the majority principle, while capitalism and socialism represented different economical policies applicable under both democratic and totalitarian rule.[30] But there was, as STRANG notes in his chapter, a political purpose with this attempt to de-ideologise democracy. It was a conscious move in 'the Great Danish Democracy Debate' and directed primarily at what Ross conceived of as communist attempts at colonising the concept. However, it was also a criticism of the liberal conception of democracy, according to which there were indisputable individual rights that social reforms were likely to violate. At a time when liberal critics such as F. A. Hayek were arguing that planned economy was *The Road to Serfdom* (1944), Ross gave a theoretical motivation for his own political conviction by proving that socialism and democracy were indeed compatible.[31]

The other editor of *Nordisk demokrati*, the theologian Hal Koch, had a different conceptualisation of democracy. Drawing on the famous Danish nineteenth-century educationalist N. F. S. Grundtvig (1783–1872), Koch emphasised enlightened discussion and education as the main features of 'the democratic way of life'.[32] To be sure, Koch and Ross have often been presented as the main combatants of the Danish democracy debate, but in this particular historical context they had a common motive: to resist communism by defending a social democratic interpretation of democracy. By using 'Nordic democracy' they were able to give national, cultural and historical legitimacy to their own account. Moreover, by the anthology *Nordisk Demokrati* they were able to gather Scandinavian support for their cause as they brought together an impressive number of distinguished Danish, Norwegian and Swedish scholars and politicians in order to present and defend the idea of a specific Nordic type of democracy, more successful – and ultimately more democratic – than other political systems of the East and the West. According to K. K. Steincke, the former Social Democratic Social Minister and Minister of Justice of Denmark, who was handed the job to write an epilogue to the volume, it was 'not the Nordic countries that should learn from the East or the West, but Russia and America that *could* learn from the Nordic democracies; the champions of peace, freedom and social politics in a chaotic and mentally deranged world'.[33] It was also the

---

30 Ross, Alf (1946) *Hvorfor Demokrati?*. København: Munksgaard. Translated to English as *Why Democracy?* Cambridge, Massachusetts: Harvard University Press, 1952.

31 Hayek, F. A. (1944) *The Road to Serfdom*. Chicago: University of Chicago Press.

32 Koch, Hal (1945) *Hvad er Demokrati?*. København: Gyldendal.

33 Steincke, K. K. (1949) 'Mellem Øst og Vest'. In Koch & Ross 1949, 432–458, at 458 (our translation), emphasis in original.

explicit wish of the editors that the volume would soon be published in English, so that the world could be informed about the 'democracy of the middle' that successfully combined the political freedom of the West with the ideals of economic and social levelling of the East.[34]

When the volume was finally remade into English under the title *Scandinavian Democracy: Development of Democratic Thought & Institutions in Denmark, Norway and Sweden* in 1958,[35] the message of the social democratic middle way reformism and class compromise had already been presented to an international audience by the Scandinavian-American anthology *Scandinavia: Between East and West* (1950).[36] As the editor of the book, Henning Friis,[37] put it, the book was 'based on the conception that Scandinavian culture is a distinctive culture somewhere between that of free-enterprise democracy in the United States and that of the Communist dictatorship in Soviet Russia'.[38] It is noteworthy that both English-language anthologies were supported by *The American–Scandinavian Foundation*. Despite the repeated emphasises on 'the middle way'[39] and the mapping of the Scandinavian countries in-between the blocs, Scandinavia was evidently regarded as nonetheless belonging to the Western hemisphere. Indeed, the editor of *Scandinavian Democracy*, J. A. Lauwerys, a University of London professor, stated that the purpose of the book was to present 'an account of the special manner in which the democratic principles upon which Western society is founded operate in Scandinavian countries'.[40] Lithgow Osborne, President of the American-Scandinavian Foundation, held in his foreword to *Scandinavia: Between East and West* that 'Scandinavian socialists are also democrats' and that he believed that they did not have 'the slightest intention of betraying their guarantees of the rights of the individual'.[41]

Despite the fact that these mid-twentieth-century volumes on Scandinavian or Nordic democracy were supported by some Western scholars like Lauwerys and by the Foundation based in New York, we cannot escape the self-applauding nature of the enterprise. It was not left unnoticed by the contemporaries either. In one of the most prominent forums of academic

34 Koch & Ross 1949, XV.
35 Lauwerys, J. A: (ed.) (1958) *Scandinavian Democracy. Development of Democratic Thought & Institutions in Denmark, Norway and Sweden*. Copenhagen: The Danish Institute, The Norwegian Office of Cultural Relations, The Swedish Institute, The American-Scandinavian Foundation.
36 Friis, Henning (ed.) (1950) *Scandinavia: Between East and West*. Ithaca and New York: Cornell University Press. It should be noted that the editor of the book explained the omission of Finland and Iceland by maintaining that these two countries were, despite their historical and cultural closeness to the Scandinavian countries, 'too different in many respects to be profitably included in this survey'. Friis 1950, ix.
37 A specialist on social policy issues, Friis was at that time Adviser in Social Science to the Danish Ministry of Social Affairs and United Nations Adviser on Social Welfare to the Government of Egypt. The book was the outgrowth of a series of lectures that were given at the New School for Social Research, New York.
38 Friis 1950, x.
39 See e.g. Friis 1950, v.
40 Lauwerys 1958, 7.
41 Osborne, Lithgow (1950) 'Foreword'. In Friis (ed.) 1950, vi–vii.

political debate, *The American Political Science Review*, the Columbia University political scientist Dankwart A. Rustow, who had written an important study on Swedish politics[42], reviewed *Scandinavian Democracy* as continuation of 'a tradition of panegyric writing which has presented the three Northern countries as so many idyllic utopias in which all the New Dealer's fondest hopes come effortlessly true'.[43] He maintained that there was no need of such uncritical praise that was inaugurated by 'American journalists', which obviously referred to the writings of Childs in the 1930s.[44] However, such was the force of Scandinavian exceptionality, that Rustow's own critical sting became seriously blunt as he motivated his criticism by claiming that the 'Scandinavian achievements in parliamentary government, economic policy, labor relations, education, science, and technology are genuine and impressive enough not to require euphemism of embellishment'.[45]

* * *

It took more than twenty years before 'Nordic democracy' was next time internationally promoted in a form of a particular anthology. For sure, the language of 'Nordic democracy' was not absent in the 1960s and 1970s but it is, nevertheless, possible to suggest that during this period 'Nordic democracy' was giving way to an emerging use of 'the Nordic Society', 'the welfare state' and 'the Nordic model'.[46] When the volume *Nordic Democracy* was published in 1981 (this time with the support from the Nordic Cultural Fund), in which also Finland and Iceland were included, the emphasis had shifted from ideological argumentation to a thorough presentation of institutional design of the five Nordic countries.[47] As indicated also by the lengthy sub-title of the compendium, *Issues and Institutions in Politics, Economy, Education, Social and Cultural Affairs*, the middle-of-the-road positioning of the early Cold War context had given way to multidimensional descriptions of exemplary and firmly established welfare societies. The language of international relations and political theories was, by and large,

---

42 Rustow, Dankwart A. (1955) *The Politics of Compromise: A Study of Parties and Cabinet Government in Sweden*. Princeton, New Jersey: Princeton University Press.

43 Rustow, Dankwart A. (1960) 'Scandinavian Democracy: Development of Democratic Thought and Institutions in Denmark, Norway, and Sweden'. *The American Political Science Review*, Vol. 54, No 2 (June 1960), 560.

44 Rustow 1960, 560.

45 Rustow 1960, 560.

46 For example, 'Nordic society' was the key category and the point of departure for the historical investigation in Eino Jutikkala's *Pohjoismaisen yhteiskunnan historiallisia juuria* (Historical Roots of the Nordic Society), which is one of the most influential Finnish studies of modern political history of the Nordic countries. See Jutikkala, Eino (1965) *Pohjoismaisen yhteiskunnan historiallisia juuria*. Porvoo: Werner Söderström Osakeyhtiö. On 'Nordic society' and 'the Nordic welfare state', see Kettunen 2005.

47 Allardt et al. (eds) (1981) *Nordic Democracy: Ideas, Issues and Institutions in Politics, Economy, Education, Social and Cultural Affairs of Denmark, Finland, Iceland, Norway, and Sweden*. Copenhagen: Det Danske Selskab.

replaced by the language of social policy and sociology. 'Nordic democracy' was now understood as virtually synonymous to 'the Nordic welfare state'.

In the foreword of the book, K. B. Andersen, former social democratic Foreign Minister and then President of the Danish Parliament, claimed that 'democracy, as we look upon it in Scandinavia, is not only a form of government but also comprises social and economic democracy as well as the democratic principles underlying justice, education, and culture, etc. This broadened concept of democracy is held in common by these five nations, not only in the sense that it has put its stamp on society in all the Nordic countries but also in that it as a form of government is not solely the vehicle for an elite but is based on the support of the people as a whole.'[48] This conceptualisation of Nordic democracy diverged considerably from the formal and procedural account defended by Tingsten and Ross in the 1940s. Yet, the belief and the message that there was something superior in the Nordic version of democracy lived on. To be sure, Andersen issued a warning of the potentially patronising tone of the book. Nevertheless, he insisted to present Nordic democracy as a model for others with 'much useful information [...] that may be applied in the task of harmonizing the often vexing relationships between society and the individual in the complex world in which we live'.[49]

'Nordic democracy' was also treated as synonymous to 'the Nordic welfare model' in the volume *Nordisk demokrati i förändring* (Nordic democracy in transition) in 1999, half a century after the first anthology. However, by now, the previous optimism and expansionism was replaced with protectionism, even sentimentality. According to the editors of the book, the prosperity and the future of the welfare state was threatened by the process of European integration and a globalising world.[50] But a revision of the social democratic vision of politics can nevertheless be noted here, as one of the editors emphasised the importance of judicial guarantees of the rights of citizens as well as the principle of the separation of powers if Nordic democracy was to survive in the future. According to him, changes in society had bypassed 'the old collectivistic view of democracy' that was based solely on the majority principle.[51] Accordingly, Nordic democracy was to be reformed in conjunction with the idea of *Rechtsstaat*.[52]

An indication of the departure from the earlier social democratic conception can also be found in *Demokrati i Norden* (2005), which was a report from the Democracy Committee of the Nordic Council of Ministers. As the title of the report indicates, the notion of a particular Nordic version of democracy was substituted by the unspecific language of 'Nordic

48 Allardt et al. 1981, i–ii.
49 Allardt et al. 1981, ii.
50 Karvonen, Lauri & Ljungberg, Elisabet (eds) (1999) *Nordisk demokrati i förändring*. Sundsvall: Demokratiinstitutet, i–ii, 395, 410–413.
51 Karvonen, Lauri (1999) 'Demokrati och samhörighet i Norden: Har vi en lysande framtid bakom oss?'. In Karvonen & Ljungberg 1999, 395–413, at 403.
52 Karvonen 1999, 404, 412.

democracies'.[53] In addition, democracy was discussed not only along the national divisions but also following some current categories of democratic theory such as 'representative democracy', 'elite democracy', 'participatory democracy', 'deliberative democracy', and 'living democracy'.[54] The Democracy Committee also used the figure 'Nordic democracy' in some occasions. In its recommendations it was maintained that '[t]he Nordic countries and autonomous areas are facing a number of challenges which simultaneously deepen and counteract the development of Nordic democracy'.[55] Moreover, it was stated that '[b]oth local referendums and popular initiatives are deeply rooted aspects of Nordic local democracy'.[56] But these were rare findings and it seems that 'Nordic democracy' had lost ground as the majority of the Nordic countries had become members of the European Union and as the Nordic welfare state had lost some of its previous status as an international beacon.[57]

However, this is not the whole picture. In 2002, the Nordic Council's 50th anniversary was celebrated under the title 'Nordic Democracy 2020'. Not only the title but also many speeches given by members of the Council and other key-note speakers in the jubilee meeting indicated that the idea of a particular Nordic democracy was not, and should not be, dead. At the same time as the virtuous effects of gradual democratisation and broad popular participation in politics as well as the welfare policy were pointed out, the overall spirit of the event was nevertheless a concern over the consequences of European integration and globalisation. In order for Nordic democracy to maintain its status as a model for the rest of the world – it was once again openly spelled out – a number of challenges such as the consequences of global market economy, the decreased turnout in elections, the democracy deficit on national level, and the problems caused by immigration had to be tackled.[58] Although not representative, an important sceptic voice was raised by Carl Bildt, the former conservative Prime Minister of Sweden and the UN envoy in Kosovo at that time, who pointed out that the Nordic countries

---

53 *Demokrati i Norden* (2005). København: Nordisk Ministerråd, 157.

54 *Demokrati i Norden* 2005, 17–24.

55 *Demokrati i Norden* 2005, 157. Our translation.

56 *Demokrati i Norden* 2005, 167. Our translation.

57 This is not to say that arguments concerning the democratic character of the Nordic countries were unimportant in the political campaigns concerning the EU membership in the Nordic countries in the 1990s when Sweden and Finland joined the union and Norway decided not to join. For an illuminating analysis regarding the Swedish case in the early 1990s, see Trägårdh, Lars (2002) 'Sweden and the EU: Welfare state nationalism and the spectre of "Europe"'. In Lene Hansen and Ole Wæever (eds) *European Integration and National Identity: The challenge of the Nordic states.* London: Routledge, 168–169. On the decreased role of the Nordic countries as bridge-builders after the Cold War era, see Arter, David (2008) *Scandinavian politics today. Second edition.* Manchester: Manchester University Press, 334.

58 It should be pointed out that most of the participants in the jubilee meeting were active politicians and not scholars, which marks the nature of the comments made in the occasion. It should also be pointed out that opinions regarding the pros and contras of European integration and global markets varied as did the participants' party political commitments. See *Nordisk demokrati 2020: Rapport fra Nordisk Råds temamøde om demokrati,* København: Nordisk Ministerråd, 2002.

really did not have such an important positive role as model countries as it was often assumed.[59] It is quite obvious that, at that time, the idea of Nordic democracy had to be related to a European framework.

* * *

The literature explicit on Nordic or Scandinavian democracy analysed above is, we think, sufficient in enabling us to discern some major characteristics attached to the notion of 'Nordic democracy'. The rhetoric of 'Nordic democracy' was motivated by the changing geopolitical circumstances, it included a social aspect strongly related to the welfare state, it was anchored in the idea of a common Nordic democratic tradition, and it rested on an idea of a shared set of Nordic values. However, before we proceed to a discussion of these characteristics we want to raise the important question of the geographical extent of 'Norden' which has been far from an uncomplicated issue in the literature on 'Nordic democracy'.

The advocates of Nordic democracy had to face the problem of forging three to five different nations into a single Nordic political culture – and this against the background of the failed project of common Scandinavian nation-building in the 1860s.[60] As pointed out in HEMSTAD's chapter in this volume, the relationship between the Scandinavian countries in terms of close cooperation has many times been problematic, which may be one explanation for the preference of 'Nordic' over 'Scandinavian' democracy. Hemstad pays particular attention to the dissolution of the personal union between Sweden and Norway in 1905 and its consequences. Despite this problematic background, the introduction of 'Nordic democracy' in the 1930s took place with references made to 'Scandinavianism'. This time, however, it was the social democratic 'labour Scandinavianism', which was able to make the rhetorical link to nineteenth-century romanticism.

It was no coincidence that the Day of Nordic Democracy was celebrated in Malmö, a short boat trip from the Danish capital Copenhagen. The labour movements and the social democratic parties in Denmark and Sweden could easily find a common chord in their revisionist and national agenda in the early 1930s. While Denmark since the late nineteenth century had been the most advanced Nordic country when it came to urbanisation, industrialisation as well as welfare policies (in the form of social insurances), it was from the 1930s onwards Sweden that represented the Nordic horizon of expectation, or what a 'Nordic country' should look like. It was also mainly Sweden that reached international recognition as a model democracy, for example in Childs' analyses during the 1930s. The image of Sweden as a model country, or as an image of the future, remained for long a central part of the political discussion not only in Sweden itself, but also in the neighbouring countries, particularly in Finland.

59 *Nordisk demokrati 2020* 2002, 24–25.
60 Østergård, Uffe (1997) 'The Geopolitics of Nordic Identity: From Composite States to Nation States'. In Øystein Sørensen and Bo Stråth (eds) *The Cultural Construction of Norden*. Oslo: Scandinavian University Press, 25–71, at 39.

The difference between the 'Scandinavian countries' and 'Nordic countries' is sometimes downplayed in the analysed literature. In geographic terms it is commonly understood that Sweden, Norway, and Denmark are 'the Scandinavian countries', while 'the Nordic countries' also include Finland and Iceland. In political terms the difference was many times pointed out as well. It is clear that, for example, Childs discussed the Scandinavian and not the Nordic countries as he emphasised the strong labour movement of Sweden, Denmark and Norway. Simon, to name another example, explicitly noted in his *The Smaller Democracies* that Finland was 'a democracy in the making' whereas the three Scandinavian countries had contributed with the 'Scandinavian achievement'.[61]

In his chapter, KURUNMÄKI raises the question whether 'Nordic democracy' was, in the 1930s, consciously preferred over 'Scandinavian democracy' in order to include also Finland. The language strife between the Finnish-speaking and Swedish-speaking population as well as the wave of right-wing extremism in Finland made the country suspicious to many Scandinavian eyes, while likewise Sweden (which was more or less identified with Scandinavia at large in the Finnish mindset) often was equally suspicious to many Finns. However, Finland was, if somewhat hesitantly, included in the group of Nordic democracies, not least due to geopolitical considerations, good party contacts between Finnish and Swedish social democrats, and the commonly held opinion that Finland, which had been a part of the Swedish kingdom for over six hundred years (before it became a part of the Russian empire in 1809 and before the country gained the status of an independent state in 1917) nonetheless shared a political tradition of freedom and popular participation as well as the legal system and the Lutheran state religion with Scandinavia.

During the Second World War, Finland's alignment with Germany at a time when both Denmark and Norway were occupied by the Nazis posed new problems for the advocates of Nordic cooperation. However, as HECKER-STAMPEHL argues, these problems were countered by pointing out Finland's historical and cultural belonging to the Nordic countries. In fact, the rhetoric of 'Nordic democracy' was here taken in use in order to ensure that Finland would end up on the right side once the war was over. But despite these efforts, which were put forward mainly by the programmatic Nordic Associations, Finland was not represented in the literature on Nordic democracy after the Second World War. This is arguably due to Finland's unsettled position as a country with a specific security pact with the Soviet Union in the emerging Cold War. Initial Soviet opposition was also the reason why Finland joined the Nordic Council not at its first session in 1953 but with a two year delay (Stalin's death had triggered the 'thaw'). This is not to say that 'Nordic democracy' did not play any role in Finland at the time. On the contrary, in the Finnish political discourse during the Cold War, the Nordic connection and 'Nordic democracy' were important ways by which it could be argued that Finland did not belong to the Eastern Block.[62]

61 Simon 1939, 155–175.
62 Kettunen 2005, 56.

The best example of the rhetorical use of 'Nordic democracy' in this sense is arguably the speech held by Finnish President Urho Kekkonen on occasion of Soviet government leader Nikita Khrushchev visiting Helsinki in autumn 1960. As discussed by KOIKKALAINEN, the Finnish President maintained that even if the rest of Europe was to turn communist, Finland would 'remain a traditional Nordic democracy' if the majority of the Finnish people so wished, which he believed they would.[63] It was a clear positioning of Finland's political culture in a Nordic tradition with a variety of implicit connotations, not least of overall Western orientation, as well as a clear and direct marker of distance towards communist dictatorship at a time of intimate official Finnish–Soviet friendship by the highest Finnish official vis-à-vis the highest Soviet representative. The ultimate question was Finland's position in the ideological struggle of the Cold War.

As mentioned earlier, the 1981 volume *Nordic Democracy* finally covered also Finland as well as Iceland. Indeed, Iceland is another country whose position outside the Scandinavian core had made it less visible in the literature on Nordic democracy. However, this did not hinder the analysed literature to trace the origins of Scandinavian or Nordic democracy in the Icelandic Sagas.[64] So, if Finland was a complicated case, and if Iceland, however sidestepped in the mid-twentieth century, provided the ancient source of Nordic democracy, the case of Norway was actually most troubling for those who promoted the idea of Nordic democracy in the 1930s. To a certain extent, the Norwegian reluctance towards Nordic co-operation can be seen in the light of a suspicion of Swedish imperialistic ambitions stemming from the Swedish–Norwegian Union.[65] Moreover, as the very concept of democracy was intimately connected to the national cause in Norway, there was little place for the rhetoric of 'Nordic democracy'. Furthermore, it is also important to emphasise that the Norwegian Labour Party – the only Nordic social democratic party to have been the member of the Moscow steered Comintern (the Third International) between 1921 and 1923 – had a considerably more radical profile than its Nordic counterparts until the mid-1930s. As a matter of fact, the representatives of the Norwegian Labour Party were accepted only as guests in the meetings of the Nordic Cooperation Committee of the Labour Movement before the Norwegian party joined the social democratic Second International in 1938.[66] It does therefore not come as a great surprise that out of the Nordic Social Democratic leaders

---

63 Kekkonen, Urho (1973) [1960] 'Finland Sticks to Her Traditional Democracy'. In *Neutrality: The Finnish Position*, 2nd exp. ed. London: Heinemann, 83–86, at 84. In this translation, the wording was 'Scandinavian democracy', but the original Finnish-language version reads 'Nordic democracy'. See Kekkonen, Urho (1967)[1960] 'Suomi pysyy perinteellisen kansanvallan pohjalla'. In *Puheita ja kirjoituksia, vol. 2: Puheita presidenttikaudelta 1956–1967*. Helsinki: Weilin+Göös, 117–119, at 118.

64 See Andersson, Ingvar (1949) 'Äldre demokratisk tradition i Norden och dess fortsatta utformning i Sverige. In Koch & Ross 1949, 9; Andersson, Ingvar (1958) 'Early Democratic Traditions in Scandinavia'. In Lauwerys 1958, 72.

65 See Fure, Odd-Bjørn (1996) *Norsk utenrikspolitikks historie, Bind 3. Mellomkrigstid, 1920–1940*. Oslo: Universitetsforlaget, Chapter 5.

66 See Wahlbäck & Blidberg 1986, 5–6.

speaking on the Day of Nordic Democracy in 1935, only the fresh Prime Minister of Norway, Johan Nygaardsvold, raised doubts about the notion of 'Nordic democracy'. Nygaardsvold was concerned that the concept contained a certain element of conservatism, which he regarded alien to the inherently progressive labour movement.[67] On the other hand, the very fact that Nygaardsvold nevertheless participated in the meeting was a sign of the new Nordic orientation of the Norwegian Labour party, even if the notion 'Nordic democracy' failed to gain any persuasive power in the Norwegian context at this point in time.

* * *

'Nordic democracy' has been intimately connected with the social aspect of democracy, implying social and economic equality associated with the emerging welfare state and, in more practical terms, collective bargaining on the labour market. Despite the seemingly de-partisan use of 'Nordic democracy' after the Second World War, it always remained closely linked to social democracy.

In the 1930s, the emphasis of 'Nordic' over 'social' aimed at giving historical and cultural legitimacy to the social democratic standpoint. In this sense, 'Nordic democracy' was related to the concept of 'the people's home' (*folkhemmet*) – the social democratic metaphor that had a conservative background.[68] As KURUNMÄKI shows in his chapter, 'the people's home' and 'Nordic democracy' were sometimes used as synonyms by Swedish Social Democrats in the 1930s. Both concepts denoted social equality and solidarity between citizens, emphasising the idea of national cohesion in the face of internal and external threats. In this sense, 'Nordic democracy' and 'the people's home' were charged with the same culturally nationalistic connotations.[69] The importance of national solidarity, unity, or even homogeneity did not disappear with the Second World War. In 1966 Tingsten maintained that the Scandinavian countries were 'happy democracies' as they were characterised by an extraordinary homogeneity as to nationality, language and religion.[70]

Moreover, 'Nordic democracy' was also a way of depoliticising social democracy and presenting it as the pragmatic, rational, and orderly running of political matters. According to Gunnar Myrdal, for example, the success of the Scandinavian democracies was largely due to the fact that the political

67 See *Fyra tal om nordisk demokrati* 1935, 29–30.
68 See Götz, Norbert (2001) *Ungleiche Geschwister: Die Konstruktion von national-sozialistischer Volksgemeinschaft und schwedischem Volksheim.* Baden-Baden: Nomos; Götz, Norbert (2004) 'The Modern Home Sweet Home'. In Kurt Almqvist and Kay Glans (eds) *The Swedish Success Story?* Stockholm: Axel and Margaret Ax:son Johnson Foundation, 97-107, 300-302.
69 See also Kayser Nielsen, Niels (2009) *Bonde, stat og hjem: Nordisk demokrati og nationalisme – fra pietismen til 2. verdenskrig.* Århus: Aarhus Universitetsforlag, 429–451.
70 Tingsten, Herbert (1966) *Från idéer till idyll – den lyckliga demokratien.* Stockholm: Norstedt, 12.

discussion in Scandinavia did not concern the fundamentals, but rather the mere expediency of different avenues of action.[71] While Myrdal sought to de-politicise 'Nordic democracy' through social engineering, Tingsten is known as one of the early advocates of the 'end of ideology' thesis. His approach to ideologies was to prove that they were based on erroneous descriptions of facts. That is, although evaluative attitudes, according to his philosophical commitment, could not be criticised within the realm of (political) science, Tingsten succeeded in finding a way to study and refute political ideologies as statements and interpretations of empirical facts.[72] This rationalistic view of politics was proclaimed also in his article on Nordic democracy, in which he greeted Nordic democracy of its anti-rhetorical nature in comparison to the political styles in countries like France and England, where the parliamentary debates were often of a theatrical character.[73] However, the political nature and intentions of these rhetorical attempts to depoliticise the political discussion should not escape anyone.

The image of happy and rational democracies of the North was not a matter of home-made branding alone. As STADIUS shows in his chapter on Spanish travel letters and diplomat reports at the turn of the nineteenth century, the Nordic countries were portrayed in positive light with regard to modernity, equality and democratic political life. The Spanish descriptions, while being a part of domestic political game, presented the Nordic countries in a way that is reminiscent to the positive picture delivered later on by Childs. One particular topic to which the Spanish commentators paid much attention was women's high social status and political rights in the Nordic countries. Not least thanks to Ibsen, it was commonly presumed outside *Norden* that equality between men and women was greater in the Nordic countries than elsewhere. Stadius also points at the ways in which the Finnish introduction of universal suffrage in 1906 was used as an argument in Spanish discussions.

Given the emphasis on the principle of equality that has been associated with the figure of Nordic democracy, it is important to note that the rhetorical link to gendered political rights has been rather vague in the explicit literature on Nordic democracy. Although some of the discussed volumes do mention early women's associations and the breakthrough of women's right to vote in parliamentary elections, gender has not formed a major part of the concept 'Nordic democracy'. For example, the celebration of the Day of Nordic Democracy in 1935 did not make any particular notice of the role of women in the Nordic pattern of democracy.[74] In *Nordisk demokrati* (1949), gender issues were approached under the section 'family' in a chapter that critically discussed the housewife's position and argued in favour of a more equal relationship between husband and wife, as well as in favour of institutionalised education of children and women's entrance in the waged labour market. In terms of explicit rhetoric, there was nothing

---

71 Myrdal 1939, 8.
72 Tingsten, Herbert (1941) *Idékritik*. Stockholm: Bonnier. See Strang's contribution to this volume.
73 Tingsten 1938, 41.
74 See *Fyra tal om nordisk demokrati* 1935.

about 'Nordic democracy' in this piece.[75] In the 1958 English-language edition, *Scandinavian Democracy*, the chapter was dropped.

It could probably be argued that the launch and establishment of 'Nordic democracy' during the 1930s and 1940s occurred both too late and too early with regard to the gender issue. It was too late for women's suffrage to be any longer a controversial issue and it was too early for modern political feminism to leave its mark. The sociological and comparative approach that marked the 1981 volume *Nordic Democracy* did give room for notions that pointed out a high degree of women's participation in parliamentary elections, level of education, economic activity, and general position in society, when the Nordic countries were considered within an international context. However, this score was regarded as a result of progressive social policy and high standard of living, that is, the welfare state, more than as an outcome of something that was termed as 'Nordic democracy'.[76] In *Nordisk demokrati i förändring* (1999), it was also 'the welfare state' and 'Nordic model' instead of 'Nordic democracy' that was the point of departure in the article dealing with women's place in parliamentary politics.[77] Indeed, perhaps the self-applauding rhetoric of 'Nordic democracy' was alien also to modern political feminism. The political position of women in the Nordic countries has generally been discussed in more critical terms, as an 'unfinished democracy'.[78] However, a more optimistic picture was sketched in *Women in Nordic Politics* (1995) in which a Nordic particularity in terms of shared cultural values, Nordic cooperation, and social democratic policies was pointed out to give support to the view that the gap between men and women was successively closing.[79] A less positive picture was again painted in the volume *Equal Democracies? Gender and Politics in the Nordic Countries* (1999), in which the image of the Nordic countries as unity and as an oasis of equality was questioned.[80]

* * *

In the literature analysed in this chapter, Nordic democracy has often been anchored to the idea of an ancient democratic tradition, characterised by

75 v. Hofsten, Birgitta (1949) 'Familjen'. In Koch & Ross 1949, 377–394.

76 See Haavio-Mannila, Elina (1981) 'The Position of Women'. In Allardt et al. 1981, 555-588, at 586.

77 Christensen, Ann-Dorte & Nina C. Raaum (1999) 'Kvinner i parlamentarisk politikk'. In Karvonen & Ljungberg 1999, 153–192. In the article, inspired by democratisation theories of Stein Rokkan, hinders and hiatus of democratisation of women's role in parliamentary politics, as well as differences between the Nordic countries, is pointed out in an elaborate manner.

78 Haavio-Mannila, Elina et al. (eds) (1983) *Unfinished Democracy: Women in Nordic Politics*. Oxford: Pergamon Press.

79 Karvonen, Lauri and Per Selle (1995) 'Introduction: Scandinavia: a case apart'. In Lauri Karvonen and Per Selle (eds) *Women in Nordic Politics: Closing the Gap*. Aldershot: Dartmouth, 3–23.

80 Bergqvist, Christina (1999) 'The Nordic Countries – One Model or Several?'. In Christina Bergqvist et al. (eds) *Equal Democracies? Gender and Politics in the Nordic Countries*, Oslo: Scandinavian University Press, 3–11.

representative assemblies at local communities, *Tings*, freedom of the peasants, and consensual and egalitarian political culture. In contrast to mainstream understandings of the background reference, or the birthplace, of democracy, 'Nordic democracy' has no rhetorical link to the Athenian democracy or, for that matter, to Roman Republic.[81] Instead of pointing out free men in city-states, *polis* or *res publica*, this particular democracy has been traced back into the Viking Age and the assemblies of free peasants.[82] This is also what Robert A. Dahl means when he writes that 'democracy seems to have been invented more than once, and in more than one place'.[83] For him, Scandinavia was one the birthplaces of democracy alongside the commercial Lowlands, Swiss mountain valleys, and the parliament of medieval England.[84]

However critical and dispassionate the attempts at discussing the historical basis of the Nordic political tradition might have been, they have often ended up as contributions to the narrative of particularly democratic past of Nordic political culture. For example, in *Scandinavian Democracy*, Ingvar Andersson, a historian and member of the Swedish Academy, warned of an anachronistic view as he discussed early modern democratic traditions in Scandinavia. He held that 'it would be very difficult to point to those features of early Scandinavian history which foreshadow modern democracy as practiced today in the Nordic countries'.[85] Moreover, Andersson attempted to 'offset recent and often highly idealized versions of the ancient political liberties in Scandinavia'.[86] But despite these cautious remarks, he nevertheless stated that during the Age of Liberty (1719–1772) 'pre-democratic' features of Sweden were turned to fully democratic ones in the modern sense. Without 'pre-democratic' institutions, no Age of Liberty either, was Andersson's argument.[87] Even bolder was his concluding remark that 'although Denmark and Norway did not present the same unbroken and direct line of "pre-democratic" traditions as Sweden, it is not difficult to find ties and connections between later democratic developments and the ideals of the early period'.[88] It is, indeed, characteristic to this rhetoric of democratic history that 'the early period', to which Andersson referred, was left undefined.

---

81 This is especially noteworthy against the background that there have been significant currents in Nordic political life that have found the political inspiration in the classical Greek and Roman political culture, not least during the Swedish Age of Liberty in the eighteenth century, which has been, as we noted, the very point of reference in the literature of Nordic democracy. Moreover, the Ancient notion of public virtues and a civic-minded citizen were idealised in particular during the rule of Gustavus III in the late eighteenth century, the era that followed the Age of Liberty.

82 See also Jakobsen, Uffe (2009) 'The Conception of "Nordic Democracy" and European Judicial Integration'. *Nordisk tidsskrift for menneskerettigheter* Vol. 27, No. 2, 221–241, at 229.

83 Dahl, Robert A. (1998) *On Democracy*. New Haven: Yale University Press, 9.

84 Dahl 1998, 17-20.

85 Andersson 1958, 69–93, at 69.

86 Andersson 1958, 72.

87 Andersson 1958, 88–89.

88 Andersson 1958, 93.

In the 1981 volume *Nordic Democracy*, Sigurđur Líndal, Professor of Law and the editor of *Saga Íslands*, made a similar effort to bridge the gap between the past and the present by re-describing the past in a positive manner so as to create a fitting background for the present view of Nordic democracy. Despite his critical account of yeoman freedom and his emphasis on a contest between the king and the privileged classes, and despite his notion that modern democracy in the Nordic countries is far from a wholly home-grown product, he nevertheless concluded by maintaining that 'there are distinct threads in modern Nordic democracy which extend all the way back to the Viking Age, and which tie the history of Nordic democracy together. This is perhaps why democracy has found such firm footing in the Nordic nations of today, and has shown such consistent development there since early in the nineteenth century.'[89]

As these examples show, the idea that there actually is something special with the political tradition in *Norden* has been enduring even in critical historical accounts.[90] To determine whether these statements gain support from current historical research and whether they make a culture democratic is, as previously emphasised, outside the scope of our interest in this book. But the ways in which historical references have been used in the making of 'Nordic democracy' deserve special attention. In this volume, HALLBERG shows that the idea of a freeholding peasant, the ancient yeoman, was cultivated in eighteenth-century Swedish political debates concerning estate privileges in order to advance arguments in daily political controversies, as it was given a positively evaluated content that was in contradiction to the present state of affairs. The radical writers of the 1760s and 1770s can be viewed as early rhetoricians of the 'democratic spirit' of ancient Swedish politics. Similar attempts at rhetorically tailoring a pre-democratic past for the notion of 'Nordic democracy' are discussed in several articles in the present volume. Both KURUNMÄKI and HECKER-STAMPEHL note the several

89 Líndal, Sigurđur (1981) 'Early Democratic Traditions in the Nordic Countries'. In Allardt et al. 1981, 15–41, quoted from 40–41.
90 This can be seen also in the volume *The Cultural Construction of Norden* (1997), in which a critical discussion of the role of different historical narratives and elements in the construction of the free and egalitarian *Norden* – the independent peasants, the egalitarian ideals of education, pietism and Lutheranism as moral codes, and the myths of a glorious historical past – ultimately seems to end up as a contribution to, rather than a deconstruction of, the narrative of a Nordic democratic *Sonderweg*. The editors of the book conclusively maintain that in the Nordic countries there was a unique democratic political culture which enabled the Nordic countries, better than elsewhere, to contain the tension between freedom and equality. See Sørensen, Øystein and Bo Stråth (1997) 'Introduction: The Cultural Construction of Norden'. In Sørensen and Stråth 1997, 1–24, at 3. In the review of the book, Pauli Kettunen maintained that while a peasant myth with strong connection to the concept of democracy existed in all Nordic countries, its status as narrative or as an attempt to deliver a factual description was often left unclear by the authors of the book. At the very least, Kettunen argued, it should be acknowledged that the peasant myth could have been, and that is actually has been, used for different political purposes than merely as a basis for a social democratic welfare state. For example, after the Finnish civil war in 1918, the winning white side referred to the peasant myth as part of an anti-revolutionary call for 'social peace'. See Kettunen, Pauli (1999) 'A Return to the Figure of the Free Nordic Peasant'. *Acta Sociologica*, Vol. 42, 259–269, at 262, 264.

references to a democratic tradition of the Nordic countries made by the advocates of 'Nordic democracy' in order to ground their arguments in the 1930s and during the wartime. Hecker-Stampehl's analysis of wartime publications on Nordic cooperation shows that an idealised picture of historically rooted Nordic freedom and democracy was made a crucial part of moral defence in the Nordic countries. Likewise, KOIKKALAINEN explores how the President of Finland, Urho Kekkonen, in many different ways utilised the figure of the freeholding peasant, characteristic to the Finnish agrarian republican tradition, in his rhetoric during the Cold War.

While it is certainly true that the narrative of a particular Nordic democratic tradition was not constructed *ex nihilo*, we want to emphasise the rhetorical role it has played in twentieth-century contexts.[91] We are interested in the instrumentality of the narrative of Nordic democracy. In our reading, it is not surprising that 'Nordic democracy' was given historical roots; what is important to note, however, is that the historical roots the Social Democrats attached to it did not differ in any considerable manner from those included in canonical national narratives. As discussed by KURUNMÄKI in chapter two, the Social Democrats quite easily rejected the initial critique by the Swedish and Finnish Conservatives in the 1930s, that the label 'Nordic democracy' was anti-national, by a successful pairing of 'Nordic' and 'Swedish' or 'Finnish'.

* * *

Our findings point at one more consensual aspect of the rhetoric of Nordic democracy: the idea of shared values. On the one hand, the idea of shared values was used to denote simply the respect for the rules of the game in parliamentary democracy. However, such a minimal definition did not make any democracy Nordic. On the other hand, these shared values were also presented as something that separated the Nordic countries from the rest of the world in different (geo-)political situations. They inspired the democratic path during the totalitarian epoch; they were the backbone in the wartime rhetoric; they served as a moral beacon during the Cold War, and they were also the foundation on which a progressive welfare policy could be built. Shared values were culturally shaped, a way of life and a mentality.

With the help of shared values it was possible to overcome ideological and national divisions. It was possible to claim that these shared values made five different countries into one unit, yet allowing these countries to be taken as separate national units with peculiar characteristics. As discussed by KURUNMÄKI and HECKER-STAMPEHL, this notion of shared values as the backbone of Nordic political culture was not merely cultivated by the social democrats during the 1930s and 1940s. In the time of crisis, several prominent non-socialists re-described the 'tradition of Nordic freedom', which had been an important identity marker for them, into

---

91 For a rather similar conclusion, based mainly on Danish sources, see Jakobsen 2009, 221–241.

'a tradition of Nordic democracy'. As Kurunmäki suggests in his chapter, it is even possible to view the adaptation of the rhetoric of 'Nordic democracy' as having crucially contributed to the Finnish and Swedish Conservatives' acceptance of parliamentary democracy in the 1930s.

STRANG shows in his chapter that the idea of shared values as the foundation of democracy also became part of the theoretical elaborations of many influential Scandinavian philosophers. The interesting crux here is that these very same philosophers followed the controversial Uppsala philosopher Axel Hägerström (1868–1939) in rejecting the possibility of objective values. The influential disciples of Hägerström – Ingemar Hedenius, Herbert Tingsten, Alf Ross, and Gunnar Myrdal – were accused of representing a (value) nihilistic philosophical view that paved the way for totalitarian doctrines. Under such charges these followers of Hägerström motivated their commitment to democracy by using the culturally nationalistic 'Nordic democracy' as a stepping stone. They claimed that people could have historically rooted shared values without needing to believe that these values were objective, absolute or even true. As Strang notes, this rhetorical move gave additional, philosophical, legitimacy to 'Nordic democracy' at the same time as it helped these intellectuals to establish themselves as leading national philosophers at a time when positivistic and relativistic theories were questioned elsewhere.

Now, when we finally try to estimate and explain the career of the figure 'Nordic democracy', our first conclusion remains that it has to a large extent given way to 'the welfare state' and to 'the Nordic model' during the last two or three decades of the twentieth century. The success of 'the Nordic welfare state' has made 'Nordic democracy' an attribute of the welfare state rather than a forceful catch phrase in its own right. Whether a weakened appeal of 'the welfare state' would bring 'Nordic democracy' back to the fore is unlikely to happen, however. It was the tensed world that gave the primary motivation for the labelling of Nordic democracy, and it also terminated its success as a category of democratic regimes. In our view, the Cold War division of the ideological and geopolitical blocks eventually provided too little space for 'Nordic democracy' to establish itself internationally. When the Cold War was over, there was even less international interest. The geopolitical motivation for the rhetoric of 'Nordic democracy' has more or less disappeared, as there no longer are two opposing sides to profile oneself as a superior middle way in-between.

In the age of European integration, 'Nordic democracy' has lost much of its momentum as a spearhead. Now it is primarily about defending the domestic national and Nordic traditions of democracy and welfare in the face of external threats of modernisation.[92] One might even argue that 'Nordic democracy', as well as 'the Nordic Welfare State', have become nostalgic figures – the future is no longer conceptualised in terms of *Norden* or Nordic.[93] In the debates on European integration, it was the sceptics that

92 Cf. Hansen, Lene (2002) 'Conclusion'. In Hansen and Ole Wæever 2002, 224.
93 Kettunen 2005, 31.

tried to play the Nordic card, referring to Nordic co-operation as a more democratic and *'folklig'* form of international collaboration.[94] But although concerns about democracy deficit in the European Union are common in the Nordic countries today – Norway and Iceland are not member states in the union and Finland is the only Nordic country in the European Monetary Union – the issue of European Union has arguably been treated more as a question of the future of the welfare state than as question of the future of Nordic democracy.

We also think that the idea of shared values as the core characteristic of Nordic democracy is moving from having been strength to weakness with regard to the success of 'Nordic democracy'. In the 1930s, it was indeed quite meaningful to claim that 'Nordic democracy' was based on shared values when the surrounding Europe was turning to totalitarian regimes; during the Cold War the idea of shared values could find certain legitimacy in the middle position that 'Nordic democracy' was claimed to represent; in the era of expansive welfare policies, it was possible to think that there were common values that were, if not shared by all but at least by most people within the welfare state. Today, none of these contexts of the idea of shared values exist. In the recent discussion on the integration of immigrants in the Nordic countries, especially in the debate on the Mohammed-caricatures in Denmark, *Norden* was largely an absent category. The populist right either adopted a strictly nationalistic rhetoric, or they tried to polarise Western values against those of the immigrants. For those defending the ethos of multiculturalism, on the other hand, the idea of Nordic shared values seemed to be far too particular. Indeed, in a globalised world, it seems to us, shared values have either become a self-evident Western nominator of democracy or an obsolete and problematic category in a multicultural society.

However, if history is to teach us something it is that nothing is certain and that history matters as the source for political arguments. It remains to be seen whether the history of 'Nordic democracy' in the twentieth century can serve as a legitimising source for future politics. The advocates of 'Nordic democracy' used the past in their rhetoric, and history will most certainly be selectively used again and again. The future of democracy is to a high degree also about the re-descriptions of its past.

BIBLIOGRAPHY

Allardt et al. (eds) (1981) *Nordic Democracy: Ideas, Issues and Institutions in Politics, Economy, Education, Social and Cultural Affairs of Denmark, Finland, Iceland, Norway, and Sweden.* Copenhagen: Det Danske Selskab.

Andersson, Ingvar (1949) 'Äldre demokratisk tradition i Norden och dess fortsatta utformning i Sverige. In Koch, Hal & Ross, Alf (eds) *Nordisk demokrati.* Oslo: Halvorsen & Larsen, Stockholm: Natur och Kultur, København: Westermann.

Andersson, Ingvar (1958) 'Early Democratic Traditions in Scandinavia'. In Lauwerys, J. A: (ed.) *Scandinavian Democracy. Development of Democratic Thought &*

---

94 See Trägårdh 2002, 130–181, at 165–169.

Institutions in Denmark, Norway and Sweden. Copenhagen: The Danish Institute, The Norwegian Office of Cultural Relations, The Swedish Institute, The American-Scandinavian Foundation.

Arter, David (2008) *Scandinavian politics today. Second edition.* Manchester: Manchester University Press.

Bergqvist, Christina (1999) 'The Nordic Countries – One Model or Several?'. In Christina Bergqvist et al. (eds) *Equal Democracies? Gender and Politics in the Nordic Countries,* Oslo: Scandinavian University Press.

Childs, Marquis W. (1934) *Sweden: Where Capitalism Is Controlled.* New York: The John Day Company.

Childs, Marquis W. (1936) *Sweden: The Middle Way.* New Haven: Yale University Press

Childs, Marquis W. (1937/38) 'Sweden Revisited'. *Yale Review* N.S. 27/1

Childs, Marquis W. (1938) *This Is Democracy: Collective Bargaining in Scandinavia.* New Haven: Yale University Press.

Christensen, Ann-Dorte & Nina C. Raaum (1999) 'Kvinner i parlamentarisk politikk'. In Karvonen, Lauri & Ljungberg, Elisabet (eds) *Nordisk demokrati i förändring.* Sundsvall: Demokratiinstitutet.

Dahl, Robert A. (1998) *On Democracy.* New Haven: Yale University Press.

Demokrati i Norden (2005). København: Nordisk Ministerråd.

Flora, Peter with Stein Kuhnle and Derek Urwin (eds) (1999) *State Formation, Nation-Building, and Mass Politics in Europe: The Theory of Stein Rokkan. Based on his collected works.* Oxford: Oxford University Press.

Friis, Henning (ed.) (1950) *Scandinavia: Between East and West.* Ithaca and New York: Cornell University Press.

Frisch, Hartvig (1933) *Pest over Europa – Bolschevisme, Fascisme og Nazisme.* Copenhagen: Henrik Koppels Forlag.

Fure, Odd-Bjørn (1996) *Norsk utenrikspolitikks historie, Bind 3. Mellomkrigstid, 1920–1940.* Oslo: Universitetsforlaget.

Fyra tal om Nordisk Demokrati (1935). Stockholm: Frihets förlag.

Greaves, H. R. G. and C. P. Mayhew (1938) 'Constitution'. In Cole, Margaret and Charles Smith (eds) *Democratic Sweden: A Volume of Studies prepared by Members of the New Fabian Research Bureau.* London: Routledge.

Götz, Norbert (2001) *Ungleiche Geschwister: Die Konstruktion von nationalsozialistischer Volksgemeinschaft und schwedischem Volksheim.* Baden-Baden: Nomos.

Götz, Norbert (2004) 'The Modern Home Sweet Home'. In Kurt Almqvist and Kay Glans (eds): *The Swedish Success Story?* Stockholm: Axel and Margaret Ax:son Johnson Foundation..

Götz, Norbert (2008) '"Blue-eyed Angels" at the League of Nations: The Genevese Construction of Norden'. In Norbert Götz and Heidi Haggrén (eds) *Regional Cooperation and International Organizations: The Nordic Model in Transnational Alignment.* London: Routledge.

Haavio-Mannila, Elina (1981) 'The Position of Women'. In Allardt et al. (eds) *Nordic Democracy: Ideas, Issues and Institutions in Politics, Economy, Education, Social and Cultural Affairs of Denmark, Finland, Iceland, Norway, and Sweden.* Copenhagen: Det Danske Selsab.

Haavio-Mannila, Elina et al. (eds) (1983) *Unfinished Democracy: Women in Nordic Politics.* Oxford: Pergamon Press.

Hansen, Lene (2002) 'Conclusion'. In Lene Hansen and Ole Wæever (eds) *European Integration and National Identity: The challenge of the Nordic states.* London: Routledge.

Hansson, P. Albin (1935) *Demokrati.* Stockholm: Tidens Förlag.

Hayek, F.A. (1944) *The Road to Serfdom.* Chicago: University of Chicago Press.

Held, David (1996) *Models of Democracy. Second Edition.* Cambridge: Polity Press.

v. Hofsten, Birgitta (1949) 'Familjen'. In Koch, Hal & Ross, Alf (eds) *Nordisk demokrati.* Oslo: Halvorsen & Larsen, Stockholm: Natur och Kultur, København: Westermann.

Jakobsen, Uffe (2009) 'The Conception of "Nordic Democracy" and European Judicial Integration'. *Nordisk tidsskrift for menneskerettigheter* Vol. 27, Nr 2, 221–241.

Jutikkala, Eino (1965) *Pohjoismaisen yhteiskunnan historiallisia juuria.* Porvoo: Werner Söderström Osakeyhtiö.

Karvonen, Lauri and Selle, Per (1995) 'Introduction: Scandinavia: a case apart'. In Lauri Karvonen and Per Selle (eds) *Women in Nordic Politics: Closing the Gap.* Aldershot: Dartmouth.

Karvonen, Lauri & Ljungberg, Elisabet (eds) (1999) *Nordisk demokrati i förändring.* Sundsvall: Demokratiinstitutet.

Karvonen, Lauri (1999) 'Demokrati och samhörighet i Norden: Har vi en lysande framtid bakom oss?'. In Karvonen, Lauri & Ljungberg, Elisabet (eds) *Nordisk demokrati i förändring.* Sundsvall: Demokratiinstitutet.

Kayser Nielsen, Niels (2009) *Bonde, stat og hjem: Nordisk demokrati og nationalisme – fra pietismen til 2. verdenskrig.* Århus: Aarhus Universitetsforlag.

Kekkonen, Urho (1967)[1960] 'Suomi pysyy perinteellisen kansanvallan pohjalla'. In *Puheita ja kirjoituksia, vol. 2: Puheita presidenttikaudelta 1956–1967.* Helsinki: Weilin+Göös.

Kekkonen, Urho (1973)[1960] 'Finland Sticks to Her Traditional Democracy', In *Neutrality: The Finnish Position,* 2nd exp. ed. London: Heinemann.

Kettunen, Pauli (1999) 'A Return to the Figure of the Free Nordic Peasant'. *Acta Sociologica* 42, 259–269.

Kettunen, Pauli (2005) 'The Power of International Comparison – A Perspective on the Making and Challenging of the Nordic Welfare State'. In Niels Finn Christiansen, Klaus Petersen, Nils Edling, Per Haave (eds) *The Nordic Model of Welfare – a Historical Reappraisal,* Copenhagen: Museum Tusculanum Press.

Koch, Hal (1945) *Hvad er Demokrati?.* København: Gyldendal.

Koch, Hal & Ross, Alf (eds) (1949) *Nordisk demokrati.* Oslo: Halvorsen & Larsen, Stockholm: Natur och Kultur, København: Westermann.

Koselleck, Reinhart (1972) 'Einleitung'. In Otto Brunner, Werner Conze & Reinhart Koselleck (eds) *Geschichtliche Grundbegriffe. Historisches Lexikon zur politisch-sozialen Sprache in Deutschland,* vol. 1, Stuttgart: Ernst Klett.

Koselleck, Reinhart (2002) *The Practice of Conceptual History: Timing History, Spacing Concepts.* Stanford: Stanford University Press.

Lauwerys, J. A: (ed.) (1958) *Scandinavian Democracy. Development of Democratic Thought & Institutions in Denmark, Norway and Sweden.* Copenhagen: The Danish Institute, The Norwegian Office of Cultural Relations, The Swedish Institute, The American-Scandinavian Foundation.

Lijphart, Arend (1984) *Democracies: Patterns of Majoritarian and Consensus Government in Twenty-One Countries.* New Haven and London: Yale University Press.

Líndal, Sigurdur (1981) 'Early Democratic Traditions in the Nordic Countries'. In Allardt et al. (eds) *Nordic Democracy: Ideas, Issues and Institutions in Politics, Economy, Education, Social and Cultural Affairs of Denmark, Finland, Iceland, Norway, and Sweden.* Copenhagen: Det Danske Selsab.

Maier, Christian et al. (1972) 'Demokratie'. In Otto Brunner, Werner Conze and Reinhart Koselleck (eds) *Geschichtliche Grundbegriffe. Historisches Lexikon zur politisch-sozialen Sprache in Deutschland,* vol. 1, Stuttgart: Ernst Klett.

Majander, Mikko (2004) *Pohjoismaa vai kansandemokratia? Sosiaalidemokraatit, kommunistit ja Suomen kansainvälinen asema 1944–51.* Helsinki: Suomalaisen Kirjallisuuden Seura.

Myrdal, Gunnar (1939) *Maintaining Democracy in Sweden, I With Dictators as Neighbors, II. The Defences of Democracy.* A Bonnier reprint from *Survey Graphic – Magazine of Social Interpretation,* May–June, 4.

McKeon, Richard & Rokkan, Stein (eds) (1951) *Democracy in a World of Tensions. A Symposium prepared by UNESCO.* Paris: UNESCO.

Nordisk demokrati 2020: Rapport fra Nordisk Råds temamøde om demokrati, København: Nordisk Ministerråd, 2002.

Osborne, Lithgow (1950) 'Foreword'. In Friis, Henning (ed.) *Scandinavia: Between East and West*. Ithaca and New York: Cornell University Press.

Palonen, Kari (1999) 'Rhetorical and Temporal Perspectives on Conceptual Change', *Finnish Yearbook of Political Thought*, Vol. 3, 41–59.

Ross, Alf (1946) *Hvorfor Demokrati?*. København: Munksgaard.

Rustow, Dankwart A. (1955) *The Politics of Compromise: A Study of Parties and Cabinet Government in Sweden*. Princeton, New Jersey: Princeton University Press.

Rustow, Dankwart A. (1960) 'Scandinavian Democracy: Development of Democratic Thought and Institutions in Denmark, Norway, and Sweden'. *The American Political Science Review*, Vol. 54, No 2 (June 1960), 559–560.

Ruth, Arne (1984) 'The Second New Nation: The Mythology of Modern Sweden'. *Daedalus*, Vol. 113, No. 2, 53–96.

Simon, Ernest Darwin (1939) *The Smaller Democracies*. London: Victor Gollancz.

Skinner, Quentin (1996) *Reason and rhetoric in the philosophy of Hobbes*. Cambridge: Cambridge University Press.

Skinner, Quentin (2002) *Visions of Politics. Volume I: Regarding Method*. Cambridge: Cambridge University Press.

Steincke, K. K. (1949) 'Mellem Øst og Vest'. In Koch, Hal & Ross, Alf (eds) *Nordisk demokrati*. Oslo: Halvorsen & Larsen, Stockholm: Natur och Kultur, København: Westermann.

Sørensen, Øystein and Stråth, Bo (1997) 'Introduction: The Cultural Construction of Norden'. In Øystein Sørensen and Bo Stråth (eds): *The Cultural Construction of Norden*. Oslo [et al.]: Scandinavian University Press.

Tingsten, Herbert (1933) *Demokratins seger och kris. Vår egen tids historia 1880–1930*. Utgiven av Yngve Lorents. Stockholm: Albert Bonniers Förlag.

Tingsten, Herbert (1937) *Political Behaviour – Studies in Election Statistics*. London: P. S. King & Son.

Tingsten, Herbert (1938) 'Nordisk demokrati'. *Nordens kalender*. Vol. 9, 41–50.

Tingsten, Herbert (1941) *Idékritik*. Stockholm: Bonnier.

Tingsten, Herbert (1945) *Demokratiens problem*. Stockholm: Norstedts.

Tingsten, Herbert (1966) *Från idéer till idyll – den lyckliga demokratien*. Stockholm: Norstedt.

Trägårdh, Lars (2002) 'Sweden and the EU: Welfare state nationalism and the spectre of "Europe"'. In Lene Hansen and Ole Wæever (eds) *European Integration and National Identity: The challenge of the Nordic states*. London: Routledge.

Wahlbäck, Krister and Blidberg, Kersti (1986) *Samråd i kristid: Protokoll från den Nordiska Arbetarrörelsens Samarbetskommitté 1932–1946*. Stockholm: Kungl. Samfundet för utgivandet av handskrifter rörande Skandinaviens historia.

Østergård, Uffe (1997) 'The Geopolitics of Nordic Identity: From Composite States to Nation States'. In Øystein Sørensen and Bo Stråth (eds) *The Cultural Construction of Norden*. Oslo: Scandinavian University Press.

JUSSI KURUNMÄKI

'Nordic Democracy' in 1935

On the Finnish and Swedish Rhetoric of Democracy

In August 1935, two and a half years after Hitler's takeover in Germany and on the eve of the Italian invasion in Abyssinia, the Social Democratic parties of Sweden, Denmark, Finland, Norway, and Iceland manifested their engagement in democracy on the 'Day of Nordic Democracy' in Malmö, Sweden. The festival was arranged by the Swedish Social Democratic Youth organisation at the same time as the Socialist Youth International was having a congress in the neighbouring Danish capital, Copenhagen. About 20 000 people were gathered to celebrate Nordic democracy and socialist internationalism.[1] Per Albin Hansson, the Swedish Prime Minister and leader of the Social Democratic Party appealed to the Social Democratic Youth that it would 'take care that Sweden and *Norden* would keep its position among the free people, and that *Norden* would become a mighty agitator against dictatorship and in favour of democracy – democracy within the people and between the peoples'.[2] According to him, Nordic democracy needed careful cultivation not only because it was good for the Nordic countries but also because it presented a model for other countries.[3] It was a cry for democracy in a proud tenor, and it was not the first time for Hansson. Democracy was a recurring topic for him in the early 1930s. In February 1935, he had addressed Danish students in Copenhagen, maintaining that the setbacks

---

1 The speeches of Per Albin Hansson (Sweden), Väinö Tanner (Finland), H. P. Hansen (Denmark), and Johan Nygaardsvold (Norway) were soon published in a pamphlet. Among the keynote speakers were also Jón Baldvinsson, the president of the Icelandic Parliament and the leader of the Social Democratic Party, and Koos Vorrink (the Netherlands), the chairman of the Socialist Youth International. *Fyra tal om nordisk demokrati* (1935). Stockholm: Frihets Förlag. On the speakers in the festival, see *Arbetet*, 26 August, 1935; *Dagens Nyheter*, 26 August, 1935; *Sydsvenska Dagbladet Snällposten*, 26 August, 1935; *Frihet* 16/1935, 5.

2 *Fyra tal om nordisk demokrati* 1935, 11. (All translations by the author if not mentioned otherwise.)

3 *Fyra tal om nordisk demokrati* 1935, 5.

met by democracy in other countries had made Nordic democracy conscious of its own value and raised strong interest in the rest of the world.[4]

The fact that democracy was in crisis was felt everywhere, as noted, for example, by the Swedish political scientist Herbert Tingsten in his influential *Demokratins seger och kris* (Democracy's Victory and Crisis) (1933).[5] For sure, it is easy to see why this was the case. Dictatorial or autocratic rule was put into effect in most European countries, the dictatorships led by Stalin, Mussolini, and Hitler being only the most spectacular examples.[6] Against this background, it may appear as self-evident yet idealistic when Torgny Segerstedt, professor and a liberal Swedish publicist, maintained that the key criterion of democracy was the principle of freedom. In his passionate apology for democracy, *Demokrati och diktatur* (Democracy and Dictatorship) (1933), Segerstedt argued that tolerance and freedom of opinion were the cornerstones of democracy and not its weakness, as was so often claimed. For him, democracy was sustainable because of its ability to meet criticism and remain unfinished. This in opposition to dictatorship, in which freedom was suppressed by force and individualism substituted by collectivism.[7]

However, freedom of opinion and the principle of tolerance were regarded as the weak points of democracy not only in pejorative opinions of democracy but also in many pro-democratic accounts. What had happened to the Weimar Republic was all too alarming an example of the fact that a democratic system could host and feed its own enemies. For example, Urho Kekkonen, one of the young intellectuals within the Finnish-language

---

4   Hansson, Per Albin (1948) [1935] 'Nordisk demokrati'. In Rolf Edberg (ed.) (1948) *Demokratisk linje. Tal och artiklar av Hjalmar Branting och Per Albin Hansson.* Stockholm: Tidens Förlag, 206-207. The speeches held in Copenhagen and Malmö were published also in Hansson, P. Albin (1935) *Demokrati*, Stockholm: Tidens Förlag. 217-230, 268–274. Hansson touched upon the topic also in December 1934, although without explicit rhetoric of 'Nordic democracy', in his speech on the workers' Scandinavianism (*arbetarskandinavism*) in Copenhagen. He had pointed out democracy's firm position in *Norden* also in his speech in Stockholm on First of May in 1933. See Hansson 1935, 107, 177. On the workers' Scandinavianism, see Ruth Hemstad's article in this volume.

5   Tingsten, Herbert (1933) *Demokratiens seger och kris. Vår egen tids historia 1880–1930.* Utgiven av Yngve Lorents. Stockholm: Albert Bonniers Förlag, 17–18.

6   For example, there were military coups in Bulgaria (1923), Portugal, Lithuania, and Poland (1926). In Yugoslavia a monarchical autocracy was put into effect in 1929, and in Greece monarchy was restored in 1935. In Austria democratic institutions were 'killed from above' by the prime minister Dollfuss in 1934, Estonia and Latvia following the pattern shortly afterwards. See Capoccia, Giovanni (2005) *Defending Democracy. Reactions to Extremism in Interwar Europe.* Baltimore and London: The Johns Hopkins University Press, 6–9; Linz, Juan J. and Stepan, Alfred (eds) (1978) *The Breakdown of Democratic Regimes.* Baltimore and London: The Johns Hopkins University Press; Bessel, Richard (1997) 'The crisis of modern democracy, 1919-39'. In David Potter, David Goldblatt, Margaret Kiloh, Paul Lewis (eds) *Democratisation.* Cambridge: Polity Press in association with The Open University, 71–94; Stern, Fritz (1997) 'The new democracies in crisis in interwar Europe'. In Axel Hadenius (ed.) *Democracy's victory and crisis.* Cambridge: Cambridge University Press, 15–23.

7   Segerstedt, Torgny (1933) *Demokrati och diktatur.* Stockholm: Albert Bonniers Förlag, 5–22.

nationalist movement and a rising name in the Finnish Agrarian Party, pointed out the German case in his *Demokratian itsepuolustus* (The Self-Defence of Democracy) (1934). According to him, freedom and coercion made two sides of democracy, but too much freedom was dangerous for democracy, as the German case just had shown. By criticising liberalism and emphasising the aspects of coercion and order as well as firm leadership, Kekkonen used many of the arguments that were used against democracy. However, his conclusion pointed out the importance of liberties and tolerance as he maintained that only groups which respected the rights of political minorities should be given voice in a democracy.[8]

These two examples, arguably the most famous Swedish and Finnish apologies in favour of democracy in the thirties, should primarily be understood as illustrative of two different discourses on the defence of democracy rather than a sharp distinction between Swedish and Finnish characteristics with regard to the rhetoric of democracy. It would be too venturing to maintain that in Sweden it was freedom that was the topic of democracy and in Finland it was order. However, we cannot ignore the fact that in particular Kekkonen's lengthy essay was written against the special Finnish background. The influence of the Soviet Union in Finnish left-wing politics[9] and, in particular, the extremist right-wing Lapua movement that was mobilised against communism have made Finnish interwar politics a notable case in the literature on the crisis of democracy, because the serious extremist challenge was, in fact, defeated. It should be pointed out that, out of those European countries that gained independence after the First World

---

8 See Kekkonen, Urho (1973) [1934] 'Demokratian itsepuolustus'. In *Puheita ja kirjoituksia IV*. Helsinki: Weilin+Göös, 29-110; see also Hyvärinen, Matti (2003) 'Valta'. In Matti Hyvärinen, Jussi Kurunmäki, Kari Palonen, Tuija Pulkkinen & Henrik Stenius (eds) *Käsitteet liikkeessä. Suomen poliittisen kulttuurin käsitehistoria*. Tampere: Vastapaino, 101–103; Tuikka, Timo J. (2007) *'Kekkosen konstit'. Urho Kekkosen historia- ja politiikkakäsitykset teoriasta käytäntöön 1933–1981*. Jyväskylä: University of Jyväskylä, 70–87; Uino, Ari (1985) *Nuori Urho Kekkonen. Poliittisen ja yhteiskunnallisen kasvun vuodet (1900-1936)*. Helsinki: Kirjayhtymä, 327–340. Kekkonen had a good insight in German politics as he had visited the country in 1931–1932 while preparing his doctoral dissertation on municipal elections. See Kekkonen, Urho (1981) *Vuosisatani I*. Helsinki: Suuri Suomalainen Kirjakerho, 220-233. Kekkonen became the most influential Finnish politician in post-war-era Finland, being the President of Finland in 1956–1981. For Kekkonen's role in Finnish politics and his rhetoric of Nordic democracy after the Second World War, see the chapter written by Petri Koikkalainen in this volume.

9 The Finnish Communist Party was founded in Moscow after the 1918 Finnish Civil War. It operated underground or under other party names and cover organisations. Its party programme was thoroughly revolutionary, rejecting any concessions made to 'parliamentary democracy' and viewing the 1918 Civil War as an unsuccessful revolution that ought to be completed in the future. It can also be noted that the ideological leader of the Finnish communists in Moscow, Otto Ville Kuusinen, was one of the leaders of the Communistic International and had a prominent position in the Soviet hierarchy. See Hodgson, John H. (1967) *Communism in Finland. A History and Interpretation*. Princeton, New Jersey: Princeton University Press, 81-120; Rentola, Kimmo (1998) 'Finnish Communism, O. W. Kuusinen, and Their Two Native Countries'. In Tauno Saarela and Kimmo Rentola (eds) *Communism: National & International*. Helsinki: SHS, 159–170.

War, only Finland and Czechoslovakia did not become dictatorships by the mid-thirties.[10]

The Lapua movement challenged the Finnish political system in 1929–1932. It was, at the beginning, backed by influential factions within the non-socialist parties, and, throughout its existence, by many military officers and industrialists. The movement managed to get the government changed and the laws that prohibited any political activities of the communists passed in the re-elected parliament. In 1932, the movement made an armed revolt against the political system, demanding the government to resign. However, the state leadership and in particular President Svinhufvud, the prominent conservative who had gained his newly elevated position to a large extent thanks to the Lapua movement, stood against the revolting leaders of the movement. As a matter of fact, the communist laws that the Lapua movement managed to get through were used against the movement as it was banned in 1932.[11] During the heydays of the Lapua movement, the Finnish government made plans that would have reduced the power of the parliament and increased the power of the president. There were also calculations that would have changed the system of representation so that economic and educational interests, as it was held, would have gotten special representation in the parliament. After the Lapua movement was dissolved, the right-wing ideas of corporative representation and populist nationalism were furthered by the People's Patriotic Movement which homed in the Conservative Party before it was thrown out from the party in 1934.[12]

The Swedish experience of the crisis of democracy was quite different. There were, of course, communists and home-made Nazis in Sweden as well, but these factions never managed to set the political system in proof.[13] While Finland has been discussed as a survivor in the literature

10 See Capoccia 2005, 6-9, 41–46; see also Alapuro, Risto and Allardt, Erik (1978) 'The Lapua Movement: The Threat of Rightist Takeover in Finland, 1930–32'. In Juan J. Linz and Alfred Stepan (eds) *The Breakdown of Democratic Regimes: Europe*. Baltimore and London: The Johns Hopkins University Press, 122–141.

11 See Alapuro and Allardt 1978, 122–141; Siltala, Juha (1985) *Lapuanliike ja kyyditykset 1930*. Helsinki: Kustannusosakeyhtiö Otava; Capoccia 2005, 155–176; Uola, Mikko (2006) 'Parlamentaarisen demokratian haastajat 1920- ja 1930-luvuilla'. In Vesa Vares, Mikko Uola, Mikko Majander: *Kansanvalta koetuksella. Suomen Eduskunta 100 vuotta 3*. Helsinki: Edita, 190–246.

12 See Uola 2006, 213-214, 250-254; Vares, Vesa (2007) 'Kokoomus ja demokratian kriisi'. In Vesa Vares and Ari Uino: *Suomalaiskansallinen Kokoomus. Kansallisen Kokoomuspuolueen historia 1929–1944*. Helsinki: Edita, 35–37, 106–107, 118–119. In the 1933 parliamentary elections the Conservative Party lost ten seats. Moreover, the People's Patriotic Movement formed its own parliamentary group and took 14 representatives away from the Conservatives. The party thus went down from 42 seats to 18. The winner of the elections was the Social Democratic Party, gaining 12 more seats and resulting in 78 out of the total 200 seats. The Agrarian Party formed the biggest non-socialist parliamentary group by its 53 seats. See Jääskeläinen, Mauno (1973) 'Itsenäisyyden ajan eduskunta 1919–1938'. In *Suomen kansanedustuslaitoksen historia VII*, Helsinki: Eduskunnan historiakomitea, 250.

13 The most significant faction in this respect was the youth organisation of the Conservative Party, Sweden's National League of Youth (*Sveriges nationella ungdomsförbund*, SNU), which, due to its support of the Nazi ideology, was excluded from the party in 1934.

of democratisation and interwar crisis, Sweden has been regarded as an example of a country where democratic institutions were firmly rooted and the crisis tackled by the politics of compromise led by the Social Democrats. It is a picture of successful social democratic reformism, often associated with a 'Keynesian' economic policy even before Keynes had formulated his theories on public investment and before the Rooseveltian 'New Deal' was put into practice.[14]

This picture was clearly in the making on the Day of Nordic Democracy. According to Hansson, it was thanks to the strong position Social Democratic Parties had in the Nordic countries, and thanks to these parties' capacity to build 'a democratic coalition' with 'bourgeois democracy', that these countries were able to present themselves as exemplary countries to the rest of the world. He held that it was in particular due to the social democratic economic policy that the Nordic countries were so successful in their defence of democracy.[15] It should be noted, however, that Hansson was speaking about Sweden and not about all the Nordic countries as he credited the social democratic *krispolitik* – the policy that was based on public investments and subsidies for agriculture, a result of the compromise between the Social Democratic Party and the Agrarian Party in 1933.[16] The *krispolitik* came to bear an important symbolic effect in the social democratic narrative of Swedish political history, marking the beginning

Three members of the party's parliamentary group followed the youth organisation and formed a group of its own in 1935–1936. However, neither the National League nor the three small National Socialist parties succeeded in winning any seats in the elections to the Riksdag. See Olsson, Stefan (2000) *Den svenska högerns anpassning till demokratin.* Uppsala: Uppsala University, 243–254; Nilsson, Torbjörn (2004) *Mellan arv och utopi: Moderata vägval under hundra år, 1904–2004.* Stockholm: Santérus Förlag, 171–173. For a thorough analysis of the Swedish Nazism, see Lööw, Helene (1990) *Hakkorset och Wasakärven: En studie av nationalsocialismen i Sverige 1924–1950.* Göteborg: Göteborgs universitet. On fascism and National Socialism in the Scandinavian countries, see Lindström, Ulf (1985) *Fascism in Scandinavia 1920–1940.* Stockholm: Almqvist & Wiksell International. As for the Swedish communists, they were divided into two factions in 1929, the minority continuing under the rule of the Third International, Comintern. See, Björlin, Lars (1997) 'För svensk arbetarklass eller sovjetisk utrikespolitik? Den kommunistiska rörelsen i Sverige och förbindelserna med Moskva 1920–1970'. In Sune Jungar & Bent Jensen (eds) *Sovjetunionen och Norden – konflikt, kontakt, influenser.* Helsinki: FHS, 212.

14 See Hilson, Mary (2007) 'Scandinavia'. In Robert Gerwarth (ed.) *Twisted Paths. Europe 1914–1945.* Oxford: Oxford University Press, 20–31; Ertman, Thomas (1998) 'Democracy and Dictatorship in Interwar Western Europe Revisited'. *World Politics* 50.3, 475–505. For a classic example of Sweden as the success story of democracy, see Rustow, Dankwart A. (1955) *The Politics of Compromise: A Study of Parties and Cabinet Government in Sweden.* Princeton: Princeton University Press; Rustow, Dankwart A. (1970) 'Transitions to Democracy: Toward a Dynamic Model'. *Comparative Politics,* Vol. 2, No. 3, 337–363. See also the introductory chapter in this volume.

15 *Fyra tal om nordisk demokrati* 1935, 8–10.

16 In the 1933 parliamentary elections the Social Democratic Party and the Agrarian Party together gained a majority of seats both in the Second (the lower) and the First Chamber, the numbers being 104 + 36 out of 230 in the Second Chamber and 58 + 18 out of 150 in the First Chamber. See Schück, Herman et al. (eds) (1985) *Riksdagen genom tiderna.* Stockholm: Sveriges Riksdag, Riksbankens Jubileumsfond, 33–333.

of a new epoch.[17] The image of a new era of the peasant-socialist coalition and planned economy was carefully promoted and elevated by the Social Democrats to signify the modern Sweden.[18]

For Väinö Tanner, the Finnish speaker on the Day of Nordic Democracy and leader of the Finnish Social Democratic Party, the crisis felt was of a different kind. It dealt with the faith of the existing political system and not any particular policy. Despite this difference, he nevertheless applied the Swedish way to the Finnish case in his rhetoric as he credited his own party of having participated in a successful defence of Finnish democracy. According to him, there had been serious plans in Finland to make the political system a dictatorship, but the Social Democrats had been able to build up, together with 'democratically minded bourgeois circles', a strong enough defence of democracy.[19] The leading Finnish Social Democrats saw themselves as the main defenders of democracy and parliamentarism in the country.[20] Tanner maintained that '[w]hen we give the democratic system our unconditional support it is our conviction that it is the best possible system of government. Its deepest aim is a government for the people and by the people'.[21]

As for the role of the Social Democrats in the defence of democracy in Finland, Tanner was speaking more about how the things should have been than how the situation really had developed. Although Tanner had belonged during the Lapua days to a political faction, 'the democratic front', that was formed in order to reject any attempts to install a dictatorship in Finland, the Social Democrats did not make any core of the defence of the political system.[22] The party had actually run a serious risk of being banned during the heydays of the Lapua movement.[23] It is thus no surprise that the

17 See e.g. Hilson 2007, 21.
18 However, it has been argued that the new economic policy had quite little to do with the recovery of Swedish economy, and that it was not a particularly controversial policy, as supportive measures with regard to agriculture were suggested also by the bourgeois parties. Moreover, it has been pointed out that, for example, both Denmark and Britain saw lab-lib compromises before Sweden entered into the labour-agrarian cooperation. See, e.g., Isaksson, Anders (2000) *Per Albin IV: Landsfadern*. Stockholm: Wahlström & Widstrand, 198–210, 229–242, 261.
19 *Fyra tal om nordisk demokrati* 1935, 12, 16–17.
20 See also Kettunen, Pauli (1980) 'Den finländska socialdemokratins demokratiuppfattning mellan inbördeskriget och lapporörelsens framträdande'. *Historisk Tidskrift för Finland*, 148; Kettunen, Pauli (1986) *Poliittinen like ja sosiaalinen kollektiivisuus. Tutkimus sosialidemokratiasta ja ammattiyhdistysliikkeestä Suomessa 1918–1930*. Helsinki: SHS, 261, 307, 314–315; Siltala 1985, 485–495.
21 *Fyra tal om nordisk demokrati* 1935, 13.
22 On the 'democratic front', see Kulha, Keijo (1989) *Sanasotaa ja sovittelua. Helsingin Sanomain poliittinen linja itsenäistymisestä talvisotaan*. Helsinki: Helsingin Sanomat, 157. Another faction, the legalist association 'Pro patria et lege' was formed by the Agrarian, Liberal, and Swedish People's parties' 'democratic-republican' circles, and it was explicitly stated that the Social Democrats should be excluded. See Uino, Ari (1983) 'Pro patria et lege – isänmaan ja lain puolesta -järjestö'. *Historiallinen Aikakauskirja* 3, 1983, 198–207; see also Mylly, Juhani (1989) *Maalaisliitto-Keskustapuolueen historia 2*. Helsinki: Kirjayhtymä, 285–290.
23 See Soikkanen, Hannu (1975) *Kohti kansanvaltaa 1. 1899–1937. Suomen Sosialidemokraattinen Puolue 75 vuotta*. Helsinki: Suomen Sosialidemokraattinen Puolue, 527–537.

Finnish Social Democrats viewed Sweden as exemplary, for it was there the Social Democrats governed with a newly launched progressive reform policy. Accordingly, K. A. Fagerholm, the Finnish Social Democrat who regularly wrote in the Swedish Young Socialists' paper, *Frihet* (Freedom), held in 1933 that '*Norden* would be the stronghold of democracy', because the labour movement in these countries was strong and united, with the exception of Finland where, according to him, the Communists had divided the movement.[24]

The contested concept of 'Nordic democracy'

'Nordic democracy' was presented by the Social Democrats as an antidote to the extremes on the Right and the Left, as well as an efficient social and economic policy that consolidated the nation. Despite the neutral ethos that the word 'Nordic' was intended to denote, the partisan aspect of the social democratic rhetoric was not left unnoticed. For example, the leading conservative newspaper in Sweden, *Svenska Dagbladet*, had a news item about the demonstration in Malmö, in which it was ironically explained, 'how the Social Democrats had saved democracy in Sweden'.[25] Another conservative paper, *Sydsvenska Dagbladet*, maintained that the Social Democrats' appeals to democracy were 'empty and hollow' as long as the party continued with its reluctant, even hostile, attitude towards the military defence of the country.[26] *Uusi Suomi*, the leading conservative daily newspaper in Finland, held that 'the demonstration in Malmö was a brutal misuse of the word democracy for the purpose of party propaganda'. According to the paper, 'the day of Nordic democracy was in fact the day of Nordic Social Democracy, on which the Nordic youth was trained in advancing socialism, the meaning of which was the destruction of Nordic democracy and its ancient ideals of freedom'.[27] It was also held that the sham rhetoric of democracy was meant to weaken the real democracy so that it would be unable to defend itself in the face of socialist revolution.[28] *Ajan Suunta*, the party organ of the Finnish right-wing extremist People's Patriotic Movement, which was the successor of the banned Lapua movement, viewed the social democratic rhetoric of Nordic democracy as orchestrated from Moscow and as a part of the new policy of the Communistic International that encouraged social democratic and liberal bourgeois parties to join the communists in a common 'popular front' against fascism. The fact that the leaders of the social democratic parties spoke in the name of individual freedom was ridiculed in the paper, which outright labelled these parties as Marxist and, consequently, as revolutionary.[29]

---

24   *Frihet* 9/1933, 5–6.
25   *Svenska Dagbladet*, 26 August, 1935.
26   Quoted in *Svenska Dagbladet*, 27 August, 1935.
27   *Uusi Suomi*, 29 August, 1935.
28   *Uusi Suomi*, 29 August, 1935.
29   *Ajan Suunta*, 30 August, 1935.

Now, it should be noted that *Uusi Suomi*, the paper that had only lately openly supported the Lapua movement and the People's Patriotic Movement, referred to 'Nordic democracy' in its attack on the social democratic use of the very same expression. This is not to say that 'democracy' was in vogue in the right-wing populist quarters, only to point out that there was a conservative conception of democracy that was regarded as particularly Nordic of its character. Moreover, it is important to note that the Social Democrats' effort to launch 'Nordic democracy' could be contested from the left-wing side as well. As a matter of fact, the social democratic parties' rhetorical identification on the Day of Nordic Democracy was not the first attempt of promoting 'Nordic democracy' from the left-wing angle.

If a godfather of the Finnish rhetoric of 'Nordic democracy' must be named, it was not Tanner, nor any other from within the party leadership, but the editor of the cultural-radical weekly *Tulenkantajat* (The Torch Bearers), Erkki Vala. In 1933, the paper that was the forum of a small but in terms of cultural debates quite influential group of left-wing and liberal radicals and literati, started a campaign, demanding Western cultural and political orientation in Finland. In this agenda the rhetoric of 'Nordic democracy' had a crucial role. A couple of months before Hitler came into power in Germany and during the winter when the People's Patriotic Movement took a considerable hold on the Conservative Party in Finland, Vala started a rhetorical manoeuvre which to a considerable degree resembled the rhetorical campaign in which the Finnish Social Democratic Party engaged with a couple of years later. For him, the Nordic countries and the Anglo-Saxon countries were the guardians of Western civilisation in the time of continental reaction and, in particular, Germany going in to darkness.[30] On the one hand, Vala naturalised Nordic democracy by claiming that it had existed for hundreds of years; on the other hand, he positioned his political opponents in Finland, and many times Finland as a whole, outside this democratic Nordic community.[31] He held, for example, that 'one has begun to advocate German and Italian ideas as national in here, whereas one has labelled as antinational the Nordic democracy that has reigned for hundreds of years in our country'.[32] In his rhetoric Finland moved into and out from Nordic democracy, depending on his argument at hands. The point was to demand democracy in Finland by making comparative references to the Nordic democracy that, according to him, the Scandinavian countries cultivated.

In 1935, when the promotion of 'Nordic democracy' had been taken over by the Social Democratic Party leadership, Vala and *Tulenkantajat* made 'Nordic democracy' a rhetorical tool in the purpose of criticising the

---

30 *Tulenkantajat* No 3, 3 January, 1933; No 10, 11 March, 1933; No 11, 18 March, 1933. On *Tulenkantajat* and the Nordic political and cultural orientation in Finland, see also Elmgren, Ainur (2008) *Den allrakäraste fienden. Svenska stereotyper i finländsk press 1918–1939*. Lund: Sekel, 53–55, 103–139.

31 *Tulenkantajat* No 5, 4 February, 1933; No 17, 29 April, 1933; No 18, 6 May, 1933; No 25, 5 August, 1933.

32 *Tulenkantajat* No 5, February 4, 1933.

Finnish government and, in particular, the Social Democratic party leader Tanner.[33] Thus, it was held in the paper that the increased Finnish interest in cooperation with the Scandinavian countries was a positive sign as such, but the picture Tanner had painted on the Day of Nordic Democracy was wrong. According to Vala, the defence of democracy had not yet proved to be successful in Finland, contrary to what Tanner had claimed. Moreover, he held that the Social Democratic Party was cooperating with the bourgeois government that was limiting democratic rights rather than defending them.[34] Two months later, Vala bluntly maintained that 'talks about cooperation with the Scandinavian democratic countries were empty and hollow, because Finland was a fascistic country whereas the Scandinavian countries were democratic ones'.[35]

The contested concept of 'democracy'

The rhetoric of Nordic democracy needs to be understood as a part of a general contest over the meaning of 'democracy'. Two interrelated aspects of this contest can be pointed out. On the one hand, there was the question whether or not democracy was acceptable at all; on the other hand, the contest was about the correct meaning of the concept. In the 1930s, it was not entirely uncommon to reject democracy, and it was quite common to criticise democracy without any positively evaluated and alternative use of the very word. Many conservatives viewed the crisis of democracy as a result of the internal weakness and, consequently, dysfunctions of democracy itself and, as caused particularly by the Left.[36] However, more common than to deny any virtuous content of the concept of democracy was to make a distinction between good and bad democracy. As one analyst of Swedish conservative ideology has noted, it was common to take 'democracy' as a necessary part of the game, yet, at the same time, treat it as a sub-category of 'the people's power' or 'the government of the people'.[37] When seen this way, it was possible to claim that one was in fact in favour of democracy although one rejected the idea of parliamentary government. Consequently,

33 The government, led by T. M. Kivimäki, The Progressive Party (Liberals), was a bourgeois composition supported by the parliamentary groups of the Progressive Party and the Swedish People's Party. It was most of the time criticised by the Conservatives despite the fact that the party belonged to the government coalition. The ministry could actually stay in office with the help of a tactical support from the Social Democratic Party.
34 *Tulenkantajat* No 35, 31 August, 1935.
35 *Tulenkantajat* No 39, 28 September, 1935.
36 For example, the Swedish conservative leader Arvid Lindman described Hitler's takeover in Germany not in the first place as a threat to democracy but as an illness-symptom of democracy. In a similar vein, *Svenska landsbygden*, the paper close to the Agrarian Party, held that National Socialism was a consequence of democracy's devices, such as misuse of power, minority parliamentarism, and the tyranny of labour organisations. See Torstendahl, Rolf (1969) *Mellan nykonservatism och liberalism. Idébrytningar inom högern och bondepartierna 1918–1934*. Stockholm: Svenska bokförlaget, 97, 106.
37 Torstendahl 1969, 103.

one version of the critique of democracy was to claim that the source of the legitimacy of the political system was the people when understood as the plebiscite that gave the authority to a 'strong man' who would represent the people and thus be a democratic leader.[38] For example, 'a strong man's politics on the Swedish ground' was contrasted to 'the foggy and unclear concept of democracy' in an article published in the Conservative Party's weekly *Medborgaren* (The Citizen). The unsigned article was explicit in denouncing parliamentarism as the source of this fogginess of democracy.[39] The critique of parliamentarism was also evident in the rhetoric of J. K. Paasikivi, the leader of the Finnish Conservative Party, whose main task was to wash off the right-wing extremism that the People's Patriotic Movement imposed on the Conservatives.[40] He referred particularly to the Scandinavian countries, when he stated that parliamentarism functioned badly because the governments were based on an occasional and shifting support from parliament.[41]

On the Day of Nordic Democracy, Tanner rejected such a view and held that in the Scandinavian countries the governments had been sustainable and executed their tasks in an exemplary way.[42] To some extent, both Paasikivi and Tanner were right. In Sweden, interwar parliamentarism was based on the government having only shifting majorities at parliament and therefore it has been characterised as 'negative parliamentarism' but the system itself functioned rather well, the medial age of a cabinet being close to two years between 1920 and 1932. In Finland, where there were no less than 19 ministries between 1917 and 1932, parliamentary life was characterised by the cleavage that originated from the 1918 Civil War between the 'Reds'

38 This was the core idea in Carl Schmitt's famous critique of parliamentary democracy as elaborated in *Die geistesgeschichtliche Lage des heutigen Parlamentarismus*, published in two editions in 1923 and 1926. See Schmitt, Carl (1988) [1926] *The Crisis of Parliamentary Democracy*, translated by Ellen Kennedy. Cambridge Massachusetts, and London, England: The MIT Press.
39 *Medborgaren* N:r 10, 1933, 360–361. In another article, 'true democracy' was then set against 'class parties' and associated with 'free individuals', 'freedom and laws', 'conviction', 'citizen, citizenry state and citizenry mind'. *Medborgaren* N:r 6, 1933, 201–202.
40 Paasikivi was a grand old man in Finnish political life. He had belonged to the Finnish-language nationalist party and supported the introduction of universal suffrage in 1906; he was one of the key persons in the process that led to the declaration of independence in 1917. He was also one of the leading advocates of monarchy in 1918, the position that was defeated after Germany's capitulation in the world war. In the 1920s and 1930s Paasikivi was one of the leading men in banking and economics in Finland. He was the Finnish Ambassador in Stockholm in 1936–1940. He was the President of Finland 1946–1956.
41 Paasikivi, Juho Kusti (1956) [1935] 'Ajankohtaisia kysymyksiä'. In *Paasikiven linja II. Juho Kusti Paasikiven puheita ja esitelmiä vuosilta 1923–1942*. Porvoo, Helsinki: Werner Söderström Osakeyhtiö, 75–76.
42 *Fyra tal om nordisk demokrati* 1935, 14. The Finnish Social Democrats maintained also that it was not correct to claim that the parliamentary system resulted in a weak executive. According to them, several examples showed that governments lasted longer in democracies than in dictatorships. Denmark and Sweden were particularly mentioned as such examples. *Valtiopäivät 1935, pöytäkirjat II*. Helsinki, 1648–1654. Quotation on p. 1653. On the same argument, see *Frihet* 10/1935, 7.

and 'Whites' and, consequently, by restrictions made to the Communists' participation in the parliamentary life. Moreover, the fundamental unity that was claimed in the name of the 'White Finland' did not materialise in the bourgeois parliamentary politics either. It should also be noted that much of the executive power was placed in the hand of the president in the 1919 Constitution, which made the parliamentary government a less prominent actor in the system than was the case in Sweden.[43]

It was common to criticise modern parliamentarism by pointing out the difference between it and the classical English parliamentarism that was developed in the context of remarkably restricted voting rights. According to this view, parliamentarism did not work properly in a mass-society with universal suffrage.[44] Despite this critique, however, both the Finnish and Swedish Conservative Parties started to take a more positive stand to parliamentary democracy around the middle of the 1930s. The shift was to a large extent provoked by the internal divisions in the parties in both countries. In Finland, the reorientation was driven, in particular, by Paasikivi who notwithstanding his criticism of parliamentarism defended the principle of democracy, though pointing out that, in a system of millions of voters, agitation, demagogy, and propaganda threatened the idealised picture of democracy.[45] In Sweden, negative views of democracy were abandoned in particular among a new generation of conservatives whose influence within the party increased as the party was breaking up with its Nazi-inspired youth organisation in 1934. It was even held in an article published in *Medborgaren* that 'democracy' should be made a key word in the party programme. What was needed, it was argued, was to adopt 'democracy in its real meaning, that is, government through the people' and not the social democrats' class politics which made 'freedom' an empty word.[46] The political scientist Gunnar Heckscher was probably the leading intellectual among these young Swedish conservatives, whose aim was to redirect the party's view of

43   Nyman, Olle (1947) *Svensk parlamentarism 1932–1936. Från minoritetsparlamentarism till majoritetskoalition.* Uppsala: Uppsala univestitet (distributed by Almqvist & Wiksell), 1–16; von Sydow, Björn (1990) 'Parlamentarismens utveckling'. In *Att styra riket. Regeringskansliet 1840–1990.* Stockholm: Departementshistoriekommittén, Allmänna Förlaget, 73–75; Nousianen, Jaakko (2006) 'Suomalainen parlamentarismi'. In Antero Jyränki and Jaakko Nousiainen: *Eduskunnan muuttuva asema. Suomen Eduskunta 100 vuotta 2.* Edita: Helsinki, 204-208; Nousiainen, Jaakko (1985) *Suomen presidentit valtiollisina johtajina: K. J. Ståhlebrgista Mauno Koivistoon.* Porvoo-Helsinki-Juva: Werner Söderström Osakeyhtiö, 115.
44   Paasikivi 1956 [1934], 49–50; Paasikivi 1956 [1935], 72–73; *Medborgaren* N:r 10, 1933, 360–361.
45   Paasikivi 1956 [1935], 73–74.
46   *Medborgaren* N:r 5, 1935, 156–158. Sven-Ulric Palme, one of the young conservatives, accused the opponents of democracy of their hypocritical stand when they took use of 'the crisis of democracy' in their rhetoric. By referring to Tingsten's *Democracy's Victory and Crisis,* Palme argued that instead of maintaining an idealised view of democracy one should see it as an unfinished project that had different practical applications in different situations. The problems that the system of parliamentary government obviously had were not fatal but, instead, a sign of a democracy which was based on a sense of reality and not on an illusionary search for the truth. *Medborgaren* N:r 3, 1934, 103–107.

democracy.[47] He developed a positive historical view of parliamentarism by presenting a historical account of English parliamentarism and concluding that, despite the fact that parliamentarism and democracy were two different concepts and despite the fact that parliamentarism had its greatest period at the time when hardly anyone thought of mass-democracy, there were still some signs in the continental liberal thought which had shown that these two concepts were combinable.[48]

In *Demokratins seger och kris* Tingsten viewed the crisis of democracy as a consequence of the decline of shared values. For him, contestation and possibility for political struggle were inherent characteristics of parliamentary democracy in a liberal state. In order for democracy to sustain the contestation, it needed a common ground of shared values with regard to the rules of the game.[49] In a similar vein, Paasikivi held that parliamentary democracy could function properly only if all parties shared the same principled attitudes toward the political system and society.[50] However, the difference between the Swedish social democratic political scientist and the Finnish conservative politician (with a doctoral degree in jurisprudence) was that the former made a distinction that separated the Social Democrats from the Communists and thus regarded social democracy as democratic ideology,[51] whereas the latter saw social democracy and communism as eventually based on the same ideology. According to Paasikivi, a democratic system was sustainable only on the condition that social democratic parties either would grow considerably smaller or that they would abandon the Marxist doctrine and take an open and positive view of the foundations of the contemporary society. As it was in the present situation, Paasikivi held, the Social Democrats participated in the 'the parliamentary game' on the condition that they did not get any parliamentary majority. If they would get it and still continued to play the game, he added, they were then not faithful to their principles.[52] It is important to note that, while the Finnish Social Democrats were strongly condemned by Paasikivi as advocates of the idea of class struggle and, accordingly, of German Marxism, he nevertheless saw some positive signs in the Swedish social democracy. He referred to 'a Swedish socialist leader' who had made the distinction between Marxism and socialism. In this account, the materialistic view of history and the

47 Heckscher paved the way to 'liberal conservatism' within the party. See Möller, Tommy (2004) *Mellan ljusblå och mörkblå. Gunnar Heckscher som högerledare.* Stockholm: SNS Förlag, 56. Heckscher was the leader of the Conservative Party in 1961–1965.

48 Heckscher, Gunnar (1937) *Parlamentarism och demokrati i England.* Stockholm: Hugo Gebers Förlag, 323–324. The book was based on university lectures held in 1935–1936.

49 Tingsten 1933, 22, 60–61. In 1935, Tingsten held that different ideologies had different conceptualisations, which resulted in the notion that words like 'democracy' and 'freedom' had entirely different meanings in countries like Russia, Italy, and Germany. See Tingsten, Herbert (1935) 'Installationsföreläsning den 15 april 1935'. In *Samhällskrisen och socialvetenskaperna: Två installationsföreläsningar.* Stockholm: Kooperativa förbundets bokförlag, 48–49, 56, 62–63.

50 Paasikivi 1956 [1935], 75–76.

51 Tingsten 1933, 48-59, 86–118.

52 Paasikivi 1956 [1935], 76.

idea of class struggle as well as theories of surplus and pauperisation were abandoned. Moreover, there was room for private enterprises in the system that was sketched in Sweden.[53]

Whatever his own party's commitment to democracy may have been, Paasikivi's critique of the Social Democrats' unsolved relationship with parliamentary democracy was in many regards understandable. It should be pointed out that the Finnish Social Democrats' positive view of 'parliamentary democracy' had been far from unanimous when the party had recreated its political profile after the Civil War, although the issue was crucial in making the division between the Finnish Social Democrats and the Communists in 1918–1920.[54] Throughout the 1920s, the party was more focused on parliamentary politics and cooperative associations than on the labour union, in which the Communists still had much influence.[55] With regard to parliamentary politics, an important step was taken by the Finnish Social Democrats in 1926-1927 when Tanner was the prime minister of the Social Democratic cabinet. Both the theoretical position of Kautsky and the practical experiences of Swedish and Danish Social Democrats were weighed when the party decided on the building of the government. Regarding the labour union, the Social Democrats left the union in 1930 as it was dominated by the Communists.[56] Despite these signs of moderation, the Social Democrats cultivated the rhetoric of class struggle and socialism, which did not go unnoticed among the non-socialists. The Social Democrats' credibility in bourgeois quarters was weakened also by the fact that there was always a faction or two on the leftmost outpost of the party.

It is actually quite easy to see why the Conservatives were negative in their comments on the Day of Nordic Democracy, when we take into account that Hansson stated in the occasion that democracy should be spread to all levels of social life before it was possible to maintain that 'democracy prevailed completely'.[57] Even more provocative must have been an article in *Frihet* (Freedom), the periodical that usually represented a moderate line within the party. It was, namely, held in the paper that the purpose of the Day of Nordic Democracy was to advance socialism. It was proclaimed that 'to fight for Democracy and to defend Democracy are the first steps in our struggle for Socialism'.[58] Moreover, the article read that 'where the foundation of Democracy has been laid down and made secure, Socialism can continue its march to victory' and that 'when Democracy is being threatened and has been lost in several quarters, we realize its value more clearly'.[59] Although the periodical was making a link between democracy and socialism that actually was, and remained to be up till the 1980s, quite common for the

---

53 Paasikivi 1956 [1934], 51. See also Vares 2007, 211.
54 See Soikkanen 1975, 366.
55 In Sweden, the Social Democrats had much closer tie with the union than was the case in Finland. See Kettunen 1986, passim.
56 See Soikkanen 1975, 445–460, 492–493; Kettunen 1980, 141–143; Kettunen 1986, 314.
57 *Fyra tal om nordisk demokrati* 1935, 6.
58 *Frihet* 16/1935, 3.
59 *Frihet* 16/1935, 3.

Social Democrats, the fact remains that the Social Democratic parole of socialism easily gave to their bourgeois rivalries the impression that their commitment to democracy, and thus Nordic democracy, served merely instrumental purposes. It did not help either that a certain aspect of instrumentality was built in the Marxist Socialists' view of parliamentary democracy, because they were committed to the idea of bourgeois class domination and, eventually, to the idea of world historical progress toward socialism, characterised by class struggle.

Both the Kautskyan socialism and the Leninist communism were based on the idea of class struggle.[60] The Kautskyan socialism, on which social democracy drew, made the case against 'bourgeois democracy' or 'capitalist democracy' due to the existing inequalities but, nevertheless, defended 'liberal' principles of democracy as a means of gaining more fairness in economic conditions.[61] In the Communists' view, meanwhile, parliament was useful only as a forum for revolutionary propaganda. Accordingly, parliament could be used only in advancing of the destruction of the political system and, thus, the very parliament itself.[62] In Finland, the Communists' public activity being banned, the sceptical or even pejorative view of parliamentary democracy was articulated in the periodical of the Academic Socialist Society, *Soihtu* (The Torch), which was the forum of an intern opposition within the Social Democratic Party.[63] It was held in the periodical, for example, that a socialist party should reject any participation in the procedures of a democratic republic and aim at the dictatorship of the proletariat instead. It was also held that 'democracy' and 'dictatorship' meant the same thing in bourgeois democracy and that the socialist strategy should take use of the freedoms of the bourgeois democracy. The only real democracy was thus 'proletarian' or 'socialistic' democracy. [64]

In the Comintern's policy the Communists' first target was quite often not the Conservatives or the bourgeois liberals, not even the fascists or the Nazis, but the 'social fascists' – the Social Democrats – because they had split the

---

60   It should be noted that the there were, of course, several variations of Marxist thought, Austro-Marxism being an important one. For a detailed analysis of ideological differences within the Marxist tradition in the 1920s and early 1930s, see Kettunen 1986, 90–104, 231–315.

61   On one influential account in this respect, see Laski, Harold, J. (1933) *Democracy in Crisis*. London: George Allen & Unwin Ltd.

62   See Saarela, Tauno (1998) 'International and National in the Communist Movement'. In Tauno Saarela and Kimmo Rentola (eds) *Communism: National & International*. Helsinki: SHS, 33.

63   The party majority that was gathered around Tanner was more or less constantly at pains in trying to figure out as to how much *Soihtu* was under the direct influence of the Communists. Although there were left-wing intellectuals of different colour gathered around the periodical, the Social Democratic party cut off formal contacts with the Academic Socialist Society in 1937. See Soikkanen 1975, 559, 576–583. It should be noted that many of the key persons around *Tulenkantajat* appeared regularly in *Soihtu*. For example, Erkki Vala was active in both publications.

64   *Soihtu* 1931, 19; 1/1932, 14; 5/1932, 10–13; 2/1934, 35-36; 4–5/1934, 85. In fact, one article concerning a party meeting openly ridiculed 'social democracy' by emphasising the latter part of the compound word (sosiali*demokratia*) every time as the party line was criticised. *Soihtu* 4–5/1934, 84–90.

proletariat and thus, among other things, cleared the road for the Nazis.[65] Although the Nazis' coming into power could in principle be interpreted as proof of the fragility of the capitalist system and as a step toward the proletarian revolution, it was a major problem for the Communists who looked at the world with Soviet geopolitics in mind. The Soviet communists no longer could afford to picture all other parties as their enemies. Instead of being 'social fascists', the Social Democrats – and even bourgeois middle parties – were invited to create a 'popular front' against fascism. The new strategy emerged in 1934–1935 and was officially launched in the summer of 1935.[66] After the doctrine of a 'popular front' was launched, 'true' democracy still had a strictly demarcated proletarian content, but the 'petite bourgeoisie' and 'democratic parties' were treated sometimes not merely as reasons for fascism but also as its victims.[67]

The idea of a popular front was rejected by the leading Social Democrats in Sweden and Finland. The problem was, as it was held in the Swedish social democratic journal *Tiden* (Time), that the Communists had for a long time preached on the futility of democracy and that they in this sense differed insignificantly from the advocates of a dictatorship of other colour. What the Communists now tried to do was to defend democracy in order to make it possible for them to demolish it later on. Moreover, it was held that the Social Democrats viewed 'a bourgeois middle-ground' much more committed to democracy than 'five tons of resolutions from Moscow'.[68]

Compared to Finland, the Communists did not have any considerable influence in the Swedish labour movement.[69] However, it was important for the Social Democratic Party leadership to try to mark the difference between themselves and the Communists, not least due to the internal rivalry within the Social Democratic Party itself.[70] In Finland, the Social Democrats had an even more urgent need of upholding the line of demarcation between themselves and the Communists than in Sweden due to the popularity of the Communists in the workers' associations and due to the pressure from the bourgeois parties.[71] An illuminating example of the Social Democrats'

---

65 See Majander, Mikko (1998) 'The Soviet view on Social Democracy. From Lenin to the End of the Stalin Era'. In Tauno Saarela and Kimmo Rentola (eds) *Communism: National & International*. Helsinki: SHS, 61–66, 74–77, 81–82.

66 Majander 1998, 83–84; with regard to the Swedish communists, see Björlin 1997, 217–220.

67 *Soihtu*, marraskuu (November) 1935, 106–109.

68 *Tiden* 1935, 473–482, quotations at 482.

69 See Björlin 1997, 201–220.

70 See *Frihet* 7/1934, 5–6; *Frihet* 18/1934, 5–6; *Frihet* 22/1934, 5–6; *Frihet* 21/1935, 2. Organisations that were regarded as being under the influence of the communists were excluded from the party in 1933. See Isaksson 2000, 150.

71 See e.g. Soikkanen 1975, 590. The pressure from the Right made the party to restate the nature of their membership of the Socialist International. It was decided in the 1933 party congress that the party would follow its own judgement rather than the decisions of the International. Soikkanen 1975, 543; Paasivirta, Juhani (1988) *Finland and Europe. The early years of independence 1917–1939*. Helsinki: SHS, 393. In Sweden, the same revision was made in 1932. See Isaksson 2000, 203. The Socialist International was the successor of the Second International, which had been dominated by Kautsky and dissolved in 1914 due to the war.

position was that Tanner had regarded the emergence of the Lapua movement at first as a consequence of communism in Finland. He saw the movement as a reaction to the 'senseless and childish action of the Communists'.[72] To him, both the Communists and the 'right-wing-Bolsheviks' took orders from foreign governments. At the same time as Tanner defended the Marxist character of his own party, he nevertheless argued in favour of cooperation between the Social Democrats and bourgeois parties that were committed to democracy.[73] It was the question of the very cooperation he had emphasised when he addressed his audience on the Day of Nordic Democracy.

Despite the pressed situation of the Finnish Social Democrats in the early thirties, and despite the criticism the party line gained from the left-wing socialists, Tanner actually had something to show which would support his view of the key role he gave to his own party. A couple of months before his attendance in the festival that celebrated Nordic democracy he had been making investigations for the Finnish government, aiming at a closer cooperation in foreign policy between Finland and Sweden. As will be shown below, the foreign policy rapprochement increased the possibility for the Social Democrats' rhetoric of 'Nordic democracy' to take hold among the bourgeois parties in Finland.

The Scandinavian orientation in Finland

The 'Scandinavian orientation'[74] of Finnish foreign policy, which was announced by the Finnish government in December 1935, needs to be seen as an important background for the rhetoric of 'Nordic democracy' in Finland. The bourgeois government was not thrilled by this rhetoric but the reorientation created a favourable political climate for such rhetoric, although it was not 'democracy' but 'neutrality', 'peace' and 'defence' that were the key words in use when the new foreign policy orientation was presented in parliament.[75] There is no doubt that the motivation behind the

72   Tanner, Väinö (1956) [1930] *Itsenäisen Suomen arkea. Valikoima puheita.* Helsinki: Kustannusosakeyhtiö Tammi, 129. See also Kettunen 1986, 309–310; Siltala 1985, 486. This opinion was not always coherent, however. For example, K. H. Wiik, the party secretary and the most influential left-wing socialist in the party, criticised in 1930 'bourgeois democratic circles' of viewing fascism and communism as identical threat to democracy. See Kettunen 1986, 311. It can be noted that, in the Social Democrats' view, the Communists had betrayed the cause of the working class – the same accusation as the Communists directed toward the Social Democrats in the contest over the right meaning of 'the working class' – and therefore they were regarded as being wrong, whereas the fascists were seen as enemies of the working class and thus being inherently wrong.

73   Tanner 1956 [1933], 179–193; see Kettunen 1980, 142. 'Right-wing Bolshevism' was used as early as in 1922 by the liberal *Helsingin Sanomat* in an article that denounced Finnish supporters of Italian fascism. See Hyvämäki, Lauri (1968) 'Fascismin "tulo Suomeen" 1922–23'. *Historiallinen Aikakauskirja* N:o 2, 118.

74   'Scandinavian orientation' and 'Nordic orientation' were used synonymously in Finnish discussions, the former being more common.

75   According to Prime Minister Kivimäki, Sweden had the best chance in the Finnish neighbourhood to remain a neutral country in the case of war; and because neutrality

new policy was security. The international political scene in Europe was dramatically changing, and it was quite commonly felt in small countries like Finland and the Scandinavian countries that the status of the League of Nations was in decline. The world organisation had in many eyes begun to appear as a factor that might draw small countries into troubles rather than be a guarantee against them.[76] The exit of Germany from the League of Nations in 1933 and the Italian invasion of Abyssinia in 1935, which was the most acute international crisis at the time, underlined the weakness of the international arrangement. This change undermined much of the Finnish foreign policy premises.

In the League of Nations Finland had been aligned with France and been committed to the idea of security guarantees, whereas Sweden and the other Scandinavian countries had shared Britain's view of disarmament as the main strategy. This difference was diminishing in 1935, when France made a pact with the Soviet Union. An earlier interest in cooperation with the Baltic States and Poland, 'the Border States', which had had its momentum in the early 1920s, was more or less abandoned as the Soviet Union started to propose security guarantee arrangements with these countries. When a rapprochement with Germany was also conceived as too risky, there was a growing sense of isolation among those responsible for Finnish international relations and security. To this problem, closer cooperation with the Scandinavian countries seemed like a viable solution.[77]

It was certainly not uncommon in Finland to view Germany as a potential ally, but the political and military leadership regarded Hitler's international moves as too risky for Finland to be involved. Ideological arguments in favour of a German orientation were not commonly presented either.[78] It is true, however, that in 1933 Finnish conservative newspapers expressed a rather positive view of the German Nazis, but it dealt more with hopes of the return of pre-1918 nationalism and conservatism in Germany than

---

was also the goal of Finnish policy, 'it was only natural that the Finnish orientation was toward Scandinavia'. *Valtiopäivät 1935, Pöytäkirjat III*. Helsinki, 2514.

76 For example, the Swedish Foreign Minister Rickard Sandler expressed this caution in his speech on Swedish foreign policy options in December 1935. See Sandler, Rickard (1935) *Svenska utrikesärenden: Anföranden 1934–35*. Stockholm: Tidens förlag, 167.

77 See Selén, Kari (1974) *Genevestä Tukholmaan. Suomen turvallisuuspolitiikan painopisteen siirtyminen Kansainliitosta pohjoismaiseen yhteistyöhön 1931–1936*, Historiallisia tutkimuksia 94. Helsinki: Suomen Historiallinen Seura, 132–135, 155; Soikkanen, Timo (1983) *Kansallinen eheytyminen - myytti vai todellisuus?: ulko- ja sisäpolitiikan linjat ja vuorovaikutus Suomessa vuosina 1933–1939*. Turku: University of Turku, 28; Kaukiainen, Leena (1984) 'From Reluctancy to Activity. Finland's Way to the Nordic Family during 1920's and 1930's. *Scandinavian Journal of History*, 9:2, 201–219; Paasivirta 1988, 396–402, 456; Salmon, Patrick (1997) *Scandinavia and the great powers 1890–1940*. Cambridge: Cambridge University Press, 189–199. On Swedish views regarding collective security arrangements, see Stråth, Bo (1993) *Folkhemmet mot Europa. Ett historiskt perspektiv på 90-talet*. Stockholm: Tiden, 189; Stråth, Bo (2000) 'Poverty, Neutrality and Welfare: Three Key Concepts in the Modern Foundation Myth of Sweden'. In Bo Stråth (ed.) *Myth and Memory in the Construction of Community. Historical Patterns in Europe and Beyond*. Brussels: P.I.E.-Peter Lang S.A., 387–388.

78 Soikkanen 1983, 30–33.

with an outspoken sympathy for the Nazi ideology.[79] Apart from the papers of the People's Patriotic Movement, such enthusiasm soon disappeared as Hitler's methods became more apparent. The Left and the bourgeois liberals were by and large consequent in their criticism of the Nazis and the Italian fascism.[80] On many international issues the social democratic papers showed sympathy for Soviet initiatives as they were marking their contempt regarding Hitler's Germany. This was strongly criticised by the Right, which was harsh in its critique of the Soviet Union.[81]

The existence and politics of the Soviet Union must be seen as the main geopolitical factor behind the Scandinavian orientation in Finland. The Soviet Union was conceived of as the outmost problem in Finland, not least due to the Soviet involvement in Finnish politics through the Finnish Communist Party.[82] Another problem for the Finnish-Soviet relationship was caused by the fact that there was a loud, dominantly academic, nationalistic movement in Finland that proclaimed togetherness between Finland and the Finnish-speaking (or linguistically related) population which lived within the Soviet borders. The collectivisation and resettlement of this population was strongly criticised in Finland and viewed as a violation against the Tartu Peace Treaty between the countries from 1920. The Soviet government, in turn, accused the Finnish government of supporting the idea of 'Great-Finland' as well as the illegal actions of the Lapua movement.[83] However,

79 See e.g. Selén, Kari (1980) *C. G. E. Mannerheim ja hänen puolustusneuvostonsa 1931–1939*. Helsinki: Kustannusosakeyhtiö Otava, 220–221; Vares 2007, 16, 168–170, 201. There had been a strong orientation toward Germany in Finland in 1918, when German troops assisted the Whites in the Civil War. A German Duke was actually requested to become the King of Finland. The collapse of the German Reich, however, made these monarchist plans impossible and Finland became a republic. It should be mentioned that there was a common sympathy for German conservatism and nationalism among the Conservatives also in Sweden. As regards to the first impressions of the Nazi power in Germany, the Swedish conservatives were not particularly different from the Finnish ones. The conservative papers tended to regard Nazism as a reaction against the Treaty of Versailles, and as the power that had succeeded in stopping the influence of the Communists and the Socialists. Some members of the Agrarian Party also welcomed Hitler but, in the main, the Agrarians were against the Nazis. In general, German politics was regarded as more alarming than that of the Soviet Union. The German government actually complained about the critical articles that were published in liberal and left-wing papers, but the Swedish government explained that the freedom of press made it impossible for the government to direct and control the media. See Tingsten, Herbert (1949) *The Debate on the Foreign Policy of Sweden* (translated by Joan Bulman). London: Oxford University Press, 173–176; Torbacke, Jarl (1972) *Dagens Nyheter och demokratins kris 1922–1936. Friheten är vår lösen*. Stockholm: Bonniers, 252; Lönnroth, Erik (1959) *Den svenska utrikespolitikens historia: V 1919–1939*. Stockholm: Norstedts, 129, 163–166.
80 Paasivirta 1988, 392-394.
81 Soikkanen 1983, 32-33.
82 See Vihavainen, Timo (1997) 'Sovjetbilden i Finland – ett fall för sig'. In Sune Jungar & Bent Jensen (eds) *Sovjetunionen och Norden – konflikt, kontakt, influenser*. Helsinki: FHS, 133-138.
83 See Korhonen, Keijo (1971) *Turvallisuuden pettäessä. Suomi neuvostodiplomatiassa Tartosta talvisotaan II 1933–1939*. Helsinki: Kustannusosakeyhtiö Tammi, 85; Paasivirta 1988, 398–399.

the main problem in the 1930s was that the Soviet government viewed Finland as taking sides with Germany. Despite the 1932 non-aggression treaty between Finland and the Soviet Union, the relationship between the countries continued to be chilly. In 1935, the Soviet envoy in Helsinki informed the Finnish Prime Minister that, in the case of a European crisis, the Red Army might be forced to occupy a part of Finland in order to defend the Soviet Union against Germany.[84]

In Stalin's view, Finland belonged with the Baltic countries and not with the Nordic ones.[85] This attitude can be seen also in the comment published by the Soviet government's paper *Izvestija* a day before (sic) the statement of Finland's Scandinavian orientation. According to the paper, the whole thing was a sham operation, the purpose of which was to veil the Finnish cooperation with Germany and, moreover, to enlist the Scandinavian countries on the hazardous policy of Finland.[86] The Soviet government took the rapprochement as an orchestrated attempt by Germany to block the Soviet Union's contact with the Baltic Sea area. The attempt of coup d'état, which took place in Estonia at the same time as the Finnish government announced the new foreign policy orientation and in which some Finnish nationalistic activists and right-wing extremists in fact were involved, only underlined Soviet fears of the increased German influence in the area.[87] From the Finnish government's perspective, one particular problem was that the Soviet view was in some international comments taken as correct. For example, there was a rumour spreading in April 1935 at the League of Nations' headquarter in Geneva telling that Germany had given Finland guarantees of military help in case of Soviet attack.[88]

The Scandinavian orientation of Finland was planned and put into effect within a small circle at the political top.[89] However, a special role in the rapprochement was given to the Social Democrats, for it was Tanner who, due to his personal contacts with the Swedish Social Democrats in power,

---

84   Korhonen 1971, 124; see also Paasivirta 1988, 387–388, 398–400, 462.

85   Korhonen 1971, 26; Selén 1980, 192. In Comintern strategy, Finland had also been placed in the same group with the Baltic states and Poland, whereas the Scandinavian countries formed a separate group. See Salmon 1997, 227–228.

86   Korhonen 1971, 131; see also Lönnroth 1959, 131; Soikkanen 1983, 73.

87   See Korhonen 1971, 107–109, 129–131.

88   Korhonen 1971, 122. Moreover, shortly after the foreign policy statement, the Finnish representative in Geneva, Rudolf Holsti, who strongly advocated Finland's commitment to the League of Nations, privately let know that Finland's Scandinavian orientation was taken as a bluff 'in everywhere'. (Korhonen 1971, 133).

89   The most important actors in Finnish reorientation were president Svinhufvud, Foreign Minister Hackzell, Prime Minister Kivimäki, the chairman of Economy Committee, J. K. Paasikivi, and the chairman of the Defence Council, C. G. Mannerheim. In Sweden the key persons were Foreign Minister Rickard Sandler, Swedish Ambassador in Helsinki von Heidenstam, and the chairman of the Swedish-Finnish Association General Linder. See Soikkanen 1983, 38. A period of active diplomacy preceded the statement. In 1934, the Foreign Ministers of Sweden and Finland paid visits in the respective countries and Finland participated for the first time in the Scandinavian meeting of Foreign Ministers. See Soikkanen 1983, 25–28, 44–45, 70–77; Selén 1974, 132, 226–227; Lönnroth 1959, 135–136.

was appointed by the government to make the preparatory investigations.[90] In May 1935, Tanner met Prime Minister Hansson, Minister of Foreign Affairs Rickard Sandler and Social Minister Gustav Möller in Stockholm. The two governmental memoranda Tanner had with him emphasised Finnish commitment to stable democracy and neutrality as well as common interests with the Scandinavian countries. Moreover, Sweden was quite bluntly asked to decide whether it wanted to lead an active Nordic cooperation in order to defend the neutrality of the Nordic countries or whether it preferred *Norden* to be divided.[91]

The Swedish leadership welcomed the Finnish initiative but was not willing to enter into any formal defence alliance.[92] The tensed international atmosphere had made the Swedish Government more interested than before in a security strategy based on geographical considerations, despite the country's commitment to the League of Nations. The emphasis on collective security and the policy of sanctions was successively replaced by the idea of national neutrality, which, in turn, gave way to the idea of a Nordic orientation.[93] In the rhetoric of the Swedish Social Democrats, the maintenance of the disarmament strategy – which they in fact were modifying toward a military defence strategy[94] – was linked with Nordic cooperation. Therefore, it was only natural to publish a pamphlet entitled 'Defence and Democracy', in which it was argued under the subtitle 'The defence question and Nordic democracy' that 'the Nordic democracies' needed to create a defence front that was not primarily based on military forces but instead on values that cannot be beaten by violent means.[95]

The Swedish Foreign Minister Rickard Sandler was a key figure on the Swedish side of the rapprochement.[96] For him, '*Norden*' was a concept that had a distinguished political content beyond a mere geographical meaning.[97] When the Finnish Foreign Minister paid a visit to Stockholm in 1934, Sandler pointed out the tradition of Nordic self-governance and

---

90 Tanner, Väinö (1966) *Kahden maailmansodan välissä. Muistelmia 20- ja 30-luvuilta.* Helsinki: Kustannusosakeyhtiö Tammi, 168. See also Hakalehto, Ilkka (1973) *Väinö Tanner. Taipumaton tie.* Helsinki: Kirjayhtymä, 167; Soikkanen 1975, 590–591. It has been held that it was General Mannerheim, the chairman of the Defence Council and 'White General' of the 1918 Finnish Civil War, who actually was behind the decision to send Tanner to Stockholm. Selén 1974, 235; Paavolainen, Jaakko (1984) *Väinö Tanner. Sillanrakentaja. Elämäkerta vuosilta 1924–1936, 3.* Helsinki: Kustannusosakeyhtiö Tammi, 343; Soikkanen 1983, 38.

91 Tanner 1966, 169; Selén 1974, 236–237; Soikkanen 1983, 41.

92 On Tanner's account of the Swedish response, see Tanner 1966, 168–173.

93 af Malmborg, Mikael (2001) *Neutrality and State-Building in Sweden.* Basingstoke: Palgrave, 127–134; see also Soikkanen 1983, 28, 74; Stråth 1993, 193–194; Stråth 2000, 393.

94 See e.g. Isaksson 2000, 189–190, 322.

95 Vougt, Allan (1935) *Försvaret och demokratin.* Stockholm: Tidens Förlag, 39–40.

96 It has even been maintained that Sandler was drawing Finland into the cooperation with Sweden. See Kaukiainen 1984, 215.

97 In a speech given at a Nordic festival in 1934, Sandler likened the idea of *Norden* to the freedom of will. Sandler, Rickard (1934) *Ett utrikespolitiskt program: Anföranden 1933–34.* Stockholm: Tidens förlag, 34.

freedom as the common ground between the two countries.[98] Moreover, 'the common Nordic ground', 'the Nordic cultural sphere', and 'shared values' were explicit rhetorical means of identification in Sandler's speeches that he gave in meetings with his Finnish and Scandinavian colleagues in 1934 and 1935.[99] The concept of *Norden* was associated with the concepts of freedom and individuality, based on the Lutheran religion, and with the vision of the independent and diligent spirit of the people.[100]

Consequently, the image of *Norden* that was put forward was traditional and conservative rather than radical and progressive. It is obvious that the objective of these speeches was to create a feeling of togetherness rather than to point out the exact political meaning of '*Norden*' or to bring about any party controversy on the issue of Nordic cooperation – a point Sandler made himself.[101] Moreover, there is no doubt that Sandler wanted to avoid topics that would have caused irritation in Finland. In a speech that he gave in the meeting with the Finnish Foreign Minister in 1934, the overall message was to downplay the significance of the fact that Finland, in terms of language, was very different from the Scandinavian countries.[102] It was symptomatic, however, for although the Åland controversy between Finland and Sweden had more or less been resolved by the mid-1930s,[103] there was still a long-lasting language conflict between the Finnish-language nationalists and a Swedish-language minority in Finland which troubled the relations between the two countries. Not only the most radical 'pure-Finns' (*aitosuomalaiset*)[104] but also many others in Finland saw Swedish expressions of sympathy for the Swedish language in Finland, encouraged by the Swedish People's Party in Finland, as an illegitimate involvement in domestic Finnish affairs. The issue influenced all political matters in Finland.[105] In Sweden the

---

98 Sandler, Rickard (1936) *Svenska utrikesärenden: Anföranden 1934–35*. Stockholm: Tidens förlag, 6.
99 Sandler 1936, 9, 12, 17. On rhetorical identification and division, see Burke, Kenneth (1950) *A Rhetoric of Motives*. New York: Prentice-Hall, 45–46.
100 Sandler 1936, 14, 16–19.
101 Sandler 1936, 32.
102 Sandler 1936, 5–12.
103 Åland, a group of islands close to the Swedish coast, belonged to the Grand Duchy of Finland when Finland was a part of the Russian Empire. In 1918, the majority of the people in Åland had wanted the islands to become a part of Sweden, supported heavily by the Swedish government. However, the League of Nations decided in 1921 that Åland would be a part of Finland also in the future. In the mid-thirties, the Åland question pulled Finland and Sweden closer to each other as there was a strong interest in both countries to get the islands' demilitarised status withdrawn. See Paasivirta 1988, 293–300; Tingsten 1949, 83–137.
104 'Pure-Finnishness' was a language-based nationalist ideology that had its bastions in the Agrarian Party and in the Academic Karelia Society.
105 See, Selén 1974, 228–230; Selén 1980, 206–212; Kaukiainen 1984, 213–214; Paasivirta 1988, 390, 402–403. Swedish had been the language of administration, education, and politics in Finland till the late nineteenth century, when the Finnish-language nationalist movement successively managed to adjust the language conditions to be more in accordance with the proportional share (which was ca. 10 to 1) of native speakers. In terms of political influence, the turning point was the 1906 Parliamentary Reform which abolished the estate-based representation and introduced universal and equal suffrage

language question was viewed as a sign of unfortunate cultural isolationism of Finland and, in many accounts, as a nationalist current similar to right-wing extremism in continental Europe.[106] It was associated with the Lapua movement, although the movement's radicalism was not primarily based on the language issue. While the conservative press in Sweden had a more understanding view of the Lapua movement due to its anti-communism, the Swedish Social Democrats saw it as an alarming attack on democracy.[107]

In the Swedish Social Democrats' view the existence of the Finnish right-wing extremism and language-nationalism was taken as an argument in favour rather than against the collaboration with Finland. In other words, it was possible to see Finland's joining the Scandinavian countries as a victory for Scandinavian democracy. Accordingly, the Swedish social democratic paper *Arbetet* pictured a 'Scandia Major', which would be able to cooperate within the League of Nations. Moreover, it was hoped that the relations between Finland and the Soviet Union would become better due to the new course of the Finnish foreign policy.[108] However, this was not likely to happen, as can be seen from the reaction of the Moscow-steered Swedish Communists who outright denounced the rapprochement.[109] On the political right, in turn, a cautious tone was voiced as *Svenska Dagladet* made a point against the social democratic government by emphasising the importance of military cooperation and by holding that there should not be any illusions regarding the international significance of *Norden*.[110]

In Finland, the only party having a consistently negative view of the rapprochement was the People's Patriotic Movement, even though the party stated that Finland needed all the military help from Sweden it could get.[111] The party organ *Ajan Suunta* maintained that it was impossible to get a lasting understanding between Finland and the Scandinavian countries as long as these countries' politics rested on Marxist ground.[112] In the rhetoric of the People's Patriotic Movement the Scandinavian countries were often viewed as proto-communist states that paved the way for the

in Finland. On the 1906 reform, see Kurunmäki, Jussi (2008) 'The Breakthrough of Universal Suffrage in Finland, 1905–1906'. In Kari Palonen, Tuija Pulkkinen & José María Rosales (eds) *The Ashgate Research Companion to the Politics of Democratisation in Europe*. London: Ashgate, 355–370.

106 See, Lönnroth 1959,129; Tingsten 1949, 140, 224.

107 Tingsten 1949, 149. A couple of months after the revolt incident to which the Lapua movement had culminated in 1932, Gustav Möller had held at the Nordic festival of the Social Democratic Youth in Helsinki that it would be 'a terrible accident for the whole *Norden* if Finland would become a terrorised dictatorship instead of being the outpost of democracy and freedom'. *Frihet* 14/1932.

108 *Arbetet*, December 10, 1935.

109 *Kommunistisk Tidskrift* 1934, 87–90, 109–110, 145–151; *Kommunistisk Tidskrift* 1935, 111–113. The 'national' faction of the Communists took the rapprochement as a violation against Swedish neutrality, provoked by Moscow and supported by Britain and Germany. See *Folkets Dagblad*, 7 December, 1935.

110 *Svenska Dagbladet*, 7 December, 1935.

111 *Valtiopäivät 1935, Pöytäkirjat III*, 2519–2520.

112 Sulevo 1973, 62 [*Ajan Suunta*, 7 December 7, 1935].

Soviet dominance in Europe and, in particular, Finland.[113] The Conservative Party, being in principle positive to the rapprochement, was nevertheless concerned about the 'passive pacifism', which, as the party's parliamentary group put it, characterised Scandinavian politics.[114] It is possible to see that the party had some ideological difficulties in joining the orientation that had been planned with the support of Paasikivi and actively put into practice by Foreign Minister Hackzell, a member of the Conservative Party. The fact that the Scandinavian countries were governed by the Social Democrats had to be ignored or explained away so that it looked less important with regard to Finnish foreign policy. The influential conservative paper *Aamulehti*, for example, held that 'the majority of the people in Scandinavia were, like in our country, bourgeois, although diluted by socialistic influences'.[115]

While the strong position of socialism in Scandinavia was difficult to cope with for the Finnish Conservatives, the Agrarian Party saw the rapprochement through language-nationalist lenses. Not that the Finnish Agrarians had any sympathy for social democracy as ideology, but the main concern was nevertheless the influence that the Scandinavian orientation would exert in the Finnish language conflict. With the exception of the right-wing extremists, the party had been the most reluctant in improving the political relationship with Sweden. The biggest non-socialist party in the country was more than any other party marked by the 'pure-Finnish' ideology. Accordingly, any increased cooperation between Finland and Sweden was rejected in *Suomalainen Suomi* (Finnish Finland), the periodical that was a forum for many pure-Finn intellectuals belonging to the Agrarian Party. 'Anti-national Scandinavism' was an often used label to denote those who lent support to the rapprochement and did not take radical stand on the language issue. 'Nordic cooperation' was portrayed as necessitating the abortion of natural development of Finnish nationality and the Finnish nation-state.[116] That the rapprochement was most eagerly promoted by the Swedish Foreign Minister – a 'Marxist' – was also pointed out.[117] No wonder then that *Suomalainen Suomi* published after the governmental announcement an article that was harsh in its critique, stating that it was false to claim that Finland's belonging to Western civilization was conditioned by Finland's belonging to Scandinavia. It was held that the rapprochement was the result of Scandinavistic propaganda and based on Swedish nationalism, Soviet-friendly socialism, and the bilingual front in Finland. Moreover, the article viewed the Scandinavian orientation as dangerous in terms of security policy, because one could not trust in Swedish willingness and ability to defend Finland in case of a Soviet attack.[118]

113 See also Paasivirta 1988, 447–452; Soikkanen 1983, 36, 44, 47.
114 *Valtiopäivät 1935, Pöytäkirjat III*, 2518–2519.
115 Quoted in Sulevo 1973, 64 [*Aamulehti*, 1 January, 1936].
116 *Suomalainen Suomi* N:o 2, 1934, 64–66; *Suomalainen Suomi* N:o 4, 1934, 184; *Suomalainen Suomi* N:o 6, 1934, 287–289.
117 See e.g. *Suomalainen Suomi* N:o 5, 1934, 240.
118 *Suomalainen Suomi* N:o 1, 1936, 1–5.

Against this background it is noteworthy that the Agrarian Party did not criticise the Scandinavian orientation more than by pointing out the importance of the Baltic countries for Finnish foreign policy when the topic was debated in parliament.[119] No doubt, the party's parliamentary group was not as radical as the young intellectuals who so strongly committed themselves to the language issue. It should also be noted that the party, although conservative on many value issues, was radical rather than conservative in its view of democracy, based on the idea of freeholding peasants as the ground for republican self-government. It was the small peasants rather than big farmers that served as the self-image of the party. If it had not been for the language issue and the memory of the Civil War, there would not have been many hinders for political collaboration with the Social Democrats. In fact, the Social Democrats had made initiatives for such collaboration, pointing out the examples of Sweden and Denmark, but these enquiries had been rejected by the Agrarians.[120] By 1935, some openings for this direction may be discerned, however. In 1935, at the same time as the government's foreign policy announcement was in the making, an influential Agrarian paper was ready to publish a series of articles in which the idea of a peasant-worker front was put forward, anticipating the government coalition of the Agrarians, the Social Democrats, and the Liberals in 1937.[121]

Not surprisingly, the most outspoken support for the new foreign policy came from the Swedish People's Party. According to the party's parliamentary group, it was only natural that the Finnish orientation was towards Scandinavia as there was a Swedish-speaking population in Finland and because Finland and Sweden shared a common history and the cultural ties it entailed.[122] Such a view was backed by the Swedish-language intellectuals who maintained, for example, that the position of Swedish language in Finland and Finland's willingness to belong to the Nordic countries were the preconditions for Finland being a Western civilised country, a country based on humanism and not on dictatorial and brutal doctrines.[123] According to one Swedish-language nationalist, as a cultural-historical category, Finland was a Swedish creation.[124]

It is important to note that emphasising cultural ties and similarities between the countries was not merely a faculty of the Swedish People's Party. If the circumstances were right, almost anyone could point at such connections. Therefore it was quite natural that President Svinhufvud, a man who was highly respected among the Finnish-language nationalists,

---

119 *Valtiopäivät 1935, Pöytäkirjat III*, 2517–2518.
120 See Mylly 1989, 359.
121 See Hokkanen, Kari (2006) *Ilkan vuosisata*. Seinäjoki: Etelä-Pohjanmaan lehtiseura, 101–102. Kekkonen presented in 1934 the Swedish cooperation between the Social Democrats and the Agrarians as one possible model for his party. See Mylly 1989, 358–360.
122 *Valtiopäivät 1935, Pöytäkirjat III*, 2518. See also Schauman, Henrik and Lilius, Patrik (1992) *Från Lappo till Vinterkriget. Svenska folkpartiet III 1930–1939*. Helsingfors: Svenska folkpartiet, 256.
123 E.g. *Nya Argus*, Nr 3, 1935, 27–29.
124 Hornborg, Eirik (1932) 'Nordens östgräns'. *Nordens Kalender* 1932, 57–64.

referred to a centuries-long common development with the Nordic countries in 'political, social and cultural' regards in his greetings to the Nordic Associations in 1931.[125] Importantly, Prime Minister Kivimäki held in his announcement in parliament that Finland was tied to Scandinavia in terms of 'geography, history, economic policy, culture and, as a consequence, similar world view'.[126] However, the rhetoric of togetherness that was used to legitimate the new orientation did not necessarily need to connote democracy. It is therefore noteworthy that the dominantly non-socialist and in many ways conservative Swedish People's Party welcomed the Scandinavian orientation with reference made to democracy as it was held that 'the political system was based on the democratic ground in all these countries'.[127] Being a language-based political party, the Swedish People's Party contained factions that pulled in different ideological directions. A somewhat radical and liberal direction was voiced in the journal Nya Argus in which a clear distance to totalitarian doctrines was proclaimed. In this purpose the idea of Nordic democracy and freedom was contrasted with the Nazi formula 'Der nordische Gedanke'.[128] Consequently, both tactical and ideological reasons suggest that the social democratic conception of Nordic democracy was not unattractive for the liberals and radicals within and around the party, although it is difficult to judge as to what extent the liberal faction of the Swedish-language intellectuals actually needed the social democratic inspiration in their furthering 'Nordic democracy'. What is possible to note, however, is that that the Swedish People's Party had cooperated with the Social Democrats in maintaining or withdrawing the support of a cabinet in many occasions, the most notable cases being the Social Democratic minority cabinet in 1926–1927 and the actual Kivimäki cabinet. A conservative Finnish-language nationalist could easily see an anti-national pattern in such cooperation.

It is quite evident, nevertheless, that the Scandinavian orientation actually came to be associated with the Social Democrats' notion of 'Nordic democracy' much thanks to a convenient timing. The rapprochement was declared only a couple of days before the prime ministers of Sweden, Norway and Denmark visited Helsinki in their capacity as Social Democratic party leaders. It is unclear as to how coincidental this simultaneousness was, but it is quite obvious that both the government and the Social Democrats were well aware of it. For the government it was a potential prestige problem but also a possibility for getting good publicity for the new strategy.[129] For the

---

125 Nordens Kalender 1932, 7.
126 Valtiopäivät 1935, Pöytäkirjat III, 2514.
127 Valtiopäivät 1935, Pöytäkirjat III, 2518.
128 Nya Argus Nr 14, 1935, 181–183. The explicit formulations denoting the Nordic position were: 'democratic base'; 'the ground for Nordic culture and societal life ... freedom and democracy'.
129 As a matter of fact, some briefing was felt necessary from the Finnish government's side so that the occasion would not turn to a prestige problem for the bourgeois government. The Foreign Ministry consulted the Social Democrats several weeks before the meeting, worrying about the impact of the visit to political opinion in Finland if the Finnish Prime Minister did not get enough attention during the visit. See Paavolainen 1984, 347.

Social Democrats it offered a good opportunity to declare their commitment to Nordic democracy.[130] So much so that the Social Democrats' instant comment with regard to the Scandinavian orientation actually dealt with 'Nordic democracy' which referred to the upcoming meeting of the social democratic party leaders in Helsinki and not to the government's new policy. According to the social democratic parliamentary group, the Social Democrats' Nordic meeting was a sign of the 'common spirit of Nordic democracy', which would gain more authority due to the government's announcement of the foreign policy reorientation.[131] The order of things was thus that Finnish foreign policy orientation helped the Finnish Social Democrats' agenda and not the other way round. However, the parliamentary group of the party was critical towards the security policy arguments of the new orientation. According to them, the Nordic orientation must not lead to a decreased role of the League of Nations in Finnish foreign policy. It was also stated that the Nordic orientation required a democratic political life in Finland.[132] *Suomen Sosialidemokraatti*, the party organ, did everything to show how central a role the party had in the new foreign policy orientation. The paper underlined that it was the Social Democratic Party that supported the new orientation most, although all the 'democratic parties' should take care of the progress of the new foreign policy.[133] According to the paper, the Nordic party congress took place in the name of 'Nordic cooperation and democracy'.[134] In the speech given in the occasion, the editor of the paper concluded that the three Scandinavian countries formed a solid ground for democracy thanks to the social democratic governments, and that the Finnish working class had belonged to Scandinavia since the days of the former leader of the Swedish Social Democrats, Hjalmar Branting, who had assisted the Finns to write their first party program in 1899.[135] Hence, the point was to show that the success of Scandinavian social democracy meant Finnish success as well.[136]

When trying to frame the limits of the rhetoric of 'Nordic democracy', it is important to note that the tone was altogether different in the radical socialistic papers *Soihtu*, *Tulenkantajat* and *Kirjallisuuslehti* (The Journal of Literature). In *Soihtu*, the government's Scandinavian orientation was not questioned as such but it was turned to a critique of the government's earlier policy and of the support Tanner had given to the government. The overall judgement of the Finnish Social Democrats' commitment to the Scandinavian orientation was negative rather than positive. It was feared that the influence of Scandinavian social democracy would hinder the formation of popular front against fascism and that it would make Finnish social democracy too

---

130 The Social Democrats' critical view of the defence political aspect of the statement had actually postponed the publication of the government's statement, which was planned to have taken place earlier in the autumn of 1935. See Soikkanen 1975, 591.

131 *Valtiopäivät 1935, Pöytäkirjat III*, 2516.

132 *Valtiopäivät 1935, Pöytäkirjat III*, 2515–2517.

133 *Suomen Sosialidemokraatti*, 8 December, 1935.

134 *Suomen Sosialidemokraatti*, 9 December, 1935.

135 *Suomen Sosialidemokraatti*, 9 December, 1935. See also Soikkanen 1975, 40.

136 *Suomen Sosialidemokraatti*, 9 December, 1935.

Scandinavian and thus bring about 'extreme reformism'.[137] Consequently, 'Nordic democracy', as used by the party leadership, marked the lack of real democracy: socialism. In *Tulenkantajat*, the Finnish reorientation and the Scandinavian social democracy were welcomed in the manner that could have been from a social democratic paper had it not been the case that the main target of criticism was the party leader Tanner himself.[138] It should also be pointed out that the editor of *Tulenkantajat*, Erkki Vala, had become a supporter of the idea of popular front, which did not allow for any explicit rhetoric of 'Nordic democracy' any longer.[139] In two years time, the paper had abandoned one of its favourite phrases. *Kirjallisuuslehti*, the forum for the left-wing literati, actually saw the foreign policy orientation toward Scandinavia as a sign of a tactical retreat of Finnish militarism and caused by the popular front. While this could be seen as a victory for the popular front, the radical paper nevertheless warned about the risk that these militarists would try to pull the Scandinavian countries into their suspect affairs. In this non-signed article, the author emphasised the importance of Scandinavian neutrality, the policy of the League of Nations, and the freedom of the people.[140]

The fact that the foreign policy reorientation was discussed in Finnish papers together with the Nordic Social Democratic meeting gave the rhetoric of 'Nordic democracy' a platform it would not have had otherwise. For example, *Helsingin Sanomat*, the leading liberal paper that had a good insight in Kivimäki's government, picked up the rhetoric of 'Nordic democracy', when it defended the government's foreign policy. It is noteworthy that the Social Democrats' Nordic congress was greeted in the paper and that the paper presented a strong appeal for Nordic democracy. In the editorial article that was published both in Finnish and in Swedish, the paper maintained that 'Nordic liberty and Nordic democracy create, in our view, an unbreakable front against the takeover plans of both communism and fascism, if the parties and governments that formed the vanguard in defending democracy would keep a clear distance with these ideologies and avoid any infection from them'.[141] Hence, the point was made against any influence of radical socialism and the idea of a popular front in the conception of Nordic democracy. The point was noted but not taken by the aforementioned writer in *Kirjallisuuslehti*, who rejected the idea that 'Scandinavian democracy' could be equated with 'the freedom of an individual'.[142]

In order to try to explain *Helsingin Sanomat*'s positive stand, we need to take into account that the paper had been a central actor in Finnish pro-democratic grouping during the Lapua challenge, organised among some

---

137 *Soihtu* 8/1935, 134, 146–148, 160.
138 *Tulenkantajat* No 49, 7 December, 1935; No 50, 14 December, 1935.
139 *Tulenkantajat* No 35, 31 August, 1935.
140 *Kirjallisuuslehti*, Neljäs vuosikerta, numerot 18–24, Jouluna 1935, 440–442. The editor-in-chief of the journal was Jarno Pennanen, who moved toward the Communists in the mid-1930s.
141 *Helsingin Sanomat*, 6 December, 1935.
142 *Kirjallisuuslehti*, 1935, 442.

key persons of the middle-field parties, that is, the Liberals, the Agrarians, the Swedish People's Party, and, notably, the Social Democrats. In liberal papers, the language of democracy was a crucial part of their self-image and political positioning.[143] To add a Nordic dimension to the conception of democracy that was conceived of as being a part of Western political culture was not particularly difficult for a paper like *Helsingin Sanomat* that was quite moderate in the language strife and thus not part of the loud anti-Scandinavian press opinion in Finland.[144]

The Conservative's *Uusi Suomi* did not take as positive stand as did the liberal paper, but it is worth to note that it published the speeches that had been held at the Social Democrats' Nordic meeting. As a consequence, the paper was, without any explicit criticism, filled with the language of democracy that was associated with the Social Democrats and the Nordic countries.[145] Moreover, the Swedish People's Party's *Hufvudstadsbladet* presented the three social democratic prime ministers in a very sympathetic way, emphasising their non-revolutionary sentiment and popular anchorage.[146] It may be too venturing to claim that the non-socialist Swedish-language flagship was buying the social democratic view wholesale, but the paper nevertheless associated the Scandinavian orientation with 'consolidating democracy' and 'enlightened democratic government' as well as with 'inherited view of popular freedom', 'liberty', and 'peaceful development and progress'.[147] The bourgeois party paper was taking stand for democracy while aided by the Social Democrats in their Scandinavian orientation.

This particular language of democracy circulated between Finland and Sweden, for it was common to refer and quote other countries' papers both in Finland and in Sweden. *Dagens Nyheter*, the Swedish liberal daily, delivered a positive view of the Nordic Social Democratic meeting to its readers by quoting at length *Helsingin Sanomat*'s appraisal of Nordic democracy.[148] In Finnish newspapers, an optimistic view was regenerated by making references to Swedish press comments. *Uusi Suomi* quoted the Swedish paper *Stockholms Tidningen* in which it was held that after the Finnish statement the Nordic countries would present themselves in an international arena as united, sharing the same ideals and spirit. *Uusi Suomi* quoted also *Dagens Nyheter* in which the Finnish statement was seen as a clarification that rejected the Soviet press agency's claim that Finland was planning to join Poland and Germany in her foreign policy. By this practice of making quotations, the Finnish conservative paper could then put forward

---

143 See Kulha 1989, 151–200; see also Vahtera, Raimo (2005) *Matkan määränä kansan menestys. 1905–2005 Turun Sanomat.* Turku: TS-Yhtymä, 101–127; Suistola, Jouni (1999) *Kaleva. Sata vuotta kansan kaikuja.* Oulu: Kaleva Kustannus, 114–116.

144 See Kulha 1989, 188.

145 *Uusi Suomi*, 8 December, 1935.

146 *Hufvudstadsbladet*, 6 December, 1935.

147 *Hufvudstadsbladet*, 6 December, 1935. Against the background of the language issue in Finland it is less surprising, though, that the paper also emphasised the importance of national unity and was critical to those who did not see the real meaning of the popular freedom, which Finland had received from the Scandinavian countries.

148 *Dagens Nyheter*, 6 December, 1935.

the idea that Finland was becoming under the 'moral and political influence' of the Scandinavian countries.[149]

To sum up, we can note that, although 'Nordic democracy' had predominantly social democratic connotations, it broke out onto the bourgeois side of the political field, in particular, when it was synchronised with the geopolitical motives of the political and military elite in Finland. When being connected to foreign policy cooperation, the reception of 'Nordic democracy' was thus quite different from the negative picture that the Conservatives had painted only a couple of months earlier in connection with the Day of Nordic Democracy. Nonetheless, it would be a mistake to view the emergence of the rhetoric of 'Nordic democracy' merely as a consequence of Finnish-Swedish foreign policy calculations, for there actually existed a non-social democratic conception of democracy that was understood as particularly Nordic of its character in both Sweden and Finland.

Democracy inherited

In 1935, Kekkonen, the author of *Demokratian itsepuolustus* (The Self-Defence of Democracy), paid attention to the fact that democracy and dictatorship were in several occasions during the summer of 1935 viewed especially from the Nordic perspective. As he wrote in *Suomalainen Suomi*, the purpose had been to show that the political and societal life in the Nordic countries had for centuries been based on democratic ground. To Kekkonen, this was correct, although he was unsatisfied by the fact that this democracy had not been able to solve the Finnish nationality problem. However, he was careful to point out that the promotion of the Finnish nationality was not to be blended with the doctrines of dictatorship. What Kekkonen was aiming at was to warn against any speculations that would make it possible to position Nordic democracy against the champions of the Finnish nationality.[150]

Kekkonen's remark suggests that the idea of Nordic democracy was much more widely spread in Finland than what amounts to the Social Democrats and, as we have seen, a couple of liberal and Swedish-language papers and periodicals. In other words, it indicates that it could mean that one was painting oneself into a corner if one was arguing too radically against a democracy that was taken as Nordic in character. Accordingly, while it is true that 'Nordic democracy' was not a catch phrase for the non-socialists, it is important to pay attention to the notion of a specific Nordic world view also in non-social democratic regards. We have seen that the Prime Minister of Finland referred to such a world view in his speech on the Scandinavian orientation. Paasikivi, to take another example, referred to 'our Nordic way of thinking' as he motivated his party's divorce from the People's Patriotic Movement.[151] We can also recall the conservative *Uusi Suomi*'s use of

---

149 *Uusi Suomi*, 6 December, 1935.
150 *Suomalainen Suomi* N:o 5, 1935, 236–239.
151 Paasikivi 1956 [1936], 94.

'Nordic democracy' in its critique of the Social Democrats' use of the same phrase.

In Sweden, the Nordic particularity was emphasised by the Swedish editor of *Nordisk Tidskrift* (Nordic Journal), Nils Herlitz, Professor of Constitutional and Administrative Law at Stockholm University College. After the Nazi takeover in Germany, he wrote or republished a number of articles and books focusing on the topics of Swedish self-government, Swedish freedom, and Swedish popular state.[152] Herlitz was arguably the foremost non-socialist protagonist of the idea of *Norden* in Swedish public life. His rhetoric of democracy can be seen as the case in point as regards to the non-socialist juxtaposition of the concepts of 'self-government' and 'democracy' towards the mid-1930s. Although the key concepts that he employed were mostly 'self-government' and 'Swedish' instead of 'democracy' and 'Nordic', he nevertheless moved quite freely between 'self-government' and 'democracy' as well as between 'Sweden' and 'Norden'.[153] According to him, the crisis of democracy and the consequent measures that needed to be taken did not need not to be the same in countries like Portugal, Italy or Greece, on the one hand, and in the Nordic countries, on the other.[154] The fact that democracy was not in an immediate crisis in the Nordic countries was, for him, due to certain characteristics of the Nordic countries: in these countries individual freedom was respected; people had the principle of equality 'in their blood'; the peoples owned an ancient culture of rights and rule of law; these countries were nationally united; and their people were mature enough to put the common good above private egoism.[155] His rhetoric of democracy was a variation of a neo-roman or republican language of political virtues, public freedom, and common good. It was also well in line with Swedish egalitarian conservative nationalism that can be traced back to the famous nineteenth-century Swedish historians Erik Gustaf Geijer and Harald Hjärne.[156]

The Nordic durability in the face of the crisis of democracy had also been pointed out by one of the leading Finnish conservative politicians, Paavo Virkkunen. As early as in 1927, he regarded parliamentarism as democracy's highest form, and defended it against the dictatorial and anti-

---

152 See Herlitz, Nils (1933) *Svensk självstyrelse*. Stockholm: Hugo Gebers Förlag; Herlitz, Nils (1934a) *Den svenska folkstaten*. Stockholm; Herlitz, Nils (1934b) *Svensk självstyre förr och nu*. Stockholm.

153 See e.g. Herlitz 1934b, 9; Herlitz 1933, 9–10, 278.

154 Herlitz 1933, 277–278.

155 Herlitz 1933, 278–279.

156 On neo-Roman political thought and republicanism, see Skinner, Quentin (1998) *Liberty Before Liberalism*. Cambridge: Cambridge University Press; Viroli, Maurizio (1995) *For Love of Country. An Essay on Patriotism and Nationalism*. Oxford: Clarendon Press. On Geijer, see e.g. Kurunmäki, Jussi (2000) *Representation, Nation and Time. The Political Rhetoric of the 1866 Parliamentary Reform in Sweden*. Jyväskylä: University of Jyväskylä, 136–147. On Hjärne, see Elvander, Nils (1961) *Harald Hjärne och konservatismen. Konservativ idédebatt i Sverige 1866–1922*. Stockholm: Almqvist & Wiksell.

parliamentarian doctrines of Italian fascism and Soviet communism.[157] Virkkunen's main point was that parliamentarism had the best chance to survive and develop in countries that had an ancient tradition of popular freedom. Accordingly, parliamentarism was in trouble in the Latin countries but did rather well in the Germanic (sic) countries, in which citizenry rights were based on the Lutheran individualism in contrast to the Catholic collectivism and dependence on authorities.[158] What is more, he argued that the well-being of Finnish parliamentarism was due to the Finnish political culture being based on the historical Nordic tradition. Downplaying the relevance of the language issue and the cleavage caused (or exemplified) by the civil war, he emphasised Finnish national unity as a characteristic advantage for the Finnish and Nordic political life.[159] According to him, 'Nordic parliamentarism' was based on a strong position of the peasants in these countries. In Finland, he continued, the people were one and united, a string of generations, and the civilised elite was raised by the common people, thus sharing its values.[160]

In 1935, however, Virkkunen's view of the Finnish parliamentary politics was much more negative than before. He had belonged in the early thirties to the faction within the party that was sympathetic to the Lapua movement and the People's Patriotic Movement, and now he excluded both the Social Democrats and the Swedish People's Party from the national unity. According to him, the former party represented class interests that were international of their nature, whereas the latter party was anti-national in its language policy. What was more, he held, the Swedish People's Party had cooperated with the Social Democrats, causing serious instability and weakness in the Finnish parliamentarism. This being the case, Virkkunen concluded, it was utterly important that all nationally minded parties would join together in defending a patriotic front and, consequently, Finnish parliamentarism.[161] Now, it is possible to view this as a message that was sent, in particular, to the Agrarians, telling that they should not opt for any cooperation with the Social Democrats as had happened in Sweden. It is important to note, nevertheless, that the core nominator and the basis of the Finnish national unity and 'vital democracy' in Virkkunen's account was still the tradition of Nordic liberty.[162]

The image of democratic tradition was particularly enhanced in 1935 as it was the year when the Swedish Parliament was celebrated due to its five-hundred-years' history. The commemoration was accompanied with political language in which the importance of political representation and

---

157 Virkkunen, Paavo (1927) 'Parlamentarismin pula nykyaikana. Suomen valtiollisen elämän kannalta'. *Valvoja-aika*, 287–313. Virkkunen was the Speaker of Parliament at several parliaments and the leader of the Conservative Party in 1932–1934.
158 Virkkunen 1927, 292.
159 Virkkunen 1927, 298, 307.
160 Virkkunen 1927, 308–313.
161 Virkkunen, Paavo (1935) 'Katsaus Eduskunnan työhön Suomen itsenäisyyden ensimmäisenä jaksona, kokemuksia ja toivomuksia'. In *Politiikkaa ja merkkimiehiä*. Helsinki: Suomalaisen Kirjallisuuden Seuran Kirjapaino Oy, 27–66.
162 Virkkunen 1935, 64–65.

parliamentary democracy was expressed. Gunnar Heckscher, for instance, emphasised the existence of a long tradition of political representation in Sweden and associated this tradition with 'Swedish democracy'.[163] The celebration of the Swedish Riksdag offered also a convenient possibility for some Finnish politicians to emphasise Finland's belonging to democratic Nordic countries. It was held that the political tradition in Finland was shaped by an almost four centuries long era of Finnish representation at Riksdag, an era which ended in 1809. As a matter of fact, it is in the speeches held by the Finnish guests on the festive occasions in Sweden it is possible to find some of the most straightforward arguments for the particularity of Nordic democracy. For example, Oskari Mantere, the Liberal minister in Kivimäki's cabinet, associated 'individual freedom that was limited by law' and 'democratic constitution' with 'the Nordic people'.[164] In addition, the Finnish parliament held in its address of congratulation that 'the freedom and the spirit of togetherness in the Nordic democracies' made these countries strong enough to stand against the changes of political representation which had in many countries destroyed citizens' freedoms.[165]

It is important to note that the commemoration suited also well in the Social Democrats' agenda. On the Day of Nordic Democracy Hansson maintained that the Riksdag had been the ground for people's anchoring in democracy in Sweden.[166] According to an article in *Tiden*, moreover, political representation in Sweden had been developing throughout centuries and rested at the moment 'on the most extended democratic ground'. It was held that democracy was 'firm and stable' in the country thanks to the long history of political representation. It meant that the political and economic crises, which had crushed democratic institutions in other countries, had not been able to disturb 'Swedish – and Nordic – democracy'.[167] The Swedish Social Democrats wanted to emphasise their role in the breakthrough of democracy and, at the same time, point out the democratic tradition that had existed before their own role became decisive.[168] Hansson's speech on the Day of Nordic Democracy is illustrative in this sense. He held that there was good soil for democracy in Sweden because of the mores of the people and the popular tradition of the country.[169] The concept that linked the past with the present was 'freedom', the very concept the Conservatives claimed as their domain.[170] For example, an article in *Tiden* explained that the success of

163 *Medborgaren* N:r 5, 1935, 162.
164 Quoted in Hildebrand, Karl & Hallin, Eric (eds) (1936) *Riksdagens minnesfest 1935.* Stockholm: P. A. Norstedt & Söner, 87–88.
165 Hildebrand & Hallin 1936, 131–133. It can be noted that this commitment to the Nordic countries and their democracy were expressed half a year before the government's foreign policy announcement.
166 *Fyra tal om nordisk demokrati* 1935, 6.
167 *Tiden* 1935, 233–236.
168 It was held that the breakthrough had taken place in 1918 when universal suffrage for both men and women was accepted. The labour movement had been a central factor in the struggle for democracy, and the current strong position of the Social Democrats was the outcome of that democracy. *Tiden* 1935, 234–236.
169 *Fyra tal om nordisk demokrati* 1935, 6.
170 See e.g. Lindman, Arvid (1935) *Frihet eller förtryck?* Stockholm.

the labour movement in the struggle for democracy was due to the fact that, in contrast to most other countries, the Swedish labour movement was born and grown 'in the soil of freedom'. It was thus held that 'our democracy is of rather young origin but our freedom is old'.[171] It should be noted that in these Swedish notions of democratic tradition it was the Swedish tradition that was in question. The above presented quotation 'the Swedish – and Nordic – democracy' underlines rather than denies such a conclusion. It was as if one had not to forget the Nordic aspect.

In Finland the tradition was conceived of as democratic because it was Nordic by being a part of the Swedish tradition. On the Day of Nordic Democracy, Tanner held that the Nordic countries were supporters of the people's power by nature. Both the peasant and the worker had always been free.[172] In the Nordic meeting of the Social Democratic Parties in Helsinki, he argued that all the Nordic countries shared a strong tradition of democracy, which, in fact, separated them from most of the other European countries.[173] He held that in 'new democracies' the ideas of freedom had not had time to get rooted and to create a tradition that would have been strong enough in order to this tradition to be able to defend democracy.[174] Hence, Tanner did not regard Finland as a 'new democracy' thanks to the country being a Nordic country with the Nordic tradition of democracy.[175]

An important discord to these greetings of the democratic character of political tradition came from Raoul Palmgren, the Finnish radical socialist and intellectual who belonged to the *Soihtu* group. He noted that the Scandinavian orientation had made the question of Nordic freedom and democracy real in Finland. However, he added, one should be careful not to make this emphasis on democracy an empty phrase. According to him, it was a superficial view and not in accordance with the facts; it was a mistake to elevate Nordic democracy above the class struggle perspective. For him, the Scandinavian countries were still capitalistic countries and their democracy was bourgeois despite the fact that the labour movement was strong in these countries.[176] True, this may not be surprising, as it was based on a radical interpretation of the Marxist class struggle doctrine. It is nevertheless important to note the somewhat double-edged way Palmgren questioned the very idea of Nordic democratic tradition that was built on the idea of peasant freedom. His point was that the historical position of a peasant in the Nordic countries revealed a condition that needed to be understood in terms of feudal dependence and not as freedom. When he gave an explanation to this false view of Nordic freedom, he, however, underlined the relatively

---

171 *Tiden* 1934, 521–522.
172 *Fyra tal om nordisk demokrati* 1935, 19.
173 Tanner 1956 [1935], 232–235. See also *Suomen Sosialidemokraatti*, 9 December, 1935.
174 *Fyra tal om nordisk demokrati* 1935, 13; see also Tingsten 1933, 59; *Tiden* 1933, 484.
175 There were, of course, also statements in which the Finnish particularity was emphasised. For example, a Finnish social democratic member of the parliament greeted his home country's 'ancient democratic customs', which had made the people mature enough to liberate themselves from the rule of both Sweden and Russia. *Valtiopäivät 1935, pöytäkirjat II*, 1648–1654.
176 *Soihtu* 1/1936, 13–14, 28.

strong position of the peasants in Sweden and Finland.[177] According to him, the peasants had throughout history been numerous, strong and freedom-loving. What is more, they had been able to gain certain democratic rights. Yet, it did not mean democracy, according to him. Palmgren was busy to note that it was the class society that was in question. His message was that 'in order to be a good Marxist and dialectician' one had to keep in mind that democratic rights can be only limited in the capitalistic system and that the only way to get these rights has been through a struggle. To him, the existing democracy was the result of class struggle, but it was merely an abstract democracy; the full democracy necessitated a further struggle.[178] Hence, Palmgren actually advocated a radicalised version of the social democratic conception of Nordic democracy in which the existence of Nordic democracy was made highly conditional of its character, pointing at demands for socialisation in the nearest future.

After the Second World War, Palmgren was one of the main, if not the foremost, left-wing intellectuals aiming at combining the internationalist class perspective with the main national narrative of the Finnish history writing.[179] In Sweden, the path was opened in the 1920s most notably by the social democratic ideologist Nils Karleby whose interpretation of Swedish social democracy as inherently national movement came to influence the Swedish Social Democrats' self-understanding in the years to come. The fact that the Swedish social democracy was Marxist of its character was not, according to him, due to any extensive reading of Marx in Sweden but, rather, due to the simple fact that Marx was right in his analysis of the modern society.[180] More than Karleby, however, the national orientation has been attached to Hansson, who not only took use of national-patriotic references in his political speeches but also made the topic of national belonging and patriotic sentiment one of the main aspects of his political message.[181] Hansson's rhetoric of 'Nordic democracy' needs to be understood as a part of this national orientation.

The best known and most influential national move the Social Democrats made was the takeover of the metaphor *folkhem*, 'the people's home', in the 1920s.[182] *Folkhem* was originally a conservative metaphor that was

177 Today, it has become almost a commonplace to point out the constructed character of the democratic tradition in the Nordic countries. However, it has been difficult to live without. See Kettunen, 1999.

178 *Soihtu* 1/1936, 14, 28.

179 See Palmgren, Raoul (1948) *Suuri linja: Arwidssoninsta vallankumouksellisiin sosialisteihin: Kansallisia tutkielmia.* Helsinki: Kansan kulttuuri.

180 Karleby, Nils (1928) [1926] *Socialismen inför verkligheten: Studier över socialdemokratisk åskådning och nutidspolitik.* Stockholm: Tidens Förlag (4. reprint), 104–124; see especially p. 106. See also Linderborg, Åsa (2001) *Socialdemokraterna skriver historia: Historieskrivning som ideologisk maktresurs 1892–2000.* Stockholm: Atlas, 195, 235.

181 This can be seen for example in the collection of Hansson's speeches and writings that were published under the title 'Demokrati' in order to mark his 50-years birthday. See Hansson 1935.

182 For an elaborated analysis of the concept of *folkhem*, see Götz, Norbert (2001) *Ungleiche Geschwister. Die Konstruktion von nationalsozialistischer Volksgemeinschaft*

invented at the beginning of the twentieth century, and it was meant to capture a social conservative view of togetherness in which different layers of people and different social interests would make a harmonious whole under a patriarchal supervision of the existing state power. The purpose was to enhance the concept of nation as the bulwark against the class conscious workers. Hansson had already in 1921 claimed that Sweden was to be made a good home for every Swedish people on a democratic ground.[183] The social and economic aspect of the home metaphor was elaborated throughout the 1920s, and in 1928 Hansson famously held in a parliamentary speech that 'the keystone of a good home was that there should not be any privileged nor pressured, no pets nor stepchildren'.[184] It meant that the social and economic barriers should be broken down. Despite these additional dimensions, *folkhem* was nevertheless based on the very principle of parliamentary democracy. According to an article in *Tiden*, the institution of political representation was not only the ground for democracy but it was also the basis of 'national consciousness', 'the unity of the people', and 'the people's home'.[185]

The takeover of *folkhem* was accompanied with the Social Democrats' adaptation of national heroes such as the peasant leader Engelbrekt (the presumed founder of the Riksdag) and the King Gustavus Vasa, to name but a few.[186] There is no doubt that the Social Democrats tried to wash off the class party character from the party. For example, it was argued in *Frihet*, in 1934, that 'the Swedish social democracy has always regarded the nation positively'.[187] A couple of months later the same ambition was described in terms of a change as one article in the same periodical was entitled: 'From class movement to the people's movement'.[188] The current parliamentary cooperation between the Social Democrats and the Agrarians did not make the adoption of the idea of peasant freedom and the celebration of Engelbrekt more difficult than before, to say the least.[189]

und schwedischem Volksheim, Baden-Baden: Nomos Verlagsgesellschaft, 190–271; see also Götz, Norbert (2004) 'The modern Home Sweet Home'. In Kurt Almqvist & Kay Glans (eds) *The Swedish Success Story?* Stockholm: Axel and Margaret Ax:son Johnson Foundation, 97–107; Stråth 2000, 386–388; Isaksson, Anders (1996) *Per Albin III: Partiledaren.* Stockholm: Wahlström & Widstrand, 172–192.

183 See Isaksson 1996, 188–189.

184 Hansson 1935, 19–20.

185 *Tiden* 1935, 235.

186 For a detailed analysis, see Linderborg 2001, 265–328; see also Kayser Nielsen, Niels (2009) *Bonde, stat og hjem: Nordisk demokrati og nationalisme – fra pietismen til 2. Verdenskrig.* Aarhus: Aarhus Universitetsförlag; Kayser Nielsen, Niels (2004) 'Demokrati og kulturel nationalisme i Norden i mellemkrigstiden - en realpolitisk højredrejning?' *Historisk tidskrift* 4/2004, 581–603; Isaksson 2000, 316–317.

187 *Frihet* 15/1934, 2.

188 *Frihet* 18/1934, 5–6.

189 See also Isaksson 2000, 261–263, 283. However, this parliamentary cooperation can also be seen as a step away from the idea of unitary and indivisible national interest, because it was based on the acknowledgement of particular interest groups – the workers and the agrarians – who reached a compromise. See Kettunen, Pauli (1997) 'The Society of Virtuous Circles'. In Pauli Kettunen and Hanna Eskola (eds) *Models, Modernity and the Myrdals.* Helsinki: Renvall Institute, 153–173.

The Finnish phrase 'the reunification of our people' (*kansamme eheyttäminen*) was in many regards meant to have a similar effect as the Swedish 'people's home'.[190] It contained the idea of social reforms as a means of creating a common spirit of togetherness among the people, and especially among the workers who felt that they were left without such a connection. On the one hand, it was meant to idealise the Finnish peasant as the proper citizen in the system of 'the people's power'. In this bourgeois conception the labour movement could hardly be included as long as it kept with the idea of class interests.[191] On the other hand, 'reunification' could refer to a corporatist system of political representation and even to a quest for dictatorship. This was the case with the political scientist Yrjö Ruutu who lent a great influence on the generation of young intellectuals in interwar Finland, not least those involved in the Academic Karelia Society. In his thought a combination of social reforms, occupational corporatism in political representation, and 'pure-Finnishness' were forged in 'national socialism' or 'state socialism'.[192] However, the rhetoric of reunification was not particularly appealing in many quarters in the mid-1930s. In addition to the conceived class and language divisions, there was a strong paternalistic tradition in Finnish political culture, which, so to speak, resisted any efforts to unite the people. Paradoxically, the reunification was blocked by the idea of the indivisible people. In other words, the Finnish rhetoric of the people dealt to a considerable degree with the claim for the right to speak in the name of the people which already was conceived of as one and unitary.[193] Those who did not fit in were not regarded as 'our people'.

190 See Klinge, Matti (1983) *Vihan veljistä valtiososialismiin: Yhteiskunnallisia ja kansallisia näkemyksiä 1910- ja 1920-luvuilta* (toinen painos). Porvoo–Helsinki–Juva: WSOY, 142.

191 See Kettunen, Pauli (2008) *Globalisaatio ja kansallinen me: Kansallisen katseen historiallinen kritiikki*. Tampere: Vastapaino, 84; see also Siltala 1985, 477–479.

192 Despite the choice of the words 'national' and 'socialism', and despite Ruutu's critique of parliamentary democracy and defence of the historical legitimisation of dictatorship, it cannot be equated with the Nazi ideology. More correct is to see similarities with the Swedish political scientist Rudolf Kjellén's idea of the organic character of state and the representation of societal interests, as well as with the corporative ideas of syndicalism and fascism. In the course of the 1930s, after he had seen the aggressive nature of dictatorships in Italy and Germany as well as the violent character of the Lapua movement, Ruutu's 'energetic' view of the state was transformed into a defence of social democratic position. In the mid-thirties, Ruutu was ready to regard the Social Democrats as nationally minded and, at the same time, give some positive thought to the internationalism of the Marxist tradition. By 1937, he had become a defender of parliamentary democracy and joined the Social Democratic Party. See Kangaspuro, Markku (1999) 'Yrjö Ruudun kansallinen sosialismi'. In Pertti Karkama & Hanne Koivisto (eds) *Ajan paineessa: Kirjoituksia 1930-luvun suomalaisesta aatemaailmasta*. Helsinki: SKS, 194–210; see also Klinge 1983, 132–152. On Ruutu's energetic theory of the state, see Borg, Olavi (ed.) (2000) *Valtio-opin historiaa Platonista nykyaikaan Y. Ruudun tulkitsemana*. Tampere: Tampereen yliopisto, 301–314.

193 See Kurunmäki, Jussi (2005) 'A parliament for the unity of the people. On the rhetoric of legitimisation in the debate over Finnish parliamentary reform in 1906'. In Lars-Folke Landgrén and Pirkko Hautamäki (eds) *People, Citizen, Nation*. Helsinki: Renvall Institute, 116–131.

When the conception of the people was 'closed' on political and/or linguistic grounds (Whites vs. Reds, Finnish vs. Swedish), the concept of democracy had a character of being all-inclusive and strictly demarcating at the same time. It was so not least due to the fact that the word *kansanvalta* (the people's power) was used in Finnish more often than the word *demokratia* when 'democracy' was in question.[194] *Kansanvalta* was a direct translation of *demos* (the people) and *kratos* (rule, power) and thus not peculiar as such. The remarkable thing, however, is that the word for the demos-people, *kansa*, is also the root-word for the nation (*kansakunta*) (as well as for the citizen, *kansalainen*). 'Democracy' in Finnish could therefore literally speaking mean both the power of the demos and the power of the nation. To be sure, these two poles – the sovereign people and the national people – make the two sides of the concept of democracy,[195] but the semantic closeness of 'the people' and 'the nation' in Finnish made the radical-democratic and nationalist connotations of democracy not only equally possible but also equally apparent. Consequently, *kansanvalta* was used also by those who would never have used *demokratia* in a positively evaluated meaning. No surprise then that even the Lapua movement claimed that it was defending 'the people's power' against communism.[196]

When *kansanvalta* was understood in terms of national unity and national sovereignty, it was easier to associate it with 'Nordic democracy'. Both 'Nordic democracy' and *kansanvalta* expressed the idea of popular self-governance in terms of national unity, which was projected a long way back in history. It means that when a Finnish Social Democrat used the expression *pohjoismainen kansanvalta* it most probably bore connotations which pointed at ideas of political, social and economic equality but it also contained images of commonly shared national tradition. When a conservative picked up the same expression, it could bear connotations which referred to a popular access to political decision-making and the principle of equality but most probably, however, the main point was to put forward the idea of self-governing people, an independent nation with a tradition of Nordic peasant freedom. Sometimes the two sides were mutually exclusive, as was the case when *Uusi Suomi* associated 'Nordic democracy' with 'ancient ideals of freedom' and opposed it to the social democratic use of the phrase.[197]

194 Hyvärinen 2003, 83; see also Kettunen 2008, 81–84. As Hyvärinen notes, the word *demokratia* took the dominant position only after the Second World War in Finland. However, it should be pointed out that some pure-Finn intellectuals, especially Kekkonen and the political scientist Jussi Teljo, had elaborate discussions on *demokratia* in *Suomalainen Suomi* in the early 1930s.
195 See Yack, Bernard (2001) 'Popular Sovereignty and Nationalism'. *Political Theory*, Vol. 29, No. 4, 517–536; Canovan, Margaret (1996) *Nationhood and Political Theory*. Cheltenham, UK, Northampton, MA; USA: Edward Elgar, 16–26.
196 See Vares 2007, 20; Siltala, 451–452.
197 *Uusi Suomi*, 29 August, 1935.

Concluding remarks

The rhetoric of 'Nordic democracy' needs to be understood within the context of the general crisis of democracy. The social democratic use of 'Nordic democracy' in the middle of the 1930s was in the first place meant to mark the difference between the Nordic countries and the autocratic or dictatorial Europe. However, this rhetoric dealt with much more than drawing a line of demarcation vis-à-vis the rest of the Europe. It was part of the contest over the meaning of the concept of democracy between the Social Democrats and their political rivalries as well as, importantly, within the social democratic ideology itself. Despite the fact that the arrangement of the Day of Nordic Democracy was well in line with the Marxist tradition of international festivals and anniversaries, and despite the fact that the festival was announced beforehand as being a manifest for socialism, the emergent use of 'Nordic democracy' should not be understood merely as a socialist or Marxist manifestation.[198] Besides being a manifestation against fascism and communism, it should be viewed as the Social Democrats' attempt of naturalising their relationship with dominating national narratives of history and, importantly, as their commitment to parliamentary democracy, often called as 'bourgeois democracy'.

For the Social Democrats, 'Nordic democracy' had a geopolitical rationale and in an important way a conserving aim. It marked a willingness to defend the existing institutions of democracy and it referred to a particular democratic tradition. Thanks to this tradition, it was held, there existed a set of shared values that were favourable to the maintenance of democracy. It has been maintained that the early 1930s was the period when Sweden was social-democratised and the Social Democrats were 'Swedishised'. For sure, the goal of the Social Democrats was still in socialism but the way to reach the goal was no longer in taking some drastic political actions but in an in-programmed feature of the progress of society that was steered by the social democratic reform policy.[199] The Social Democrats' rhetoric of Nordic democracy was a part of this ideological transformation.

198 As mentioned in the previous chapter, there were several occasions arranged by the Social Democrats in the 1930s that went under the label 'Day of Nordic Democracy'.
199 See Isaksson 2000, 151, 202. Pauli Kettunen has maintained that the Swedish social democratic ideology was based on the idea of a 'virtuous circle' of social equality, economic growth and enhanced democracy within the framework of nationstate, when the foundations of the welfare state policy were laid down. In other words, it was thought that the society was able to anticipate, criticise and revise itself on its way to socialism through reforms that were made possible by the class compromise between the labour movement and the Agrarians. See Kettunen, Pauli (2004) 'The Notion of Nordic Model as a Framework for Comparative Knowledge'. In Jani Marjanen, Henrik Stenius and Jussi Vauhkonen (eds) Research on the Study of the Nordic Welfare State. Helsinki: Renvall Institute, 129–130. For example, Gunnar Myrdal wrote in 1932 that social policy and the social democratic ideology was a compromise between liberal and socialist ideas. His recapitulation of social democracy clearly distinguished it from the historical determinism that was built in the Marxist thought, although substituting it with a strong belief in scientific and rational development of policy-making, which, obviously, did not make it free from deterministic implications. See Myrdal, Gunnar

The fact that it was 'Nordic democracy' instead of 'Scandinavian democracy' that was used in 1935 can at least in part be understood as a consequence of Finland's foreign policy reorientation which lent additional support to the view that Finland belonged culturally to the same group of countries as the Scandinavian countries. However, with or without Finland, 'Nordic' had yet another aspects which made it more convenient than 'Scandinavian'. It could be taken as something older and more genuine than 'Scandinavian'. The emergence of 'Nordism' in the late nineteenth century, after the political bankruptcy of the pan-Scandinavian movement, made the concept of 'Nordic' not only commonly used in different occasions but also lent it some political added value by denoting a particular political culture, religion, and social structure rather than geographic area.[200] The idea of political freedom, however contested, was so well grounded in the concept that not even the Nazis' systematic use of the romantic German expression 'Nordisch'[201] raised any questions when the Social Democrats chose to use the word 'Nordic'.[202]

The rhetoric of 'Nordic democracy' gave the Social Democrats an opportunity to present their view of democracy as nationally anchored without having to use the very word 'national', which was the word belonging to the rhetorical arsenal of conservatives despite the Social Democrats' increased attachment to national language. 'Nordic democracy' helped the Social Democrats to enhance their alignment with the national political tradition by making an implicit equation between 'Nordic' and 'Swedish'/ 'Finnish'. It has been noted that 'Nordic' developed in conjunction with the modern nationalisms that underpin the modern nationstates. According to this observation, 'Nordic' and the national should be viewed as entangled concepts rather than opposite ones. 'Nordic' has referred to something that is transnational but nevertheless it has left room for something that is national so as to exemplifying a particular aspect of the Nordicness.[203] In other words, it was possible to play the national card two times at once by using 'Nordic' instead of 'Scandinavian'.

While it can be concluded that 'Nordic democracy' was to some extent a conserving rhetorical figure for the Social Democrats, it is nevertheless important to point out the progressive side of the rhetoric of 'Nordic democracy'. By putting the national, social and economic aspects together, this rhetoric was close to the social democratic idea of the people's home. Consequently, 'Nordic democracy' was also meant to be something more

(1932a) 'Socialpolitikens dilemma I'. *Spektrum*, N:r 3, 1932, 1–13; Myrdal, Gunnar (1932b) 'Socialpolitikens dilemma II', *Spektrum* N:r 4, 13–31.

200 See Østergård, Uffe (1997) 'The Geopolitics of Nordic Identity – From Composite States to Nation States'. In Øystein Sørensen and Bo Stråth (eds) *The Cultural Construction of Norden*. Oslo – Stockholm – Copenhagen – Oxford – Boston: Scandinavian University Press, 25, 31–48.

201 See also Østergård 1997, 32.

202 Moreover, as noted, the liberal Swedish-language periodical in Finland made an explicit contrast between 'Nordic' and 'Nordisch'.

203 Hansen, Lene (2002) 'Introduction'. In Lene Hansen and Ole Wæver (eds) *European Integration and National Identity*, London and New York: Routledge, 12.

than just bourgeois democracy. It was thought that parliamentary democracy was a stage in political progress which was to be defended so that it would be possible to take more steps toward a full democracy. 'Nordic democracy' referred both to the existing system and to a future goal. It can be asked, then, whether the idea of Nordic democracy nevertheless was the idea of popular front in disguise. The Comintern-promoted idea of popular front against fascism made success in many liberal and left circles across Europe and particularly in France, and there certainly were those who advocated both 'Nordic democracy' and popular front, as was the case with Erkki Vala and his *Tulenkantajat*. Yet, it is quite clear that the motivation for the Social Democrats' emphasis on 'Nordic democracy' was to draw a line of demarcation vis-à-vis the Communists rather than to unite the entire left by buying the Soviet initiative.

The Social Democrats' commitment to the Marxist thought and the cause of the working class, and the internationalism it entailed as well as their flagging in favour of pacifism, made it difficult for the Conservatives to welcome the social democratic 'Nordic democracy' without strong reservations. The problem was not merely that 'Nordic democracy' was propagated by the Social Democrats; a further problem was that the Conservatives did not always know what to think about democracy in general.[204] This confused attitude can be discerned in the statement of the leader of the Swedish Conservatives, Arvid Lindman, who held that the country did not need more talk about democracy but, instead, 'real national democracy'.[205] As noted, however, a more positive view of democracy gained ground when the ideas of dictatorship were put into practice in Germany and when these ideas infected the youth in their own party. In this situation the doctrines of dictatorship were defined as anti-national and thus unsuitable both in Finland and in Sweden. It has even been argued, regarding Sweden, that it was no longer possible for anyone to represent extreme conservative ideas without becoming labelled as a supporter of the continental ideas of dictatorship.[206]

As a consequence, it became common to speak favourably of national democracy in conservative quarters. Although 'national democracy' was sometimes presented as an alternative to 'Nordic democracy', the very idea of national democracy opened the backdoor for the idea of Nordic democracy to come in. The national aspect of 'Nordic democracy' lent support to the idea of the tradition of freedom and popular rule. Although it cannot be shown that the Conservatives generally adopted the language of 'Nordic democracy' in the mid-thirties, it is possible to see that when the political tradition was in question it was quite natural also for the Conservatives – also for those who had struggled against parliamentary democratisation – to regard the national culture as Nordic and thus democratic. As for

---

204 It has been maintained that the Swedish political right came to an instrumental adaptation of democracy rather than to a principled advocates of democracy by the mid-thirties. See Möller 2004, 59.

205 Lindman 1935a, 16.

206 Torstendahl 1969, 206.

the Liberals and the bourgeois middle-ground parties, 'parliamentary democracy' was well-anchored. These parties and their papers regarded themselves as the main guardians of democracy during the time of crisis.[207] Eventually, it cannot be taken as a great surprise that the liberal 'bourgeois democracy' and the social democratic 'Nordic democracy' found each other, when the international ideological and geopolitical situation was combined with an internal crisis in Finland. To maintain that democracy was Nordic of its character was never really a problem for the Liberals or the Agrarians, although they were concerned of the Social Democrats' factious motives in using the phrase.

There has been a tendency in the explanations given to the survival of democratic systems in the Scandinavian countries to view it as an outcome of social democratic reformism and the compromise between the Social Democrats and the Agrarians. In this social democratic or 'welfare-statist' account the role of the Liberal and Conservative parties has been underestimated and sometimes ignored.[208] In order to capture the significance of the rhetoric of 'Nordic democracy', we had better to understand it not only as the Social Democrats' way of confirming their moderation with regard to democracy but we should also view it in connection to the move the political right made toward the political middle-ground. As for many Conservatives, the Nordic character of democracy was an important reason for democracy being acceptable and in a need of defence, despite all criticism they thought democracy deserved. Hence, if the Social Democrats nationalised their view of democracy by making it Nordic, the Conservatives democratised their ideological standpoint by interpreting it as an outcome of national tradition that was Nordic and democratic. For the Conservatives, democracy was acceptable because it was historical; for the Social Democrats, history was given a democratic re-description and democracy was given a national content.

BIBLIOGRAPHY

Ajan Suunta 1935.

Alapuro, Risto and Allardt, Erik (1978) 'The Lapua Movement: The Threat of Rightist Takeover in Finland, 1930–32'. In Juan J. Linz and Alfred Stepan (eds) *The Breakdown of Democratic Regimes: Europe*. Baltimore and London: The Johns Hopkins University Press.

Arbetet 1935.

Bessel, Richard (1997) 'The crisis of modern democracy, 1919–39'. In David Potter, David Goldblatt, Margaret Kiloh, Paul Lewis (eds) *Democratisation*. Cambridge: Polity Press in association with The Open University.

Björlin, Lars (1997) 'För svensk arbetarklass eller sovjetisk utrikespolitik? Den kommunistiska rörelsen i Sverige och förbindelserna med Moskva 1920–1970'. In Sune Jungar & Bent Jensen (eds) *Sovjetunionen och Norden – konflikt, kontakt, influenser*. Helsinki: FHS.

207 See e.g. Kulha 1989; Torbacke 1972.
208 A recent example of this line of interpretation can be found in Hilson 2007.

Borg, Olavi (ed.) (2000) *Valtio-opin historiaa Platonista nykyaikaan Y. Ruudun tulkitsemana*. Tampere: Tampereen yliopisto.

Burke, Kenneth (1950) *A Rhetoric of Motives*. New York: Prentice-Hall.

Canovan, Margaret (1996) *Nationhood and Political Theory*. Cheltenham, UK, Northampton, MA; USA: Edward Elgar.

Capoccia, Giovanni (2005) *Defending Democracy. Reactions to Extremism in Interwar Europe*. Baltimore and London: The Johns Hopkins University Press.

Dagens Nyheter 1935.

Elmgren, Ainur (2008) *Den allrakäraste fienden. Svenska stereotyper i finländsk press 1918–1939*. Lund: Sekel.

Elvander, Nils (1961) *Harald Hjärne och konservatismen. Konservativ idédebatt i Sverige 1866–1922*. Stockholm: Almqvist & Wiksell.

Ertman, Thomas (1998) 'Democracy and Dictatorship in Interwar Western Europe Revisited'. *World Politics* 50.3, 475–505.

Folkets Dagblad 1935.

Frihet 1932–1935.

Fyra tal om nordisk demokrati (1935). Stockholm: Frihets Förlag.

Götz, Norbert (2001) *Ungleiche Geschwister. Die Konstruktion von nationalsozialistischer Volksgemeinschaft und schwedischem Volksheim*, Baden-Baden: Nomos Verlagsgesellschaft.

Götz, Norbert (2004) 'The modern Home Sweet Home'. In Kurt Almqvist & Kay Glans (eds) *The Swedish Success Story?* Stockholm: Axel and Margaret Ax:son Johnson Foundation.

Hakalehto, Ilkka (1973) *Väinö Tanner. Taipumaton tie*. Helsinki: Kirjayhtymä.

Hansen, Lene (2002) 'Introduction'. In Lene Hansen and Ole Wæver (eds) *European Integration and National Identity*, London and New York: Routledge.

Hansson, P. Albin (1935) *Demokrati*. Stockholm: Tidens Förlag.

Hansson, Per Albin (1948) [1935] 'Nordisk demokrati'. In Rolf Edberg (ed.) (1948) *Demokratisk linje. Tal och artiklar av Hjalmar Branting och Per Albin Hansson*. Stockholm: Tidens Förlag.

Heckscher, Gunnar (1937) *Parlamentarism och demokrati i England*. Stockholm: Hugo Gebers Förlag.

Helsingin Sanomat 1935.

Herlitz, Nils (1933) *Svensk självstyrelse*. Stockholm: Hugo Gebers Förlag.

Herlitz, Nils (1934a) *Den svenska folkstaten*. Stockholm.

Herlitz, Nils (1934b) *Svensk självstyre förr och nu*. Stockholm.

Hildebrand, Karl & Hallin, Eric (eds) (1936) *Riksdagens minnesfest 1935*. Stockholm: P. A. Norstedt & Söner.

Hilson, Mary (2007) 'Scandinavia'. In Robert Gerwarth (ed.) *Twisted Paths. Europe 1914–1945*. Oxford: Oxford University Press.

Hodgson, John H. (1967) *Communism in Finland. A History and Interpretation*. Princeton, New Jersey: Princeton University Press.

Hokkanen, Kari (2006) *Ilkan vuosisata*. Seinäjoki: Etelä-Pohjanmaan lehtiseura.

Hornborg, Eirik (1932) 'Nordens östgräns'. *Nordens Kalender*, 57–64.

Hufvudstadsbladet 1935.

Hyvämäki, Lauri (1968) 'Fascismin "tulo Suomeen" 1922–23'. *Historiallinen Aikakauskirja* N:o 2.

Hyvärinen, Matti (2003) 'Valta'. In Matti Hyvärinen, Jussi Kurunmäki, Kari Palonen, Tuija Pulkkinen & Henrik Stenius (eds) *Käsitteet liikkeessä. Suomen poliittisen kulttuurin käsitehistoria*. Tampere: Vastapaino.

Isaksson, Anders (1996) *Per Albin III: Partiledaren*. Stockholm: Wahlström & Widstrand.

Isaksson, Anders (2000) *Per Albin IV: Landsfadern*. Stockholm: Wahlström & Widstrand.

Jääskeläinen, Mauno (1973) 'Itsenäisyyden ajan eduskunta 1919–1938'. In *Suomen kansanedustuslaitoksen historia VII*, Helsinki: Eduskunnan historiakomitea.

Kangaspuro, Markku (1999) 'Yrjö Ruudun kansallinen sosialismi'. In Pertti Karkama & Hanne Koivisto (eds) *Ajan paineessa: Kirjoituksia 1930-luvun suomalaisesta aatemaailmasta*. Helsinki: SKS.

Karleby, Nils (1928) [1926] *Socialismen inför verkligheten: Studier över socialdemokratisk åskådning och nutidspolitik*. Stockholm: Tidens Förlag (4. reprint).

Kaukiainen, Leena (1984) 'From Reluctancy to Activity. Finland's Way to the Nordic Family during 1920's and 1930's. *Scandinavian Journal of History*, 9:2, 201–219.

Kayser Nielsen, Niels (2004) 'Demokrati og kulturel nationalisme i Norden i mellem-krigstiden – en realpolitisk højredrejning?' *Historisk tidskrift* 4/2004, 581–603.

Kayser Nielsen, Niels (2009) *Bonde, stat og hjem: Nordisk demokrati og nationalisme – fra pietismen til 2. Verdenskrig*. Aarhus: Aarhus Universitetsförlag.

Kekkonen, Urho (1973) [1934] 'Demokratian itsepuolustus'. In *Puheita ja kirjoituksia IV*. Helsinki: Weilin+Göös.

Kekkonen, Urho (1981) *Vuosisatani I*. Helsinki: Suuri Suomelainen Kirjakerho.

Kettunen, Pauli (1980) 'Den finländska socialdemokratins demokratiuppfattning mellan inbördeskriget och lapporörelsens framträdande'. *Historisk Tidskrift för Finland*.

Kettunen, Pauli (1986) *Poliittinen like ja sosiaalinen kollektiivisuus. Tutkimus sosiali-demokratiasta ja ammattiyhdistysliikkeestä Suomessa 1918–1930*. Helsinki: SHS.

Kettunen, Pauli (1997) 'The Society of Virtuous Circles'. In Pauli Kettunen and Hanna Eskola (eds) *Models, Modernity and the Myrdals*. Helsinki: Renvall Institute.

Kettunen, Pauli (2004) 'The Notion of Nordic Model as a Framework for Comparative Knowledge'. In Jani Marjanen, Henrik Stenius and Jussi Vauhkonen (eds): *Research on the Study of the Nordic Welfare State*. Helsinki: Renvall Institute.

Kettunen, Pauli (2008) *Globalisaatio ja kansallinen me: Kansallisen katseen historialli-nen kritiikki*. Tampere: Vastapaino.

Kirjallisuuslehti 1935.

Klinge, Matti (1983) *Vihan veljistä valtiososialismiin: Yhteiskunnallisia ja kansallisia näkemyksiä 1910- ja 1920-luvuilta* (toinen painos). Porvoo–Helsinki–Juva: WSOY.

Kommunistisk Tidskrift 1934–1935.

Korhonen, Keijo (1971) *Turvallisuuden pettäessä. Suomi neuvostodiplomatiassa Tartos-ta talvisotaan II 1933–1939*. Helsinki: Kustannusosakeyhtiö Tammi.

Kulha, Keijo (1989) *Sanasotaa ja sovittelua. Helsingin Sanomain poliittinen linja itsenäistymisestä talvisotaan*. Helsinki: Helsingin Sanomat.

Kurunmäki, Jussi (2000) *Representation, Nation and Time. The Political Rhetoric of the 1866 Parliamentary Reform in Sweden*. Jyväskylä: University of Jyväskylä.

Kurunmäki, Jussi (2005) 'A parliament for the unity of the people. On the rhetoric of legitimisation in the debate over Finnish parliamentary reform in 1906'. In Lars-Folke Landgrén and Pirkko Hautamäki (eds) *People, Citizen, Nation*. Helsinki: Renvall Institute.

Kurunmäki, Jussi (2008) 'The Breakthrough of Universal Suffrage in Finland, 1905–1906'. In Kari Palonen, Tuija Pulkkinen & José María Rosales (eds) *The Ashgate Research Companion to the Politics of Democratisation in Europe*. London: Ashgate.

Laski, Harold, J. (1933) *Democracy in Crisis*. London: George Allen & Unwin Ltd.

Linderborg, Åsa (2001) *Socialdemokraterna skriver historia: Historieskrivning som ideologisk maktresurs 1892–2000*. Stockholm: Atlas.

Lindman, Arvid (1935) *Frihet eller förtryck?* Stockholm.

Lindström, Ulf (1985) *Fascism in Scandinavia 1920–1940*. Stockholm: Almqvist & Wiksell International.

Linz, Juan J. and Stepan, Alfred (eds) (1978) *The Breakdown of Democratic Regimes*. Baltimore and London: The Johns Hopkins University Press.

Lönnroth, Erik (1959) *Den svenska utrikespolitikens historia: V 1919–1939*. Stockholm: Norstedts.

Lööw, Helene (1990) *Hakkorset och Wasakärven: En studie av nationalsocialismen i Sverige 1924–1950*. Göteborg: Göteborgs universitet.

Majander, Mikko (1998) 'The Soviet view on Social Democracy. From Lenin to the End of the Stalin Era'. In Tauno Saarela and Kimmo Rentola (eds) *Communism: National & International*. Helsinki: SHS.

af Malmborg, Mikael (2001) *Neutrality and State-Building in Sweden*. Basingstoke: Palgrave.

Medborgaren 1933–1935.

Mylly, Juhani (1989) *Maalaisliitto-Keskustapuolueen historia 2*. Helsinki: Kirjayhtymä.

Myrdal, Gunnar (1932a) 'Socialpolitikens dilemma I'. *Spektrum*, N:r 3, 1–13.

Myrdal, Gunnar (1932b) 'Socialpolitikens dilemma II', *Spektrum* N:r 4, 13–31.

Möller, Tommy (2004) *Mellan ljusblå och mörkblå. Gunnar Heckscher som högerledare*. Stockholm: SNS Förlag.

Nilsson, Torbjörn (2004) *Mellan arv och utopi: Moderata vägval under hundra år, 1904–2004*. Stockholm: Santérus Förlag.

Nousiainen, Jaakko (1985) *Suomen presidentit valtiollisina johtajina: K. J. Ståhlebrgista Mauno Koivistoon*. Porvoo–Helsinki–Juva: Werner Söderström Osakeyhtiö.

Nousianen, Jaakko (2006) 'Suomalainen parlamentarismi'. In Antero Jyränki and Jaakko Nousiainen: *Eduskunnan muuttuva asema. Suomen Eduskunta 100 vuotta 2*. Edita: Helsinki.

Nya Argus 1935.

Nyman, Olle (1947) *Svensk parlamentarism 1932–1936. Från minoritetsparlamentarism till majoritetskoalition*. Uppsala: Uppsala univestitet (distributed by Almqvist & Wiksell).

Olsson, Stefan (2000) *Den svenska högerns anpassning till demokratin*. Uppsala: Uppsala University.

Paasikivi, Juho Kusti (1956) [1935] 'Ajankohtaisia kysymyksiä'. In *Paasikiven linja II. Juho Kusti Paasikiven puheita ja esitelmiä vuosilta 1923–1942*. Porvoo, Helsinki: Werner Söderström Osakeyhtiö.

Paasivirta, Juhani (1988) *Finland and Europe. The early years of independence 1917–1939*. Helsinki: SHS.

Paavolainen, Jaakko (1984) *Väinö Tanner. Sillanrakentaja. Elämäkerta vuosilta 1924–1936*, 3. Helsinki: Kustannusosakeyhtiö Tammi.

Palmgren, Raoul (1948) *Suuri linja: Arwidssoninsta vallankumouksellisiin sosialisteihin: Kansallisia tutkielmia*. Helsinki: Kansan kulttuuri.

Rentola, Kimmo (1998) 'Finnish Communism, O. W. Kuusinen, and Their Two Native Countries'. In Tauno Saarela and Kimmo Rentola (eds) *Communism: National & International*. Helsinki: SHS.

Segerstedt, Torgny (1933) *Demokrati och diktatur*. Stockholm: Albert Bonniers Förlag.

Rustow, Dankwart A. (1955) *The Politics of Compromise: A Study of Parties and Cabinet Government in Sweden*. Princeton: Princeton University Press.

Rustow, Dankwart A. (1970) 'Transitions to Democracy: Toward a Dynamic Model'. *Comparative Politics*, Vol. 2, No. 3, 337–363.

Saarela, Tauno (1998) 'International and National in the Communist Movement'. In Tauno Saarela and Kimmo Rentola (eds) *Communism: National & International*. Helsinki: SHS.

Salmon, Patrick (1997) *Scandinavia and the great powers 1890–1940*. Cambridge: Cambridge University Press.

Sandler, Rickard (1934) *Ett utrikespolitiskt program: Anföranden 1933–34*. Stockholm: Tidens förlag.

Sandler, Rickard (1935) *Svenska utrikesärenden: Anföranden 1934–35*. Stockholm: Tidens förlag.

Sandler, Rickard (1936) *Svenska utrikesärenden: Anföranden 1934–35*. Stockholm: Tidens förlag.

Schauman, Henrik and Lilius, Patrik (1992) *Från Lappo till Vinterkriget. Svenska folkpartiet III 1930–1939*. Helsingfors: Svenska folkpartiet.

Schmitt, Carl (1988) [1926] *The Crisis of Parliamentary Democracy*, translated by Ellen Kennedy. Cambridge Massachusetts, and London, England: The MIT Press.

Schück, Herman et al. (eds) (1985) *Riksdagen genom tiderna*. Stockholm: Sveriges Riksdag, Riksbankens Jubileumsfond.

Selén, Kari (1974) *Genevestä Tukholmaan. Suomen turvallisuuspolitiikan painopisteen siirtyminen Kansainliitosta pohjoismaiseen yhteistyöhön 1931–1936*, Historiallisia tutkimuksia 94. Helsinki: Suomen Historiallinen Seura.

Selén, Kari (1980) *C. G. E. Mannerheim ja hänen puolustusneuvostonsa 1931–1939*. Helsinki: Kustannusosakeyhtiö Otava.

Siltala, Juha (1985) *Lapuanliike ja kyyditykset 1930*. Helsinki: Kustannusosakeyhtiö Otava.

Skinner, Quentin (1998) *Liberty Before Liberalism*. Cambridge: Cambridge University Press.

Soihtu 1931–1936.

Soikkanen, Hannu (1975) *Kohti kansanvaltaa 1. 1899–1937. Suomen Sosialidemokraattinen Puolue 75 vuotta*. Helsinki: Suomen Sosialidemokraattinen Puolue.

Soikkanen, Timo (1983) *Kansallinen eheytyminen – myytti vai todellisuus?: ulko- ja sisäpolitiikan linjat ja vuorovaikutus Suomessa vuosina 1933–1939*. Turku: University of Turku.

Stern, Fritz (1997) 'The new democracies in crisis in interwar Europe'. In Axel Hadenius (ed.) *Democracy's victory and crisis*. Cambridge: Cambridge University Press, 15–23.

Stråth, Bo (1993) *Folkhemmet mot Europa. Ett historiskt perspektiv på 90-talet*. Stockholm: Tiden.

Stråth, Bo (2000) 'Poverty, Neutrality and Welfare: Three Key Concepts in the Modern Foundation Myth of Sweden'. In Bo Stråth (ed.) *Myth and Memory in the Construction of Community. Historical Patterns in Europe and Beyond*. Brussels: P.I.E.-Peter Lang S.A.

Suistola, Jouni (1999) *Kaleva. Sata vuotta kansan kaikuja*. Oulu: Kaleva Kustannus.

Suomalainen Suomi 1934–1936.

Suomen Sosialidemokraatti 1935.

Svenska Dagbladet 1935.

Sydsvenska Dagbladet Snällposten 1935.

von Sydow, Björn (1990) 'Parlamentarismens utveckling'. In *Att styra riket. Regeringskansliet 1840–1990*. Stockholm: Departementshistoriekommittén, Allmänna Förlaget.

Tanner, Väinö (1956) [1930] *Itsenäisen Suomen arkea. Valikoima puheita*. Helsinki: Kustannusosakeyhtiö Tammi.

Tanner, Väinö (1966) *Kahden maailmansodan välissä. Muistelmia 20- ja 30-luvuilta*. Helsinki: Kustannusosakeyhtiö Tammi.

Tiden 1933–1935.

Tingsten, Herbert (1933) *Demokratiens seger och kris. Vår egen tids historia 1880–1930*. Utgiven av Yngve Lorents. Stockholm: Albert Bonniers Förlag.

Tingsten, Herbert (1935) 'Installationsföreläsning den 15 april 1935'. In *Samhällskrisen och socialvetenskaperna: Två installationsföreläsningar*. Stockholm: Kooperativa förbundets bokförlag.

Tingsten, Herbert (1949) *The Debate on the Foreign Policy of Sweden* (translated by Joan Bulman). London: Oxford University Press.

Torbacke, Jarl (1972) *Dagens Nyheter och demokratins kris 1922–1936. Friheten är vår lösen*. Stockholm: Bonniers.

Torstendahl, Rolf (1969) *Mellan nykonservatism och liberalism. Idébrytningar inom högern och bondepartierna 1918–1934*. Stockholm: Svenska bokförlaget.

Tuikka, Timo J. (2007) *'Kekkosen konstit'. Urho Kekkosen historia- ja politiikkakäsitykset teoriasta käytäntöön 1933–1981*. Jyväskylä: University of Jyväskylä.

Tulenkantajat 1933–1935.

Uino, Ari (1983) 'Pro patria et lege – isänmaan ja lain puolesta -järjestö'. *Historiallinen Aikakauskirja* 3, 1983, 198–207.

Uino, Ari (1985) *Nuori Urho Kekkonen. Poliittisen ja yhteiskunnallisen kasvun vuodet (1900–1936)*. Helsinki: Kirjayhtymä.

Uola, Mikko (2006) 'Parlamentaarisen demokratian haastajat 1920- ja 1930-luvuilla'. In Vesa Vares, Mikko Uola, Mikko Majander: *Kansanvalta koetuksella. Suomen Eduskunta 100 vuotta 3*. Helsinki: Edita.

Uusi Suomi 1935.

Vahtera, Raimo (2005) *Matkan määränä kansan menestys. 1905–2005 Turun Sanomat*. Turku: TS-Yhtymä.

Valtiopäivät 1935, Pöytäkirjat II. Helsinki.

Valtiopäivät 1935, Pöytäkirjat III. Helsinki.

Vares, Vesa (2007) 'Kokoomus ja demokratian kriisi'. In Vesa Vares and Ari Uino: *Suomalaiskansallinen Kokoomus. Kansallisen Kokoomuspuolueen historia 1929–1944*. Helsinki: Edita.

Vihavainen, Timo (1997) 'Sovjetbilden i Finland – ett fall för sig'. In Sune Jungar & Bent Jensen (eds) *Sovjetunionen och Norden – konflikt, kontakt, influenser*. Helsinki: FHS.

Virkkunen, Paavo (1927) 'Parlamentarismin pula nykyaikana. Suomen valtiollisen elämän kannalta'. *Valvoja-aika*, 287–313.

Virkkunen, Paavo (1935) 'Katsaus Eduskunnan työhön Suomen itsenäisyyden ensimmäisenä jaksona, kokemuksia ja toivomuksia'. In *Politiikkaa ja merkkimiehiä*. Helsinki: Suomalaisen Kirjallisuuden Seuran Kirjapaino Oy.

Viroli, Maurizio (1995) *For Love of Country. An Essay on Patriotism and Nationalism*. Oxford: Clarendon Press.

Vougt, Allan (1935) *Försvaret och demokratin*. Stockholm: Tidens Förlag.

Yack, Bernard (2001) 'Popular Sovereignty and Nationalism'. *Political Theory*, Vol. 29, No. 4, 517–536.

Østergård, Uffe (1997) 'The Geopolitics of Nordic Identity – From Composite States to Nation States'. In Øystein Sørensen and Bo Stråth (eds) *The Cultural Construction of Norden*. Oslo – Stockholm – Copenhagen – Oxford – Boston: Scandinavian University Press.

JOHAN STRANG[1]

Why 'Nordic Democracy'?

The Scandinavian Value Nihilists and the Crisis of Democracy

In 1941, as a critical reaction to the shattering events on the European continent, the Swedish philosopher Alf Ahlberg stated that 'value nihilism is the spiritual background of National Socialism'.[2] According to him, value nihilism was undermining the community of shared values (*värdegemenskap*) which was necessary for democracy and the peaceful coexistence of human beings. In the same way that the relativism of the ancient Sophist had evolved into a nihilism that eventually wrecked the democracy of Athens, modern relativism was now about to ruin the very foundations of the contemporary democracies. 'As long as value relativism was an academic affair, it appeared rather harmless. All changed when world history itself pursued its consequences. That is where we are now.'[3]

Ahlberg's line of reasoning was by no means unique. It was part of a Swedish and Scandinavian debate that, in turn, paralleled an international discussion during the 1930s and 1940s in which 'relativism' was equated with nihilism and blamed for the rise of totalitarianism and the politics of power. The Second World War provoked something of a renaissance of objectivist value theories among philosophers of the Western world; it has been claimed for example that the famous relativist legal theorist Gustav Radbruch converted from positivism to natural law philosophy as a result of his experiences of Nazism.[4] On the other hand, there were also intellectuals

---

1   This is a revised and extended version of my article Strang, Johan (2009a) 'The Scandinavian Value Nihilists and the crisis of democracy in the 1930s and 40s'. *Nordeuropaforum*, Vol. 19, Issue 1, 37–63.

2   This and all subsequent translations from the Scandinavian languages are mine. The Scandinavian original will be given in footnotes. '...den allmänna värdenihilism, som är den andliga bakgrunden till nationalsocialismen.' Ahlberg, Alf (1941) 'Maktfilosofi och värdenihilism'. In Alf Ahlberg et. al. (eds) *Varför det svenska folket reagerar*. Stockholm: Natur och kultur, 24.

3   'Så länge värderelativismen bara var en akademisk angelägenhet kunde den förefalla tämligen harmlös. Annorlunda blev det, när världshistorien själv drog ut konsekvenserna. Där befinna vi oss nu.' Ahlberg 1941, 14–15.

4   Radbruch's conversion has been the subject of repeated discussion by legal historians. A fairly recent contribution is Mertens, Thomas (2003) 'Nazism, Legal Positivism and Radbruch's thesis on Statutory Injustice'. *Law and Critique*, Vol. 14, Issue 3, 277–295.

who were making the opposite point, that the very idea of democracy implied a relativistic *Weltanschauung* while philosophical and political absolutism were connected. This argument was famously raised by Hans Kelsen in *Vom Wesen und Wert der Demokratie* (1929),[5] and repeated in various forms by Kelsen himself, as well as by other prominent relativists, such as Bertrand Russell and the logical empiricists, in the years following the Second World War.[6]

The discussion on the nature of the connection between democracy and relativism took different forms in different contexts, but the comparatively loud presence of moral relativism (or non-cognitivism) in the Scandinavian intellectual debates of the 1930s and 40s makes the Nordic countries a particularly interesting case. The primary target of Ahlberg's charges was neither Kelsen, Russell nor the logical empiricists, but the adherents of Axel Hägerström, the founder of the so-called Uppsala School in philosophy. Hägerström was famous for his value theory according to which moral judgements are cognitively meaningless; they cannot be true or false as they always involve a feeling. While Hägerström himself, as well as some of his ardent disciples, seemed to believe that his value theory would lead to a more forgiving and humane moral attitude, which would 'rise as a Phoenix bird from the ashes',[7] its many critics pejoratively labelled the theory 'value nihilism' (*värdenihilism*) and argued that it was responsible for the collapse of European culture and for the rise of totalitarian and antidemocratic ideas.[8] The accusations were particularly numerous after Hägerström's death in 1939 and the posthumous publication of a collection of his moral philosophical essays, *Socialfilosofiska uppsatser* (1939). In newspaper articles and reviews variously entitled 'Prof Hägerström and the World Crisis' or even 'Hitler and Hägerström' it was suggested that the value nihilistic theory had left people in a spiritual void which was now being exploited by destructive forces armed with military power.[9]

The situation called for a response from Hägerström's democratically minded followers, and on these pages I will discuss how a group of younger Scandinavian intellectuals confronted the problem of value nihilism and

5   Kelsen, Hans (1981) [1929] *Vom Wesen und Wert der Demokratie*. Aalen: Scientia, 1981, 98–104.

6   Kelsen, Hans (1948) 'Absolutism and Relativism in Philosophy'. *The American Political Science Review*. Vol. 42, Issue 5, 906–914; Russell, Bertrand (1947) *Philosophy and Politics*. London: Cambridge University Press; Frank, Philipp (1951) *Relativity – A Richer Truth*. London: Jonathan Cape.

7   '...att den, en fågel Fenix, skall födas på nytt ur det gamlas aska med friare och fjärrsyntare blick'. Hägerström, Axel (1911) 'Om moraliska föreställnings sanning'. In Hägerström, Axel (1939) *Socialfilosofiska uppsatser*. Stockholm: Bonniers, 35–65, at 62.

8   According to the received view, it was the philosopher John Landquist who launched the term 'value nihilism' ('*värdenihilism*') in 1931. See Marc-Wogau, Konrad (1968) *Studier till Axel Hägerströms filosofi*. Stockholm: Prisma, 202.

9   Källström, Harald (1940) 'Prof Hägerström och världskrisen'. *Göteborgs Morgonpost*, 27 January 1940; Lönnqvist, C (1940) 'Hitler och Hägerström'. *Göteborgs Handels- och Sjöfartstidning*, 3 July 1940. See Källström, Staffan (1986) *Den gode nihilisten – Axel Hägerström och striderna kring uppsalafilosofin*. Stockholm: Raben & Sjögren, 110–116.

democracy in the 1930s and 40s.[10] The primary aim of this article is not to assess the theoretical validity of their arguments as attempts to solve the alleged perennial question about the justification of democracy, but to look at how they tried to overcome a problem that emerged as a result of a particular historical situation; that is, how they struggled to consolidate a value nihilistic philosophical standpoint with a democratic political conviction. This was something that required an innovative re-description of both the value nihilistic theory and of democracy.

The central aim of this chapter is to discuss the ways in which the Scandinavian value nihilists utilised and contributed to the image and rhetoric of 'Nordic democracy' in their discussions of democracy. It is important to acknowledge the peculiarities of the Scandinavian political development in the 1930s and 40s, which differed considerably from both the European continent and the Anglo-Saxon world. Even if liberalism arguably failed to maintain its dominance, fascist movements remained rather insignificant. Instead it was social democracy that emerged as a dominant political force with a radically revisionist programme. But this did not mean that the Nordic countries were exempt from the culturally nationalistic rhetoric that reigned on the continent. In the Nordic countries, national and 'völkish' symbols were not the sole property of the right wing or the Conservatives, but the subjects of rhetorical struggles between different political movements seeking to represent the nation, its people (*folk*) and its heritage. The Swedish liberals changed their name to *Folkpartiet* (the people's party) in 1934, and the Social Democrats abandoned class-based rhetoric in favour of the politics of '*folkhemmet*' (the people's home) during the late 1920s and 30s.[11] Indeed, the revisionist Social Democratic programme of the 1930s was thoroughly marked by what Sheri Berman has labelled a 'communitarian' emphasis on the unity of the nation and its people.[12]

However, while this cultural nationalism or communitarian rhetoric in many other regions facilitated an aggressive totalitarianism, the Nordic *Sonderweg* was, as emphasised by Niels Kayser Nielsen, that 'democracy' itself was made an intrinsic part of this national and Nordic cultural heritage, which in turn made fascist or anti-democratic propaganda on a culturally nationalistic basis very difficult.[13] Democracy was 'rooted in the very soul of the people', firmly anchored in the historical figure of the free

---

10 In this article I will not go into the related, but separate, discussion of the political consequences of Scandinavian Legal Realism. See Bjarup, Jes (2005) 'The Philosophy of Scandinavian Legal Realism'. *Ratio Juris*. Vol. 18, Issue 1, 1–15; Blandhol, Sverre (1999) *Juridisk ideologi – Alf Ross' kritikk av naturretten*. København: Jurist- og Økonomforbundets forlag; Strang, Johan (2009b) 'Two Generations of Scandinavian Legal Realists'. *Retfærd*. Vol. 32, Issue 1, 62–82.

11 Götz, Norbert (2001) *Ungleiche Geschwister - die Konstruktion von nationalsozialistischer Volksgemeinschaft und schwedischem Volksheim*. Baden-Baden: Nomos.

12 Berman, Sheri (2006) *The Primacy of Politics – Social Democracy and the Making of Europe's Twentieth Century*. Cambridge: Cambridge University Press.

13 Kayser Nielsen, Niels (2004) 'Demokrati og kulturel nationalisme i Norden i mellemkrigstiden – en realpolitisk højredrejning'. *Historisk tidskrift*. Vol. 124, Issue 4, 581–603.

Nordic peasant.[14] In Scandinavia, therefore, the discussion on the political implications of relativism was taking place in a context in which democracy was considered to be part of the national culture, while totalitarianism was considered to be essentially 'foreign'. Thus, the central argument in this chapter is that the Scandinavian value nihilists tried, in different ways, to consolidate their value nihilistic belief with this culturally nationalistic rhetoric of *folkhemmet* and 'Nordic democracy'. Ultimately they argued democracy would prevail in the Nordic countries because of the strong cultural unity of the Nordic nations, and because of the strong roots of democracy and freedom in the history, culture and spirit of the people of the Northern lands.

I will focus on a group of Scandinavian intellectuals that can be counted among the innovating ideologists or national strategists that contributed to the way in which democracy was conceptualised in the Nordic countries in the 1930s and 40s.[15] The philosopher Ingemar Hedenius (1908–1982), the political scientist Herbert Tingsten (1896–1973), the philosopher of law Alf Ross (1899–1979) and the economist and social scientist Gunnar Myrdal (1898–1987) shared the value nihilistic starting point and were recognised as vehement opponents of totalitarianism in the years before and after the Second World War. While Hedenius established himself as the leading moral philosopher in Sweden, both within academia as the Professor of Practical Philosophy at the University of Uppsala (1947–1973) and in the public debate as an active participant in discussions on religious and moral issues,[16] Tingsten and Ross have been depicted as the most influential theoreticians of democracy in the Nordic countries of the past century.[17] Tingsten, professor in political science in Stockholm (1935–1946) and editor in chief of the leading liberal newspaper *Dagens Nyheter* (1946–1960), wrote a number of significant expositions of democracy, most notably *Demokratins seger och kris* (1933) and *Demokratiens problem* (1945), and Ross, professor in jurisprudence in Copenhagen (1938–1969), was one of the main participants in the great Danish democracy debate in the years following the German occupation, mainly through his influential *Hvorfor Demokrati?* (1946).[18] Gunnar Myrdal was professor in economics

---

14 Trägårdh, Lars (2002) 'Sweden and the EU – Welfare state nationalism and the spectre of "Europe"'. In Lene Hansen & Ole Wæver (eds) *European integration and national identity – The challenge of the Nordic States*. London: Routledge, 130–181, here at p. 139. See also Øystein Sørensen & Bo Stråth (eds) (1997) *The Cultural Construction of Norden*. Oslo: Scandinavian University Press.

15 I borrow the idea of innovating ideologists from Quentin Skinner and the concept of national strategist from Rune Slagstad. See Skinner, Quentin (2002) *Visions of Politics, vol. 1: Regarding Method*. Cambridge: Cambridge University Press, 149; Slagstad, Rune (1998) *De nasjonale strateger*. Oslo: Pax, 2001.

16 Nordin, Svante (2004) *Ingemar Hedenius – en filosof och hans tid*. Stockholm: Natur och kultur.

17 Nergelius, Joakim (1996) *Konstitutionellt rättighetsskydd – svensk rätt i komparativt perspektiv*. Stockholm: Fritzes, 133.

18 Tingsten, Herbert (1933) *Demokratiens seger och kris (Vår egen tids historia 1880–1930, vol 1)*. Stockholm: Bonniers; Tingsten, Herbert (1945) *Demokratiens problem*. Stockholm: Norstedts; Ross, Alf (1946) *Hvorfor Demokrati?* København: Munksgaard.

in Stockholm (1933–1947 and 1960–1967), Nobel laureate in 1972, and a leading, albeit very controversial ideologist of the Social Democratic Party in Sweden. Together with his wife Alva Myrdal, he has become an almost mythological figure that more than anyone else epitomises the rationalistic ethos of planning and social engineering.

Hedenius – science and politics

Hedenius, Tingsten and Ross were by no means uncritical disciples of Hägerström. Rather, there are good reasons to argue that they formed, or belonged to, a group of intellectuals who were abandoning Hägerström in favour of recent developments in international analytical philosophy.[19] But Hägerström, Uppsala philosophy and, in particular, value nihilism, had gained a recognised position in the Swedish intellectual debate, epitomising a modern, progressive and scientific way of thinking,[20] and thus it formed an intellectual legacy that Hedenius, Tingsten and Ross were keen on making their own. When Hägerström died in 1939 Hedenius quickly emerged as the main proponent of the value nihilistic theory in Sweden. He defended the theory against criticisms raised by Ernst Cassirer, arguing that Cassirer had misleadingly equated value nihilism with the *homomensura*-thesis of the Ancient Sophists.[21] Hedenius also wrote a series of semi-popular articles on Hägerström and the value nihilistic theory in the Social Democratic journal *Tiden* in 1940–1942, some of which were gathered together in the book *Om rätt och moral* (1941). The Swedish intellectual historian Svante Nordin has correctly emphasised that the value theory Hedenius was defending was technically and rhetorically more similar to the emotive or non-cognitive theories of Alfred Ayer (1936), Rudolf Carnap (1935) and Bertrand Russell (1935) than to Hägerström.[22] But by explicitly ascribing the theory to Hägerström and by adopting the pejorative label 'value nihilism' launched

19 The relation of Gunnar Myrdal to Hägerström was even more distant, but it was arguably also marked by a stronger adoration.
20 Källström, Staffan (1984) *Värdenihilism och vetenskap – Uppsalafilosofin i forskning och samhälle under 1920- och 30-talen*. Göteborg: Acta Universitatis Gothoburgensis; Källström 1986.
21 Cassirer, Ernst (1939) *Axel Hägerström – eine Studie zur schwedischen Philosophie der Gegenwart*. Göteborg: Elander; Hedenius, Ingemar (1939) 'Über den alogischen Character der sog. Werturteile. Bemerkungen zu Ernst Cassirer: Axel Hägerström. Eine Studie zur schwedishen Philosophie der Gegenwart'. *Theoria*. Vol. 5, Issue 3, 314–329.
22 Hägerström's value nihilistic theory is often regarded as the first example of the non-cognitivist or emotivist theories later associated with the logical empiricists (e.g. Ayer, Alfred (1958) [1936] *Language, Truth and Logic*. London: Victor Gollancz; Carnap, Rudolf (1935) *Philosophy and Logical Syntax*. London: Kegan Paul). However, while the logical empiricists based their theory on the principle of verification and logical analysis, Hägerström's version was rooted in the act-psychological terminology of Austrian *Werttheorie* (Brentano & Ehrenfelds). See, for example, Petersson, Bo (1973) *Axel Hägerströms värdeteori*. Uppsala: Uppsala universitet; Nordin, Svante (1983) *Från Hägerström till Hedenius – den moderna svenska filosofin*. Lund: Doxa, 149–152.

by Hägerström's critics, Hedenius palpably pursued the now vacant position as the leading proponent of the value nihilistic theory in Sweden.[23]

Already Hedenius's first article in *Tiden* 1940, 'Om Hägerströms filosofi' provoked a worried response. Anders Örne, a Social Democratic Member of Parliament and the general director of the Post Office Administration, claimed that the philosophy of the Uppsala School formed 'a theoretical foundation for the advance of the modern totalitarian states' and that the consistent value nihilist must hold that 'the Finns, who are presently fighting for their political freedom and self-government, are putting their lives at stake for sheer superstition'.[24] In a ferocious reply, Hedenius retorted that even if it might be conceivable that a philosophical theory *causes* someone to believe one thing or the other, it would surely be crazy to suggest that Hägerström had *caused* the political developments in Italy, Germany and Russia. Rather, in claiming that Uppsala philosophy formed a theoretical foundation for the totalitarian states, Örne had to be indicating a logical connection of some sort. But, Hedenius continued, it is a grave misunderstanding to believe that the value nihilistic theory can form a theoretical foundation for a destructive morality, because the basic idea of value nihilism is that a scientific theory cannot form a foundation for any morality at all.[25]

In the book *Om rätt och moral* (1941), Hedenius used a similar strategy in refuting the allegations that value nihilism implied a practical nihilism. He argued that the basic tenet of practical nihilism, 'everything is allowed', is a normative statement, that is, a valuation, and as such theoretically meaningless according to the value nihilistic theory itself.[26] Hedenius also confronted Alf Ahlberg's claim that value nihilism was paving the way for anarchy and despotism by undermining the shared values on which civilisation and democracy were based. While Ahlberg was perfectly correct in claiming that shared values are a prerequisite for the peaceful coexistence of human beings, Hedenius thought he was mistaken in believing that these values had to be thought of as absolute, true or objective.[27] There is hardly any proof, Hedenius claimed, that people who live in peaceful co-existence with each other nurse ideas that are in any way contradictory to value nihilism; in fact, Hedenius continued, most people have not thought about these things in a properly theoretical and philosophical manner. Neither did Hedenius think that there was any convincing empirical evidence suggesting

23 Strang, Johan (2006) 'Arvet efter Kaila och Hägerström – den analytiska filosofin i Finland och Sverige'. In Stefan Nygård & Johan Strang (2006) *Mellan idealism och analytisk filosofi – den moderna filosofin i Finland och Sverige*. Helsingfors & Stockholm: Svenska litteratursällskapet & Atlantis.

24 'en teoretisk grundval för de moderna diktaturstaternas framfart' and 'att finnarna, som för närvarande kämpa för sin politiska frihet och sin statsliga självbestämmanderätt [...], blott kämpa för idel vidskepelse'. Örne, Anders (1940) 'Uppsalafilosofin – reflexioner av en lekman'. *Tiden*. Vol. 32, Issue 3, 167–173, here 167 & 171.

25 Hedenius, Ingemar (1940) 'Hägerström och diktaturstaternas framfart'. *Tiden*. Vol. 32, Issue 3, 174–178, here at 177.

26 Hedenius, Ingemar (1967) [1941] *Om rätt och moral*. Stockholm: Wahlström & Widstrand, 145–146.

27 Hedenius, 1967 [194] 147–148.

that the value nihilistic theory had degenerating effects on the actual moral attitudes of the philosophers or intellectuals that actually supported the theory. 'Being personally acquainted with a rather significant share of those concerned', Hedenius dared to testify that many value nihilists were, in fact, quite decent and moral people.[28]

Hedenius's basic strategy in refuting the allegations of a connection between value nihilism and totalitarianism was to emphasise the rift between scientific theory and political ideology. In Nordin's words, Hedenius transformed value nihilism from a culturally revolutionary programme to an academic affair, with little or no consequences for cultural or political life in general.[29] Value nihilism is a philosophical theory, Hedenius argued, and, as such, it bore no necessary relation to any particular political attitude; in fact, properly understood, value nihilism itself denies the possibility of such a relation. However, as a consequence of this rigorous demarcation between science and politics, Hedenius was also forced to distance himself from the optimistic belief in the emancipatory effects of value nihilism suggested by Hägerström and his more ardent disciples. Even if Hedenius succeeded in overcoming the explicit connections between value nihilism and totalitarianism, his manoeuvre seemed to have a downside that committed him to silence. What could a value nihilist possibly say in defence of democracy?

Hedenius did not directly touch upon the problem of democracy in the articles in *Tiden* or in the book *Om rätt och moral*, but this was something he was given the chance to do in the anthology *Nordisk demokrati* (1949), edited by the Danes Hal Koch and Alf Ross. The explicit task of Hedenius's essay 'Filosofiska skäl för demokratien' (Philosophical reasons for democracy) was to consider the prospects for a value nihilistically sound defence of democracy. Hedenius started his exposition by pointing to the apparent conflict between his philosophical conviction and the common idea that philosophy should be able to provide fundamental arguments in support of democracy. From the logical-analytical and empirical perspective of modern scientific philosophy, Hedenius argued, it was impossible to give objective reasons in support of a political system. Therefore, Hedenius continued, it was rather obvious that the traditional arguments for democracy, as presented by Rousseau and Bentham, were 'invalid and sometimes even confusing'.[30] Not only did they fail to prove that democracy promotes 'freedom' and 'the common good', they actually believed that 'freedom' and 'the common good' were objective or absolute values. In other words, they did not realise that 'no facts about reality can give logical reasons for anything being

---

28 'Efter egen bekantskap med en ganska stor del av de personer det gäller, kan jag våga påståendet, att det icke finns skäl för antagandet, att någon av dem skulle ha varit mer moralisk, om han omfattat t. ex. en värdeobjektivistisk teori'. Hedenius (1967) [1941], 146.

29 Nordin 1983, 151.

30 'resonerade på ett i våra ögon alldeles felaktigt och ibland rent av förvirrande sätt'. Hedenius, Ingemar (1949) 'Filosofiska skäl för demokratien'. In Koch & Ross (eds.) *Nordisk Demokrati*. København: Munksgaard, 207–224, here at 209.

valuable'.[31] From a value nihilistic point of view, Hedenius argued, the only way one can give philosophical reasons in support of democracy is by pointing to certain actual features of democracy which one *presupposes* that the persons to whom the argument is directed actually like. For instance, a scholar might be able to prove that democracy leads to greater 'freedom' and 'equality' for the population, but this does not persuade someone who does not like freedom and equality. The truth or validity of these basic values can not be proven, but have to be taken for granted.[32]

It might seem like a strange idea that only people that previously support certain values can be reached by arguments in favour of democracy. However, as Ola Sigurdson has observed, this idea of shared values actually formed a corner stone of Hedenius's moral philosophy.[33] But it was not an idea that was original to Hedenius or to the Scandinavian value nihilists, rather, on this particular point Hedenius followed a line of thought central to many of the famous advocates of emotivism or non-cognitivism. For example, in his *Language, Truth and Logic* (1936) Ayer explicitly declared that 'argument on moral questions is possible only if some system of values is presupposed'.[34] If we don't share the same values, the discussion collapses into a meaningless confrontation of irreconcilable world-views. We might feel that our opponent has an underdeveloped moral sense, but we do not have any arguments to prove him wrong. In 'Filosofiska skäl för demokratien' Hedenius extended the idea further by arguing that all our beliefs are based upon basic principles which have been chosen without evidence. It is not a feature that is special to moral and ethical beliefs; it also holds true for theoretical assumptions about reality. Our knowledge ultimately depends on a set of axiomatic principles which must be chosen without evidence. Some principles have to be the first ones; there is no way of escaping the choice.[35]

This axiomatic way of thinking was rather common among scientists and philosophers in the early twentieth century, but it was seldom explicitly discussed in relation to ethics.[36] Still, it does seem to have been an underlying assumption of many value nihilists that a meaningful moral discussion required shared moral axioms. The pressing problem for such a conception

---

31 'inga fakta om verkligheten kan ge *logiskt* tvingande bevis för att något är i och för sig värdefullt'. Hedenius 1949, 210.

32 Hedenius 1949, 211.

33 Sigurdson, Ola (2000) *Den lyckliga filosofin – etik och politik hos Hägerström, Tingsten, makarna Myrdal och Hedenius*. Stockholm/Stehag: Brutus Östlings bokförlag Symposion, 177–179 & 242–243.

34 Ayer 1958 [1936], 111.

35 Hedenius 1949, 211–212.

36 Hans Reichenbach is an exception in talking explicitly about the necessity of 'moral axioms' in ethics. Every ethical argument, he argues, must contain one ethical premise which is not derived by the same argument, and every ethical system must contain some ethical axioms which are not derivable from the system. These basic ethical axioms, Reichenbach continues in emotivist/value nihilist fashion, are not statements (they cannot be true or false), but directives or imperatives used in order to influence the behaviour of other people. Reichenbach, Hans (1951) *The Rise of Scientific Philosophy*. Berkeley: The University of California Press, 279–283.

of ethics is, however, to give an account of, or to discuss, the content or nature of these basic values. On this particular point, the value nihilists seemed to lean towards an individualist, voluntarist and almost existentialist conception according to which the choice of basic moral principles is a very personal affair. In this sense, the value nihilistic claim that moral issues are non-cognitive was not intended as an argument for the superiority of science, but rather as an argument against unwarranted uses of science and reason in an area in which it did not belong. It was an attempt to defend personal autonomy on moral issues.[37]

On the other hand, the actual choices of people, that is, the actual valuations of individuals or groups of people, were, of course, empirical matters of fact which could be established by means of an empirical statistical or sociological analysis, and in this sense, the value nihilists undoubtedly represented a 'scientistic' view on ethics. Mostly however, such valuations were taken as more or less self-evident. Hedenius, for example, merely stated that the evaluative background for democracy was part of a greater net, or system, of attitudes that characterises our culture and our attitude towards life;[38] that this community of shared values (*värdegemenskap*) was the result of the experiences and struggles of previous generations and that these values have become indisputable for large parts of humanity.[39] The moral values presupposed by the philosopher in his arguments for democracy, Hedenius claimed, are not accidental, but form a 'cornerstone of our culture'.[40] Even if Hedenius did not give a more precise definition of this 'culture', he apparently had no doubts that the audience of the book *Nordisk Demokrati* belonged to the same culture and shared the same basic values. He concluded his article in *Nordisk Demokrati* by asking whether the reasons he had presented in favour of democracy were so convincing that it would be impossible to live a satisfactory life without democracy. His conclusion was that this was undoubtedly the case, 'for us', thereby ultimately appealing to a shared set of Nordic values in his account of the philosophical reasons in support of democracy.[41]

Tingsten – unscientific ideologies

Tingsten did not share his friend Hedenius's immediate connection with Hägerström's philosophy. In his autobiography, Tingsten says that he read only Hägerström's more popular writings, and that his acquaintance with hägerströmian philosophy was largely second hand, and it is often argued that the hägerströmian influence on Tingsten was of a rather general

---

37 On such an interpretation of Carnap's emotivism, see Uebel, Thomas (2005) 'Political philosophy of science in logical empiricism: the left Vienna Circle'. *Studies in History and Philosophy of Science*. Vol. 36, No. 4, 762–764.
38 Hedenius 1949, 213.
39 Hedenius 1967 [1941], 142.
40 'en kärnpunkt i vår kultur'. Hedenius 1949, 213.
41 'Onekligen är det så: för oss.' Hedenius 1949, 224.

character.[42] However, following Bernt Skovdal it might be feasible to take the second-hand nature of these hägerströmian influences seriously, and classify Tingsten as an 'associated member' of the critical group of younger Uppsala philosophers who were replacing Hägerström's ideas with those found in international trends in analytic philosophy.[43] From this perspective, Skovdal assumes that Tingsten was quite familiar with the recent discussions of the value nihilistic theory and even presents a rather convincing case that Tingsten adhered to a version of value nihilism that resembled Hedenius's semantic, or linguistic, version more than Hägerström's psychological one.[44]

Skovdal is probably correct in so far as it is justified to say that Tingsten actually advocated a particular, philosophically elaborated, value theory. Mostly, however, it seemed as if the value nihilistic ideas and slogans formed something of a self-evident starting point in Tingsten's scholarship.[45] This attitude was apparent not least in Tingsten's outspoken scepticism regarding the possibilities of justifying democracy. In both of his major works on democracy, namely *Demokratiens seger och kris* (1933) and *Demokratiens problem* (1945), Tingsten disapproved of the traditional justifications of democracy as he thought they were ultimately based either on the metaphysics of natural law philosophy, or on concealed personal political valuations.[46] But neither did Tingsten find Kelsen's attempt to construe a defence of democracy on the basis of a relativistic philosophy any more convincing. According to Tingsten, Kelsen's argument was based on an unwarranted psychological premise that a person who is convinced of the absolute truth of their standpoint is more likely to resort to undemocratic means of realising their conviction than someone of a more relativist frame of mind. More precisely, Tingsten continued, Kelsen failed to clarify the decisive difference between an absolutist and a relativist attitude. It had to be something more significant than the claim that an absolutist view is more vigorously supported than a relativist view, as this would merely support the preposterous claim that a democratic order rests on the weak political passion of its population.[47] Finally, Tingsten claimed, there is hardly anything inherent in relativism that excludes an undemocratic attitude; by contrast, there were also many fascists that used 'relativism' as an argument in favour of their political stance. Summing up, Tingsten complained that Kelsen, well-known for his great achievements in exposing political valuations underpinning other political theories, relapsed into making the same mistake himself, when trying to rationalise a pacifist, anti-revolutionary, liberal or reform-socialist attitude.[48]

42   Tingsten, Herbert (1961) *Mitt liv – Ungdomsåren*. Stockholm: Wahlström & Widstrand, 145. See Lundborg, Johan (1991) *Ideologiernas och religionens död – en analys av Herbert Tingstens ideologi- och religionskritik*. Nora: Nya Doxa, 24 & 27

43   'associerad medlem'. Skovdal, Bernt (1992) *Tingsten, totalitarismen och ideologierna*. Stockholm/Stehag: Brutus Östlings bokförlag Symposion, 134.

44   Skovdal 1992, 106–122.

45   Källström 1984, 147.

46   Tingsten 1933, 21–32; Tingsten 1945, 59–90.

47   Tingsten 1933, 26–28; Tingsten 1945, 85–87.

48   Tingsten 1933, 28–29.

This was undoubtedly something that Tingsten wanted to avoid himself, and like many value nihilists, he believed that moral and political questions ultimately came down to personal convictions and voluntaristic decisions that could not be justified or even discussed within the realm of science. Skovdal has observed that one of the few times that Tingsten tried to make a moral appeal in support of democracy, in a speech to students in Uppsala in 1948, he did so by stressing that 'we must consciously act in accordance with our valuations' and by emphasising that 'we are alone, and the responsibility is ours'; in fact he even referred to Sartre at this point.[49] But despite the fact that Tingsten believed it was evident that 'the "proofs" for the value of democracy, in the dogmatic form they have traditionally been presented, are invalid', he still thought that that they contained 'a core of truth'.[50] For example, Tingsten argued, the claim of the natural and absolute equality of men can be understood as a critical statement pointing to the fact that there are no rational reasons for the privileges of the nobility. In fact, Tingsten continued, historically most of the advances of democracy have been made by revealing untenable features in the existing order. Suffrage has gradually been extended when it has become considered irrational or nonsensical to deny a certain group of people, for example, women or the poor, the right to participate in elections. On the whole, Tingsten argued, 'the democratic line in the debate has appeared less as an ideology than as a critique of ideologies and traditions'.[51] In this way, for Tingsten the rational and scientific criticism of ideologies formed a central part of the democratic attitude.

However, from the point of view of value nihilism such criticism seems to involve a problem similar to that involved in the justification of democracy: if it is impossible to justify scientifically a democratic standpoint, it must be equally impossible to criticise a totalitarian ideology. This challenge was the starting point for Tingsten's most elaborate discussion of his ideology-critical programme, namely the essay 'De politiska ideologierna i vetenskaplig debatt' (The political ideologies in scientific debate) (1941). 'It is often asserted', Tingsten argued, 'that ideologies are valuations, and that they therefore cannot be criticised; the question of truth and falsity does not exist when it comes to valuations'.[52] However, analysing ideologies, Tingsten continued, you will find that they are not essentially valuations, but rather

---

49 'Vi måste medvetet handla utifrån våra värderingar [...] Vi är ensamma, och ansvaret är vårt'. Tingsten, Herbert (1948) *Argument*. Stockholm: Bonniers, 303; Skovdal 1992, 404. Also Hedenius noticed that the democratic conviction of his friend Tingsten was in some way existentialistic in nature, and that Tingsten was convinced that any attempt at justifying democracy was futile. Hedenius, Ingemar (1973): *Herbert Tingsten – Människan och demokraten*. Stockholm: Norstedts, 103-105.

50 '...en kärna av sanning'. Tingsten 1945, 90.

51 'Den demokratiska linjen har i debatten mindre framstått som en ideologi än som en kritik av ideologier och traditioner.' Tingsten 1945, 97.

52 'Ofta påstås att de politiska ideologierna utgöra värderingar och på denna grund äro undandragna debatt; när det gäller värderingar föreligger ju inte sanningsfrågan'. Tingsten, Herbert (1941) *Idékritik*. Stockholm: Bonniers, 12.

statements about facts.[53] Thus, value nihilism does not render ideologies immune to scientific analysis and criticism, as long as it is the theoretical and empirical assumptions and the logical coherence of the ideology that are discussed.[54] Some ideologies, Tingsten argued, can be criticised on the basis of their more or less explicit metaphysical assumption of the existence of a supreme being or a natural law; some, typically originating in the philosophies of Hegel and Marx, for their teleological conceptions of history; and some for their assumptions of biological differences between nationalities, races or social classes.[55] But Tingsten not only used his ideology-critical method on totalitarian ideologies, he also used it as part of his critical analysis of less authoritarian political ideologies, such as conservatism and social democracy.[56] As Tingsten embraced the idea that the democratic line in the debate was rational criticism, 'ideologies' in general soon became something that had to die if democracy was to prevail.[57] In *Den svenska socialdemokratiens idéutveckling* (1941) he argued that the Swedish Social Democrats were gradually overcoming (albeit in a rather dawdling tempo) the untenable Marxist ideology in favour of a liberal welfare ideology.[58] At the time still a member of the Social Democratic Party himself, Tingsten's historical interpretation was undoubtedly intended as a political move in favour of the development he described, and accordingly, it spurred negative reactions from more Marxist members of the party.[59]

Tingsten's way of enabling rational or scientific criticism of ideologies on the grounds that they are essentially characterised, not by their valuations, but by their statements of facts, has been subject to much discussion both by Tingsten's contemporaries and by historians.[60] But it has not been noticed that Tingsten's move, in fact, corresponded to the standard way in which value nihilists accounted for moral reasoning and disagreement. A basic objection to a non-cognitive or subjectivist/relativist moral theory, raised already by G. E. Moore, was that it failed to explain the fact that we do in fact engage in meaningful discussions on moral issues, and occasionally even change our views as a result of these debates. If moral judgements are

---

53 'Men en undersökning av några politiskt viktiga ideologier visar omedelbart att de icke huvudsakligen utgöra serier av värderingar. Verklighetsomdömen spela huvudrollen.' Tingsten 1941, 12.

54 For a typology of Tingsten's different ways of refuting ideologies, see Lundborg 1991, 57–86.

55 Tingsten 1941, 13–15.

56 Tingsten, Herbert (1939) *De konservativa idéerna*. Stockholm: Bonniers; Tingsten, Herbert (1967) [1941] *Den svenska socialdemokratiens idéutveckling*. Stockholm: Aldus. See also Lundborg 1991, 52–55; Skovdal 1992, 69–74.

57 Johansson, Alf W. (1995) *Herbert Tingsten och det kalla kriget*. Stockholm: Tiden, 27–31; Skovdal 1992, 13 and chapter 1.

58 Tingsten 1967 [1941], 353–366.

59 See Linderborg, Åsa (2001) *Socialdemokraterna skriver historia – historieskrivning som ideologisk maktresurs 1892-2000*. Stockholm: Atlas, 204-217; Johansson 1995, 246–250.

60 For an analysis of the debate between Tingsten and the political scientist (later to become the leader of the Swedish Conservatives) Gunnar Heckscher on the possibility of scientifically criticising ideologies, see Lundborg 1991, 52–56; Skovdal 1992, 69–74.

to be understood as mere expressions of feelings, this is impossible as there is nothing in the debate that can be acknowledged as true or false.[61] The standard reply of the value nihilist is to argue that these discussions do not concern valuation, but rather the interpretation of facts. For example, two persons debating abortion surely agree on the valuation that 'killing human beings is evil', the issue at stake is rather the definition of 'a living human being'. In his *Language, Truth, and Logic* (1936) Ayer famously challenged his readers to give an example of a moral discussion that could not, in this way, be reduced to a logical or empirical question; carefully analysed, he claimed, every discussion or debate that appears to be moral or ethical, will actually turn out to be a discussion of facts rather than values.[62] Thus, there was an interesting tension in the value nihilist doctrine, between the call for an autonomous moral, liberated from the strains of traditional dogmatic moral systems, and a form of scientism that claimed that the questions that remained truly autonomously moral in character were rather limited in number. This tension was undoubtedly also characteristic of Tingsten's defence of democracy by means of a scientific/rational criticism of all its competitors.

After the war, in *Demokratiens problem* (1945), Tingsten launched his famous idea of democracy as an 'over-ideology' (*överideologi*) – 'you are a democrat and at the same time a conservative, liberal or socialist'.[63] This was not merely a means of depoliticising democracy at a stage when it had become the preferred ideology of all. It was also a way of claiming that 'democracy' concerns the *form* of government, and not the *content* or direction of political decisions. In the political debate, the democrat is primarily defined as a socialist, liberal or conservative, precisely as the totalitarian is primarily a socialist, nationalist or conservative. But while the totalitarian ideology is based on the suppression of its ideological competitors, the basic paradox of democracy is that you might have to accept and even defend a government that endorses political ideas that contradicts your own. The democratic 'over-ideology' entails that the population is prepared to confine itself to the decisions of the majority, and that it therefore requires, Tingsten believed, that people on a fundamental level share the same values.[64]

It is important to notice, however, that Tingsten did not come up with the idea of shared values as a prerequisite for democracy after the war, when democracy had emerged victorious and become the preferred (over-) ideology of all. As early as in 1933 he had argued that a set of shared values is just as important for democratic practice as a common language is for communication. If people are not prepared to accept political decisions and compromises, democracy does not stand a chance.[65] Similarly, in a political

---

61 See Moore's famous essay 'The Nature of Moral Philosophy' in Moore, George Edward (1922) *Philosophical Studies*. London: Routledge & Kegan Paul, 310–339.
62 Ayer 1958 [1936], 110–112.
63 'Man är demokrat, men därjämte konservativ, liberal eller socialist.' Tingsten 1945, 57.
64 Tingsten 1945, 57–58.
65 Tingsten 1933, 61.

dictionary from 1937, Tingsten declared that 'democracy ultimately rests on a certain community of shared values'.[66] Moreover, he also explicitly linked the rise of totalitarianism with the annihilation of this community of shared values. In his inaugural lecture in 1935 Tingsten claimed that the radicalisation of political life, and the rise of totalitarian parties, was challenging the shared values on which the democratic system rests.[67] Similarly a few years later, Tingsten argued that the crisis of democracy on the European continent was a result of rising economic and social conflicts, which had 'disturbed the community of shared values that democracy is ultimately based upon'.[68] Instead of voting in parliamentary elections, the conflicting parties had resorted to revolution and open battle.

The idea that democracy requires some kind of fundamental agreement was no novelty in political thinking. Tingsten himself traced its origins to Rousseau's conception of majority rule as the best approximation of the general will.[69] Neither was the idea original among political theoreticians contemporary to Tingsten. Among those referred to in *Demokratiens problem*, Joseph Schumpeter and Ernest Barker most explicitly stressed the need for some kind of 'agreement on fundamentals'. In his influential *Capitalism, Socialism and Democracy* (1942) Schumpeter argued that 'democracy cannot be expected to function satisfactorily unless the vast majority of people in all classes are resolved to abide by the rules of the democratic game' which, in turn, required that 'they are substantially agreed on the fundamentals of their institutional structure'.[70] Quite similarly, the liberal British political scientist Barker argued in his *Reflections on Government* (1942) that democracy requires a 'mental habit of agreement upon a number of axioms' concerning democratic procedure, such as 'the majority principle' and 'the principle of compromise'.[71]

The origin of Tingsten's emphasis of shared values is probably primarily to be found in contemporaneous democratic theory, but there is nevertheless an interesting similarity to Hedenius's idea that shared values are a prerequisite for moral discussion. For both Hedenius and Tingsten, the absence of shared

66 'Demokratien vilar ytterst på en viss värdegemenskap.' Gunnar Dahlberg & Herbert Tingsten (eds) (1937) *Svensk politisk uppslagsbok*. Stockholm: Svensk litteratur, 104. It is surely fair to assume that it was Tingsten, rather than Dahlberg, who was responsible for these paragraphs.

67 Tingsten, Herbert (1935) 'Statskunskapen och den politiska utvecklingen'. In Gunnar Myrdal & Herbert Tingsten, *Samhällskrisen och socialvetenskaperna*. Stockholm: Kooperativa förbundets bokförlag, 59.

68 'Den värdegemenskap, på vilken demokratin ytterst vilar, har rubbats.' Tingsten, Herbert (1938) 'Nordisk demokrati'. *Nordens kalender*, 41–50, here at 48–50.

69 Tingsten 1938, 65.

70 Schumpeter, Joseph A. (1942) *Capitalism, Socialism, and Democracy*. London: Harper & Brothers, 295, 301.

71 Barker, Ernest (1942) *Reflections on Government*. London: Oxford University Press, 63–69. As a third axiom Barker discussed something he called 'the agreement to differ', by which he meant not only that people had to recognise that the fundamental friendship between people should not be disturbed by political disagreement, but also that people had to agree on which topics they would disagree, that is, on which questions they found important.

values would mean that it would be impossible to reach a common ground for understanding, and that disagreements could not be solved by means of discussion. It might be more than a matter of language that, by using '*värdegemenskap*', Tingsten emphasised more strongly than Schumpeter and Barker that the agreement is a moral one, that it is *values* that have to be shared. But like Hedenius, Tingsten was rather ambivalent in his description of the nature of these values.[72] When talking about the 'over-ideology' thesis, Tingsten maintained primarily that the values that have to be shared are simply the ones cherishing the formal democratic procedure itself. If democratic and socialist values come in to conflict a true democrat would always choose democracy. In this sense the idea of shared values amounts to little more than the claim that democracy requires that the population shares a positive evaluation of democracy. On the other hand, Tingsten also frequently indicated that democracy requires that people share values of a more substantial kind as well. For example, in *Demokratiens problem*, Tingsten argued that one of the main challenges of contemporary democracy was the preservation of community (*gemenskap*) despite the many conflicts that might be present in a society. As such dangerous disintegrating elements Tingsten listed religious and national differences, gender issues, as well as economic and social conflicts.[73] According to Tingsten, democracy could only prevail if such conflicts are resolved before they burst.

It should be emphasised that this 'communitarian' perspective was by no means original to Tingsten; Barker claimed in very similar terms that a certain national and social homogeneity had to be seen as a material condition for democracy.[74] However, in Tingsten's writings it was often used in connection with a discussion of the reasons for the success of democracy in Sweden and the Nordic countries. In the article 'Nordisk Demokrati' (1938) Tingsten claimed that the Nordic political debate, in contrast to the continental one, was characterised by a dismissal of extreme political standpoints; everyone agrees on the main issues and the political parties tend to gravitate towards the middle of the political spectrum.[75] Two years later Tingsten included the strong national unity, the lack of minorities, as well as the long tradition of representative government, civic liberties and an effective and respected administration, among the main reasons for the success of democracy in the Nordic countries.[76] Later, in 1966, Tingsten explicitly connected the idea of shared values to social, cultural and historical factors, referring to the 'almost remarkable national, linguistic and religious homogeneity' as the main explanation for the success of democracy in the Scandinavian countries.[77]

---

72   Boström, Bengt-Ove (1988) *Samtal om demokratin*. Lund: Doxa, 152–153.
73   Tingsten 1945, 133–163.
74   Barker 1942, 60–63.
75   Tingsten 1938, 48–50.
76   Tingsten, Herbert (1940) 'Folkstyret i Norden'. In Petander, Karl (ed.) *Nordisk Gemenskap*. Stockholm: Kooperativa förbundets bokförlag, 50–83, here at 83.
77   '...en nästan enastående homogenitet i fråga om nationalitet, språk och religion'. Tingsten, Herbert (1966) *Från idéer till idyll – den lyckliga demokratien*. Stockholm: Norstedts, 12.

While 'democracy' in Tingsten's view was an over-ideology that concerned the form of government only and not the political direction, but it nevertheless required shared values in order to be successful. The success of the phrase 'Nordic democracy' was arguably that it combined form and content in one image, while simultaneously giving it a cultural anchorage.

Alf Ross – what is democracy?

The Danish legal philosopher Alf Ross came to Uppsala to study under Hägerström in 1928 after he had failed to get his Kelsen-inspired doctoral thesis accepted at the University of Copenhagen. Hägerström's moral and legal philosophy made a huge impact on Ross and the value nihilistic theory remained a central trait in his scholarship throughout his career, although in the 1940s he, like Hedenius, supplemented or even replaced Hägerströmian arguments with ideas and techniques borrowed mainly from logical empiricism.[78] In 1946 Ross published what he called 'his modest contribution to Denmark's fight for freedom and independence', *Hvorfor Demokrati?* (Why Democracy?). The title of the book was, however, somewhat misleading as Ross already declared in the preface that he would not try to convince the reader in the name of any imagined authority of science that a particular attitude was correct.[79] In a manner that resembled Hedenius, Ross argued that if someone does not like democracy, freedom or peace, there is no logical way to prove that he is wrong. But Ross emphasised that this does not lead to resignation in the face of totalitarianism. A person that refutes the idea that values can be scientifically proven does not have to fall back into indifference. Ross claimed 'because a point of view is a point of view and not a scientific truth, it naturally does not follow from this that one cannot have some point of view', and continued with a personal declaration: 'I know very well what I shall stand for and fight for. Only I do not imagine myself, or try to make others believe, that it can be scientifically proved that my point of view is the "right" one'.[80]

In this way, Ross tried, like Tingsten, to turn the value nihilistic theory into a defence of personal autonomy, and the choice between democracy and totalitarianism into a very personal affair, something that each individual ultimately had to make up his own mind about and carry the responsibility for. But Ross also seems to have thought, like Hedenius, that it was possible to appeal to these valuations as matters of fact. In order to be effective, Ross argued, the defence of democracy must 'start from the available historical valuations that have actually been held by large groups of people'.[81] Like

---

78 Blandhol 1999, 29–45; Dalberg-Larsen, Jørgen (2003) *Dansk Retsfilosofi – udviklingslinjer og portrætter.* København: Jurist- og Økonomforbundets forlag, 46–67; Strang 2009b, 74–77.

79 '…mit beskedne Bidrag til Danmarks Frihedskamp'. Ross 1946, 7 (Danish original). Unless otherwise stated, I am referring to the English translation: Ross, Alf (1952) *Why Democracy?* Cambridge Massachusetts.

80 Ross 1952 [1946], 93–94.

81 Ross 1952 [1946], 94.

Hedenius, Ross believed that shared values are a prerequisite for a successful, and indeed meaningful, moral argument.

Ross's main strategy in defending democracy, however, was not to appeal to the personal responsibility of the citizens or to a set of shared values, but rather to clarify what actually was at stake in the choice between democracy and totalitarianism. Ross seemed to think that many opponents of democracy did not really understand the difference between totalitarianism and democracy, and that they would change their minds if the erroneous conceptions were corrected. This was something that could be done within the realm of political science because while 'the points of view themselves cannot be discussed, the understanding of the facts that constitute the prerequisite for the points of view can be'.[82] *Hvorfor Demokrati?* was therefore largely a discussion of the meaning of the concept 'democracy' and Ross distinguished between three different understandings of democracy: (1) formal democracy, (2) real, or economic, democracy and (3) democracy as an attitude or way of life. However, Ross strongly emphasised that it was the first of these, the formal or political meaning of democracy, which was the heart of the concept. Democracy, Ross argued, echoing Tingsten, 'indicates a *how*, not a *what*'. 'It indicates how political decisions are made, not what these decisions are in substance. It designates a method for the establishment of the "political will", not its object, end, or means.' The measure of the degree to which a form of government is democratic, Ross continued, is the majority principle.[83]

It has been rendered somewhat surprising that Ross (and Tingsten) endorsed such a formal and procedural account of democracy at this point in time, when the experiences of Nazism might have provoked a stronger emphasis on the individual rights of citizens and minorities. In Ross's view individual rights were merely prerequisites for a well-functioning majority principle, and thus inherently secondary to it. Joakim Nergelius and Lars Adam Rehof have both presumed that Ross's reluctance to include material considerations in his concept of democracy was connected to the value nihilistic theory on one hand, and the experiences of materially defined totalitarian regimes on the other.[84] The first idea seems to be that, as the value nihilists did not believe in the objective truth of values or in the existence of 'natural rights', they were inclined not to include them in their definition of democracy. However, even if the value nihilistic theory might have formed a psychological barrier, it hardly constituted an insurmountable logical obstacle for a more material definition of democracy. There was nothing in value nihilism that made a more moral or normative definition of democracy impossible, as long as these values were not presented as scientifically established truths.[85] Indeed, the high regard given to the majority principle

---

82   Ross 1952 [1946], 93.

83   Ross 1952 [1946], 75–76, 91–94.

84   Nergelius 1996, 138; Rehof, Lars Adam (1991) 'På sporet af pragmatismen i dansk retspleje'. In Peter Blume, Ditlev Tamm & Vibeke Vindeløv (eds) *Suum cuique – retsvidenskablige afhandlinger, Københavns Universitet 1991*. København: Jurist- og Økonomforbundets forlag, 30–49, here at 41–42.

85   And, perhaps more importantly, even if the Scandinavian Legal Realists, following the legal philosophy of Hägerström, were rather sceptical of the concept of individual

must also be conceived of as something of an evaluation. Moreover, some philosophers that sympathised with value nihilism nevertheless opposed a restricted formal conception of democracy, perhaps most notably the Danish philosopher and communist Jørgen Jørgensen who included political, juridical, social, cultural as well as economic aspects in what he called 'the wide democracy' (*det brede demokrati*).[86]

But Nergelius and Rehof are undoubtedly right in claiming that the formal account of democracy was motivated by the totalitarian threat; however, the decisive factor was arguably not so much the experience of Nazism, but rather the rising threat of Communism during the immediate post-war period. *Hvorfor Demokrati?* was written as a contribution to the great Danish democracy debate in the years following the Second World War, and the three conceptions of democracy (formal democracy, economical democracy and democracy as a way of life) that Ross discussed represented the three major standpoints in this debate.[87] The idea of democracy as a way of life was advocated by the theologian Hal Koch, who argued that peaceful conversation aiming at an acceptable compromise was the essence of democracy.[88] Ross did not make an issue of criticising Koch's notion of democracy. Although often presented as the main antagonists, Koch and Ross were more of allies in the Danish Democracy Debate. They both supported Social Democracy and collaborated as editors of the anthology *Nordisk Demokrati* (1949).[89] Rather, by emphasising that democracy concerned the form and not the content of political decisions, Ross was primarily trying to refute what he conceived as communistic attempts to extend, or even colonise, the concept of democracy by talking about 'economic democracy' or 'real democracy' like Jørgensen. According to Ross, the Danish communists adopted Soviet-Russian rhetorical tactics of confusing democracy with a particular economical politics that would more appropriately be denoted by the term 'socialism'.[90] The opposite of 'democracy' is 'autocracy' and the opposite of 'socialism' is 'capitalism', Ross argued, and it is possible to combine these in any way one pleases.[91]

Thus, the formal account of democracy advocated by Ross closely resembled Tingsten's idea of an over-ideology, and it also involved an analogous 'communitarian' emphasis of shared values. In an article in *Tiden* in 1947 Ross argued that shared values and the sense of belonging

rights, Ross (and Hedenius) belonged to a second generation of Legal Realists who criticised Hägerström and his more ardent disciples for dispatching the whole concept of (individual) rights. The mission of Ross (and Hedenius) was, rather, to make it possible to talk about individual rights despite the 'realistic' or 'positivistic' outlook. See Blandhol 1999, 95–109; Strang 2009b.

86 Jørgensen, Jørgen (1945) *Det Demokratiske Samfund – Grundtræk af en Analyse.* København: Tiden.

87 A number of central articles from the Danish Democracy Debate have been gathered in Søren Hein Rasmussen & Niels Kayser Nielsen (eds) (2003) *Strid om demokratiet – Artikler fra en dansk debat.* Århus: Aarhus Universitetsforlag.

88 Koch, Hal (1945) *Hvad er Demokrati?* København: Gyldendal.

89 Koch & Ross 1949.

90 Ross 1952 [1946], 142.

91 Ross 1952 [1946], 233.

to the same community constitute the framework that unites the minority with the majority and makes it possible for them to accept their decisions.[92] Conversely, if a certain group of people, on a very fundamental level, disagree with the rest of the population, they will feel little or no respect for the decisions of the majority, and thus democracy itself will be in danger. In *Hvorfor Demokrati?* Ross argued that such conflicts, involving for example religious and national minorities, can only be resolved if the minority conforms to the majority or if they create a separate political community.[93] Moreover, Ross also connected the idea of shared values to his struggle against the communists, arguing that democracy would deteriorate if a socialist majority of 51 per cent swiftly attempted to carry out a sweeping economic and social revolution. The minority would most likely opt out of the democratic community as they would no longer feel that they shared the same basic values as the majority. Thus, even though Ross pointed out the problems and limitations of majoritarianism, he did not immediately connect them to a stronger emphasis on constitutional rights. Rather, his response was to trust in communitarian solidarity, arguing that the only way of introducing socialism and a planned economy was to do it piecemeal in order not to disturb the community of shared values.[94]

Tingsten and Ross shared the formal understanding of democracy and both of them stressed the necessity of shared values, but their views clashed in the post-war debate on the compatibility of socialism and democracy. Tingsten, who had been a member of the Swedish Social Democratic Labour Party in the 1930s, became one of their loudest critics after the war. Inspired by reading F. A. Hayek's *The Road to Serfdom* Tingsten became very attentive to the problems of realising socialism under democratic rule, and repeatedly accused the Swedish Social Democrats for neglecting the inherent dangers of a planned economy.[95] For Ross, on the other hand, criticism of the communists aimed at making room for a position that was socialist and democratic – that is, social democratic. These sympathies, visible between the lines in *Hvorfor Demokrati?*, were explicitly pronounced in a number of partisan publications in the late 1940s.[96] It soon became almost as important

---

92 Ross, Alf (1947) 'Socialismen och demokratin'. *Tiden*. Vol. 39, Issue 7, 392–404.

93 Ross 1952 [1946], 143–144.

94 Ross 1952 [1946], 291; Ross 1947, 397.

95 Tingsten 1945, 298-238. Besides the influence from Hayek, which Tingsten emphasises himself – for example in the afterword of the 1967 edition of *Socialdemokratiens idéutveckling*, (Tingsten 1967 [1941], 389–391), Tingsten's conversion from Social Democracy has also been explained as a result of his own studies of Social Democratic ideology in the early 1940s, in combination with a general dissatisfaction with both the politics and, perhaps even more importantly, the dominant role of the Social Democrats in Sweden. See Johansson 1995, 246–250.

96 Ross, Alf (1945b) *Kommunismen og Demokratiet*. København: Fremad; Ross, Alf (1945a) 'Hvorfor jeg stemmer paa socialdemokratiet'. *SocialDemokraten*. 25 October 1945; Ross, Alf (1948) 'Kan man være socialist uden at være marxist?' *Verdens Gang*. Vol. 2, 255-258. Ross's relation to social democracy was, however, by no means unproblematic. Most apparently, as Henning Fonsmark has noticed, the concept of 'economic democracy', that Ross emphatically criticised, appeared on almost every page of the economic chapter of the social democratic mission statement *Fremtidens*

for Ross to respond to Hayek's liberal challenge as it had been to stand up against the communists.

Ross paid special attention to Hayek's argument that a planned economy required a moral scale according to which different political actions and reforms would be prioritised. According to Hayek, it is impossible for the citizens of a nation to agree on such a scale, which inevitably means that politics will be taken over by experts, that democratic control will be diminished, and totalitarianism will prevail.[97] Ross denied that a planned economy had to be based on an objective philosophical moral standard; rather, he argued, the plan can be established through the 'usual democratic majority procedure', and, thus, it represents 'the manifold evaluations, wishes, and considerations which actually live traditionally and assert themselves in a community'.[98] In this way Ross tried to connect the voluntaristic aspect of value nihilism directly to the democratic procedure. As individuals are fundamentally autonomous on moral issues, the only way to deal with the situation is by voting and letting the majority rule. On the other hand, Ross undoubtedly believed that the democratic elaboration of an economic plan requires that people share the same values, at least to the extent that makes the acceptance of the decisions of the majority possible, otherwise the plan would endanger the democratic community. Thus one of the basic differences between Hayek and Ross was their views on the extent to which it is possible for a population to share the same values. While Hayek seemed to believe that the number of uncontested issues that can be subjected to planning in a democratically justifiable manner was rather limited,[99] Ross was quite optimistic. If construction materials are scarce, Ross argued, it is easy to agree that proper housing must be prioritised over summer residences; equally it is easy to agree that 'the import of necessary raw materials must have priority over nuts and jam'.[100] Moreover, Ross was not merely optimistic regarding the possibility of people agreeing, there was also undoubtedly a considerable trait of scientism in his view. Referring to Karl Mannheim and Schumpeter, Ross argued that it is likely that an increasing number of issues will be rendered unpolitical as a result of economic levelling and scientific progress, which in turn will make the construction of a plan even less problematic.[101]

Given Ross's social democratic credo, it is perhaps not very surprising that he transformed the idea of shared values from a prerequisite for democracy to a basis for effective economic planning. It is more surprising

Danmark in 1945. Much later, when the Social Democrats collaborated with the socialists (*Socialistisk Folkeparti*) in the 1966 elections, Ross announced that he no longer supported them. See Fonsmark, Henning (1990) *Historien om den danske utopi.* København: Gyldendal, 62–65.

97   Ross 1952 [1946], 181–183; Hayek, F. A. (1944) *The Road to Serfdom.* Chicago: The University of Chicago Press, 1994, 63–70.
98   Ross 1952 [1946], 184; Ross 1947, 401.
99   Hayek 1944, 68–70.
100 'Man enes ogsaa let om, at Import af vigtige Raavarer maa gaa forud for Nødder og Marmelade.' Ross 1946, 276 (in the Danish original).
101 Ross 1952 [1946], 185 & 189.

that Tingsten, as a leading liberal voice in Sweden, continued to embrace the idea of shared values despite the fact that many other renowned liberal intellectuals, such as Hayek and Isaiah Berlin, endorsed moral pluralism and stressed that people as a matter of fact support different and incompatible values.[102] This difference was mirrored in their different conceptions of democracy. While Tingsten believed that democracy was essentially majority rule and thus thought that shared values was a necessary prerequisite for a well-functioning democratic society, Hayek was more concerned with the protection of individual freedom and the rights of citizens in a value pluralistic world characterised by disagreement rather than agreement. It is hardly insignificant that Tingsten looked upon things with Swedish eyes, while Hayek was writing as an Austrian refugee in Britain.

But the difference between Tingsten and Hayek can also be seen as a clash over whether priority should be given to liberalism or democracy. In his *Road to Serfdom* Hayek explicitly stated that democracy, unlike liberalism, should not be conceived of as an intrinsic value.[103] For Hayek, democracy was merely a means of realising peace and individual freedom. If forced to choose between democracy and liberalism he would have taken the latter, while Tingsten undoubtedly, true to his over-ideology thesis, would have preferred the first. Tingsten shared with Ross the formal conception of democracy, the view that the majority principle was the defining characteristic of democracy, and also the idea that democracy therefore ultimately required that the population shared the same basic values. For them, democracy remained an over-ideology that was by no means synonymous with liberalism or socialism, but had to be prioritised over them both.

Gunnar Myrdal – planning for democracy

One of Tingsten's main targets as a liberal critic of social democracy after the Second World War was his old friend Gunnar Myrdal who, as a Social Democratic trade minister in the late 1940s and as a renowned economist and social scientist, was considered to be one of the main advocates of social and economic planning in Sweden.[104] Given their profound disagreement on the issue of planning, it is certainly quite ironic that in 1972 Myrdal shared the Nobel Prize in economics with Hayek. But even though they disagreed on both the outcome and the political evaluation of planning, Myrdal and Hayek shared an almost deterministic view according to which the road towards increasing economic and social planning was almost an inevitable and irreversible process. When people have become accustomed to planning, Myrdal argued in 1951, there is no turning back. 'Planning is our destiny. We have to make the most out of the world we have, and

---

102 Berlin, Isaiah (1958) *Two Concepts of Liberty.* Oxford: Clarendon.
103 Hayek 1944, 78–79.
104 Lewin 1967, 319.

we also have to make our social and economic plans better and better.'[105] Myrdal was not, of course, impressed by the arguments that planning would endanger freedom or democracy; in 1951, he brushed aside the allegations that economic and social planning (*planhushållning*) would lead to a police state as mere 'rubbish'.[106] According to Myrdal, there was little empirical evidence that supported such a claim; in the countries in which totalitarianism had prevailed, economic planning and social engineering had not been implemented to any significant extent. Instead what was decisive, Myrdal claimed, was the fact that these countries had much shorter histories as democracies than Scandinavia, where democracy was strongly rooted in a historical development that has proceeded for centuries. Our democracy, Myrdal concluded, has survived brutal economic crises and 'it will certainly endure more planning'.[107]

Thus, Myrdal utilised references to the democratic traditions of the North in his defence of the compatibility of planning and democracy similar to those used by Tingsten and Ross in their defence of Nordic democracy against the threats of fascist and communist totalitarianism. Moreover, Myrdal also seemed to support a similar idea of the importance of shared values. For sure, he did not believe that there was, or should be, complete political agreement in a democratic society such as Scandinavia or the United States; in fact, he argued, there was 'disagreement on all questions'. But echoing Tingsten's over-ideology thesis Myrdal claimed that these disagreements did 'not concern the fundamentals'.[108] Even though people are bound to disagree on the implementation of a certain policy, or even on a more principal level on the choice between liberalism and socialism, a well-functioning democracy still requires that there was agreement at a more basic level. Speaking about the United States, Myrdal claimed in communitarian terms that 'the cultural unity of the nation consists...in the fact that *most Americans have most valuations in common*' and that 'this cultural unity is the indispensable basis for discussion between individuals and groups. It is the floor upon which the democratic process goes on.'[109]

For Myrdal planning was not a threat to democracy. In fact, according to him, quite the opposite was the case: planning was a necessary part of the defence of democracy. This line of thought was most explicitly formulated in two articles from 1939 in the American progressive and liberal (in the American sense of the word) journal *Survey Graphic – Magazine for*

---

105 Myrdal, Gunnar (1951) 'Utvecklingen mot planhushållning'. *Tiden*. Vol. 43, Issue 3, 148

106 Myrdal 1951, 149.

107 'Utan tvivel kan den uthärda mera planhushålling'. Myrdal 1951, 149. The article was a translation of a speech that Myrdal gave in Manchester in 1950, and therefore, by 'us' and 'our' Myrdal referred to both Scandinavia and Great Britain.

108 Myrdal, Gunnar (1939a) 'With dictators as neigbors'. In Gunnar Myrdal, *Maintaining Democracy in Sweden – Two Articles by Gunnar Myrdal*. Reprinted from *Survey Graphic – Magazine for Social Interpretation* by Albert Bonnier Publishing House, 1–8, here at 8.

109 Myrdal, Gunnar (1944) *An American Dilemma – the Negro Problem and Modern Democracy*. New York: Harper & Brothers, xlviii. Emphasis in original.

Social Interpretation where Myrdal discussed the reasons for the apparent success of democracy in Scandinavia despite the precarious geopolitical situation of the region. In this situation, 'having Soviet Russia at our back, Nazi Germany at our front…our inherited democratic system is running in keen competition with the dictatorial systems of our mighty neighbors', Myrdal argued, it was more apparent in Scandinavia than anywhere else, that 'the frontier of democracy lies within our boundaries, and not at our borderlines'.[110] The Nordic countries are too small to be able to but up an *external* defence that would make them safe in a military sense, and therefore, the only way for them to defend their democratic sovereignty is by strengthening their *internal* defence by making the population immune to Communist and Nazi propaganda. And this was, according to Myrdal, something that the Scandinavians had managed to do with great success: the labour movement was practically free of Communist contamination and the intellectuals were flirting with neither Communism nor Nazism – 'neither ism has ever had a single adherent [in Sweden] who could pretend to any expert knowledge or real literary capacity'. The main reason for this success was, Myrdal claimed confidently, the fact that the Swedish government 'delivered the goods' – that it had proven itself highly competent in tackling economic problems.[111] Sweden, Norway and Denmark, Myrdal argued, were closer than any other country 'to a completion of the symptomatic or curative stage of social policy'. Instead of just focusing on alleviating the symptoms, the aim had become to prevent social problems from arising in the first place, through active and comprehensive unemployment, health, housing, and population policies.[112]

The idea that social reforms were needed in order to quench the totalitarian threat was, of course, rather common in Europe at the time. The difference was, perhaps, that Myrdal was able to use the argument, not as a warning, but as a description of past events, of the successful Scandinavian policies of economic planning and social engineering. However, being a disciple of Hägerström, the idea of policy planning formed a peculiar methodological problem for Myrdal. How could he, as an economic or political scientist, provide theoretical arguments in favour of a particular plan or policy? It seemed to be a clear cut case of normative science, something Myrdal himself, on Hägerströmian premises, had vehemently criticised in his *The Political Element in the Development of Economic Theory* (*Vetenskap och politik i nationalekonomien*, 1929). Myrdal did not look for the solution along the same lines as Ross, emphasising the strict division of labour between politics and science. For Myrdal, the idea of a disinterested social science was 'pure nonsense',[113] and instead he tried to formulate a theory that would make room for practical political suggestions within the realm of science itself. After all, Myrdal argued, social scientists are more familiar with social problems than politicians and the general public, and

110 Myrdal 1939a, 3–4
111 Myrdal 1939a, 4
112 Myrdal 1939a, 5–7.
113 Myrdal 1944, 1064

therefore they should be able to direct their studies themselves, without the time-consuming procedure of political decision making.[114] But such a view seems to realise Hayek's fears that those in charge of planning would start to implement their own valuations, which, in effect, would mean that totalitarianism would be introduced.

There are good reasons to suspect that Myrdal thought that it was perfectly legitimate for social scientists to do 'political propaganda' by taking their own personal valuations as a starting point for study as long as they were explicit about it and did not present the valuations as scientific truths. This was explicitly stated by Gunnar Myrdal's wife Alva Myrdal in her book *Nation and Family* (1941). However, she emphasised that such a study, would only have a very limited significance as the valuations might not be supported by politicians or the general public.[115] That the value premises were explicitly stated was not enough, they also had to be relevant to the particular study. Gunnar Myrdal's basic idea, hinted at already in 1929, but more extensively developed in the methodological appendixes of *An American Dilemma* (1944), was that the social scientist should try to develop an 'instrumental norm' on the basis of valuations actually present in the society under study. These valuations should then be explicitly accounted for and used as the basic value premises for the policies suggested.

Even though Myrdal arguably struggled somewhat to find a method by which the valuations of a population could be determined – attempting a number of different solutions, ranging from opinion polls to eclectic cultural analyses[116] – he did put the idea into effect in his own studies. Most notably, the basic argument of *An American Dilemma* (1944) was that racial segregation in the US violated the basic values of the American nation – something Myrdal called 'the American Creed'.[117] Similarly, in *Kris i befolkningsfrågan* (1934), Alva and Gunnar Myrdal argued that the value premises they presupposed were not strictly party-political, but widely held among Swedes.[118] And more thoroughly, in *Nation and Family* (1941), which was a rewritten English version of *Kris i befolkningsfrågan* for an American audience, Alva Myrdal elaborated something which could be called a 'Scandinavian Creed', a system of evaluative standpoints which formed the basis for the social political programme she presented in the book. Among the values appreciated in Scandinavia, she mentioned 'the freedom of the individual', 'a high standard of living', 'economic equality', and 'a positive evaluation of children, family, and marriage' as well as 'a rather strong belief in the usefulness of social control exercised through

114 Myrdal 1944, 1044

115 Myrdal Alva (1998) [1941] *Nation and Family – The Swedish Experiment in Democratic Family and Population Policy*. London: Routledge, 101.

116 See Strang, Johan (2007) 'Overcoming the rift between "is" and "ought" – Gunnar Myrdal and the philosophy of social engineering'. *Ideas in history*. Vol. 2, Issue 2, 143–177.

117 See Myrdal 1944, 3–25 & 997–1064.

118 Alva Myrdal & Gunnar Myrdal (1934) *Kris i befolkningsfrågan (folkupplagan)*. Stockholm: Bonniers, 20

collective agencies, such as the state, the municipalities, and the large civic organisations'.[119]

Like Tingsten and Ross, Myrdal believed that shared values, cultural unity or even homogeneity, was a precondition for a well-functioning democracy. And he was at least as confident as Tingsten and Ross that such unanimity, unity and homogeneity actually existed in Sweden and Scandinavia. In the second *Survey Graphic*-article, 'The Defenses of Democracy', Myrdal argued that even though there were many features in Swedish democracy that other countries, particularly the United States, could learn from, Sweden had a number of advantages working in its favour. Not only was it a small country which was easier to administer than the United States, Sweden was also characterised by a 'greater racial, religious, social and cultural homogeneity of the people'.[120] According to Myrdal, in Sweden, 'the basic philosophy is common, the main direction agreed upon, and the disagreement concerns mainly the expediency of different avenues of action'.[121]

But unlike Tingsten (and, at least to some extent, Ross) Myrdal gave the idea of shared values more importance as he believed that the democratic heritage and the cultural unity and homogeneity of the Scandinavian countries made them particularly suited for planning and social engineering. If people shared the same values, economic planning and social engineering could be implemented more extensively and with less controversy. Moreover, in this connection Myrdal also claimed that one of the main benefits of modern Sweden was the fact that it had inherited 'an honest civil service' which has installed in people 'habits of unconditional obedience to the law'.[122] Similarly, in *Nation and Family*, Alva Myrdal explicitly claimed that 'the Scandinavian countries, and particularly Sweden, have by an historical accident been given a most advantageous set of prerequisites for a bold experiment in social democracy'.[123]

In this way, the issue of planning and social engineering was depoliticised and turned into a similar culturally shared 'over-ideology' as democracy itself. By such a view, the idea of a conflict between democracy and planning was, of course, a non-starter. To the contrary, the very concept of 'democracy' became itself, if not synonymous, then at least very closely associated, with 'social democracy', 'planning' and 'social engineering'. The fortune of the Nordic countries, according to Myrdal, was that their democratic heritage and cultural homogeneity facilitated a vast implementation of social engineering and economic planning, which was needed in order to keep them as effective and competitive as the totalitarian states. This was a virtuous circle which was further enhanced by the fact that, in turn, social engineering and economic

119 Myrdal 1998 [1941], 102–103
120 Myrdal, Gunnar (1939b) 'The Defenses of Democracy'. In Gunnar Myrdal, *Maintaining Democracy in Sweden – Two Articles by Gunnar Myrdal*. Reprinted from *Survey Graphic – Magazine for Social Interpretation* by Albert Bonnier Publishing House, 9–14, at 9–10.
121 Myrdal 1939a, 8.
122 Myrdal 1939b, 10
123 Myrdal 1998 [1941], 10–11.

planning could be used to preserve and improve the unity of the nation. 'Swedish democracy has by its own accomplishments during recent years strengthened even further the cultural, social and economic unity which the present generation inherited.'[124] Thus, for Myrdal, economic planning and social engineering were not merely instruments by which democracy could be defended, they were a continuation of the Nordic democratic legacy; the best way in which this legacy could be managed and developed further. 'Nordic democracy' was not only a sentimental figure denoting the fortunate preconditions that Social Democrats like Myrdal inherited; it was also very much a figure of the future. It is therefore characteristic that Alva Myrdal claimed that 'if democracy could not develop successfully in Scandinavia, given by historical chance quite exceptionally advantageous conditions, it will probably not work anywhere else'.[125]

Conclusions – the value nihilists and 'Nordic democracy'

There are of course many points that can be, and have been, raised against the ideas of Hedenius, Tingsten, Ross and Myrdal. The value nihilistic theory, which they conceived of as a more or less conclusive achievement of modern scientific philosophy, has since proven far from indisputable. The philosophical debate between moral realists and non-cognitivists is as vivid as ever, although not as explicitly connected to political currents as it was in the 1930s and 1940s.[126] Democracy, on the other hand, has undoubtedly become an over-ideology supported by all, but the formal or procedural account defended by Tingsten and Ross has – even in Scandinavia – been challenged by scholars who more strongly emphasise the importance of constitutional rights.[127] Finally, the emphasis of shared values certainly mirrors contemporary challenges for both ethics and democracy in an age of globalisation. But where the philosophers and social scientists of today look for ways to establish communication and dialogue between different value systems and cultures, the Scandinavian value nihilists seemed to think that everyone basically agreed, and that if people did not agree further discussion was fruitless. Indeed, one of the main problems with the accounts of Hedenius, Tingsten and Ross was that they hardly ever ventured to discuss the values that they thought were almost universally shared. Instead, they tended to take them more or less for granted. Myrdal was perhaps exceptional in this sense, but even he thought that Nordic values were rather self-evident, if not universal, in character. It is easy to follow Gunnar Skirbekk in his remark that there was little place for (normative) moral discussions in the Nordic countries after the Second World War – it

---

124 Myrdal 1939a, 8
125 Myrdal 1998 [1941], 15
126 For a reasonably updated account of the debate, see Miller, Alexander (2003) *An Introduction to Contemporary Metaethics*. Cambridge: Polity Press.
127 One of the most forceful recent claims is Nergelius 1996.

was as if 'the normative problem already had been solved' and the question that remained was merely the instrumental *how* of social engineering.[128]

From an international perspective it might appear as striking that in Scandinavia, the rise of totalitarianism and the catastrophe of the Second World War did not lead to a rejection of positivistic thinking and relativistic moral theories. To the contrary, the Scandinavian value nihilists were, as a matter of fact, able to strengthen their positions in the 1930s and 1940s, and in 1949 Hedenius confidently claimed that the modern nihilistic philosophy which he represented formed 'an important part of the spiritual culture of the Nordic countries'.[129] Of course, to a large extent the explanation for this curiosity has to be institutional. While positivist philosophers were driven from the European continent in to exile, the Scandinavian value nihilists attained key positions both at universities and were thus able to influence a whole generation of students. Many of them were also active in the public debate, as authors of a number of widely read books, and as writers and columnists in important publications such as *Tiden* and *Dagens Nyheter*.

However, a significant part of the explanation must also be that the value nihilists did rather well in consolidating their philosophy with contemporary political ideas, not least in the debate on democracy and value nihilism. By emphasising the rift between science and politics, Hedenius was able to defeat the allegations of a connection to totalitarianism while simultaneously updating value nihilism with the latest international philosophical trends. Tingsten succeeded in overcoming the restraints of value nihilism to develop a critical method which revealed (the totalitarian) ideologies to be irrational and erroneous. Ross demarcated 'democracy' in a way that refuted communist attempts at colonising the concept without censuring socialist politics under democratic forms. And Myrdal found a way of making values operative within his programme of social engineering despite the strict division between facts and values.

Not least the idea of shared values can be said to have been rather fortunate in terms of its historical-political context. The value nihilists were of course far from alone in stressing the significance of shared values in a democratic community. As noted above, international theoreticians such as Schumpeter and Barker made similar claims, and in Sweden Ahlberg's criticism of value nihilism was based on an assumption that the theory undermined the shared values that were a precondition for democracy. From this perspective, the task for the value nihilists was to find a place for the idea of shared values within the framework of their own philosophy, and this was what Hedenius did when pointing to the fact that people can share values even if they do not believe that these values are objective, absolute or true. However, the idea of shared values was undoubtedly also connected

128 'Hos oss, mærkeleg nok, utløyste ikkje krigen ei slik ny normativ gjennomtenking. Hos oss var spørsmålet primært *korleis* det heile kunne skje… Det normative spørsmålet var liksom allereie løyst. Alle gode nordmenn visste kva som var rett og rangt.' Skirbekk, Gunnar (1984) '"I refleksjonens mangel…" Om vekslande intellektuelle elitar i norsk etterkrigstid'. *Nytt Norsk Tidsskrift*. Vol. 1, Issue 1, 21–37, at 31.
129 'en icke oviktig beståndsdel i Nordens andliga kultur'. Hedenius 1949, 207.

to the 'communitarian' or culturally nationalistic rhetoric prevalent in Scandinavian political language at this point in time. It is noteworthy that the universalistic 'positivist' philosophy, and the value nihilistic theory, did not prevent Hedenius, Tingsten, Ross and Myrdal from contributing to this rhetoric. Even though they were often very critical towards '*völkish*' ideas, refuting them as idealistic metaphysics, they were still able to refer to a Nordic democratic heritage and to the (alleged) homogeneity of their countries as part of their defence of democracy. But there were differences in the ways in which the communitarian or culturally nationalistic rhetoric was utilised by the value nihilists. For Tingsten, 'Nordic democracy' referred primarily to the past and present success of democracy in Scandinavia, to the Nordic democratic heritage and to the present fight against totalitarianism. For those sympathetic to social democracy, namely Ross and Myrdal, it was also a way of claiming the future. It was a mobilising concept that denoted a future society emerging from the social democratic policies of economic planning and social engineering.

BIBLIOGRAPHY

Ahlberg, Alf (1941) 'Maktfilosofi och värdenihilism'. In Alf Ahlberg et. al. (eds) *Varför det svenska folket reagerar*. Stockholm: Natur och kultur.

Ayer, Alfred (1958) [1936] *Language, Truth and Logic*. London: Victor Gollancz.

Barker, Ernest (1942) *Reflections on Government*. London: Oxford University Press.

Berlin, Isaiah (1958) *Two Concepts of Liberty*. Oxford: Clarendon.

Berman, Sheri (2006) *The Primacy of Politics – Social Democracy and the Making of Europe's Twentieth Century*. Cambridge: Cambridge University Press.

Bjarup, Jes (2005) 'The Philosophy of Scandinavian Legal Realism'. *Ratio Juris*. Vol. 18, Issue 1, 1–15.

Blandhol, Sverre (1999) *Juridisk ideologi – Alf Ross' kritikk av naturretten*. København: Jurist- og Økonomforbundets forlag.

Boström, Bengt-Ove (1988) *Samtal om demokratin*. Lund: Doxa.

Carnap, Rudolf (1935) *Philosophy and Logical Syntax*. London: Kegan Paul.

Cassirer, Ernst (1939) *Axel Hägerström – eine Studie zur schwedischen Philosophie der Gegenwart*. Göteborg: Elander.

Dahlberg, Gunnar & Tingsten, Herbert (eds) (1937) *Svensk politisk uppslagsbok*. Stockholm: Svensk litteratur.

Dalberg-Larsen, Jørgen (2003) *Dansk Retsfilosofi – udviklingslinjer og portrætter*. København: Jurist- og Økonomforbundets forlag.

Fonsmark, Henning (1990) *Historien om den danske utopi*. København: Gyldendal.

Frank, Philipp (1951) *Relativity – A Richer Truth*. London: Jonathan Cape.

Götz, Norbert (2001) *Ungleiche Geschwister - die Konstruktion von nationalsozialistischer Volksgemeinschaft und schwedischem Volksheim*. Baden-Baden: Nomos.

Hägerström, Axel (1911) 'Om moraliska föreställningars sanning'. In Hägerström, Axel (1939) *Socialfilosofiska uppsatser*. Stockholm: Bonniers, 35–65.

Hayek, F. A. (1944) *The road to serfdom*. Chicago: The University of Chicago Press, 1994.

Hedenius, Ingemar (1939) 'Über den alogischen Character der sog. Werturteile. Bemerkungen zu Ernst Cassirer: Axel Hägerström. Eine Studie zur schwedishen Philosophie der Gegenwart'. *Theoria*. Vol. 5, Issue 3, 314–329.

Hedenius, Ingemar (1940) 'Hägerström och diktaturstaternas framfart'. *Tiden*. Vol. 32, Issue 3, 174–178.

Hedenius, Ingemar (1967) [1941] *Om rätt och moral.* Stockholm: Wahlström & Widstrand.

Hedenius, Ingemar (1949) 'Filosofiska skäl för demokratien'. In Koch & Ross (eds.) *Nordisk Demokrati.* København: Munksgaard, 207–224.

Hedenius, Ingemar (1973): *Herbert Tingsten – Människan och demokraten.* Stockholm: Norstedts.

Hein Rasmussen, Søren & Kayser Nielsen, Niels (eds) (2003) *Strid om demokratiet – Artikler fra en dansk debat.* Århus: Aarhus Universitetsforlag.

Johansson, Alf W (1995) *Herbert Tingsten och det kalla kriget.* Stockholm: Tiden.

Jørgensen, Jørgen (1945) *Det Demokratiske Samfund – Grundtræk af en Analyse.* København: Tiden.

Kelsen, Hans (1981) [1929] *Vom Wesen und Wert der Demokratie.* Aalen: Scientia.

Kelsen, Hans (1948) 'Absolutism and Relativism in Philosophy'. *The American Political Science Review.* Vol. 42, Issue 5, 906–914.

Kayser Nielsen, Niels (2004) 'Demokrati og kulturel nationalisme i Norden i mellem-krigstiden – en realpolitisk højredrejning'. *Historisk tidskrift.* Vol. 124, Issue 4, 581–603.

Koch, Hal (1945) *Hvad er Demokrati?* København: Gyldendal.

Källström, Harald (1940) 'Prof Hägerström och världskrisen'. *Göteborgs Morgonpost,* 27 January 1940.

Källström, Staffan (1984) *Värdenihilism och vetenskap – Uppsalafilosofin i forskning och samhälle under 1920- och 30-talen.* Göteborg: Acta Universitatis Gothoburgensis.

Källström, Staffan (1986) *Den gode nihilisten – Axel Hägerström och striderna kring uppsalafilosofin.* Stockholm: Raben & Sjögren, 110–116.

Linderborg, Åsa (2001) *Socialdemokraterna skriver historia – historieskrivning som ideologisk maktresurs 1892–2000.* Stockholm: Atlas.

Lundborg, Johan (1991) *Ideologiernas och religionens död – en analys av Herbert Tingstens ideologi- och religionskritik.* Nora: Nya Doxa.

Lönnqvist, C (1940) 'Hitler och Hägerström'. *Göteborgs Handels- och Sjöfartstidning,* 3 July 1940.

Marc-Wogau, Konrad (1968) *Studier till Axel Hägerströms filosofi.* Stockholm: Prisma, 202.

Mertens, Thomas (2003) 'Nazism, Legal Positivism and Radbruch's thesis on Statutory Injustice'. *Law and Critique,* Vol. 14, Issue 3, 277–295.

Miller, Alexander (2003) *An Introduction to Contemporary Metaethics.* Cambridge: Polity Press.

Moore, George Edward (1922) *Philosophical Studies.* London: Routledge & Kegan Paul

Myrdal, Alva (1998) [1941] *Nation and Family – The Swedish Experiment in Democratic Family and Population Policy.* London: Routledge.

Myrdal, Alva & Myrdal, Gunnar (1934) *Kris i befolkningsfrågan (folkupplagan).* Stockholm: Bonniers.

Myrdal, Gunnar (1939a) 'With dictators as neigbors'. In Gunnar Myrdal, *Maintaining Democracy in Sweden – Two Articles by Gunnar Myrdal.* Reprinted from *Survey Graphic – Magazine for Social Interpretation* by Albert Bonnier Publishing House, 1–8.

Myrdal, Gunnar (1939b) 'The Defenses of Democracy'. In Gunnar Myrdal, *Maintaining Democracy in Sweden – Two Articles by Gunnar Myrdal.* Reprinted from *Survey Graphic – Magazine for Social Interpretation* by Albert Bonnier Publishing House, 9–14.

Myrdal, Gunnar (1944) *An American Dilemma – the Negro Problem and Modern Democracy.* New York: Harper & Brothers.

Myrdal, Gunnar (1951) 'Utvecklingen mot planhushållning'. *Tiden.* Vol. 43, Issue 3.

Nergelius, Joakim (1996) *Konstitutionellt rättighetsskydd – svensk rätt i komparativt perspektiv.* Stockholm: Fritzes.

Nordin, Svante (1983) *Från Hägerström till Hedenius – den moderna svenska filosofin.* Lund: Doxa.

111

Nordin, Svante (2004) *Ingemar Hedenius – en filosof och hans tid*. Stockholm: Natur och kultur.

Petersson, Bo (1973) *Axel Hägerströms värdeteori*. Uppsala: Uppsala universitet.

Rehof, Lars Adam (1991) 'På sporet af pragmatismen i dansk retspleje'. In Peter Blume, Ditlev Tamm & Vibeke Vindeløv (eds) *Suum cuique – retsvidenskablige afhandlinger, Københavns Universitet 1991*. København: Jurist- og Økonomforbundets forlag, 30–49.

Reichenbach, Hans (1951) *The Rise of Scientific Philosophy*. Berkeley: The University of California Press.

Ross, Alf (1945a) 'Hvorfor jeg stemmer paa socialdemokratiet'. *SocialDemokraten*. 25 October 1945.

Ross, Alf (1945b) *Kommunismen og Demokratiet*. København: Fremad.

Ross, Alf (1946) *Hvorfor Demokrati?* København: Munksgaard. (Unless otherwise stated, the references indicate the page numbers in the English translation: Ross, Alf (1952) *Why Democracy?* Cambridge Massachusetts).

Ross, Alf (1947) 'Socialismen och demokratin'. *Tiden*. Vol. 39, Issue 7.

Ross, Alf (1948) 'Kan man være socialist uden at være marxist?' *Verdens Gang*. Vol 2, 255–258

Russell, Bertrand (1947) *Philosophy and Politics*. London: Cambridge University Press

Schumpeter, Joseph A. (1942) *Capitalism, Socialism, and Democracy*. London: Harper & Brothers.

Sigurdson, Ola (2000) *Den lyckliga filosofin – etik och politik hos Hägerström, Tingsten, makarna Myrdal och Hedenius*. Stockholm/Stehag: Brutus Östlings bokförlag Symposion.

Skinner, Quentin (2002) *Visions of Politics, vol. 1: Regarding Method*. Cambridge: Cambridge University Press.

Skirbekk, Gunnar (1984) '"I refleksjonens mangel…" Om vekslande intellektuelle elitar i norsk etterkrigstid'. *Nytt Norsk Tidsskrift*. Vol. 1, Issue 1.

Skovdal, Bernt (1992) *Tingsten, totalitarismen och ideologierna*. Stockholm/Stehag: Brutus Östlings bokförlag Symposion.

Slagstad, Rune (1998) *De nasjonale strateger*. Oslo: Pax, 2001.

Strang, Johan (2006) 'Arvet efter Kaila och Hägerström – den analytiska filosofin i Finland och Sverige'. In Stefan Nygård & Johan Strang (2006) *Mellan idealism och analytisk filosofi – den moderna filosofin i Finland och Sverige*. Helsingfors & Stockholm: Svenska litteratursällskapet & Atlantis.

Strang, Johan (2007) 'Overcoming the rift between "is" and "ought" – Gunnar Myrdal and the philosophy of social engineering'. *Ideas in history*. Vol. 2, Issue 2, 143–177.

Strang, Johan (2009a) 'The Scandinavian Value Nihilists and the crisis of democracy in the 1930s and 40s'. *Nordeuropaforum*, Vol. 19, Issue 1, 37–63.

Strang, Johan (2009b) 'Two Generations of Scandinavian Legal Realists'. *Retfærd*. Vol. 32, Issue 1, 62–82.

Sørensen, Øystein & Stråth, Bo (eds) (1997) *The Cultural Construction of Norden*. Oslo: Scandinavian University Press.

Tingsten, Herbert (1933) *Demokratiens seger och kris (Vår egen tids historia 1880– 1930, vol 1)*. Stockholm: Bonniers.

Tingsten, Herbert (1935) 'Statskunskapen och den politiska utvecklingen'. In Gunnar Myrdal & Herbert Tingsten (1935) *Samhällskrisen och socialvetenskaperna*. Stockholm: Kooperativa förbundets bokförlag.

Tingsten, Herbert (1938) 'Nordisk demokrati'. *Nordens kalender*, 41–50.

Tingsten, Herbert (1939) *De konservativa idéerna*. Stockholm: Bonniers.

Tingsten, Herbert (1940) 'Folkstyret i Norden'. In Petander, Karl (ed.) *Nordisk Gemenskap*. Stockholm: Kooperativa förbundets bokförlag, 50–83.

Tingsten, Herbert (1967) [1941] *Den svenska socialdemokratiens idéutveckling*. Stockholm: Aldus.

Tingsten, Herbert (1941) *Idékritik*. Stockholm: Bonniers.

Tingsten, Herbert (1945) *Demokratiens problem*. Stockholm: Norstedts.

Tingsten, Herbert (1948) *Argument*. Stockholm: Bonniers.

Tingsten, Herbert (1961) *Mitt liv – Ungdomsåren*. Stockholm: Wahlström & Widstrand.

Tingsten, Herbert (1966) *Från idéer till idyll – den lyckliga demokratien*. Stockholm: Norstedts.

Trägårdh, Lars (2002) 'Sweden and the EU – Welfare state nationalism and the spectre of "Europe"'. In Lene Hansen & Ole Wæver (eds) *European integration and national identity – The challenge of the Nordic States*. London: Routledge, 130–181.

Uebel, Thomas (2005) 'Political philosophy of science in logical empiricism: the left Vienna Circle'. *Studies in History and Philosophy of Science*. Vol. 36, No. 4.

Örne, Anders (1940) 'Uppsalafilosofin – reflexioner av en lekman'. *Tiden*. Vol. 32, Issue 3, 167–173.

CARL MARKLUND

Sharing Values and Shaping Values

Sweden, 'Nordic Democracy' and the American Crisis of Democracy

Three elements – consensus, democracy and welfare – have been central aspects of the dominant post-war story about *Norden*. In this story, however, the Nordic countries usually appear as somehow (pre)determined to achieve consensus, democracy and welfare. Alternative routes and critical junctures, as well as mirages and visions at the 'horizon of expectation' are often overshadowed by the familiar but also rather unilinear or even 'essentializing' gaze upon the Nordic countries, from within as well as from without. It is somewhere here, in this complex of self-confidence and self-doubt about the characteristics and qualities of Nordic political culture – on the part of Nordics as well as non-Nordics – that the concept of Nordic democracy emerges and comes into play in the 'philosophical geography' which finds democracy particularly at home in the North.[1]

This chapter will take a closer look at this philosophical geography. It will do so by asking how the notion of Nordic democracy has been expressed in primarily American and to a lesser extent British and Swedish accounts of Sweden from the interwar era onwards.[2] In what ways did this interest in Sweden shift over time due to the changing needs of various

1 For the concept of 'philosophical geography', see Wolff, Larry (2006) 'The Global Perspective of Enlightened Travelers: Philosophic Geography from Siberia to the Pacific Ocean'. *European Review of History*, Vol. 13, No. 3, 437–453.
2 These American outlooks on the Nordic countries must be put in context: Americans had throughout much of the 1800s considered themselves liberated from many of the woes of the Old World, a view reinforced by the continuous flow of emigrants vouching for the superiority of the American way of life. However, as recurring financial crises hit just as hard in the USA as in Europe and as some European states proved more swift and seemingly more efficient in their response to the consequences of the Great Crash in October 1929, many Americans began to look to Great Britain as well as Fascist Italy, Nazi Germany and the Soviet Union for theoretical and practical inspiration. The American interest in the Nordic countries was paralleled by an American interest in any society that seemed to do comparatively better in the economic downturn of the early 1930s. See, for example, Schivelbusch, Wolfgang (2006) *Three New Deals: Reflections on Roosevelt's America, Mussolini's Italy, and Hitler's Germany, 1933–1939.* New York: Metropolitan Books; Rodgers, Daniel T. (1998) *Atlantic Crossings: Social Politics in a Progressive Age.* Cambridge: Harvard University Press.

actors? Does the construction of the American understanding of Nordic democracy challenge or confirm the established narratives of the Nordic countries mentioned above? In asking these questions, the chapter seeks to find the link between the Nordic countries and democracy in the context of the wider 'crisis of democracy' during the interwar years and in particular the American version of this crisis.

The difference between the crisis of democracy in America and in Europe is not an idle one: seen from the perspective of the European crisis of democracy, the prime achievement of the Nordic countries was their general commitment to political democracy. As shown by several of the contributions to this volume, this underlined Nordic self-identification during the Second World War. Seen from the perspective of the American crisis of democracy, however, more specific aspects of democracy, such as 'economic democracy', 'industrial democracy' and 'planning democracy', proved more inspiring, for a variety of reasons.

American references to Nordic democracy seldom implied any particular ideology of democracy on the part of the Nordics. Instead, the Nordic countries seemed to embody a particularly democratic practice of conciliation – a practice of consensus, cooperation, and tolerance, without which democracy would indeed become a mere formality, a dead letter, which some of democracy's most vocal and influential critics in Europe indeed argued it had already become.

In order to trace the origin of this American interest in Nordic democracy in general and the industrial democracy of Sweden in particular, the present chapter first follows some of the earliest associations between the Nordic countries and democracy in Anglo-American academic literature. It attempts to situate the rhetorical function of this association within the context of the American crisis of democracy during the interwar years. The chapter then briefly outlines the differences and similarities between the American crisis of democracy and the European one. It then goes on to compare this American notion of Swedish industrial democracy with some Swedish attempts to add planning democracy and economic democracy – for example, egalitarian social policy and welfare state formation – to the already firmly established image of Swedish industrial democracy in the USA. This image of Sweden as a prime site for both industrial democracy and planning democracy is then followed through the immediate post-war decades as it becomes conceptually associated with corporatism and gradually construed as a largely satisfied 'happy democracy' of 'created harmony'.[3] In American eyes, Sweden had shifted from being an example of a particular brand of 'democracy' into becoming a showcase for a special kind of 'socialism'.

---

3 See, for example, Tingsten, Herbert (1966) *Från idéer till idyll: den lyckliga demokratien.* Stockholm: Norstedt; Myrdal, Gunnar (1961) [1960] *Beyond the Welfare State: Economic Planning in the Welfare States and its International Implications.* New Haven: Yale University Press, 45–60.

In conclusion, it is argued that these recurrent American references to Sweden and democracy – appreciative as well as critical ones – focused less upon political democracy than upon the economic, industrial and planning dimensions of democracy, all of which fulfilled particular roles in the American debate on democracy during the interwar and immediate post-war years.

From 'Northern democracies' to 'Northern democracy'

The earliest explicit conceptual connection between the Nordic countries on the one hand and the democratic form of governance on the other seems to have followed almost immediately upon the introduction of political democracy in all the Nordic countries by the early 1900s. During the interwar years, Denmark, Norway, Sweden and, to a lesser extent, Finland would gradually become known internationally as the 'northern democracies', not least in the USA.[4] This concept, however, merely took note of the fact that the democratic system of governance prevailed in the Nordic countries. It did not suggest that these countries in some way presented any particular 'Nordic' form of democracy.

To some observers, however, due to their coordinated activity within the League of Nations, the small Nordic countries came to exemplify 'the democratic control' of what was elsewhere in the hands of secretive diplomats and jealously guarded by great power interest. By emphasising the theory of the equality of states, the representatives of Denmark, Norway and Sweden were regularly looked upon as spokesmen for the smaller states of the world, as S. Shepard Jones pointed out on the eve of the Second World War.[5]

The connection between smallness and democracy would deepen during the 1920s and 1930s, primarily through the notion of community. Modernity was seen as producing a mass society inhabited by 'mass humans' lacking a sense of community and destiny and hence making collective action in the common interest more unlikely. While mass society was seen as more complex than earlier human societies and hence more difficult to govern with traditional means, including formal political democracy, it also, quite paradoxically, appeared to level human beings into mass humans, supposedly less individualistic and more easily. In this way, whatever the intentions of various critics of modernity and mass society for its lack of

---

4   See, for example, Loewenstein, Karl (1935) 'Autocracy Versus Democracy in Contemporary Europe, I'. *The American Political Science Review*, Vol. 29, No. 4, 571–593.

5   Arneson, Ben A. (1940) 'The Scandinavian States and the League of Nations. by S. Shepard Jones'. *The Journal of Politics*, Vol. 2, No. 1, 96–98; Jones, S. Shepard (1939) *The Scandinavian States and the League of Nations*. Princeton, NJ: Princeton University Press; Gram-Skjoldager, Karen & Tønnesson, Øyvind (2008) 'Unity and Diversity: Scandinavian Internationalism, 1914–1921'. *Contemporary European History*, Vol. 17, 301–324; and Salmon, Patrick (1997) *Scandinavia and the Great Powers, 1890–1940*. Cambridge: Cambridge University Press.

community might have been, their critique also tended to explain not only the increasing possibility of dictatorship, but also its growing necessity.[6]

Furthermore, urbanisation, industrialisation and the concentration of economic power seemed to threaten not only the virtues of democracy, but also the very culture and lifestyle which had made democracy a preferred mode of governance to begin with. Small-scale business, farming and living in villages and townships were increasingly eclipsed by gigantic corporations, farmers becoming indebted to banks, and the young moving to industrial cities. If it was ever going to be possible to re-create some sense of community, it would have to be based upon the realities of a new national mass-scale society and not on any nostalgic longing for some primordial village, now long lost. This sentiment was not necessarily a reaction to economic or political crisis, but rather to change *per se*. In the USA, for example, already during the prosperous 1920s, social scientists voiced concern that the decreasing sense of community in modern American mass culture could adversely affect American democracy and hence threaten 'American civilization'.[7]

While this criticism of mass society and this praise of the bucolic existence of small farming communities certainly had deep roots in the Western intellectual tradition, both gained a more acute edge under the influence of financial instability in the wake of the First World War culminating in the Great Crash in 1929. The alleged inability of democratic regimes to contain and control the effects of unfettered global capitalism – in addition to its many other shortcomings – added a third and even more critical edge to the mounting criticism of democracy; the promise of dictatorship. The critics of democracy argued that this form of government could not efficiently handle situations where choices and prioritizations would have to be made efficiently and quickly – either because of the cumbersome deliberative process of democracy in itself, or because the democratic system had been captured by vested interests looking out for their own needs, rather than the public interest.[8]

Here, there were important differences between the European and the American understandings of the crisis of democracy. In the American debate, the crisis of democracy primarily resulted from the perceived failure of democracy to deliver the goods (at the time identified as economic stability

---

6 Indeed, the complexity, leveling and vastness inherent in mass society in itself seemed to promote the trend towards increased authoritarianism and dictatorship as famously argued on various grounds by public intellectuals across the political spectrum. See, for example, Ortega y Gasset, José (1964) [1929] *The Revolt of the Masses*. New York: Norton; Dewey, John (1991) [1927] *The Public and Its Problems*. Athens, Ohio: Swallow Press; Lippmann, Walter (1997) [1922] *Public Opinion*. New York: Free Press Paperbacks; and Lippmann, Walter (1993) [1925] *The Phantom Public*. New Brunswick, N.J.: Transaction Publishers.

7 While most of these tendencies are identifiable in French and German sociological writings of the late 1800s, many American works of empirical sociology from the interwar years were influenced by this perspective, most notably Lynd, Robert S. & Lynd, Helen Merrell (1929) *Middletown: A Study in American Culture*. London: Constable.

8 Elements of this criticism were also common in the fascist charge against democracy, but were by no means confined to totalitarian groups.

and social security, and often subsumed under the caption of 'general welfare'). This failure of democracy had pragmatic as well as ideological consequences: Pragmatically, in order to survive, democracy needed to be made more rational to resist middle-class alienation, possibly through social planning and the reshaping of cultural values. Ideologically, in order to convince, democracy needed to be made more resilient in facing down totalitarianism, which was capitalising on middle-class alienation, possibly through cultural conditioning and propaganda.

Lacking either a strong labour movement or more radical political parties, except for some populist movements, the American crisis of democracy thus evolved into a rather technical debate on whether democracy could be brought to control the economy effectively, rather than any moral or principled political question of the precedence of democracy over dictatorship. The European crisis of democracy, by contrast, was more closely connected with the articulation of the special interests of a dominant force – be it the working class, the empire, the race, the nation or simply 'power' – in whose name dictatorship would take precedence over democracy.

The decline of democracy elsewhere contrasted with the resilience of democracy in the Nordic countries. Hence, the latter began to attract attention abroad during the course of the 1930s. In a book entitled *The Smaller Democracies* (1939), the British author E. D. Simon emphasized the value of smallness and equality for 'really democratic achievements' at a moment 'when democracy is challenged throughout the world', in the words of one reviewer. To Simon, it was above all Switzerland that showcased how 'the practical experience of administrative work shared by all members of the smaller communes creates a sense of civic responsibility and a fund of ability for administration on a wider scale'.[9]

Not only big societies seemed to veer in the direction of dictatorship, however. Less populous countries also experienced the tensions of modern mass society. They were not immune to the lure of dictatorship, in particular through the temptation to expand the executive power in the face of a crisis. In 1937, for example, Karl Loewenstein, a German legal scholar and part of the Central European intellectual exodus to the USA after the Nazi *Machtubernahme*, noted that:

> Everywhere [in Europe] constitutional government is in transition from parliamentary determination of political issues to the undisputed predominance of the executive, operating, even in the most thoroughly democratic countries, under discretionary powers which, very euphemistically, may be spoken of as "quasi-constitutional." Indicative of this trend – observable in every constitutional state without exception – are the events in the smaller democracies which more and more have become "disciplined," or even "authoritarian".[10]

9   M. B. (1939) 'The Smaller Democracies. by E. D. Simon'. *International Affairs*, Vol. 18, No. 6, 847–848.

10 Loewenstein, Karl (1937) 'Constitutional Government and Politics by Carl Joachim Friedrich'. *The American Political Science Review*, Vol. 31, No. 5, 956.

In particular, Loewenstein found that the 'smaller democracies' of Belgium, Switzerland, and Czechoslovakia, had begun to make use of what he euphemistically termed 'new governmental techniques'. Somewhat earlier, the Swedish political scientist Herbert Tingsten had noted this development in his *Les pleins pouvoirs* (1934).[11] In agreement with Tingsten, Loewenstein argued that:

> All democratic countries are at present in search of a workable formula which will guarantee the responsibility and the control of democratic leaders to and by the masses. It remains to be seen whether the traditional concepts of legality and constitutionality can be reconciled with the realistic necessities of national leadership.[12]

To Loewenstein then, the trend towards extra-ordinary authorisations and the expansion of executive power did not necessarily imply the demise of democracy in Europe. Rather, it could be seen as democracy's last ditch defence against the adverse effects of modernity and capitalism, without which democracy would be exposed to the threat of authoritarianism. In fact, democracy had much to learn from dictatorship about 'direct popular action' – 'this most fascinating and important problem of organized mass democracy where the constitutional state has so much to gain from close observation of the techniques of dictatorial states', Loewenstein contended in 1937.[13] Democracy's main fault, then, in the eyes of this transatlantic legal scholar, was that it largely failed to mobilise the masses in the way that dictatorship did. This is also why he took a particular interest in those European countries where democracy nevertheless seemed to hold on, such as in the Nordic countries. How did they manage to mobilise popular support for democracy in view of its alleged inefficiency?

Neither the prevalence of constitutional and parliamentary democracy, nor the cooperation in the League of Nations or the praise of smallness did by themselves suffice to promote a specific international image of the Nordic countries as representing any particular form of democracy. In his review of the American author Franklin D. Scott's *The United States and Scandinavia* (1950) in *the American Historical Review*, the Norwegian historian and Foreign Minister (1935–1940) Halvdan Koht aligned the primarily geopolitical notion of northern democra*cies* with the primarily socio-economic concept of northern democra*cy*.[14] By this time, the idea

---

11 Tingsten, Herbert (1934) [1930] *Les pleins pouvoirs. L'expansion des pouvoirs gouvernementaux pendant et après la Grande guerre.* Paris, Stock.

12 Loewenstein 1937, 956–957.

13 Loewenstein 1937, 955.

14 Koht, Halvdan (1950) 'Review: The United States and Scandinavia by Franklin D. Scott'. *The American Historical Review*, Vol. 56, No. 1, 73–74. The concept of 'northern democracy' had been in common use in American historical and political debate during the interwar years, but it referred to the anti-slavery ideology of Northern Democrats during the American Civil War – one of the greatest tests of American political democracy – rather than any particular form of democracy on the part of the Nordic states. See, for example, Foner, Eric (1980) *Politics and Ideology in the Age of the Civil War.* New

that the northern democracies – primarily understood as the Scandinavian countries, Denmark, Norway, and Sweden – exhibited a particular form of northern democracy had become firmly established and was readily accepted. The chapter will in the following seek to find what had happened in the meantime to explain this merging of concepts, this cultural-substantive rather than geographical-formal association between democracy and the Nordic countries.

Capital and labour: collective bargaining and industrial democracy

Largely due to the popularity of his 1936 book *Sweden: The Middle Way*, but also to counter the somewhat unrealistic expectations which the readers of his earlier book pinned on Sweden, the American journalist Marquis W. Childs returned to the topic of Sweden in *This is Democracy* (1938).[15]

In this book, Childs noted that the perceived peacefulness of the Nordic countries was largely a much cherished myth abroad. According to the statistics of the International Labour Office (ILO), the Nordic countries in fact had experienced some of the world's highest losses of man-hours due to conflict on the labour market in the preceding decade.[16] Instead, 'these northern democracies' were indeed democratic 'with all the virtues and all the faults inherent in the democratic form'. As such, they not only represented an experiment in a theoretical sense – indeed, all democracies could be understood as continuous experiments, according to Childs – but also in more practical terms as their democratic form of government would only be able to survive if it could cope with the tensions brought about by modernity.[17] They, too, had their fair share of conflict, and this is what made their experience well worth studying abroad.

According to Childs, it was largely the smallness of the national market and its openness to the international market which had prompted Swedish labour and Swedish capital to bargain and cooperate, partly in spite of the many reasons for conflict, but also partly exactly due to these conflicts. But market logic was not enough, as the political collaboration between labour and 'Liberals and Farmers' showed.[18] This political collaboration would have been impossible if it had not been for the conscious strategy of the Labour movement to 'broaden' its base to include not only workers, but farmers and the middle class, too, Childs argued.[19] In Childs's mind, this

York: Oxford University Press; Bender, Thomas (1986) 'Wholes and Parts: The Need for Synthesis in American History'. *The Journal of American History*, Vol. 73, No. 1, 120–136.

15 Childs, Marquis W. (1936) *Sweden: The Middle Way*. New Haven: Yale University Press.
16 Childs, Marquis W. (1938) *This is Democracy: Collective Bargaining in Scandinavia*. New Haven: Yale University Press, xi–xii, 156.
17 Childs 1938, xvi.
18 Childs 1938, xi.
19 Childs identified the trade-union congress of 1936 as particularly important in establishing this new broader policy. Childs 1938, 16.

broader labour movement and its capacity in bridging the gaps between city and country, between the middle class and the working class and between capital and labour was the primary factor in shaping and sharing the values which provided the basis for the Swedish 'experiment' in democracy.

However, there was a rift between the conservative older generation and the younger generation on this issue. This division came to the fore in the labour exposition put on by the social democratic youth organization in Stockholm in the fall of 1937 under the theme 'Organized Labour Has the Word' where the class struggle and the revolutionary traditions of the labour movement figured prominently, symbolised by the Ådalen shootings of 1931 where troops had fired upon demonstrators and killed five people.[20]

In Childs's account, members of the Social Democratic government had to navigate a careful middle-road. This moderation sometimes came under criticism from the Left for not being socialist enough. Childs found Prime Minister Per Albin Hansson particularly 'sensitive to criticism that their policy has been too cautious'. In response to radical socialists and their demands for the socialisation of the nation's industries, Hansson argued that 'the government is building socialism into the fabric of the country's everyday life'.[21] Swedish socialism – rather than Swedish democracy, it should be noted – thus exemplified a particularly far-ranging and radical transformation of public mores, a theme which would become more prevalent in American reporting on Swedish society in the post-war decades.

Despite these challenges from within the labour movement, Hansson was deeply conscious of the need for middle-class support, Childs argued. The majority of the labour movement remained '98.9 per cent loyal to Per Albin' and 'the blue-and-yellow [i.e., Swedish national colours] line he has taken', Childs assured his readers.[22] Trade unionists had come up against the realisation that a limit had been reached in the size of the share of the national income that labour could obtain 'by present tactics and within the limits of the present economy'. If labour's share is to be increased, Childs interpreted them as saying, production must be greatly expanded – a need recognized by both labour and capital.[23] It was largely due to these considerations, Childs argued, that labour in Sweden – as in the other small Nordic countries – had turned to bargaining: first, labour had used collective wage bargaining, and second, labour had bargained 'at the polls for political power'.

In this alliance for growth, trade unionists and capitalists had begun to share the central tenets of how to conduct business and industry. Previously, Childs asserted, trade unions had primarily been striving to obtain the highest possible wage, which at times made them uncertain allies of the political branch of the labour movement. In this new capacity, as partners, both employers and trade unions began to see wages as an element of 'cost' in a business in which they themselves were share-holders, and that this was 'a business that is related directly to their own standard of living'. This

20 Childs 1938, 18–19.
21 Childs 1938, 70.
22 Childs 1938, 18.
23 Childs 1938, 159–160.

'complex relationship' had direct links to the increasing peace and unabated 'progress in the northern democracies', Childs thought.[24] Fundamentally, the new attitude among the trade unions and the labour movement more widely amounted to what Childs described as 'industrial democracy', albeit on an experimental level:

> Realizing the limitations inherent in old forms – in the narrow, craft concept – they are struggling to find new forms adapted to an industrial civilization. It is not easy. There is the dead weight of inertia, of prejudice, of ancient self-interest. But if this experiment in industrial democracy is not upset by the disaster of war, it may well bring achievements that will have significance for democracy everywhere.[25]

Industrial democracy was a long-standing concept in the Anglo-American debate on modernity, industrial relations and socialism. The concept had first been used more widely by the noted British Fabian socialists Sidney Webb and Beatrice Webb to connote a more peaceful cooperation between the two sides of the productive process, labour and capital.[26] The concept referred to a kind of economic democracy in the workplace either to complement or, in more radical versions, to replace political democracy in modern society. Industrial democracy would secure industrial peace and hence promote the productivity and profitability of private enterprise. The bigger the profits, the more evenly they could be shared between capital and labour. Hence, industrial democracy could improve the standing of the working class as well as establish a more democratic culture and economy which would – the argument went – control capitalism, humanise modernity, balance liberalism and possibly stabilise the international order, thereby preventing further imperialist wars such as the First World War. Through industrial democracy, political democracy could be liberated from the stifling influence of vested interests and turned into a truer democracy.

In a fundamental sense, industrial democracy presupposed an alliance between labour and capital which could be negotiated in each individual firm. There were indeed many attempts at brokering such agreements not only in Great Britain but in the USA as well. What seemed to the American observer unique and exemplary in Sweden was the nation-wide character of these agreements as well as the fact that they were increasingly based on a coalition between middle-class and working-class interests, i.e., reaching beyond the confines of the individual firm. Quite naturally, then, the greatest risks posed to this kind of industrial democracy could be found in whichever power that seeks to break the emerging confidence and cooperation between labour and capital. Any successful attempt at destabilising the fragile *entente* between middle class and labour class interests would also effectively destabilize industrial democracy. The strategy of the broader labour

24 Childs 1938, 138.
25 Childs 1938, 160.
26 See, for example, Webb, Sidney (1891) 'The Difficulties of Individualism'. *The Economic Journal*, Vol. 1, No. 2, 360–381.

movement was hence largely to be seen as an 'effort of labor politicians to adjust to the threat of world Fascism'.[27]

In the Nordic countries, the threat of fascism[28] united external security with internal security in complex and very tangible ways after 1933, primarily due to the economic dependence and geographical proximity of Germany. As for the external threat of fascism, the Nordic countries began in the late 1930s to regard 'collective security' as offered by the League of Nations as illusory. The combination of aggressive totalitarians and the inefficiency of the League of Nations thus fostered a closer cooperation between the Nordic countries with regard to security as well as a more explicit identification between neutrality and Nordicity on their part. While an outright attack on any of the Nordic countries did not appear to be a very credible threat at the end of the 1930s, the Austrian *Anschluss* of 1938 provided a chilling example of how a more confident Germany could assert itself vis-a-vis neighbouring countries.

Also the internal threat of fascism had to be taken seriously, as the Austrian case illustrated.[29] Certain industrial interests, Childs noted, 'look with a kind of envy on the freedom from labour trouble enjoyed by businessmen in Germany', but their numbers appeared small.[30] In the minds of Swedish (and Norwegian) Social Democrats, Childs held, the inability of the labour movement in Germany and Austria in stemming the fascist advance had resulted from 'the failure of the Left to realize what were the realities outside the closed sphere of Socialist and Marxist dogma'.[31] Labour's first task must therefore be:

> to win over the middle class. The middle class must be convinced that its advantage lies with labor. This was the mistake that German and Austrian Socialists made. They thought in terms of the proletariat, narrowly defined, a trade-union monopoly, ignoring middle-class low income groups, white-collar workers, and farmers, who had far less than the official proletariat. It is not enough merely to fight for higher trade-union wages.[32]

Again, Childs emphasized how Scandinavian labour leaders realized that the totalizing and nationalist attitude of the fascists had to be copied in order to be countered and the importance of considering 'the whole economy and our place in that economy', and not merely class interests.[33] Among other

---

27 Childs 1938, xvi.
28 In the following, 'Fascism' connotes Italian Fascism, while 'fascism' indicates fascism in general, thus including American, German, Eastern European and Scandinavian versions of right-wing extremism.
29 Preceding Childs by four years, Walter Sandelius issued the same warning. See Sandelius, Walter (1934) 'Dictatorship and Irresponsible Parliamentarism – A Study in the Government of Sweden'. *Political Science Quarterly*, Vol. 49, No. 3, 347–371.
30 Childs 1938, 74.
31 Childs 1938, 76.
32 Childs 1938, 77.
33 Childs 1938, 77.

things, this strategy necessitated a de-dramatization of the class struggle motif in the political profile and rhetoric of the labour movement.[34]

City and country: sharing values and shaping values

The challenge for this new broader labour movement not only lay in the need to bridge the gap between capital and labour and between the middle class and the working class. It also had to span the rift between the rapidly modernising city and the traditional countryside with its mostly conservative and often religious farmers. This opposition between farmer and worker and between city and country was not merely a Nordic concern. Societies all over the world sought to cope with the radical shift in production from small-scale subsistence farming to large mechanised and capital-intensive forms of agriculture for the export market. The ensuing conflict between city and country was of no little importance, in the eyes of contemporaries. Childs himself went so far as to conclude that 'here, it would seem, is one of the profound maladies from which the present-day world is suffering. And somehow a cure must be found if representative government is to survive'.[35]

This is where the 'northern democracies' could provide an opportunity to look at this problem without too many complicating factors, 'with a kind of laboratory detachment', as Childs put it: 'Partly this is because they are small countries with a homogeneous population.' But even more importantly, this sense of mission came from an emotional and moral conviction: Scandinavians simply felt deeply 'the seriousness of the problem and the urgent need for a solution', and this feeling was apparently widely shared across public opinion.[36] In Scandinavia, homogeneity and small size promoted a sense of shared values and nowhere – according to Childs – was this sense of shared convictions greater than in the opinion that the 'future of Western civilization may turn on the possibility of resolving the deep opposition between the townsman and the countryman'.[37]

At the heart of this opposition we find a rather mundane factor: in the same way as workers in advanced capitalist economies across the world typically sought higher wages and employers sought lower wages, they also strove for lower prices for food while farmers aimed for higher prices. The Swedish labour movement – like most of its international counterparts

---

34 Childs pointed for example to the connections between Swedish and Norwegian labour leaders who had spent time in the USA as members of the ultra-radical Industrial Workers of the World (I.W.W.) (e.g., Edvard Mattson and Martin Tranmael), who have become 'somewhat tempered' on their return to Scandinavia. Childs 1938, 10–11, 81.

35 Childs, for example, points to the importance for world history of the split between workers and farmers, between city and country in Germany (where small landowners supported the Nazis) and in Russia (where the *kulaks* came close to bringing the Bolsheviks' regime down). See Childs 1938, 85.

36 Childs 1938, 85.

37 Childs 1938, 85.

– had traditionally been firmly committed to free trade, while Swedish conservatives could long rely on the support of farmers by following a more protectionist trade policy, at least with regard to farming products.

The farmer-worker alliance brought in by the so-called Cow Trade in May 1933, also known as the Crisis Agreement, rested upon a compromise between these opposite interests, ensuring some state aid to agriculture in exchange for some free trade. The effect was to shore up farm purchasing power, but it also disadvantaged low income groups, especially families with children, not only among city-dwelling workers but among the rural poor as well. This tactical victory ensured that the Social Democrats remained in power. At the same time it presented the party with a strategic challenge, as this alliance maintained the disadvantage of poor labourers both in the city and in the country. How to change the situation without imperilling the newly won alliance with the farmers, or, in the words of Childs: 'How to alter political values without alienating farm support?'[38]

In Childs's account of Sweden, then, it seems as if there may have been shared values concerning the goal of bridging the gap between city and country, but there was no corresponding consensus on the means by which to bring this bridging about. The famer-labour alliance identified the poverty of the living conditions of the urban poor with the poverty of the rural poor, making it possible to shape new values where none had been shared previously. Together with the widespread concern that the Swedish population had begun to decline – a concern which Childs does not seem to have treated at any length – the shared plight of the rural and urban poor motivated the appointment by the government of the Population Commission, authorised to look into every aspect of the Swedish standard of living.[39]

The picture presented was not flattering to 'the ego of the average Swede, proud of the progressiveness of his country'. Coded in the cool rational language of medical and economic terms concerning public health, contagion and worker productivity, the reports also sparked a more emotional debate about 'minimum standards of decency' and 'shockingly low [living] standards'.[40] As a consequence, the national standard of living became a sharp political issue, based on common conceptions of what 'decency' and 'standards' really meant. The political strategy was to use shock tactics and 'startle the Swedes out of their complacency'. As the report presented by the commission and signed by 'national leaders' argued, problems such as malnutrition, overcrowding and low wages, 'surely could not be reduced to terms of mere partisanship'. Instead, the Commission identified the 'basic' problem for which, strictly speaking, there could be nothing other than 'technical' solutions, thereby bypassing a number of stifling cultural, political and social stumbling blocks, or, in Childs's interpretation:

38 Childs 1938, 91–92.
39 Childs 1938, 92.
40 Childs 1938, 94.

If the people are hungry, then feed them. Could there possibly be any political argument about that? The Socialists proposed to give free lunches to all public school children in Sweden. Not just to children in need of such feeding, for that would serve to put an undemocratic stigma on hunger, but to all children.[41]

The Commission's work, here interpreted by Childs for an Anglo-American audience, thus represented a novel connection between economy and democracy, between equality and representation, which would provide a platform for the universalist approach in social policy, later to be made one of the distinguishing trademarks of Nordic welfare-state regimes.[42] To some extent, then, the real value of the Commission was to be found in the way in which it 'objectively' identified social needs and social problems, showed the similarity of the plight of the poor in both city and country. At the same time, it pointed to shared values of decency and living standards among the well-to-do.

While the American as well as European crisis of democracy let loose a flood of various proposals on how to stem the current financial downturn and how to make liberal democracy more able to handle its consequences, the American critic Roy V. Peel was surprised at what he perceived to be a lack of radical proposals in favour of democracy in Sweden:

Where is the vast body of Swedish liberal literature corresponding to our own output during this time? There is not any. This is true, because, for one thing, nearly all Swedes are moderate, and there is therefore no need for polemical writing.[43]

Swedish supporters of democracy did not have to argue in favour of improving democracy, Peel found, as the majority of the political establishment continued to perceive it as a functional and successful form of government, despite its crisis elsewhere. The Swedish system of Royal Committees played an important role here, Peel thought, arguing that few legislative novelties are ever introduced without a previous survey of the subject by experts, drawn from all parties and representing 'all shades of opinion'.[44]

41 Childs 1938, 96.
42 Esping-Andersen, Gøsta (1990) *The Three Worlds of Welfare Capitalism*. Cambridge and Princeton: Polity Press and Princeton University Press.
43 Peel, Roy V. (1937) 'Samhallskrisen och Socialvetenskaperna by Gunnar Myrdal; Herbert Tingsten Unghoger: Politiska Essayer by Gunnar Heckscher Pontus Fahlbeck och Samhallet by Erik Arrhen'. *The American Political Science Review*, Vol. 31, No. 2, 333.
44 For example, after the contentious issue of socialisation had first been raised by the first Social Democratic government in the 1920s, it was subsequently put under scrutiny by several committees, headed by among others Richard Sandler and Torsten Nothin. The resulting reports served to shelve this political hot potato for some considerable time (it would only return in 1944 under the stewardship of Ernst Wigforss). Walter Sandelius, in 1934, called to attention that the thoroughly organized system of committees in the *Riksdag* almost worked as a second government – warranting Nils Herlitz' characterization of Sweden as an example of 'committee parliamentarism'. See Sandelius 1934, 347–371. See also Skocpol, Theda & Weir, Margaret (1985) 'State Structures and the Possibilities

As an example of this, Peel mentioned the opinions of two Swedish Social Democrats (Gunnar Myrdal and Herbert Tingsten), one representative of the Young Conservatives (Gunnar Heckscher) and one 'regular' conservative (Erik Arrhen), commenting that 'to the uninitiated, it is amazing how often the views of all these men coincide':

> Myrdal and Tingsten differ from their friends on the right, not in the measure of their devotion to democratic forms of government, but in their choice of problems to be attacked immediately. They, i.e., Myrdal and Tingsten, believe in turning all the intellectual forces in the realm to the promotion of stability and order on a higher level. They want the condition of the poor improved, they want the traditionally Swedish democratic instruments of government safe-guarded and strengthened – because they have faith in the common man – and they expect to win universal adherence to their program because they believe that it is the only intelligent way to proceed.[45]

To this American observer, the commitment of Swedish academics and experts – so influential through the system of Royal Committees – to democracy was unfailing. This becomes particularly obvious in Peel's discussion of the Swedish conservatives, who had been accused of flirting with fascist ideology. To Peel, by contrast, the programme of the conservatives was strongly liberal and their objective was 'a class-differentiated but cooperating state'. It was decidedly not fascist, according to Peel, as 'race-hate, intolerance, regimentation, etc.' had been convincingly discredited in the eyes of Swedish conservatives by the German and Italian examples.[46] In contrast to fascists, Swedish conservatives of different backgrounds accepted proportional representation, equality before the law, a measure of government intervention and 'even ultimate public planning and ownership, fundamentally because it feels that these principles are suitable for the Swedish nation with its special conditions of resource, tradition, and background'.[47] The specific Nordic penchant for democracy is underlined once more.

The difference between Left and Right in Sweden did not lie in opinions about 'the democratic form of government, academic freedom, and freedom of discussion', as 'both sides vie with each other in maintaining them', Peel noted. Rather the cleavage was to be found in presuppositions regarding the 'world' or 'life', Peel asserted.

> As Myrdal insists, conservatives, and even liberals, are bound by their hypotheses regarding the relation between classes, the limits to the

for "Keynesian" Responses to the Great Depression in Sweden, Britain and the United States.' In Dietrich Rueschemeyer, Peter B. Evans & Theda Skocpol (eds) *Bringing the State Back In*. Cambridge: Cambridge University Press.
45 Peel 1937, 333.
46 Peel 1937, 333.
47 Peel 1937, 334.

authority of the state, and the indestructibility and immutability of certain institutions, whereas the objective political scientists merely describe what exists, then recommend experimentation as a guide to further action. This is, in Sweden, the socialist view.[48]

In this sense, Peel's summary of the position of Myrdal and Tingsten largely resemble the classic understanding of Scandinavian legal realism and first generation 'Hägerströmian' value nihilism.[49] Legal realists and value nihilists typically regarded legal and moral concepts of justice, liberty or rights – in civil law and criminal law as well as in constitutional law – as devoid of any inherent value or universal meaning by themselves. These conceptions were merely the constructions and expressions of power and its drive to promote desired behaviour, mainly understood as peace and security. Within the ontological framework of Scandinavian legal realism, democracy could not represent any inherent value in itself. Its only meaning was as an expression of the power which either wished to maintain it or to do away with it.[50] As long as democracy was conceptually and rhetorically construed as a given in this Nordic society, it needed no further defence in the ontological universe of legal realists and value nihilists.

The idea that Sweden – as well as the other Nordic countries – somehow exhibited a particular affinity for democracy was therefore of paramount importance for the political culture within which legal realism, value nihilism and the welfare state began to form during the 1930s. While American as well as Swedish observers seem to have taken this assumption largely for granted, it is worth looking at some of the few attempts to explain where this expressive preference for a democratic world-view originally came from.

Noting that Sweden was not only very small and homogeneous, which fostered a sense of intimacy, but was also one of the most organised societies in the world, Childs argued that Swedish citizens had several organisations through which they could channel their energies and express their opinions and interests.[51] To Childs, this presented Swedish society with an almost unique opportunity to rejuvenate the notion of democracy and counter the challenges of modern mass society. Pointing to the paradox between liberty and discipline in modern life, Childs argued that:

---

48 Peel 1937, 334.
49 For the notion of generations among Swedish value nihilists, see Strang, Johan (2009) 'Two Generations of Scandinavian Legal Realists'. *Retfaerd*, No. 1, 62–82. See also Strang's chapter in this volume.
50 For discussions on the (dis)similarities between American legal realism and its Scandinavian counterpart, see, for example, Martin, Michael (1997) *Legal Realism: American and Scandinavian*. New York: P. Lang; Kinander, Morten (2002) *The View from Within: An Analysis and Critique of Legal Realism and Descriptive Jurisprudence*. Bergen: Univ.; Bjarup, Jes (2005) 'The Philosophy of Scandinavian Legal Realism'. *Ratio Juris*, Vol. 18, No. 1, 1–15; Lyles, Max (2006) *A Call for Scientific Purity: Axel Hägerström's Critique of Legal Science*. Stockholm: Institutet för rättshistorisk forskning.
51 'As a consumer he belongs to a cooperative which keeps his household budget in line; as a worker he belongs to a trade union or a professional organization which helps to safeguard his income; as a liberal or a socialist or a conservative he is a member of a political party and participates to some degree in public life.' Childs 1938, 34.

Despite the extent to which existence is organized, or even, perhaps, because of it, one has a strong sense of the independence of the individual. Whether individual liberties are jeopardized by the power of organized business, organized labor, or organized consumers is a matter of deep and constant concern. No other people in the world today seem so aware of the need not only to protect the ancient rights of man but to re-examine them realistically in the light of modern practice.[52]

In particular, organized labour played the most crucial role in making anonymous mass society with all its dangers of mindless consumerism or the creation of a totalitarian cult of the leader into a truly democratic life form:

> It is a long way from the little man at the bottom to these men at the top [e.g., labor leaders] who are charged with so great a responsibility, leading nearly a million and a half workers in a period of grave uncertainty. But the little man has a voice and a vote and he may go as far as his energy and capacity will take him in the movement that is his own. This is a democracy, labor's own democracy, directed by men from the ranks.[53]

But unlike the impressed observers from abroad or the scientifically detached expert members of Swedish committees, whether inspired by value nihilism or not, 'labor's own democracy' could not afford take this supposed democratic proclivity for granted either in Swedish society as a whole, or among its own rank and file. Childs was particularly impressed by the intensive attention towards education, study and self-fulfilment which made up an integral part of the Swedish labour movement at the time.

Yet, the dual commitment to objectivity on the one hand and to democracy on the other could sometimes have interesting consequences for the foreign observer: For example, the head of the *Arbetarrörelsens Bildningsförbund* (ABF, 'Workers' Education Association') in Kiruna, J. E. Westberg, a locomotive engineer in the mines and, according to Childs, 'the highest type of trade-union leader', stressed the effort made to ensure objectivity in the instruction given. When Childs asked 'What of Nazism; will the Swedish trade unions go down before some such movement as they did in Germany?', Westberg is said to have replied 'in slow, careful English', that 'we hope that our people will be so well educated that they will never accept the word of one man'.[54]

At the same time, the labour movement, just like any other organisation, had to develop its own methods for maintaining control and discipline within its own ranks. Democracy, after all, can only be exercised under responsibility. The moral and values of the emerging young new elite of the Swedish labour movement influenced the American understanding of

52 Childs 1938, 34.
53 Childs 1938, 24.
54 Childs 1938, 135.

Swedish policy-making and its particular approach towards the problem of how to make democracy work in an increasingly complex and tension-ridden world.

At Brunnsvik People's College, closely associated with both the ABF and the main trade union, Sigfrid Hansson, the brother of the Prime Minister, experimented with a relaxed attitude towards control: 'There is little or no external discipline. Rather, a kind of self-discipline is the ideal. This is expressed in a single rule of conduct: *Allting är tillåtet som inte är dumt eller fult*'.[55] 'Translated freely', Childs added, slightly erroneously, 'this is: You are allowed to do anything you want to do except those things that might be considered stupid or silly.'[56] This statement reflected the fact that the unions sent 'their best men and women' to Brunnsvik, and the honour of not only the individual but also the honour of the union demanded that these young men and women shared a common knowledge of what was *dumt eller fult*.[57]

Planning and corporatism: political democracy and economic democracy

In Sweden, as well as in Norway and Denmark, labour governments had been in power since the early and mid-1930s. In Childs' opinion, all the reforms – 'old-age pensions, workmen's compensation insurance, mass housing, state medicine, unemployment relief and public works' – undertaken by the Social Democrat government of Sweden marked less an effort by a socialist party to socialise the country, than the effort of 'democracy to adjust to the modern world'.[58] If there is any particular recommendation in terms of political democracy to be taken from the Swedish experience, it would be the 'careful parliamentary course' followed by the labour government mainly made up by the Social Democrats:

> Subject to varied and conflicting pressures both from within the country and without, they must reconcile these forces and steer a careful parliamentary course. When to yield, when to stand firm, how much to surrender, what is worth a last ditch fight, these are questions that daily perplex labor ministers of the Scandinavian states. In a world increasingly given over to absolutism they seek to govern by reason, the democratic method, realizing all the time that a political democracy cannot continue to exist unless it is possible to achieve a larger measure of economic democracy.[59]

55 Childs 1938, 106.
56 The Swedish word *fult* would normally translate into English as 'ugly' rather than 'silly'.
57 Childs 1938, 106.
58 Childs 1938, 65.
59 Childs 1938, 58.

The concept of 'economic democracy' could be used in this way to connect the programme of social reforms of the Swedish Social Democrats with political democracy, which was under threat across the globe. Social reforms towards greater economic and social equality eased the tension between capital and labour, improved the capacity of democratic government to deliver the goods, and at the same time reduced the potential support for totalitarian movements.

Tellingly, American interest in Sweden shifted during the late 1930s away from the concern with Swedish forms of industrial democracy, which preoccupied Childs, to the more concrete issues of social problems and their solution: housing policy, unemployment insurance, child care, crime prevention, population policy and family planning. In the spring of 1938, for example, *The Annals of the American Academy of Political and Social Science* dedicated a special issue to the question of 'Social Problems and Policies in Sweden' which included articles from about twenty prominent Swedish social reformers and politicians, including Bertil Ohlin, Axel Höjer, Gunnar Myrdal, Alva Myrdal and Gustav Möller, among others.[60] Here, issues of democracy played a minor role, the focus being on social problems and their practical treatment.

However, when Gunnar Myrdal was invited to hold the prestigious Godkin Lectures at Harvard University the same year, he chose *Population: A Problem for Democracy* as the theme of his talks, emphasizing the close connection between population policies, social policies and the survival of democracy.[61] Later, Alva Myrdal developed this link further in her 1941 book *Nation and Family: The Swedish Experiment in Democratic Family and Population Policy*, where she described Nordic social policies and social planning – or 'constructive social engineering' as she called it – as an effective antidote to fascist tendencies.[62] By guaranteeing a higher and more equal living standard as well as a minimum of security and public services, social policy could prevent aspiring totalitarians from finding support among impoverished workers and insecure middle classes. As such,

---

60 See *The Annals of the American Academy of Political and Social Science*, Vol. 197, No. 1 (May, 1938).

61 Myrdal, Gunnar (1940) *Population: A Problem for Democracy.* Cambridge, Mass: Harvard University Press.

62 This linking of social policy with democracy was not unique to the Myrdals. A marked increase of books and reports on Sweden could be noted in the late 1930s, further establishing the notion that Sweden had become a frontrunner of modernity. Sweden also had ample opportunity to shape the American image of the country through the Delaware Tercentenary, 1638–1938, which, among other things, commemorated the 300 years which had passed since the founding of the short-lived Swedish colony New Sweden on the banks of the Delaware River as well as the 1939–1940 World Fair in New York. See Henriksson, Fritz (1939) *Sweden's participation in the U.S. celebration of the New Sweden tercentenary.* Stockholm: Bonniers; Musiał, Kazimierz (2002) *Roots of the Scandinavian Model. Images of Progress in the Era of Modernisation.* Baden Baden: Nomos Verlagsgesellschaft.

Alva Myrdal suggested, it could even supply another reason for Germany to attack the Nordic countries, besides geopolitics and military strategy.[63]

In some sense, Alva Myrdal was prescient in this opinion, as the Second World War would eventually cause a marked shift in the American association between Sweden and democracy: On the one hand, Sweden was the only Nordic country to escape the war.[64] Hence, it remained a symbolic beacon of what had become known as the northern democracies in the preceding decade. On the other hand, the way in which Sweden managed to avoid war did promote a growing suspicion that Sweden's dealings with the other northern democracies were neither shaped by neutrality, nor by solidarity, but rather by *Realpolitik*. By inference, questions about Swedish neutrality affected the perception of Swedish democracy, as the Allied press and propaganda strove to depict the world war in terms of a conflict between democracy on the one hand and dictatorship on the other.[65]

To be sure, critical voices had been heard within Sweden and were sometimes reported abroad. For example, in a study commissioned by Britain's New Fabian Research Bureau and published in 1939 under the title *Democratic Sweden*, Gösta Bagge, Conservative Party leader and professor at the Social Institute in Stockholm, claimed that the alliance between labour and capital and between farmers and workers – which foreign observers hailed as the foundation of Swedish democracy – in practice made the 'present Government almost irremovable' due to the control of the 'Popular Front' of farmers and workers of the *Riksdag*. Seen is this way, Sweden emerged as 'a totalitarian state, as only the Government parties ruled the country; the principal difference between Sweden and Germany was that in Sweden criticisms of the Government could be made openly'.[66] Bagge's arguably exaggerated characterization can be linked to the need of the Swedish Conservatives in the late 1930s to disassociate themselves from fascism by accusing others of it, as many of the conservative youth had joined various fascist movements earlier in the 1930s.[67]

In any case, it is striking that it was primarily conservative thinkers who took an interest in the relationship between contemporary Swedish political culture and that of the emerging totalitarian states in Europe. In

---

63 Myrdal, Alva (1941) *Nation and Family: The Swedish Experiment in Democratic Family and Population Policy*. New York: Harper & Row.

64 The possible exception is Iceland, depending on how British and American 'occupation' is defined.

65 This message was of course complicated by the British, French and US alliance with the Soviet Union.

66 Cole, Margaret & Smith, Charles (eds) (1938) *Democratic Sweden: A Volume of Studies Prepared by Members of the New Fabian Research Bureau*. London: Routledge, 3, 44–45.

67 The Comintern accusation that social democracy was 'social fascism' does not seem to have spurred a similar attempt to disassociate Swedish Social Democracy from Italian Fascism as the accusation primarily dealt with the conflict between Communists and Social Democrats within the labour movement. Yet, Italian appreciation of Sweden and the Social Democratic government in the mid-1930s did prove increasingly embarrassing as the decade came to a close. See Carlomagno, Marcos Cantera (1995) *Ett folk av mänsklig granit: Sverige i den italienska utrikespolitiken 1932–1936*. Lund: Historiska Media.

a 1939 article in the American journal *Public Opinion Quarterly*, Gunnar Heckscher, at the time a political scientist at Uppsala University, described the Swedish system of organized group interests – the basis of Swedish democracy as praised by Childs and the British Fabians – as an attempt to 'create equality of bargaining power':

> There is a certain resemblance between this system – the practice of which is by no means limited to Sweden – and the corporatism of Italy, and to some extent Germany. In both cases, individualism and *laissez-faire* have been abandoned as guiding political principles.[68]

Furthermore, the relationship between individuals – 'the people' – and the government is indirect and mediated by organized interest groups. But there is a vast difference, Heckscher noted, which prevented him from repeating Bagge's ostentatious claim:

> In Italy, these organizations were created by the state, after the spontaneous group organizations had been crushed; and the new groups only have a very limited amount of self-government. In Sweden, on the other hand, the state has taken advantage of spontaneous associations, built on a democratic basis, and is enlisting their independent cooperation.[69]

Both may be called 'corporatism' and/or 'corporativism'.[70] But in Sweden it was not a result of dictatorial, hardly even legislative, action. And while these 'genuine, spontaneously organized groups' were characterized by their independence of governmental authorities, 'even if they were subject to normal police regulations, and even, as in Sweden, sometimes made to act in the interests of the government', the 'State-created corporations' in Italy and Germany were 'not permitted any real autonomy at all'.[71] Hence spontaneity was the fundamental difference between Italian Fascism and Swedish organised society, and Sweden was to be understood as characterised by an essentially 'free corporativism'.[72]

Two years later, Heckscher returned to the topic in an article together with the American scholar James J. Robbins. Now, however – as the world war was raging – Heckscher characterised the Swedish solution to the conflict between labour and capital as fundamentally liberal and decidedly democratic, and hence clearly distinct from either the German or Italian experience.

---

68 Heckscher, Gunnar (1939) 'Group Organization in Sweden'. *The Public Opinion Quarterly*, Vol. 3, No. 1, 130–135.
69 Heckscher 1939, 130–135.
70 Heckscher's usage of this concept seems to have been somewhat indecisive on this point, using both forms interchangeably, as did many of his contemporaries.
71 Robbins, James J. & Heckscher, Gunnar (1941) 'The Constitutional Theory of Autonomous Groups'. *The Journal of Politics*, Vol. 3, No. 1, 22.
72 Heckscher 1939, 130–135.

...it is well known that the uncontrolled, and apparently uncontrollable, battles between organized labor and organized capital had something to do with the emergence of Fascism in Italy as well as the financing of Nazism in Germany. The experiences of countries like Great Britain and Sweden have been of another kind. There, the representatives of capital and labor have not proved unwilling to assist the State in controlling their disputes, and the organizations of farmers have been made use of as agencies of the State in controlling the output of foodstuffs in circumstances of national danger.[73]

In fact, the Swedish experience showed to Robbins and Heckscher that constitutional, 'liberal' and hence democratic regimes were not 'as incompetent to meet the new situation presented by organised groups, as the totalitarians have argued'.[74] This observation motivated the Swede and the American to ask:

Does "corporativism" offer a way out by providing a middle course between totalitarianism and rank individualism? The totalitarian dictatorships themselves make a great show of corporativism, particularly in the constitutional field, where functional representation of some kind is often used as a substitute for what is known elsewhere as representation of the people. Does such a solution avoid the absolutist qualities of the totalitarian approach, and provide a solution to the problem of organized groups?[75]

Heckscher and Robbins concluded that a new sort of free corporativism was in the making within 'our own society' – that is, in both the USA and in Sweden:

a corporativism in which autonomous groups, grown to maturity from below, and not thrown together by some dictatorial architect overnight, share with the government of the State, openly and constitutionally, the function of promoting the interests of the community in all their variegated aspects. Perhaps such a functional government will survive long after the new Paganisms [T. S. Eliot's terms for Fascism and Nazism] have passed from the scene.[76]

Prescient as this may sound – predating Gunnar Adler-Karlsson's discussions on 'functional socialism' in the 1960s and Bo Rothstein's analysis of Swedish 'neo-corporatism' in the 1980s[77] – Heckscher's wartime analysis of Sweden

---

73 Robbins & Heckscher 1941, 16.
74 Robbins & Heckscher 1941, 16.
75 Robbins & Heckscher 1941, 22.
76 Robbins & Heckscher 1941, 26.
77 Adler-Karlsson, Gunnar (1967) *Funktionssocialism: ett alternativ till kommunism och kapitalism*. Uppsala: Fören. Verdandi; Rothstein, Bo (1988) *Social Classes and Political Institutions: The Roots of Swedish Corporatism*. Uppsala: Maktutredningen.

in terms of free corporativism also signalled a shift in the understanding of Swedish democracy: Turning away from industrial democracy – which could be negatively associated with corporatism and with the anti-democratic practices of, above all, Italian Fascism – to an emphasis of technical prowess, social progressiveness and social reforms as well as neutrality, Sweden was increasingly associated with economic democracy, planning democracy and social democracy.[78] It is in this context that we should read the varied efforts to maintain or repair the link between Swedish nationhood and the concept of democracy which took place during and just after the Second World War, with an Anglo-American world market in mind.

Conclusion

In the international appreciation of the Nordic countries during the interwar era, it was primarily the alleged capacity of the Nordic countries to transcend the disruptive tensions of modernity which elsewhere brought forth a crisis of democracy which provided the most central theme. American interest in the Swedish experience of democracy primarily pivoted around the way in which this Nordic country seemed to have bridged the various opposites of 'industrial civilization'. The most notable such oppositions concerned conflicts between old and new, tradition and modernity, large and small, city and country and – most centrally – capital and labour.

The fact that these tensions appeared to put a fatal strain on democracy elsewhere made the survival of political democracy in the Nordic countries throughout the 1930s (and in the case of Sweden throughout the Second World War) valuable in its own right. But political democracy survived the onslaught of crisis and war elsewhere, too. The casual, yet cautious way in which these tensions seemed to be accepted instead of fought against or denied in the Nordic countries made the Nordics special from the American horizon. The moderate and sober manner in which this bridging between old and new took place was frequently taken as evidence of the profoundly democratic nature of these societies. In this context, the democracy of the Nordic countries implied a sensitivity to differing opinions as well as a willingness to accommodate the ends of modernity with the means of tradition, and *vice versa*.[79]

---

78 Heckscher returned once more in a 1948 attempt at characterising the Swedish system of organised interest groups through the notion of 'pluralist democracy'. See Heckscher, Gunnar (1948) 'Pluralist Democracy: The Swedish Experience'. *Social Research*, Vol. 15, 417–461.

79 It is interesting that the predominantly critical historiography on the Swedish *folkhem* which has dominated Swedish history-writing on this epoch from the late 1980s and early 1990s onwards pinpoints the unwillingness of the radical 'reform coalitions' to take tradition and the old into account and to remake society totally anew. While this type of radicalism is indeed represented in the writings of many Swedish reformers of the time, the practical reforms within housing, child care, *etcetera* are frequently combinations of new and old.

The opposition between modernity and tradition also contained a critical tension between small and large as modernity was strongly associated with mega-cities, mass society and mass production. In short, the triumph of large-scale social organization over smaller forms of social life such as the family, the farm, the village and the parish embodied the victory of the power of modernity over the power of tradition. American discourses on modernity and American civilization had long hailed the virtues of large-scale organization. Yet, the rapid social change and increasingly frequent economic crises of the late 1800s and early 1900s also led American observers to look upon community and tradition as a necessity for democracy. As a consequence, many American debaters in the early 1900s were seriously concerned with the issue of how to defend Smalltown America against Big Industry and/or Big Government as well as how to combine the benefits of large-scale modernity with the values of small-scale tradition.

Here, small-scale Scandinavian societies could be used to showcase that smallness and tradition need not stand in opposition to large-scale modernisation.[80] The Swedish example showed how prosperity, peace and democracy are interdependent upon each other. The broader policy pursued by the labour movement, including farmers as well as workers, the middle class as well as the working class, employers as well as employees answered the need not only to overcome conflict in modernity, but also to underline the fundamental interdependence between various social interests and groups in modern society. As a consequence, the true test of democracy, its benefits as well as its drawbacks, did not primarily lie in the formal doctrine of political democracy – of participation and representativity, which totalitarians may anyway bypass and then abuse for their own purposes – but in the actual practices of deliberation and in the culture of mutual respect of opposed interests which eventually results from this practice.

What kind of democracy was then conceptualised as being Nordic? Which different dimensions of democracy were over the course of time associated with Sweden? For one thing, the association shifted from the initial geopolitical notion in the early 1930s of the northern democracies to the observation that these northern democracies also happened to be smaller democracies. Childs played a pivotal role in the late 1930s in establishing the notion that these smaller, northern democracies were particularly well suited to bolster democracy in view of the fascist challenge, precisely because of their smallness and their Nordic identity.

In particular Sweden exhibited a special form of industrial democracy – a dimension of democracy which, strictly speaking, had remained an unrealised ideal elsewhere. Swedish industrial democracy was the result of a combination of effort on the part of the labour movement towards cooperating and coordinating an already highly organised society and would not have worked had it not been for the successful broadening of the labour

---

80 Marklund, Carl (2009) 'Three Frames for the Image of Sweden: The Social Laboratory, the Middle Way, and the Swedish Model'. *Scandinavian Journal of History*, Vol. 34, No. 3, 264–285.

movement to include farmer interests and middle class interests – exactly what the labour movement had failed to do in those European states where fascism and authoritarianism had emerged triumphant.

While the features of Swedish society which allowed for this remarkable development to take place may very well have been unique, there were elements of strategy and conscious effort which could be emulated elsewhere. First, the Swedish logic of bargaining was presented as operating less through shared values than through shared fears. Having identified what was needed to combat the crisis (an alliance between labour and capital) as well as fascism (a broader labour movement), the obstacles to both this broader labour movement and an alliance between labour and capital could be isolated: jealousy and competing interests between city and country, capital and labour, and between the middle class and working class. Now, shared fears could be turned into shared values. By identifying common ground in shared understandings of minimum needs, standards of living and 'decency', through the workings of parliamentary expert committees, a relative consensus on the shape of future social policy could be worked out.[81] Once the wider goals had been set, the detailed drafting of reforms could be left to technical experts and the final implementation handed over to administrative bureaucrats, in what appears to be a textbook illustration of the Myrdalian conception of 'social engineering', which both Alva Myrdal and Gunnar Myrdal later sought to propagate in an American context.[82]

The broad alliance between farmers and workers as well as other organised group interests worked as the basis for a purposive democracy which could combat economic as well as political crises and hence ensure the survival of democracy. At the same time, however, the very success of this alliance as well as its reliance upon organised group interests could also be construed as a pseudo-fascist form of corporatism. The demand to deliver on 'democracy as promise' could be pitted against the need to safeguard 'democracy as process' with its constant deliberation between majority and minority opinions and interests.[83] Heckscher's notions of free corporativism and, later, pluralist democracy were tasked with explaining the difference between Swedish democratic corporatism and German and Italian unfree corporatisms.

In Sweden, the combination of the concept of 'democracy' with the concept of 'Nordic' signalled a particular sense of community, identity

---

81 It is noteworthy that Childs, in his description of this process – which probably was not as much a result of 'political acumen' and strategy as Childs chose to depict it – failed to mention the importance of the Swedish fear of population decline, shared by many Swedes both Left and Right during the mid-1930s but of marginal concern to most Americans at the time. Childs 1938, 101.

82 For this argument, see Marklund, Carl (2007) 'Adjusting Facts and Values, Reconciling Politics with Science? Some Notes on Social Engineering as Rhetorical Strategy in Depression-Era Sweden and the USA'. *Ideas in History*, Vol. 2, No. 2.

83 For the distinction between 'democracy as promise' and 'democracy as process', see Marklund, Carl (2008) *Bridging Politics and Science: The Concept of Social Engineering in Sweden and the USA, Circa 1890–1950*. Florence: European University Institute.

and solidarity in and among the Nordic countries. This community was not only formulated in the face of present geopolitical dangers resulting from the rise of totalitarianism in the vicinity of *Norden* and the potential internal repercussions of these tensions within *Norden*. To some extent, this conceptual combination of Nordicity with democracy relied upon the notion of a specific Nordic culture as the basis of this political form. Indeed, both foreign and Nordic accounts of the success of Nordic democracy during the 1930s often underlined the importance of homogeneity and continuity in the population for peaceful progressivism.

Hence, the notion of democracy in its Nordic formulation worked first as a means by which to de-dramatize the democratization process in its opposition to the economic, political and social order of the past and its representatives (who also relied upon the notion of a culturally specific Nordicity as the basis for their conservative political programme).[84] Second, it also turned against the ideal of a Nordic community based on race as propagated by contemporary fascists in the Nordic countries.[85] Third, it fitted nicely with the fundamental tenets of legal realism and value nihilism, largely accepting democracy as a given political preference of the Nordic peoples, shared by most if not all.

American references to Sweden and democracy – appreciative as well as critical ones – appear to have been less concerned with the survival of political democracy in Sweden than with the notion that industrial democracy could be created to solve some of the pressing tensions of modernity. Later, this image was supplanted with the notion that Sweden exhibited a specific form of planning democracy where planning was undertaken in order to strengthen democracy not weaken it.

Here, it is principled bargaining between capital and labour on the one hand and between labour and farmers on the other, combined with the parliamentary sanctioned and scientifically authorized study of actual and changing living standards which provides a living test of how to make democracy work – through the active shaping of values which may not have been initially shared by all.

BIBLIOGRAPHY

Adler-Karlsson, Gunnar (1967) *Funktionssocialism: ett alternativ till kommunism och kapitalism*. Uppsala: Fören. Verdandi.

Almgren, Birgitta (2005) *Drömmen om Norden. Nazistisk infiltration i Sverige 1933–1945*. Stockholm: Carlsson.

84 For a more detailed discussion of this argument, see Marklund, Carl & Stadius, Peter (forthcoming), 'Accept and Conform.' *Culture Unbound*.
85 Recent research efforts have sought to uncover the way in which Nordic democrats, neo-conservatives and Nordic fascism interplayed with one another in a complex game of rhetorical re-description of influence as well as rejection. See, for example, Berggren, Lena (2002) 'Swedish Fascism: Why Bother?' *Journal of Contemporary History*, Vol. 37, No. 3, 395–417; Almgren, Birgitta (2005) *Drömmen om Norden. Nazistisk infiltration i Sverige 1933–1945*. Stockholm: Carlsson.

Arneson, Ben A. (1940) 'The Scandinavian States and the League of Nations. by S. Shepard Jones'. *The Journal of Politics*, Vol. 2, No. 1, 96–98.

Bender, Thomas (1986) 'Wholes and Parts: The Need for Synthesis in American History'. *The Journal of American History*, Vol. 73, No. 1, 120–136.

Berggren, Lena (2002) 'Swedish Fascism: Why Bother?' *Journal of Contemporary History*, Vol. 37, No. 3, 395–417.

Bjarup, Jes (2005) 'The Philosophy of Scandinavian Legal Realism'. *Ratio Juris*, Vol. 18, No. 1, 1–15.

Carlomagno, Marcos Cantera (1995) *Ett folk av mänsklig granit: Sverige i den italienska utrikespolitiken 1932–1936.* Lund: Historiska Media.

Childs, Marquis W. (1936) *Sweden: The Middle Way.* New Haven: Yale University Press.

Childs, Marquis W. (1938) *This is Democracy: Collective Bargaining in Scandinavia.* New Haven: Yale University Press.

Cole, Margaret & Smith, Charles (eds) (1938) *Democratic Sweden: A Volume of Studies Prepared by Members of the New Fabian Research Bureau.* London: Routledge.

Dewey, John (1991) [1927] *The Public and Its Problems.* Athens, Ohio: Swallow Press.

Esping-Andersen, Gøsta (1990) *The Three Worlds of Welfare Capitalism.* Cambridge and Princeton: Polity Press and Princeton University Press.

Foner, Eric (1980) *Politics and Ideology in the Age of the Civil War.* New York: Oxford University Press.

Gram-Skjoldager, Karen & Tønnesson, Øyvind (2008) 'Unity and Diversity: Scandinavian Internationalism, 1914–1921'. *Contemporary European History*, Vol. 17, 301–324.

Heckscher, Gunnar (1939) 'Group Organization in Sweden'. *The Public Opinion Quarterly*, Vol. 3, No. 1, 130–135.

Heckscher, Gunnar (1948) 'Pluralist Democracy: The Swedish Experience'. *Social Research*, Vol. 15, 417–461.

Henriksson, Fritz (1939) *Sweden's participation in the U.S. celebration of the New Sweden tercentenary.* Stockholm: Bonniers.

Jones, S. Shepard (1939) *The Scandinavian States and the League of Nations.* Princeton, NJ: Princeton University Press.

Kinander, Morten (2002) *The View from Within: An Analysis and Critique of Legal Realism and Descriptive Jurisprudence.* Bergen: Univ.

Koht, Halvdan (1950) 'Review: The United States and Scandinavia by Franklin D. Scott'. *The American Historical Review*, Vol. 56, No. 1, 73–74.

Lippmann, Walter (1997) [1922] *Public Opinion.* New York: Free Press Paperbacks.

Lippmann, Walter (1993) [1925] *The Phantom Public.* New Brunswick, N.J.: Transaction Publishers.

Loewenstein, Karl (1935) 'Autocracy Versus Democracy in Contemporary Europe, I'. *The American Political Science Review*, Vol. 29, No. 4, 571–593.

Loewenstein, Karl (1937) 'Constitutional Government and Politics by Carl Joachim Friedrich'. *The American Political Science Review*, Vol. 31, No. 5, 953–957.

Lyles, Max (2006) *A Call for Scientific Purity: Axel Hägerström's Critique of Legal Science.* Stockholm: Institutet för rättshistorisk forskning.

Lynd, Robert S. & Lynd, Helen Merrell (1929) *Middletown: A Study in American Culture.* London: Constable.

M. B. (1939) 'The Smaller Democracies. by E. D. Simon'. *International Affairs*, Vol. 18, No. 6, 847–848.

Marklund, Carl (2007) 'Adjusting Facts and Values, Reconciling Politics with Science? Some Notes on Social Engineering as Rhetorical Strategy in Depression-Era Sweden and the USA'. *Ideas in History*, Vol. 2, No. 2.

Marklund, Carl (2008) *Bridging Politics and Science: The Concept of Social Engineering in Sweden and the USA, Circa 1890–1950.* Florence: European University Institute.

Marklund, Carl (2009) 'Three Frames for the Image of Sweden: The Social Laboratory, the Middle Way, and the Swedish Model'. *Scandinavian Journal of History*, Vol. 34, No. 3, 264–285.

Marklund, Carl & Stadius, Peter (forthcoming), 'Accept and Conform'. *Culture Unbound*.

Martin, Michael (1997) *Legal Realism: American and Scandinavian.* New York: P. Lang.

Musiał, Kazimierz (2002) *Roots of the Scandinavian Model. Images of Progress in the Era of Modernisation.* Baden Baden: Nomos Verlagsgesellschaft.

Myrdal, Alva (1941) *Nation and Family: The Swedish Experiment in Democratic Family and Population Policy.* New York: Harper & Row.

Myrdal, Gunnar (1940) *Population: A Problem for Democracy.* Cambridge, Mass: Harvard University Press.

Myrdal, Gunnar (1961) [1960] *Beyond the Welfare State: Economic Planning in the Welfare States and its International Implications.* New Haven: Yale University Press.

Ortega y Gasset, José (1964) [1929] *The Revolt of the Masses.* New York: Norton.

Peel, Roy V. (1937) 'Samhallskrisen och Socialvetenskaperna by Gunnar Myrdal; Herbert Tingsten Unghoger: Politiska Essayer by Gunnar Heckscher Pontus Fahlbeck och Samhallet by Erik Arrhen'. *The American Political Science Review*, Vol. 31, No. 2, 332–334.

Robbins, James J. & Heckscher, Gunnar (1941) 'The Constitutional Theory of Autonomous Groups'. *The Journal of Politics*, Vol. 3, No. 1, 3–28.

Rodgers, Daniel T. (1998) *Atlantic Crossings: Social Politics in a Progressive Age.* Cambridge: Harvard University Press.

Rothstein, Bo (1988) *Social Classes and Political Institutions: The Roots of Swedish Corporatism.* Uppsala: Maktutredningen.

Salmon, Patrick (1997) *Scandinavia and the Great Powers, 1890–1940.* Cambridge: Cambridge University Press.

Sandelius, Walter (1934) 'Dictatorship and Irresponsible Parliamentarism – A Study in the Government of Sweden'. *Political Science Quarterly*, Vol. 49, No. 3, 347–371.

Schivelbusch, Wolfgang (2006) *Three New Deals: Reflections on Roosevelt's America, Mussolini's Italy, and Hitler's Germany, 1933–1939.* New York: Metropolitan Books.

Skocpol, Theda & Weir, Margaret (1985) 'State Structures and the Possibilities for "Keynesian" Responses to the Great Depression in Sweden, Britain and the United States'. In Dietrich Rueschemeyer, Peter B. Evans & Theda Skocpol (eds) *Bringing the State Back In.* Cambridge: Cambridge University Press.

Strang, Johan (2009) 'Two Generations of Scandinavian Legal Realists'. *Retfaerd*, No. 1, 62–82.

The Annals of the American Academy of Political and Social Science, Vol. 197, No. 1 (May, 1938).

Tingsten, Herbert (1934) [1930] *Les pleins pouvoirs. L'expansion des pouvoirs gouvernementaux pendant et après la Grande guerre.* Paris, Stock.

Tingsten, Herbert (1966) *Från idéer till idyll: den lyckliga demokratien.* Stockholm: Norstedt.

Webb, Sidney (1891) 'The Difficulties of Individualism'. *The Economic Journal*, Vol. 1, No. 2, 360–381.

Wolff, Larry (2006) 'The Global Perspective of Enlightened Travelers: Philosophic Geography from Siberia to the Pacific Ocean'. *European Review of History*, Vol. 13, No. 3, 437–453.

JAN HECKER-STAMPEHL

Keeping up the Morale

Constructions of 'Nordic Democracy' during World War II

World War II was not only a time when armies clashed on the front; at home, people eagerly discussed ideas about how to reorganize Europe after the war. National reconstruction was one topic, global peacekeeping and a possible revitalisation of the League of Nations was another. Besides these, there were also Nordic and European discourses about post-war politics.[1] The nation-state had an uncertain future, and many prominent discussions dealt with plans for a renewal of the international relations framework. Throughout the war in Europe, people envisioned a better future in which nation-states would co-operate peacefully.[2] In a time of crisis, of war on different fronts, of occupation, ideas about what should happen after war flourished – on both sides of the war, in fact. The German aggressors were, by far, not as keen on devising their future rule over the territories that they had conquered as the people in the occupied but also the belligerent allied countries were. Nazi plans for a 'New Europe' remained empty phrases of agitation. The Nazis ruled over large parts of Europe, but they would not make their slogans about a 'New Order' become reality.[3]

In comparison, resistance movements against Nazi rule were much more active. World War II was not only fought on the battlefield, but also in the realm of ideologies and competing visions for the future. 'The war years are not only a struggle for power on the battlefield, but also a fight over

---

1 This article is based on the research I conducted for my doctoral thesis *Vereinigte Staaten des Nordens – Die Debatte der Norden-Vereine in Dänemark, Schweden und Finnland über ein geeintes Nordeuropa im Zweiten Weltkrieg* (United States of Norden – The debate of the Nordic associations in Denmark, Sweden and Finland on a united Northern Europe in the Second World War), Humboldt University Berlin, 2009.

2 Cf. Lipgens, Walter (1968) *Europa-Föderationspläne der Widerstandsbewegungen 1940–1945.* München: Oldenbourg (= Schriften des Forschungsinstituts der Deutschen Gesellschaft für Auswärtige Politik; 26).

3 Cf. Neulen, Hans Werner (1987) *Europa und das 3. Reich. Einigungsbestrebungen im deutschen Machtbereich.* München: Universitas Verlag; Kletzin, Birgit (2002) *Europa aus Rasse und Raum. Die nationalsozialistische Idee der Neuen Ordnung.* Münster: LIT Verlag (= Region – Nation – Europa; 2); Mazower, Mark (2008) *Hitler's Empire: Nazi Rule in Occupied Europe.* London: Allen Lane.

ideas and visions for the future.'[4] While sympathies for National Socialism dominated the picture during the early years of the war, by the German defeat at Stalingrad, plans for a future democratic Europe came to the forefront. It became clear that Nazi hegemony over Europe would not last, and gradually it became evident that its end was only a question of time – time for preparing oneself. [5]

Such plans for future politics and political reconstruction after the war were also being discussed in *Norden*.[6] Nazi sympathisers in Northern Europe reacted to National Socialist ideas and searched for *Norden*'s or their own country's place in Hitler's New Europe. In general, in the first years of the war, the expectation was that a German-led reorganisation of the European system of states was about to happen. This stance was also common among people, like Danish businessmen and civil servants, who worked in preparation for *Norden* to become a part of the Greater German Empire (*Großgermanisches Reich*).[7] The peace movements discussed international peacekeeping options and a possible Nordic contribution. The resistance movements in the German-occupied countries, individual politicians, and in the case of Norway, a whole government-in-exile discussed national reconstruction as well as new orientations for their countries' foreign policies (such as an Atlantic-oriented perspective). A very lively debate about Nordic politics and a possible post-war Nordic economic, military or even political union occurred in Denmark, Sweden and Finland. The debate caught the attention of broad circles. One important circle which had discussed ideas of Nordic co-operation before the war was the 'Nordic Labour Movements' Co-operation Committee'.[8] The main actors during the

---

4 Andersson, Jan A. (1994) *Nordiskt samarbete: Aktörer, idéer och organisering 1919– 1953.* (Lund Political Studies; 85) Lund, 113 ['Krigsåren är inte bara en kraftmätning på slagfälten utan även en kamp om idéer och framtidsvisioner.'].
5 Mazower, Mark (2002) 'Pläne für das Goldene Zeitalter'. In Mazower (ed.) *Der dunkle Kontinent. Europa im 20. Jahrhundert.* Frankfurt a.M.: Fischer-Taschenbuch-Verlag [London 1998], 267–305, at 276.
6 *Norden* is an established term in the Scandinavian languages to describe the five Nordic countries (Denmark, Finland, Iceland, Norway and Sweden) when the political community of the five is meant. I use the term in this meaning, relating to 'Norden' as a (geo-) political region in contrast to 'Northern Europe' as a geographical region and 'Scandinavia' meaning Denmark, Norway and Sweden.
7 Cf. Lund, Joachim (2004) 'Denmark and the "European New Order"', 1940–1942. *Contemporary European History* Vol. 13, Issue 3, 305–321; idem (2005) *Hitlers spisekammer. Danmark og den europæiske nyordning 1940–43.* København: Gyldendal; Meyer-Gohde, Ruth (2006) 'Dänemarks wirtschaftspolitische Reaktion auf die Besetzung des Landes 1940/41'. *NORDEUROPAforum. Zeitschrift für Politik, Wirtschaft und Kultur N.F.* Vol. 9, Issue 2, 51–70.
8 This topic has been the object of a major study and an edition of important sources covering the 1930s and 1940s: Blidberg, Kersti (1984) *Splittrad gemenskap. Kontakter och samarbete inom nordisk socialdemokratisk arbetarrörelse 1931–1945.* Stockholm: Almqvist & Wiksell (= Acta Universitatis Stockholmiensis; 32); Wahlbäck, Krister/ Blidberg, Kersti (eds) (1986) *Samråd i kristid. Protokoll från den nordiska arbetarrörelsens samarbetskommitté 1932–1946.* Stockholm: Kungl. Samfundet för utgivande av handskrifter rörande Skandinaviens historia. Handlingar; 12).

war, however, became the so-called 'Nordic Associations' (*Föreningarna Norden*).[9]

These associations, which had been established in all Nordic countries after World War I (simultaneously in Denmark, Norway and Sweden in 1919, in Iceland and Finland in 1921/24), discussed schemes for a closer co-operation between Nordic states.[10] Different forms of co-operation, such as a defence union or a customs union, represented some of the proposals for a looser form of Nordic co-operation; meanwhile, the idea of esablishing closer bonds between the Nordic countries gained a lot of ground. A volume published by three Swedish authors in 1942 under the title *United States of Norden* (*Nordens förenta stater*) gave this brainchild a name, and the programme developed in this book served as a key text for the entire debate.[11] The ideas discussed here could be characterized as a trial to outline an alternative path to Nazi hegemony over *Norden*.[12] The Nordic Associations stood firmly in favour of democracy and liberal ideas and even though they would not position themselves as opponents to National Socialism, their activity was aimed at uniting a free democratic *Norden* in a post-war world where Germany had lost the war. The Nordic Associations saw themselves as the most important pressure group and discussion forum for issues of Nordic cooperation and wanted to prepare the political agenda for the post-war period. The activities included a great many publications, lectures, courses, work in the schools, but also work behind the scenes. The Nordic Associations wanted to popularise the idea of Nordic togetherness so that a political union could more easily be created after the war. Constitutions for the federal Nordic state were drafted, but another important task was remained, which was to more precisely define what 'Norden' was.

These schemes for a Nordic union required legitimation of a cultural foundation upon which the state structures would need to be erected. *Norden* and Nordicness needed clear delineations and definitions; the uniqueness of *Norden*, and consequently the value of defending it against future aggression, would have to be defined. A new concept of 'Norden' was being elaborated in a way which, similar to processes of national identity construction, used traditions, the region's history, and the ancient character of the nation (or in this case the new, greater fatherland-to-be) to make its

---

9 For a survey on these different schemes, cf. Hecker-Stampehl, Jan (2007) 'Föderationspläne in Nordeuropa im Zweiten Weltkrieg. Ein Überblick'. In Sturm-Martin, Imke and Jan Hecker-Stampehl (eds) *Europa im Blick: westeuropäische Perspektiven im 20. Jahrhundert. Festschrift für Clemens A. Wurm*. Hamburg: Verlag Dr. Kovač, 119–139.

10 On the associations' founding and first one and a half decades of activity, cf. Janfelt, Monika (2005) *Att leva i den bästa av världar. Föreningarna Nordens syn på Norden 1919–1933*. Stockholm: Carlssons.

11 Petander, Karl, Kleen, Willy and Anders Örne (1942) *Nordens förenta stater*. Stockholm: Natur och Kultur.

12 On the contradictory conceptions of 'Nordic' and 'Norden' in National Socialist ideology and in the public discussion in *Norden,* cf. Almgren, Birgitta, Hecker-Stampehl, Jan, Piper, Ernst (2008) 'Alfred Rosenberg und die Nordische Gesellschaft – Der "nordische Gedanke" in Theorie und Praxis'. *NORDEUROPAforum. Zeitschrift für Politik, Wirtschaft und Kultur N.F.* Vol. 11, Issue 2, 7–51, here especially 24–26.

case. One of the key points in this construction was the common Nordic political culture based on liberty, democracy and peace.

The Nordic community was a political, as well as cultural, community, culture being understood in such a broad sense as to also include political culture. This community was conceived of as primordial and stable, such that it would be hardly ever be affected by new developments. Nordic togetherness was something ontological – granted by nature. The Danish author Finn T. B. Friis wrote a brochure for the Nordic Association in Denmark in 1941, called *The Nordic Cultural Community and Practical Nordic Co-operation*, in which he covered a broad variety of aspects of what he perceived to be the joint Nordic culture – with 'culture' covering language, history, manifestations of 'high culture' such as literature or music – and political culture. He distinguished between forms of organised Nordic co-operation, which one could give up and leave, and the Nordic community *per se*, which could not be abolished, since it rested upon 'a series of natural factors'. There was a political Scandinavianism, but beneath it there was what he called a 'cultural Scandinavianism, which is not made up or constructed, but which has come into existence out of itself'.[13]

The interesting point is that 'Nordic democracy' belonged in a certain way to both of these Scandinavianisms. There were old traditions which could not be abolished because, partially, that form of political activity was in accordance with Nordic man's cultural identity. The Swedish author Stefan Oljelund noticed an awakening in wartime Northern Europe to national values concerning law and order and culture which were based upon 'a feeling for ancient Nordic conceptions of law and Nordic democracy'. By turning to old traditions, the peoples in *Norden* had won the strength to fight against those forces which tried to deprive them of their liberty and independence.[14] Democracy was a means of defending the common Nordic culture and was seen as one of the most important foundations for future cooperation between the Nordic countries. The future union would be based on Nordic democracy, but it would also serve to defend Nordic democracy.

The historical, geographical and cultural roots of 'Nordic democracy'

The renowned Swedish Social Democrat intellectual Herbert Tingsten had been one of the first authors to examine the phenomenon of a common Nordic democracy while also explicitly using this term.[15] In his article 'Nordisk

---

13 Friis, Finn T. B. (1941) *Nordisk Kulturfællesskab og praktisk nordisk Samarbejde.* København: Foreningen Norden (= Nordisk Oplysning; II), 7.

14 Oljelund, Stefan (1944) *Arbetarrörelse i Norden.* Stockholm: KFs bokförlag i distribution (= Nordens serie; 6), 36 ['känsla för uråldriga nordiska rättsbegrepp och nordisk demokrati'].

15 Most authors of the texts which are being discussed here were by far not as prominent and well-known in the public as Tingsten. Most of them were commissioned by the Nordic Associations to write about certain aspects of Nordic unity and its cultural foundations. Typically, the authors combined expertise in a certain field with an affinity for Nordic co-operation and unity. A good example is the Finnish expert on international law, diplomat

demokrati' (Nordic Democracy), published in the Nordic Associations' common yearbook *Nordens kalender* in 1938, Tingsten claimed that the Nordic countries' political systems and state systems showed so many similarities that it indeed would be justified to speak of a common Nordic democracy: 'not without reason could one speak of a Nordic democratic community'. For him, the cornerstone of *Norden*'s continued existence was the very fact that the Nordic region clung to its democratic values.[16] One of the central elements of this construction of a homogeneous Nordic region was a common political culture. Nordic unity had its roots in common conceptions of democracy and the rule of law. 'Nordic democracy' was constructed as an element of the aforementioned primordial 'cultural Scandinavianism'. In this context, it is crucial to point to the understanding of political culture as an element of a broad conception of the term 'culture', since this was also the understanding of most Nordic activists.

According to Swedish author Evald Fransson, ideationally linking bonds, more than geographical factors, or alleged racial commonalities (he sharply critizised the legitimacy of racial theories), should stand as the focus of a Nordic gathering. The four most important bonds were: first, law and order and the supremacy of the rule of law; second, belief in a broad conception of liberty (of the individual, religious freedom, freedom of research etc.); third, the logical consequence of these two, democracy; and fourth, the basis of all these, a profoundly humanistic view of life.[17] Fransson admitted that, when it came to universal suffrage, Nordic democracy was not very old, but suggested the existence of democratic principles and convictions outside of the current political system:

> In the meaning of universal nation-wide and local suffrage, Nordic democracy might not be old. But the essential in this form of government has nevertheless almost always come to the fore in these nations' history. They are standing as European democracy's oldest exponents [...] from the people on the Thing to our modern democracies an unusually unbroken line of the people's authority runs in the Nordic countries. [...] The thousand years' tradition of the endeavours for constitutional rule, liberty and self-government explains, why all the Nordic countries' political parties became democratic in spirit and action so fast. If we measure the true support for democracy by the overwhelming majority of the people, the absence of bloody conflicts between social classes, Norden stands in a class of its own in the era of industrial breakthrough.[18]

Consequently, 'Nordic democracy' did not primarily refer to day-to-day policy-making but rather to its most important foundation. It was seen as a

and former prime minister Rafael Erich (1879–1946), who was also member of the Finnish Nordic Association's executive board. Cf. biographical details in Vares, Vesa (2003) Erich, Rafael (1879–1946). In Matti Klinge (ed.), *Suomen kansallisbiografia Vol. 2.* Helsinki: SKS, 617–619.

16 Tingsten, Herbert (1938) 'Nordisk demokrati'. In *Nordens kalender*, Vol. 9, 41–50, at 41.

17 Fransson, Evald (1945) *Fostran till nordisk gemenskap.* Stockholm: Geber (= Almqvist & Wiksells psykologisk-pedagogiska bibliotek; 2), 33–36.

18 Fransson 1945, 34–35.

natural element of Nordic self-understanding, as something organic, having slowly developed its present-day character. It was something pre-existing, and it did not need to be 'made' or 'adapted' – it was simply there. The Nordics did not need to be taught democracy, as they had internalized it. The Nordic societies and states of today had developed from a 'consciousness of liberty originally grown in Norden', and this notion of liberty manifested itself 'in an age-old self-government, in our days broadened into a distinct, all-embracing democracy', as Karl Petander stated in 1942. Petander, a Swedish folk high school rector and activist for the Nordic cause, was mainly active as editor and co-author of anthologies promoting the Nordic cause. He saw a social and judicial order which guaranteed everyone's freedom, the rule of law, and a blending of old traditional Nordic values with Christian and humanistic beliefs as modern representations of this old striving for individual liberty and for the *Rechtsstaat*. All these aspects of Nordic political culture deserved to be defended. On the other hand, it was exactly the Nordic heritage of liberty which had hindered a political union between the Nordic countries in the past.[19] However, as Friis put it, the idea was not to allow an unlimited and unbounded individualism to become paramount, but to protect human rights and thus the rights of every individual against abuses of state power.[20]

The secret behind the alleged internationally renowned strength of Nordic democracy[21] was, according to author Gunnar Beskow (a Swedish poet who also published political essays), 'the fact that democracy is natural for us, like probably for no other people in Europe'.[22] The reasons were, according to Beskow, Scandinavia's natural conditions and the Nordics' common history. In Northern Europe, the tradition of liberty fostered by old Germanic primitive 'tribal democracy' (*stamdemokratien*) had been preserved. This 'proto-Germanic tradition of liberty' (*urgermanska frihetstradition*) had been lost in central Europe under the influence of the Roman Empire and medieval feudalism:

> In distant, wooded Scandinavia, on the other side of the Baltic Sea, it could be maintained – the free Nordic peasant democracy continues straight on until the late Middle Ages, is partially being dissolved in the state system but not in the life-style, and leaves its heritage of a desire for freedom, a sense of responsibility and a sense of right and wrong for us in contemporary times. Parliamentarian democracy became the form sought for to preserve and improve our proto-Nordic legacy of values in the period of modern industrialism.[23]

19 Petander, Karl (1942) 'Nordens framtid'. In Petander et al. 1942, 9–39, 10–12.

20 Friis 1941, 17.

21 What I mean here is that no reliable empirical data exist on the 'internationally renowned strength of Nordic democracy'. Rather, this was a conception or perception spread by the authors I analyse in this contribution which they themselves never really managed or bothered to prove.

22 Gunnar Beskow (1941) 'Demokratins framtidslinje'. In Inga Bagger-Sjöbäck and Elsa Cedergren (eds), *Diskussion om demokratin*. Stockholm: Bonnier, 177–194, at 193.

23 Beskow 1941, 193–194 ['Ensamt i det avlägsna, skogiga Skandinavien, på andra sidan Östersjön, kunde det bibehållas – den fria nordiska bondedemokratien leder rätt in

For the Swedes (which also reads as 'Nordics'), democracy was not a foreign fashion recently adapted, but the people's right to self-determination and civil maturity, which had arisen from proto-Germanic peasant democracy. The people's representation had, after intervening periods of reduced freedom, regained its prior democratic form. The Finnish-Swedish historian and politician Eirik Hornborg claimed that in Sweden, individual liberty and basic civil rights had always been respected. Political life had 'since ancient times rested on a democratic foundation' and only a few exceptions could be found in history, during the aristocratic rule and absolutism of the seventeeth and eighteenth centuries.[24] In another text, Gunnar Beskow addressed the circumstances which aided in preserving old Nordic democratic values. He argued that only in territories with dense population did the preconditions exist for establishing systems of slavery and bondage. Geographically more diverse and far-flung countries offered much better possibilities for freedom and democracy.

> Geographically splintered countries – mountainous countries, island countries, forested countries – are destined for freedom. In Norden these conditions persisted – the remote Norden, mountainous, wooded or carved into islands by bays and sounds. In continental Europe the Germanic tribes came under Roman imperialism's impact [...]. The old Germanic tradition was cut, the settlement structure became dense enough and heavily continental so that despotism's geographic prerequisite was met. That the old Germanic heritage of freedom could endure in Norden [...] depended upon the natural geographic circumstances: scattered small settlements, isolation beyond sea and wood.[25]

According to Danish author Finn T. B. Friis, the Nordic countries' geographic position had spared their peoples from the intrusion of alien elements which could be encountered in most European and American countries. Additionally, this had an impact on how political life was shaped: 'For the smooth political development in every single state in Norden this has undoubtedly played a big role, and today's Nordic democracy is free of the numerous difficulties that lack of ethnic unity has created in many

---

i senmedeltiden, upplöses delvis i statsskicket men inte i livsföringen, och lämnar sitt arv av frihetsbehov, ansvarskänsla och rättsmedvetande åt oss i nutiden. Den parlamentariska demokratien blev den efterlängtade formen för vårt urnordiska värdearvs bevarande och förkovran, i den moderna industrialismens tid.'].

24 Hornborg, Eirik (1943) *Den nordiska tanken. Föredrag vid den nordiska festen i Jakobstad den 2 oktober 1943*. Jakobstad: Föreningen Norden, 7 ['I Sverige har även statslivet sedan urminnes tider vilat på demokratisk grundval.'].

25 Gunnar Beskow (1940) *Sveriges uppgift*. Stockholm: Bonnier, 21–22 ['Geografiskt splittrade länder – bergländer, öländer, skogsländer – destinerad till frihet. I Norden blev dessa villkor bestående – det avlägsna, bergiga, skogiga eller av fjärder och sund i öar sönderskurna Norden. På fastlandseuropa kom germanstammarna under den romerska imperialismens inflytande [...]. Den gammalgermanska traditionen bröts, och bebyggelsen blev tät och fastlandstung nog för att despotiens geografiska förutsättning skulle vara uppfylld. Att det gammalgermanska frihetsarvet kunde bestå i Norden [...], berodde på de naturgeografiska villkoren: sönderflikad småbygd, isolering bakom hav och skog.'].

other places in the world.'[26] The idea of national homogeneity (which also translated to homogeneity of *Norden*) was very prevalent – the alleged ethnic uniformity of the Nordic countries was an important reason for its political uniformity and consensus culture.

The geographic remoteness which fostered the development of democracy and local self-administration was, according to Beskow, not synonymous with cultural isolationism. The Nordic region indeed followed developments in the rest of Europe, but did not let all new things come unhindered to *Norden*: one did not allow all the new thoughts to flood *Norden*. That Nordic democracy could have developed and been maintained in its specific form was due to a mixture of a certain conservativism and, simultaneously, an openness to new ideas from outside, Beskow argued. This mixture could also be explained by geography:

> Scandinavia is in its character a group of islands, an archipelago, even though the core country is fastened to the continent by a narrow stalk – that is the key to our task and the secret of our peculiarity, which we share with e.g. Greece. *Sweden's, Norway's and Denmark's insular location.*[27]

Conceptualizing a long tradition of Nordic proto-democracy and of the historical roots of parliamentary democracy has overshadowed the fact that modern democratic practice was still relatively young in the Nordic region, as previously mentioned. Tingsten addressed the latter fact, but stated that 'the late introduction of complete rule of the people'[28] should not be interpreted as a proof of weak democratic traditions. Even before the process of democratisation had been completed, Nordic countries had experience with popular representation, widespread local self-administration and guaranteeing of citizens' individual freedoms. Even if democracy had only been implemented a few decades before World War II, it nonetheless built upon the Nordic traditions of division of power and local, restricted self-government.[29] *Norden* was thus well-prepared for a full realization of democratic rule. Tingsten also pointed out that very good preconditions for introducing democracy already existed in *Norden*:

> Social and cultural prerequisites for a political democracy existed in the Nordic states to a higher degree than in the majority of the countries

---

26 Friis 1941, 10 ['For den rolige politiske Udvikling i hver enkelt Stat i Norden har dette utvivlsomt spillet en stor Rolle, og Nutidens nordiske Demokrati er fri for de talrige Vanskeligheder, Manglen paa etnisk Enhed har skabt mange andre Steder i Verden.'].

27 Beskow 1940, 27.

28 Tingsten 1938, 43 ['fullständiga folkstyrelsens sena införande'].

29 Tingsten, Herbert (1940) 'Folkstyret i Norden'. In Karl Petander (ed.) *Nordisk gemenskap. Utgiven av Norden, Svensk förening för nordiskt samarbete.* Stockholm: Kooperativa förbundets bokförlag, 50–83, at 50. At the end of the text the fact that the manuscript was finalized in September 1939 is stated. In the table of contents the headline reads 'Folkstyrelsen i Norden'.

democratized in the first decades of the 20th century; one can point above all to the general education of the people.[30]

In the eyes of renowned Norwegian author Sigrid Undset, Norway and the Nordic countries had always been at the forefront of democracy and they would still be there after an Allied victory. In the article 'The Democracy of the Nordic People' that she wrote while in exile in the USA, she also pointed to other specifically Nordic prerequisites for the successful realization of democracy:

> We were always in the forefront of the world's progress toward the ideals of democracy, and we know that we are able to be there just because we are so small nations with a homogeneous population and therefore easier to govern well and successfully than large countries with populations of mixed racial strains. If the world after this war is heading toward universal freedom, justice, and peaceful co-operation among men, we shall be in the pioneer corps, where we belong.[31]

So strong did the discursive linkage of national identity, natural conditions, geographical determinants and democracy become, that in a review of a Danish book about democracy, the reviewer missed an explanation of the historical, natural and cultural factors and their impact on the specific form of democracy. The description of different forms of democracy had a purely informative handbook character, so the reviewer stated. 'But political forms can only really be appraised against the background of the whole *historical situation*, the character and peculiarity of the people, the geopolitical situation of the country (location, natural conditions, climate, natural resources), etc.'[32] Obivously, to speak about Nordic democracy without naming its primordial foundations and its historical precursors and roots was already deemed insufficient.

Finland and 'Nordic democracy'

Looking back at the quote by Beskow (footnote 26), it is interesting to note that Finland is not mentioned in this context. Finland usually posed some problems to the ideologists of Nordic co-operation in the 1930s and 1940s. In a time when racial questions were very much en vogue in many intellectual circles, even voices which spoke positively of Finland emphasised that the Finns belonged to a different race. It was often said that their path to democracy and stability had not been a straight one. Earlier

---

30 Tingsten 1938, 43 ['Sociala och kulturella forutsättningar för en politisk demokrati funnos i de nordiska staterna i högre grad än i flertalet under 1900-talets första decennier demokratiserade länder; framför allt kan man peka på den allmänna folkbildningen.']

31 Undset, Sigrid (1943) 'The Democracy of the Nordic People'. In *Free World* vol. 4, 211–217, at 217.

32 Lundbye, Ove (1943) 'Folkestyre'. In *Gads danske magasin* vol. 37, 32–43, at 33.

discourses about a chaotic and unreliable neighbour lingered on and were not easily forgotten, and the Lapua movement had been the severest threat to Nordic democracy within the region itself. But there were discursive strategies to link both critical and supportive voices, as we can see in the case of Beskow. He stated that in Finland, the Northern Germanic element encountered a population with a background in a 'different tribe', but that the Finns were 'bearers of a not less strong democratic tradition of liberty' and that this tradition also originated in the forest.[33] This explanation is a typical example of how Finland was discursively incorporated into the Nordic community: with a big 'although' in front. Although the Finns were of a different racial or tribal origin, they had been brought the Nordic values, among them democracy and love of freedom, via the Swedish motherland during the approximately 650 years of Swedish rule.[34] Hornborg suggested that this long historical connection even contributed to democracy's strong position in Finland to this day:

> Since Finland from her history's dawn in the 13th century and up until the Russian conquest formed a part of the Swedish realm and also after that, both during the Russian time and after achieving independence, has built her laws and her social order upon old Swedish ground, the principles of liberty, democracy and liberalism might well be as strongly rooted amongst us as in Sweden.[35]

Yet the wartime events in Finland, which included censorship and military collaboration with Nazi Germany – one of *the* enemies of democracy – greatly put into question whether Finland was part of the concept of Nordic democracy. Hornborg (who had been one of the Lapua movement's fiercest opponents) was aware of the fact that these circumstances threatened to damage Finland's image, not only among its Nordic sibling countries, but also in the Western world. The Nordic idea, and with it 'Nordic democracy', thus became political tools which helped to ensure that Finland would end up on the 'right side' once the war would be over. Finland, as Hornborg wrote, ought to commit herself to the Western principles of rule of law and apply these fully in domestic as well as foreign policy:

33 Beskow 1940, 85–86.
34 Cf. Hecker-Stampehl, Jan (2006) 'Finnland – Teil des Nordens? Das eigene Andere auf der mentalen Landkarte Nordeuropas'. In Norbert Götz, Jörg Hackmann, Jan Hecker-Stampehl (eds) (2006a) *Die Ordnung des Raums: Mentale Landkarten in der Ostseeregion.* Berlin: Berliner Wissenschaftsverlag (= Die Ostseeregion: Nördliche Dimensionen – Europäische Perspektiven; 6), 150–185; Hecker-Stampehl, Jan (2006b) 'Vorposten des Nordens? Finnland als Bollwerk des Abendlandes in Veröffentlichungen aus dem Zweiten Weltkrieg'. In Aleksanteri Suvioja and Erkki Teräväinen (eds) (2006) *Kahden kulttuurin välittäjä. Hannes Saarisen juhlakirja.* Helsinki: Helsingin yliopiston historian laitos (= Helsingin yliopiston historian laitoksen julkaisuja; 20), 313–326.
35 Hornborg 1943, 7 ['Då Finland från sin historias gryning på 1200-talet och ända till den ryska erövringen har utgjort en del av det svenska riket och också sedermera, såväl under den ryska tiden som efter självständighetens ernående, har byggt sin rätt och sin samhällsordning på gammal svensk grund, borde frihetens, demokratiens och liberalismens principer vara lika rotfasta hos oss som i Sverige.'].

It is imperative to embrace with heart and soul the Nordic-Western liberal and democratic understanding of society, which gives the individual all possible freedom within the framework of law, which sees tolerance and liberal-mindedness as something self-evident, which sees free discussion in all matters social and political and open criticism of authorities' measures as a sound and necessary counterweight to man's ineradicable disposition for jog trot, good faith and power abuse – which, in one word, is based on the old, worn-off, but never worn-out catchword: freedom based on law, freedom with responsibility.

The idea of the state under the rule of law has perhaps best been realized in the Scandinavian small states. It is the finest creation in the area of societal culture; it is the goal for countless pastgenerations' conscious or unconscious endeavours. It must also be the goal of our people's endeavour. In this the Nordic spirit is summarised.[36]

From Friis' Danish perspective, common values were the one aspect that tied Finland to the rest of Norden – the dividing line of language and race being neutralised or compensated for by common institutions, the common cultural heritage and the common conception of law and order.[37] For the chairman of the Finnish Nordic Association, Bruno Suviranta, Finland's fight to defend the North was also a defence of exactly these values and also pointed to a crucial conflict:

But [the slogan] Finland for Norden does also have another meaning, perhaps not equally self-evident for everyone. It has to imply that we form a common front in defence of Nordens spiritual heritage of freedom: the democratic order of society, freedom of thought, principles for a constitutional state, humanity. [...] Therefore we cannot simultaneously defend Norden and promote such forces which want to destroy our Nordic heritage of freedom.[38]

36 Hornborg 1943, 19. ['Det gäller att av själ och hjärta anamma den nordisk-västerländska liberala och demokratiska uppfattning av samhället, som medger den enskilda all möjlig frihet inom lagens ram, som betraktar tolerans och frisinthet såsom någonting självfallet, som anser fri diskussion i sociala och politiska frågor och öppen kritik av myndigheternas åtgärder vara en hälsosam och nödvändig motvikt mot människans outrotliga benägenhet fdör slentrian, godtycke och maktmissbruk – som, med ett ord, är grundad på det gamla, slitna men aldrig utslitna slagordet: lagbunden frihet, frihet under ansvar. // Rättsstatens idé har måhända allra bäst förverkligats i de skandinaviska småstaterna. Den är Västerlandets yppersta skapelse på samhällskulturens område, den är målet för oräkneliga gångna släktleds medvetna eller omedvetna strävanden. Den måste vara målet också för vårt folks strävan. I den sammanfattas den nordiska andan.'].
37 Friis 1941, 16f.
38 Kansallisarkisto Helsinki (Finnish National Archives Helsinki, after this KA Hki), Bruno Suvirannan kokoelma (Bruno Suviranta's archive), series 8, Puheita (Speeches) 1917–1967, Norden, puhe edustajakokouksen päivällisillä 30.9.1943 (dinner speech at a conference of delegates from the local departments of the Nordic Association, 30th September, 1943).
['Men Finland för Norden har också en annan betydelse, kanske inte lika självklar för alla. Det måste också betyda, att vi bilda gemensam front i försvar för Nordens andliga frihetsarv: det [sic] folkstyrda samhällsordningen, tankefriheten, principer om rättstat,

When Finland was close to leaving the war, the Nordic Association in Finland formulated a Nordic credo which showed how important the concept of Nordic democracy had become. It shows how the form of government and the political system were understood in the broad sense of a common Nordic culture:

> Finland's culture is decidedly Nordic and Western. We share our religion and our constitutional order with the Nordic peoples. We can successfully discuss together about social, judicial, economic and pedagogical as well as literary and artistic questions, since we stand upon the same ground.
>
> Our view upon political life is a common one. This holds true first and foremost for the civil liberty, equality before the law, and a high esteem of the sanctity of law. The form of government in all of the Nordic countries is based upon liberty, law and democracy. In Finland one has learned from experience to regard these values highly as forces which create and preserve society.[39]

The aim of this resolution was to assure both the Finnish population and Findland's Nordic sibling countries of Finland's sense of belonging to the same community and of having the same values as the Scandinavian countries. Furthermore, it served to underline Finnish self-understanding as being part of the Western democratic world – an important signal to give to the anti-Hitler coalition, especially the Western Allies. Such rhetorical commitments to Nordic and Western values were also to be found in a publication sponsored and originally initiated by the State Agency for Information (*Valtion Tiedoituslaitos*) which acted as a state censorship organ that also attempted to steer public opinion into directions which served the Finnish government's political and military goals.[40]

humaniteten. […] Vi kunna därför inte samtidigt försvara Norden och befrämja sådana krafter vilka vilja förstöra vårt nordiska frihetsarv.']

39 KA Hki, Pohjola-Norden ry:n arkisto (Nordic Association's Archive, after this PNA) I, series 16, Paikallisyhdistysten edustajainkokous 1943–1946, Protokoll fört vid Föreningen Nordens andra representantmöte i Finska Hushållningssällskapets plenisal i Åbo den 25 och 26 augusti 1944. Liite/bilaga No 4 Suomi kuuluu Pohjolaan/Finland hör till Norden ['Finlands kultur är avgjort nordisk och västerländsk. Vår religion och vår rättsordning dela vi med de nordiska folken. Vi kunna med framgång gemensamt dryfta sociala, rättsliga, ekonomiska och pedagogiska liksom också litterära och konstnärliga spörsmål, emedan vi stå på samma botten. // Vår syn på statslivet är gemensam. Främst gäller det den medborgerliga friheten, likhet inför lagen och en hög uppfattning om det rättas helgd. Statsskicket i all de nordiska länderna grundar sig på frihet, rätt och demokrati. I Finland har man av erfarenheten lärt att skatta dessa värden högt som samhällsskapande och – bevarande makter.'].

40 Tallqvist, J.O. (ed.) (1944) *Finland för Norden. Uttalanden om vårt nordiska samarbete.* Helsingfors / Finnish edition: *Suomi kuuluu Pohjolaan. Lausuntoja pohjoismaisesta yhteistyöstämme.* Helsinki. Cf. the contribution by Lindman, Sven: 'Kring vårt nordiska samhällsskick', 66–69 on democracy and political culture.

The Nordic heritage of liberty and rule of law

Two pivotal elements of a common Nordic self-perception are often summed up with the terms 'liberty' and 'rule of law'. The importance of respecting the freedom of the individual and the sanctity of the *Rechtsstaat* was repeatedly stressed in public statements and articles. 'The sense of the holiness of law and the respect for individual liberty are fundamental elements of the Nordic cultural heritage.'[41] These central principles were ascribed to a long-lasting tradition which could be traced back to the earliest medieval *corpora juris*. Medieval laws were pointed to as proof of a high esteem for humanity and quasi-constitutional rule from which modern political practice had grown. These principles had been realised early on in the form of the right of political participation, but also in personal rights, such as freedom of opinion, freedom of the press, freedom of association and assembly, and freedom of religion. These rights and principles were deemed to be the roots of the modern democratic shape of Nordic societies. They formed 'a common heritage of great antiquity' which needed to be defended against external threats, so claimed Swedish minister of Justice Thorvald Bergquist, and in a similar vein, a resolution by the Nordic Association in Finland.[42] According to the rationale of the Nordic associations, the medieval traditions of the free peasantry were the source of this liberalism. While feudal rule in a continental manner indeed was absent, notably in Sweden and Finland, the idea of the free Nordic peasant was (and partially still is) being constructed as a thread running throughout the history of *Norden*. In our case, statements like one by the Finnish Nordic association's chairman Bruno Suviranta have established a connection between modern times and ancient traditions by stating that democratic values had fallen on especially fertile ground in the Nordic countries:

> Amongst us in Norden these ideas of liberty and humanism met a fitting breeding ground, because since time immemorial the social foundation had been constituted here by the free peasantry and the democratic order. On this basis, one has continued to build through the centuries; the forms have surely changed and were developed further, but the foundation has not been altered; it has stayed the same.[43]

---

41 Ahlberg, Alf (1946) 'Kulturarvet'. In Föreningen Norden (ed.) (1946) *Nordisk samhörighet en realitet.* Stockholm: Åhlén & Söners Förlag, 123–138, at 126 ['Känslan för lagens helgd och respekt för den individuella friheten är grundläggande element i det nordiska kulturarvet'].

42 Bergquist, Thorvald (1946) 'Frihet är det bästa ting'. In Föreningen Norden 1946, 51–58, at 51 (this anthology was published after the war when Bergquist no longer was minister, but the contributions were written in 1944–1945); KA Hki, PNA I 16, Paikallisyhdistysten edustajainkokous 1943–1946, Protokoll fört vid Föreningen Nordens andra representantmöte i Finska Hushållningssällskapets plenisal i Åbo den 25 och 26 augusti 1944, liite/bilaga 4 Suomi kuuluu Pohjolaan/Finland hör till Norden.

43 Suviranta, Bruno (1943). 'Föreningen Nordens verksamhet och syften'. In *För Norden. Föreningen Nordens medlemsblad* vol, Issue 6, 21–26, at 22 ['Hos oss i Norden stötte dessa frihetens och humanismens ideer på en tjänlig jordmån, ty ända sedan urminnes tider hade här den sociala grundvalen utgjorts av den fria bonden och en demokratisk statsordning. På

Liberalism was being defined from two different angles. One was liberalism defined as the overwhelming desire for freedom among the common people, and the other was liberalism defined as freedom bound by law, which was seen as the main current of any societal life in *Norden*. Civil liberties were to be protected from the ruler's arbitrariness; in the eyes of the Nordic activists, this had also made absolutism in Northern Europe less radical and much more confined by certain rules than in Central Europe. The libertarian principles enacted in *Norden* had resulted in the division of powers and in legislature and jurisdiction paying attention to the expectations and needs of the common people, thus creating a far-reaching consensus between the authority and the people, a consensus which was the cornerstone of Nordic moral strength.[44] Interfering in these ancient rights and restricting liberty had allegedly always been stymied by strong resistance from the people. Misuse of power would have no chance whatsoever in *Norden* due to these deeply grounded conceptions and perceptions of law and its rightful application.

> The demand that these rights remain unabridged is firmly rooted among the Nordic peoples. The saying about Norden as the ancestral seat of freedom on earth is no platitude, which modern men have made up in order to illuminate their history, but within it lies a living reality. The feeling of liberty, occasionally ungovernable and demanding, is one of the features of the peoples of Norden, which comes to the fore most strongly.[45]

The people's desire for freedom manifests in central elements of Nordic political culture, such as the importance of controlling government and parliament, the transparency principle (the principle of public access to government files) or civil pariticipation in popular movements (such as the Nordic associations). The idea that all Nordic peoples were conscious of the invaluable worth of this liberalism and rule of law was widespread. These notions of 'Nordic democracy' made the Nordic activists strong opponents of the totalitarian regimes of the time, but one must concede that they were not the most outspoken anti-Fascists. For example, rather than openly or directly fighting National Socialism and its aggressive ideology, activists instead concentrated on devising a positive conception of democracy, pluralism and the rule of law. The representatives of the Nordic associations also expressed (self-) criticism and pointed to bygone periods in Nordic history where people enjoyed little personal freedom and ruler attempted to restrict local self-governance. However, 'Nordic democracy' was ultimately

---

denna grundval har man sedan byggt vidare genom århundraden; formerna ha visserligen förändrats och utvecklats men grunden har icke förändrats utan förblivit densamma'].

44 Nordström, W.E. (1942) 'Nordiska perspektiv'. In *Finsk Tidskrift* Vol. 132, 1–10, 3–5.

45 Bergquist 1946, 51–52. ['Kravet på att dessa rättigheter lämnas obeskurna är djupt grundat hos de nordiska folken. Talet om Norden som en frihetens stamort på jorden är ej ett tomt tal, som den moderna tidens människor funnit på för att skänka glans åt sin historia, utan däri ligger en levande realitet. Frihetskänslan, stundom obändig och fordrande, är ett av de mest framträdande kännetecknen för Nordens folk.'].

seen as an underlying current in the region's history, which even the fiercest absolutist or anti-democratic rulers could not eliminate. The basic principles of democracy which formed the foundation of the Nordic countries' liberal characteristics and constitutions were deemed to be unshakeable and firm.[46] In the face of the totalitarian threat, it was clear to the pro-Nordic activists of the time that military force, terror and dictatorship endangered the continued existence of Nordic liberty and Nordic democracy. Torsten Nothin, who headed the Nordic Association in Sweden, spoke the following words of warning in November 1939:

> We do not want to see the culture we have painstakingly erected smashed into pieces. We do not want to see our ancient freedom of thought and of belief or our right to steer our country as it pleases us, be trampled upon. We do not want to see our legal system, which has grown from generation to generation, be eradicated. Our spiritual strivings shall not be undone, and we *want* to cede the land, which our fathers have won for us, to those, who will come after us, *freely* as an inheritance.
> The sense for these values is deeply rooted among the Nordic peoples. It is their joint view of the world, which makes the Nordic countries among themselves take a special position in the world. Here up in the North there is a small group of people with one common feature: an uncompromising love of one's own freedom and tied to it, respect for the right of self-determination of other peoples.[47]

Some authors also pointed out that Nordic democracy was both a concept for domestic politics and for international relations. According to a train of thought which the Finnish diplomat and expert on international law Rafael Erich expressed in a publication from 1944, constitutional law on the domestic side was tied to the support for peaceful international relations and for structures of conflict resolution on the foreign policy side. In addition, the common legal tradition had facilitated the harmonisation of Nordic legislation which was started in the inter-war period. A further link between domestic and foreign politics existed in the fact that a state based on the rule of law was obliged to protect its existence against external threats.[48] Defending the principle of liberty meant, according to Suviranta,

---

46 Bergquist 1946, 55–57.
47 Universitetsbiblioteket Lund, Handskriftssektionen, Torsten Nothin, efterlämnade papper, 33, Tal 1938–1941, Tal vid Föreningen Nordens högtidsmöte Nov. 1939 ['Vi vilja ej se den kultur, som har mödosamt byggts upp, bli slagen i spillror. Vi vilja ej se vår gamla tanke- och trosfrihet eller vår rätt att själva styra och ställa i eget land trampas under fötterna. Vi vilja ej se vårt under generation efter generation framvuxna rättssystem utplånas. Våra ideella strävanden skola ej göras om intet, och den bygd, som våra fäder brutit åt oss, den *vilja vi* lämna *fri* i arv åt dem, som komma efter oss. / Känslan för dessa värden är fast rotad hos de nordiska folken. Det är denna deras gemensamma livsssyn, som gör att de nordiska folken kommit att inbördes intaga en särställning i världen. Här uppe i Norden finnes en liten grupp folk med ett gemensamt grunddrag: En okuvlig kärlek till egen frihet och en därmed förknippad respekt för andra folks självbestämningsrätt.'] (original emphasis).
48 Erich, Rafael (1944) 'Nordisk rätt och Nordens rätt.' In Tallqvist 1944, 37–40, at 40.

that the Nordics would have to close their ranks in order to guard their achievements. In this context he also pointed to the Finnish dilemma, which arose from a conflict between fending off the danger which the war meant for all Nordic countries and co-operating with the 'Third Reich'. How could one act in defence of democracy while being brother in arms with *the* enemy of democracy?

> This must also mean that we build a joint front for the defence of the intellectual heritage of freedom of Norden: the democratic order of society, freedom of thought, principles of the rule of law, humanity. A fatherland without freedom is a great word of little importance as already our famous fellow countryman Anders Chydenius put it. Therefore we cannot simultaneously defend Norden and support such forces which want to destroy our Nordic heritage of liberty.[49]

This was actually one of few hints in the general discussion to the discrepancy between Finnish rhetorics of liberty and the concurrent compromises of the Finnish position that the quasi-alliance with Nazi Germany caused. Perhaps the Finns had only become aware of their own ideals too late and not stressed them enough, as Suviranta pointed out in 1943. The longer the war lasted, the clearer it was for the Finns that they needed to stand 'on the right side' after the war, namely on the side of the Western democracies. Besides the so-called peace opposition in Finland,[50] the Nordic activists were some of the first ones to openly demand a stronger positioning of Finland as part of the democratic world. Suviranta held:

> Now the forces have to be pooled. First a broad programme of activity would have to be prepared, which could genuinely unite broad and far-reaching circles, and a public statement should be passed in which both the common foundation of culture and also the common belief in the Nordic ideals of liberty became visible: the free society, legal protection, intellectual freedom, democracy and the lawful order of society. One could have stressed these already earlier.[51]

---

49 Unpublished manuscript. KA Hki, Bruno Suvirannan kokoelma, 8, Puheita 1917–1967, Norden, puhe edustajakokouksen päivällisillä 30.9.1943. ['Det måste också betyda, att vi bilda gemensam front i försvar för Nordens andliga frihetsarv: det [sic!] folkstyrda samhällsordningen, tankefriheten, principer om rättstat, humaniteten. Ett fädernesland utan frihet är ett stord ord av liten betydelse sade sedan vår store landsman Anders Chydenius. Vi kunna därför inte samtidigt försvara Norden och befrämja sådana krafter vilka vilja förstöra vårt nordiska frihetsarv'].

50 Cf. Viitala, Heikki Mikko (1969) *Rauhanoppositio. Tutkimus poliitisesta oppositiosta Suomessa vuosina 1940–1944.* Helsinki: Kansankulttuuri.

51 KA Hki, Bruno Suvirannan kokoelma, 37, Toiminta Pohjola-Norden:issa, Norden-yhdistys 8.2.1943 ['Nyt olisi koottuva voimat yhteen. Ensimmäiseksi olisi laadittava laaja toimintaohjelma, joka todella voisi yhdistää laajat ja syvät piirit, sekä hyväksyttävä julkilausuma, jossa näkyviin sekä yhteinen kulttuuripohja sekä yhteinen usko pm. vapausihanteisiin: vapaa yhteiskunta, oikeusturva, henkinen vapaus, kansanvalta ja laillinen yhteiskuntajärjestys. Niitä olisi voinut aikaisemminkin enemmän alleviivata.'].

Besides the cultural heritage, one also repeatedly connected the terms 'freedom' and 'law' with the term 'heritage': cultural heritage, heritage of liberty, legal heritage. This expression – instead of using, for example, 'traditions' – had a much stronger emotional impact and connotations of family bonds and thus also alluded to the idea of the Nordic family of states and peoples. The term 'heritage' was much more binding than 'traditions' – a heritage must be guarded; one pays tribute to the wishes of the forefathers and one takes over the obligation to pass on the heritage to the next generation. In this case, the roots of the democratic heritage lay in ancient traditions of freedom, self-administration and constitutional or law-bound rule. As in 'real life', a heritage does not stay exactly the same. New elements are incorporated into it, and some things might get lost. But the red thread that ran from the Middle Ages until modern times had, in the eyes of the pro-Nordic activists, grown into 'Nordic democracy'. One could also sum up their view in such a manner that liberty and rule of law were the foundations of a common Nordic political culture, while 'Nordic democracy' became this political culture's most concrete and practical manifestation.

A common democratic political culture

> This peculiar feature of the Nordic world view already comes to the fore in the conception of society among the Nordic peoples. [...] Since time immemorial the authoritarian state has been foreign to their nature. The state of fellow citizens is their natural social order, which they understand and with which they identify themselves. Their philosophy of life is also rather constant. They have always felt the same will for independence and self-administration, the same passion for the freedom of thought and of faith, the same respect for the law and for the legal heritage.[52]

This quotation from 1942 comes from the chairman of the Swedish *Nordic Association*, Torsten Nothin, and can be seen as a short political credo which stands for all of the democratic pro-Nordic movement. For Nothin as well as for many other Nordic activists, the common perception of life and of a sound social order was based on liberty, pluralism and democracy. These would be cornerstones of the political edifice of a united *Norden* and they would be necessary preconditions for the creation of political unity. 'To yield a firm community between them (the Nordic peoples, JHS), first and foremost a congruence of the fundamental conception and the world

---

52 Nothin, Torsten (1942) 'Det nordiska arvet och folkrörelserna'. In *Nordens årsbok* 1942, 7–10, 9 ['Den nordiska livssynens egenart framträder redan i de nordiska folkens samhällsbegrepp. [...] Från urgamla tider har överhetsstaten varit något för dem väsensfrämmande. Det är medborgarstaten, som är deras naturliga samhällsordning, vilken de förstå och med vilken de känna samhörighet. Deras livsuppfattning har också varit ganska konstant. De ha alltid hyst samma vilja till oberoende och självstyre, samma lidelse för tankens och trons frihet, samma aktning för lagen och rättsarvet.']

view is required.'[53] Rather than seeing Northern Europe as a region defined by geography, Nothin defined *Norden* as a community of values. Those things held in the highest esteem by all Nordics were 'our language, our culture building on Nordic ground, inherited from past generations, our self-government by the people, our freedom of thought and belief, our law and order'.[54]

The liberal heritage was stressed by most authors from the different Nordic countries, who often traced this heritage back to ancient times. Thus, the democratic political culture of *Norden* could bolster its authority by invoking its longevity and long history. According to Bent Wellejus, traces of this culture could even be found during the time of the Vikings: '*Politically speaking*, we have the same attitude. We might surely recognize that democracy has its shortcomings, *but the democratic fundamental idea is deeply rooted within Nordic man since the earliest times*. Just think of the Vikings, who would answer proudly: "we have no chief, we are all free men"!'[55] The policy of the common Nordic state should be based upon the 'constitutional conception, which has been created here in Norden throughout the centuries gone. Already the Viking Age's conception of the state knew how to combine respect for the individual and for the many.'[56] as Karl Bøgholm, leading figure in the Danish pro-Nordic association *The Free North* (Det frie Nord[57]) wrote. He was convinced that the Nordic countries would not need to adapt foreign ideologies to master their political future, but that it would suffice for them to look into their own past where they would find those traditions, with the help of which they could lead a free national life.[58] In a publication about Nordic solidarity, edited by the Nordic Association in Sweden, this look into the past was further defined: popular

53 Nothin, Torsten (1943) 'Samhörighetskänslan mellan de nordiska folken'. In *Nordens Tidning*, Vol. 1, Issue 1, 4–7 + 35, at 35 ['För att dem emellan åvägabringa en fast gemenskap fordras först och främst överensstämmande i grundåskådning och livssyn.'].

54 Nothin 1943, 6 ['vårt språk, vår på nordisk grund byggande kultur, ärvd från bortgångna släkten, vårt folkliga självstyre, vår tanke- och trosfrihet, vår lag och rätt'].

55 Wellejus, Bent (1941) 'Nordens Enhed'. In *Det frie Nord* Vol. 1, Issue 3, 3 (original emphasis). Wellejus (1914–1994) was a student of law at the time of the war and one of the active members of the Association *The Free North* in Denmark.

56 Bøgholm, Karl (1942a) 'Statsforbund eller forbundsstat?'. In *Det frie Nord* Vol. 2, Issue 6a, 8–10, at 9–10. ['den statslige Retsopfattelse, der er skabt her i Norden gennem de svundne Aarhundreder. Allerede Vikingetidens Statsopfattelse forstod at forene Hensyn til den ene og de mange.'].

57 This association was founded in 1939 amidst the wave of pro-Finnish sympathy caused by the Winter War. Originally devoted to supporting Danish volunteers, it changed its direction after the Winter War ended and after Denmark had been occupied on 9 April 1940. Very soon, the association developed a programme which was pro-Nordic co-operation very akin to that of the Nordic Association of 1919. The two institutions competed with each other until the end of the war, when they united under the name of the more established Nordic Association. Cf. the memories of The Free North's chairman Erik With (1954). 'Et Tilbageblik over mit Virke som Formand for Foreningen "Det frie Nord" 1940–1945'. In V[iggo].O[scar]. Harrel (ed.) (1954) *Generalløjtnant Erik With og 'Det frie Nord'*. [København] 1954, 36–70.

58 Bøgholm, Karl (1942b) 'Nordens forenede Stater'. In *Det frie Nord* Vol. 2, Issue 6, 1 & 7–9, at 7.

self-government had its roots in local self-rule by the free peasants of the North. Surely this could not be deemed democratic, but the participation of the lower classes in political life already in the Middle Ages was seen as an important reason for strong political commitment by all social classes in the *Norden* of today. Local autonomy and the people's participation in nation-wide politics were 'insolubly tied together in our Nordic democracies' and the interleaving political, local and nation-wide arenas facilitated the resolution of practical matters. 'This way, the communal self-government has become Nordic democracy's power source and strong backbone.'[59]

The uniform democratic political culture of *Norden* was seen as one of the most important reasons why the region was so well suited for closer co-operation. Political developments in recent history had followed a stable course of continuity and change had always happened without the need for violent uprising (with the exception of Finland). The long history of the Danish and Swedish parliaments was seen as one factor which helped democracy make the breakthrough to the modern age. Parallel to many other discourses about Nordic identity, hierarchies were being established when it came to defining the North. This also holds true for the discourse concerning 'Nordic democracy', when, for example, Tingsten argued that Swedish, Norwegian and Danish democracies enjoyed greater stability and a more widespread application of democratic principles. In contrast, Finland had shown instability, violence and authoritarian tendencies; her development resembled that of Poland and the Baltic states. Thanks to Finland's overall orientation towards the Scandinavian countries, Finnish democracy aligned itself with the Nordic countries again.[60]

The Nordicness of Nordic democratic practice

Herbert Tingsten also addressed the issue of the Nordicness of Nordic democracy: 'The question does arise then, if it is justified to speak of a Nordic democracy, i.e. to which extent do the Nordic democracies show crucial common features.'[61] Besides the principles which were being formulated about Nordic democracy, statements were also being made about Nordic democracy in everyday practice. These concerned the character of political debate, certain features of the political system, and aspects of the overall conception of Nordic political culture. Already, the composition of the national parliaments, according to Tingsten, belonged 'from a social point of view [...] to the most democratic in the world'.[62] Most democratically elected representatives in other countries showed an over-representation of the higher classes of society, and while this tendency was not completely absent from the Nordic countries, it was not as extensive as in, for example,

---

59 Sävström, August and Andrén, Nils (1946) 'Det folkliga självstyret'. In Föreningen Norden 1946, 59–76, at 72–73.
60 Tingsten 1940, 56–57.
61 Tingsten 1940, 56.
62 Tingsten 1938, 41.

France or the USA. In *Norden*, different social classes or occupational groups were more often represented by their peers. Additionally, there were no restrictions on which groups were eligible for parliament and which were not. The greater participation of 'non-professional' politicians influenced the matter-of-fact-style of parliamentary debate and of overall political life.[63] The actual parliamentary work taking place in the committees of the Nordic parliaments and the opinions being discussed across party lines has made solemn speeches in the plenum superfluous. Nordic democratic practice was down-to-earth and devoid of any artificial elements. The ideal example for Tingsten was France, with its heated discussions, where 'sharp-witted and simultaneously passionate statements are typical, applause and protests egg on and confuse the speaker, at great occasions the discussion becomes a dramatic showdown between crucial ideas'.[64] The picture he painted of the Nordic countries served to stress how much Nordic democratic practice was focussed on the actual problems and their solutions, thus outlining a Nordic culture of compromise and consensus. The representative bodies had 'to a lesser degree than in many other countries served as a platform for brilliant rhetoric and dramatic settlements, but their activity has in critical periods been shaped by a dispassionate objectiveness which makes it justified to speak of a working democracy'.[65] Parliamentary debates in the Nordic countries were rhetorically not very elaborate, applause was either weak or even forbidden by parliamentary regulations; speeches in parliament that were linguistically pompous, ideologically charged or politically passionate were usually laughed at or caused estrangement. Interjections, protests or heated replies were generally unacceptable. 'The overall impression is an everyday calmness, in which boredom is being ameliorated by a comfortable and friendly comradeship.'[66]

Nordic democracy was defined as being matter-of-fact, oriented towards compromise, and free of ideological conflicts. Its main characteristics were pragmatism, consensus-orientation and de-ideologisation.[67] In the discourses about Nordic democracy, continuity and stability were closely linked to democracy. The deep roots of Nordic political culture had made it possible for the Nordic countries to remain democratic and stable. The notion that was already developing during the 1930s – namely that Norden belonged to the shrinking group of European democracies – was held on to during the war and turned into one of the important aspects of 'Nordic democracy'. The sole fact of its continued existence served to reinforce the image of its strength and again added to the image of continuity. Tingsten also claimed that the outside world was aware of Nordic democracy enduring:

63 Tingsten 1940, 75.
64 Tingsten 1940, 78.
65 Tingsten 1938, 41 ['De nordiska representationerna [...] ha i mindre grad än många andra länders tjänat som platform för lysande retorik och dramatiska uppgörelser, men deras verksamhet har under kritiska perioder präglats av en lidelsefri saklighet som ger rätt att tala om en arbetets demokrati.'].
66 Tingsten 1940, 78.
67 Cf. Friis 1941, 14–15.

The young Nordic democracies have during the latter years become internationally known in a totally different way than earlier. They have been studied and admired by foreign observers. The precondition for this is the global crisis, which all at once also became a crisis of democracy. The Nordic countries have until now gone through this crisis without at all – or at least not to a considerable degree – changing their democratic institutions, and Norden has due to come to stand out for great parts of the world as the foremost example for a successful democratic order and thus as proof for the democratic system's effectiveness and adaptability.[68]

The Dane Finn T. B. Friis – trying to restrain overly high spirits – thought of the Nordic countries as an example to the world concerning democracy: 'The thought of letting Norden *stand out as an example* seems at this moment to be highly pretentious. But may we with due modesty be allowed to reckon, that there are joint Nordic values, which, if saved, could serve the world!'[69] When dictatorship and totalitarianism dominated almost all of Europe, it was well worth preserving democratic ideals, at least somewhere. Yet it has to be questioned if *Norden* became a sanctuary for universal democracy or if this was instead a withdrawal to the special Nordic type of democracy. In any case, in the wartime the concept served the purpose of defining what Nordic was. The 'defence of democracy' was combined with both Nordic and national overtones: for example, in Denmark, democracy and the rule of law became popular topics in self-study and popular educational contexts.[70]

Conclusions

Wartime discourses about Nordic democracy were an integral part of the ongoing debate about political collaboration between the Nordic countries after the war. The hypothetical United States of *Norden* were based on democratic and parliamentarian principles. Several other crucial values were constantly discussed in connection with the concept of Nordic democracy, as illustrated by the chairman of the Danish Association *The Free North*

68 Tingsten 1940, 56 ['De unga nordiska demokratierna ha under senare år blivit internationellt kända på ett helt annat sätt än tidigare. Förutsättningen härför är den världskris, som på en gång blivit en demokratins kris. De nordiska länderna ha hittills genomgått denna kris utan att alls – eller åtminstone icke i mera väsentlig grad – ändra sina demokratiska institutioner, och Norden har därför för stora delar av världen kommit att framstå som det främsta exemplet på en framgångsrik demokratisk ordning och därmed som ett bevis på det demokratiska systemets effektivitet och anpassningsförmåga.'].

69 Friis 1941, 17 ['Tanken om at lade Norden *fremstaa som Eksempel* i Øjeblikket synes rigelig fordringsfuld. Men det maa være os tilladt i al Beskedenhed at mene, at der er fællesnordiske Værdier, som Verden kan være tjent med at bevare!'].

70 See Hecker-Stampehl, Jan (2010) Erziehung zur Demokratie. Staatsbürgerkunde im Dänischen Staatsrundfunk während der Besatzungszeit. In Norbert Götz, Jan Hecker-Stampehl, Stephan Michael Schröder (eds) *Vom alten Norden zum neuen Europa: Politische Kultur im Ostseeraum. Festschrift für Bernd Henningsen.* Berlin: Berliner Wissenschafts-Verlag, 95–116.

Erik With,[71] who opened a speech in November 1941 by talking about the 'ideal of freedom, which is a common philosophy of life for all of Norden, the freedom of the people on which the democratic peoples of Norden have erected their life and their cultural acts, the freedom based on law, which rests upon an indispensable sense of justice'.[72] The concept of Nordic democracy was thus put into a broader context and the strong emphasis which was put on liberty and the rule of law is striking. Since the authors who strove to lend 'Nordic democracy' a longer past and an ancient character were very much aware of the fact that democracy as political practice was still very young in Northern Europe, they pointed to other values which then formed the earliest historical roots. Thus it became possible to extend proto-democratic traditions back to the time of the Vikings.

The connections between liberty, the rule of law and democracy also made the delineations between different forms of government clearer. The Finnish political scientist K.R. Brotherus argued for the close connection and interdependence of these three terms:

> Liberty, democracy and, as a precondition for both of these, a high esteem of the sanctity of the law are from my point of view most typical for the Nordic conception of the state. If the sense for law is missing or strongly weakened, both the aforementioned should also go to waste. The experience from the Roman Empire's time and up till our own days shows, that a democracy without a deeply rooted constitutional consciousness will pave the way for dictatorship and thus freedom would also be doomed.[73]

As in most other constructions of identities, the construction of 'Nordic democracy' relied on history. Even though nobody claimed that the forms of local autonomy and self-administration had much in common with modern day democratic political practice, it was easy to find convincing arguments that they had contributed to the fertile ground upon which Nordic democracy had developed. This historical lineage also served to rhetorically undermine the power of resistance against the threats that were posed against democracy. There was a need to assure oneself that the Nordic democracies could last – and since there was no other weapon to use for this purpose, the

---

71 Erik With (1869–1959) was the former chief of staff of the Danish army. For biographical details, see Hedegaard, Ole A.: *En general og hans samtid. General Erik With mellem Stauning og kaos.* Fredrikssund [1990].

72 With, Erik (1941) 'Nordens Fremtid'. In *Det frie Nord* Vol. 1, Issue 3, 1 + 12, 1 ['det Frihedsideal, som er et fælles Livssyn for hele Norden, den Folkefrihed, paa hvilken Nordens demokratiske Folk har bygget deres Liv og Kulturgerning, den lovbundne Frihed, der hviler paa en umistelig Retsbevisthed.'].

73 Brotherus, K.R. (1944) 'Om nordisk statsuppfattning'. In Tallqvist 1944, 19–21, at 21 ['Friheten, demokratien och, som förutsättning för dessa båda, en hög uppfattning av det rättas helgd äro enligt mitt förmenande det mest betecknande för nordisk statsuppfattning. Om känslan för det rätta saknades eller starkt försvagades, skulle även de båda förstnämnda värdena gå till spillo. Erfarenheten från det romerska väldets tider och ända fram till våra dagar visar, att en demokrati utan ett fast rotat rättsmedvetande lägger grunden för diktatur och att därmed också friheten är dömd till undergång.'].

pro-Nordic activists used words. In the wartime rhetoric of the pro-Nordic activists 'Nordic democracy' became a cornerstone of national and regional identity construction, as well as a promise of a better life in the post-war world. One could argue that there was at least one small corner in Europe, apart from the British Isles, where democracy had managed to survive. The seeds for the self-perception of the Nordics in the Cold War times were thus partially already sown during the Second World War.

BIBLIOGRAPHY

Almgren, Birgitta, Hecker-Stampehl, Jan, Piper, Ernst (2008) 'Alfred Rosenberg und die Nordische Gesellschaft – Der "nordische Gedanke" in Theorie und Praxis'. *NORDEUROPAforum. Zeitschrift für Politik, Wirtschaft und Kultur N.F.*, Vol. 11, Issue 2, 7–51.

Beskow, Gunnar (1940) *Sveriges uppgift.* Stockholm: Bonnier.

Beskow, Gunnar (1941) 'Demokratins framtidslinje'. In Inga Bagger-Sjöbäck and Elsa Cedergren (eds), *Diskussion om demokratin.* Stockholm: Bonnier, 177–194.

Blidberg, Kersti (1984) *Splittrad gemenskap. Kontakter och samarbete inom nordisk socialdemokratisk arbetarrörelse 1931–1945.* Stockholm: Almqvist & Wiksell (= Acta Universitatis Stockholmiensis; 32).

Bøgholm, Karl (1942a) 'Statsforbund eller forbundsstat?'. *Det frie Nord* Vol. 2, Issue 6a, 8–10.

Bøgholm, Karl (1942b) 'Nordens forenede Stater.' *Det frie Nord* Vol. 2, Issue 6.

Fransson, Evald (1945) *Fostran till nordisk gemenskap.* Stockholm: Geber (= Almqvist & Wiksells psykologisk-pedagogiska bibliotek; 2).

Föreningen Norden (ed.) (1946) *Nordisk samhörighet en realitet.* Stockholm: Ählén & Söners Förlag.

Friis, Finn T.B. (1941) *Nordisk Kulturfællesskab og praktisk nordisk Samarbejde.* København: Foreningen Norden (= Nordisk Oplysning; II).

Hecker-Stampehl, Jan (2006a) 'Finnland – Teil des Nordens? Das eigene Andere auf der mentalen Landkarte Nordeuropas'. In Norbert Götz, Jörg Hackmann, Jan Hecker-Stampehl (eds) *Die Ordnung des Raums: Mentale Landkarten in der Ostseeregion.* Berlin: Berliner Wissenschaftsverlag (= Die Ostseeregion: Nördliche Dimensionen – Europäische Perspektiven; 6), 150–185.

Hecker-Stampehl, Jan (2006b) 'Vorposten des Nordens? Finnland als Bollwerk des Abendlandes in Veröffentlichungen aus dem Zweiten Weltkrieg'. In Aleksanteri Suvioja and Erkki Teräväinen (eds) *Kahden kulttuurin välittäjä. Hannes Saarisen juhlakirja.* Helsinki: Helsingin yliopiston historian laitos (= Helsingin yliopiston historian laitoksen julkaisuja; 20), 313–326.

Hecker-Stampehl, Jan (2007) 'Föderationspläne in Nordeuropa im Zweiten Weltkrieg. Ein Überblick'. In Sturm-Martin, Imke and Jan Hecker-Stampehl (eds) *Europa im Blick: westeuropäische Perspektiven im 20. Jahrhundert. Festschrift für Clemens A. Wurm.* Hamburg: Verlag Dr. Kovač, 119–139.

Hecker-Stampehl, Jan (2009) *Vereinigte Staaten des Nordens – Die Debatte der Norden-Vereine in Dänemark, Schweden und Finnland über ein geeintes Nordeuropa im Zweiten Weltkrieg.*

Hecker-Stampehl, Jan (2010) 'Erziehung zur Demokratie. Staatsbürgerkunde im Dänischen Staatsrundfunk während der Besatzungszeit'. In Norbert Götz, Jan Hecker-Stampehl, Stephan Michael Schröder (eds) *Vom alten Norden zum neuen Europa: Politische Kultur im Ostseeraum. Festschrift für Bernd Henningsen.* Berlin: Berliner Wissenschafts-Verlag, 95–116.

Hornborg, Eirik (1943) *Den nordiska tanken. Föredrag vid den nordiska festen i Jakobstad den 2 oktober 1943.* Jakobstad: Föreningen Norden.

Janfelt, Monika (2005) *Att leva i den bästa av världar. Föreningarna Nordens syn på Norden 1919–1933*. Stockholm: Carlssons.

Kletzin, Birgit (2002) *Europa aus Rasse und Raum. Die nationalsozialistische Idee der Neuen Ordnung*. Münster: LIT Verlag (= Region – Nation – Europa; 2).

Lipgens, Walter (1968) *Europa-Föderationspläne der Widerstandsbewegungen 1940– 1945*. München: Oldenbourg (= Schriften des Forschungsinstituts der Deutschen Gesellschaft für Auswärtige Politik; 26).

Lund, Joachim (2004) 'Denmark and the "European New Order", 1940–1942'. *Contemporary European History* Vol. 13, Issue 3, 305–321.

Lund, Joachim (2005) *Hitlers spisekammer. Danmark og den europæiske nyordning 1940–43*. København: Gyldendal.

Lundbye, Ove (1943) 'Folkestyre'. *Gads danske magasin* vol. 37, 32–43.

Mazower, Mark (2002) 'Pläne für das Goldene Zeitalter'. In Mazower, Mark (ed.) *Der dunkle Kontinent. Europa im 20. Jahrhundert*. Frankfurt a.M.: Fischer-Taschenbuch-Verlag [London 1998].

Mazower, Mark (2008) *Hitler's Empire: Nazi Rule in Occupied Europe*. London: Allen Lane

Meyer-Gohde, Ruth (2006) 'Dänemarks wirtschaftspolitische Reaktion auf die Besetzung des Landes 1940/41'. *NORDEUROPAforum. Zeitschrift für Politik, Wirtschaft und Kultur N.F.* Vol. 9, Issue 2, 51–70.

Neulen, Hans Werner (1987) *Europa und das 3. Reich. Einigungsbestrebungen im deutschen Machtbereich*. München: Universitas Verlag.

Nordström, W.E. (1942) Nordiska perspektiv. *Finsk Tidskrift* Vol. 132, 1–10.

Nothin, Torsten (1942) 'Det nordiska arvet och folkrörelserna'. *Nordens årsbok* 1942, 7–10.

Nothin, Torsten (1943) 'Samhörighetskänslan mellan de nordiska folken'. *Nordens Tidning* Vol. 1, Issue 1, 4–7 + 35.

Oljelund, Stefan (1944) *Arbetarrörelse i Norden*. Stockholm: KFs bokförlag i distribution (= Nordens serie; 6).

Petander, Karl, Kleen, Willy and Örne, Anders (1942) *Nordens förenta stater*. Stockholm: Natur och Kultur.

Suviranta, Bruno (1943) 'Föreningen Nordens verksamhet och syften'. In *För Norden. Föreningen Nordens medlemsblad* vol, Issue 6, 21–26.

Tallqvist, J.O. (ed.) (1944) *Finland för Norden. Uttalanden om vårt nordiska samarbete*. Helsingfors [Finnish edition: *Suomi kuuluu Pohjolaan. Lausuntoja pohjoismaisesta yhteistyöstämme*. Helsinki].

Tingsten, Herbert (1938) 'Nordisk demokrati'. *Nordens kalender*, Vol. 9, 41–50.

Tingsten, Herbert (1940) 'Folkstyret i Norden'. In Karl Petander (ed.) *Nordisk gemenskap. Utgiven av Norden, Svensk förening för nordiskt samarbete*. Stockholm: Kooperativa förbundets bokförlag.

Undset, Sigrid (1943) 'The Democracy of the Nordic People'. *Free World* vol. 4, 211–217.

Vares, Vesa (2003) 'Erich, Rafael (1879–1946)'. In Matti Klinge (ed.) *Suomen kansallisbiografia Vol. 2*. Helsinki: SKS, 617–619.

Viitala, Heikki Mikko (1969) *Rauhanoppositio. Tutkimus poliitisesta oppositiosta Suomessa vuosina 1940–1944*. Helsinki: Kansankulttuuri.

Wahlbäck, Krister, Blidberg, Kersti (eds) (1986) *Samråd i kristid. Protokoll från den nordiska arbetarrörelsens samarbetskommitté 1932–1946*. Stockholm: Kungl. Samfundet för utgivande av handskrifter rörande Skandinaviens historia. Handlingar; 12.

Wellejus, Bent (1941) 'Nordens Enhed'. *Det frie Nord* Vol. 1, Issue 3, 3.

With, Erik (1941) 'Nordens Fremtid'. *Det frie Nord* Vol. 1, Issue 3, 1 + 12.

With, Erik (1954) 'Et Tilbageblik over mit Virke som Formand for Foreningen "Det frie Nord" 1940–1945'. In V[iggo].O[scar]. Harrel (ed.) *Generalløjtnant Erik With og 'Det frie Nord'*. [København] 1954, 36–70.

JEPPE NEVERS

Reformism and 'Nordic Democracy'

A Journey in Danish Political Thought

When the notion Nordic democracy had its momentum in the 1930s, it was primarily social democrats who used the term and thereby coined its meaning. Across the borders of Scandinavia, proponents of 'Nordic democracy' shared the idea that the Nordic countries were, and should continue to be, a stronghold for democracy in Europe. Historically, 'Nordic democracy' rested upon unique traditions of openness and civic participation, and for the future, the road was open for democratic socialism. By looking back to the late nineteenth century and the succeeding decades, this chapter attempts to show why and how the concept of democracy achieved this status in social democratic thought in the interwar period.

In respect of the concept of democracy, the word and its wide range of meanings, it is a pan-European phenomenon that there is a temporal gap between the period identified by R. R. Palmer as the age of the democratic revolution and the breakthrough of the word 'democracy'. Pierre Rosanvallon has shown that, for example in French political discourse, *demokratié* was not a key concept until the period after the Bourbon Restoration.[1] In the Danish case, *demokratie* was almost exclusively used as a pejorative

---

1 Rosanvallon, Pierre (1995) 'The History of the Word 'Democracy' in France', *Journal of Democracy* no. 6/4, 140–154. Benjamin Constant, for example, never felt the need to refer to democracy. In his work, other terms and concepts suffice to describe the ways of the ideal polity. It was during this very period, however, that the term 'democracy' began to work its way back into ordinary political discourse. Yet it came to connote modern egalitarian *society*, not the political regime associated with the classical Greek and Roman republics. The semantic shift was completed in 1835, when Alexis de Tocqueville published the first volume of his *Democracy in America*. But it began much earlier, during the early years of the Bourbon Restoration, as was shown by the famous parliamentary debate of 1822 on freedom of the press. The history of the concept throughout the 18th century is covered in Dippel, Horst (1986) 'Démocratie, Démocrates'. In Reichardt, Rolf & Schmitt, Eberhard (eds.) *Handbuch politisch-sozialer Grundbegriffe in Frankreich, 1680–1820.* Vol. 6., München: Oldenburg. See also Meier, Christian et. al. (1972) 'Demokratie'. In *Geschichtliche Grundbegriffe*, vol. 1. Stuttgart: Klett. Both of these articles focus on the long-term transformation of the classical vocabulary from the mid-18th century until the mid-19th century, whereby they miss, or at least understate, the point stressed by Rosanvallon: the surprisingly late acceptance of the word as signifying a distinctly modern political order.

term until as late as the 1840s, when the fight for a free constitution was in its heyday. Among the founding fathers of the Danish Constitution of 1849, there was a general feeling that the constitution should secure a more *democratic* organisation of the state, but only radical voices with no influence on the final document identified their vision of the new order as that of a democracy; a vision often condemned by the liberal leaders as 'extreme democracy'.[2]

Among the liberals, there was no doubt that the constitution should be the founding document of a constitutional monarchy more or less in line with the classical idea of a mixed constitution, that is, a bicameral parliament being the legislative power and a sovereign King being the executive.[3] A few decades later, progressive groups increasingly demanded that the government directly appointed by the King should not be able to exercise power with a majority of the lower chamber (*Folketinget*) against it, and they began to use *Demokratiet* (the Democracy) as a label for themselves. The primary force behind this rhetorical strategy was the party *Det Forenede Venstre* ('The United Left', a party of agrarian liberals), and since 1901, the fundamental principle in Danish parliamentary politics has been that the government cannot have a parliamentarian majority against it. Thus, in the beginning of the twentieth century, *Demokrati* was no longer as radical a term as it had been in the 1840s, but still it was not on the agenda as a positive *Bewegungsbegriff*.[4] As Bernard Crick has noted about the British case: '"Democracy" was not a term to rally the country.'[5]

In the Danish case, a notable example of this lack of rhetorical appeal is that the fight for women's suffrage, in the period from the 1870s until the final alteration of the constitution in 1915, was never legitimised as a struggle for democracy.[6] Although both the Social Democrats and the non-socialists used 'democracy' as the term for the united opposition against the government, this ancient word still carried radical and negative connotations in many circles. However, this picture began to change after the First World War and the revolutions in Russia. Thus, it is not hard to argue that the concept of democracy, at least in the Danish case, has a long *Sattel-Zeit* stretching from its quiet life in classical political thought to its only gradual acceptance as a modern ideal.[7]

2 Stender-Petersen, Ole (1978) *Kjøbenhavnsposten: Organ for "det extreme Democrati".* Odense: Odense Universitetsforlag. For similar patterns in Germany, cf. Sperber, Jonathan (1991) *Rhineland Radicals: The Democratic Movement and the Revolution of 1848–1849.* Princeton: Princeton University Press.
3 Cf. Bjørn, Claus (1999) *Kampen om Grundloven.* Copenhagen: Fremad.
4 Cf. Koselleck, Reinhart (2006) *Begriffsgeschichten: Studien zur Semantik und Pragmatik der politischen und sozialen Sprache.* Frankfurt am Main: Suhrkamp, 82.
5 Crick, Bernard (2002) *Democracy: A Very Short Introduction.* Oxford: Oxford University Press, 73–75.
6 This is witnessed, for instance, by absence in almost all the articles on suffrage in the journal *Kvinden og Samfundet.*
7 For the idea of a general *Sattel-Zeit* in European political discourse, see Koselleck, Reinhart (1972) 'Einleitung'. In Brunner, Otto, Conze, Werner & Koselleck, Reinhart (eds.) *Geschichtliche Grundbegriffe.* Vol. 1, Stuttgart: Klett.

From labour unions to democratic socialism

In contrast to the British case, and mostly due to the relatively late industrialization of Danish society, there was no real socialist thought in Denmark in the first half of the nineteenth century. Although radical voices entered the political scene as early as in the 1840s,[8] socialist thought is normally considered to have risen during the second half of the nineteenth century, alongside the organization of the early labour movement. This process took place in the 1860s and then especially in the 1870s, when the number of labour unions increased dramatically.[9] Before that time, the most important theorist was Frederik Dreier. Inspired not by Marx and Engels but by Pierre-Joseph Proudhon and Max Stirner, he published a number of writings on the social problems of modern society.[10] Before his early death in 1853, Dreier also had a great influence on the leading principle of *Kjøbenhavns Arbejderforening* (Copenhagen Labour Society), which held, in a utilitarian manner, that the association was to struggle by all legal means for a 'society that will secure everyone the greatest possible outcome of one's own work as well as the full leisure of one's natural right to freedom and independence'.[11]

On a European level, the situation was more developed. In 1864, a number of workers' representatives from many European countries gathered in London to create a common platform for their cause, the First International, dominated by Karl Marx and his collaborates. In 1866, the International made contact with Carl Rejnholdt Jensen from *Kjøbenhavns Arbejderforening*, but it was in 1871 that the Danish division of the International was first established. One of the leading figures at this point was Louis Pio who also presented socialist ideology to a Danish audience that same year in his *Socialistiske Blade I–II*.[12] As shown by Jens Engberg, these writings were not very original in themselves as they were heavily inspired by the German reforming socialist Ferdinand Lassalle.[13] Although Pio identified the task of the socialist movement to be the organization of the working class followed by a struggle against capitalist society, some commentators, and especially those with close ties to the labour movement, have argued that Pio was not a revolutionary socialist but a full-blooded democratic reformist.[14] However, it should also be noted that Pio by the end of the first issue of his

---

8 See Stender-Petersen 1978.

9 Bruun, Henry (1938) *Den faglige Arbejderbevægelse i Danmark indtil Aar 1900.* Copenhagen: Kildeskriftselskabet, 576ff.

10 See Dreier, Frederik (2003) *Samlede skrifter*. Vol. 1–5, Copenhagen: C. A. Reitzel.

11 Levy, Jette Lundbo & Thing, Morten (1973) *Dansk socialistisk teori, 1850–1900*. Copenhagen: Politisk revy, 8: 'Foreningen vil ved alle lovlige Midler virke for en saadan Ordning af Samfundet, som sikrer Enhver dets størst mulige Udbytte af sin personlige Arbejdskraft og den fulde nydelse af Menneskets naturlige Ret til Frihed og Uafhængighed.'

12 Pio, Louis (1974) [1871] *Socialistiske Blade I–II*. Odense: CLIO.

13 Engberg, Jens (1979) *Til arbejdet! Liv eller død! Louis Pio og arbejderbevægelsen*. Copenhagen: Gyldendal, 78–104.

14 See, for instance, Tjørnehøj, Henning (1992) *Louis Pio – folkevækkeren*. Copenhagen: Fremad, 55.

Socialistiske Blade promised that the second would 'expose what it is that we, the workers, want and what we will push through, early or late, with the law or – without it!'[15] As for the term 'democracy', is was not used at all.

One of Pio's most important contributions to Danish history was that he used his newspaper *Socialisten* (The Socialist) to rally a huge meeting in 1872, a meeting that was disrupted and, some would say, violently confronted by the police. Pio was arrested and sentenced to six years in prison for inspiring a revolution.[16] The police's harsh strategy towards the meeting was, no doubt, influenced by the experiences from Paris in 1871. A socialist revolution was indeed a real fear at this time. This also explains why the Danish section of the First International was subsequently outlawed. Despite this, the labour movement grew stronger in the following years. However, the more radical ideology of Pio and the First International was replaced by a pragmatic strategy, focusing on everyday problems rather than abstract theory.

It was also during this period that the concept of democracy became a part of early socialist rhetoric. Even in 1872, one searches in vain for the term 'democracy' in the clash between the workers and the police, but only few years later, 'democracy' became an important part of the rhetoric of the labour movement.[17] In fact, it can be argued that Danish post-1871 socialism became 'democratic' when the labour movement decided to stress that it would only fight by legal means (*lovlige Midler*). In 1873, for instance, it was defined in *Udkast til Love for den demokratiske Arbejderforening* (Outline of Laws for the Democratic Labour Union) that '[t]he main purpose of the union is by all legal means to work for the total political and social equalization of the workers with all other classes of society'.[18] Only one year earlier, before the great meeting and before Pio was imprisoned, we can find a clearly more radical rhetoric:

> Now the poor class is rising [...] It will be a battle of life and death between the rich and the poor, between the noble and the simple, between the capitalist and the worker, between the landlord and the simple farmer, between the man with duties but no rights and the man with rights but no duties.[19]

15 Tjørnehøj 1992, 15: 'fremstille, hvad det er vi, Arbejderne, ønsker og hvad vi vil sætte igennem, sent eller tidligt, med Loven eller – uden den!'

16 In 1875, he was pardoned and resumed his political work, but shortly hereafter, in 1877, he emigrated to the United States together with a colleague of his, Poul Geleff. C. F. Tietgen, the iconic capitalist of this period, paid his travel and thus Pio was for decades considered a traitor in socialist circles.

17 As already mentioned, 'democracy' was often used by radical theorists in the years around 1850, for instance by Frederik Dreier. Thus, the index to his collected writings has more than 100 references to 'democracy'. Dreier 2003, vol. 5, 232.

18 Callesen, Gerd & Lahme, Hans-Norbert (1978) *Den danske arbejderbevægelses programmatiske dokumenter og love (1871 til 1913)*. Odense: Odense Universitetsforlag, 24: 'Foreningens Hovedformaal er ved alle lovlige Midler at virke hen til, at Arbejderne i social og politisk Henseende bliver fuldkommen ligestillede med andre Klasser i Samfundet.'

19 Callesen 1978, 21: 'Nu rejser den uformuende Klasse sig [...] Det bliver en Krig paa Liv

It should also be mentioned that a number of names and titles from the mid-1870s onwards include the concept of democracy. For instance, *Den demokratiske Arbejderforening* (The Democractic Labour Union), the newspaper *Social-Demokraten* (The Social Democrat), and most importantly *Socialdemokratiet* (The Social Democratic Party).

When Pio was released from prison in 1875, he tried to influence the new labour movement. For instance, his fascination for strong leaders led to the suggestion that the chairperson of the new party should have strong executive powers. However, this suggestion led to a severe criticism. For instance, E. W. Klein, the chairperson before Pio's release, argued: 'as soon as a party recognises certain individuals as authorities, it leaves the firm ground of democracy, because the belief in authorities, the blind obedience, the cult of persons, is un-democratic'.[20]

The Social Democratic Party and political democracy

The concept of democracy thus became a central plank of Danish socialist rhetoric during the 1870s when the labour movement decided to fight exclusively by legal means. According to Claus Bryld, a specialist on the reception of European socialism in Denmark, a profoundly democratic conviction is a basic characteristic of Danish socialism in the last decades of the nineteenth century. In many countries, Germany being the most notable example, labour parties were sidelined, but the Danish labour movement was absorbed into the political system quite early.[21] From the mid-1870s onwards, there was no real doubt that the goal was a socialist society and that the means to achieve this goal was a democratic fight. In the 1876 party congress, it was decided that '[t]he Danish Socialist Labour Party is working by all legal means towards a free state and a socialist society'.[22] This meant, in practice, demands for universal suffrage from the age of 22 and the replacement of the existing two-chamber system with a one-chamber parliament that could legislate 'directly through the people'.[23]

As noted by Bryld, this emphasis on direct rule by the people through a one-chamber parliament is different from the idea of a mixed constitution

og Død mellem den Rige og den Fattige, mellem den Fornemme og den Simple, mellem Kapitalisten og Arbejderen, mellem Godsejeren og Husmanden, mellem Manden med Rettigheder uden Pligter og Manden med Pligter uden Rettigheder.'

20 Klein, E. W. (1876) *Socialismen og dens Ledere: En En kritisk Belysning*. Copenhagen, 27: 'saasnart et Parti anerkender bestemte Personer som Autoriteter, forlader det Demokratiets Grundvold, thi Autoritetstroen, den blinde Lydighed, Personkultus, er udemokratisk'.

21 Bryld, Claus (1992) *Den demokratiske socialismes gennembrudsår: Studier i udformningen af arbejderbevægelsens politiske ideologi i Danmark 1884–1916 på den nationale og internationale baggrund*. Copenhagen: Selskabet for forskning i arbeiderbevægelsens historie, 427–428.

22 Lahme, Hans-Norbert (1976) *Det danske Socialdemokratis Gimle-Kongres 1876*. Odense, 33: 'det danske socialdemokratiske Arbejderparti [stræber] ved alle lovlige Midler efter en fri Stat og et socialistisk Samfund'.

23 Lahme 1976, 33–34.

that, broadly following the British tradition, was behind the constitution of 1849. Although the ideal was not direct democracy, but representative democracy, the social democratic leaders clearly stated that the sovereign body was the people. In the next party programme from 1888, this line of thought was developed into the position that important laws should be passed through general referenda.[24]

Although the Social Democratic Party clearly wanted to go far further than *Det forenede Venstre* (The United Left), mostly a party of farmers, they managed to cooperate on a variety of issues. In 1884, the first social democrats became members of the lower chamber, and in 1887 an article in the newspaper *Social-Demokraten* (The Social Democrat) stated that the experiences of the first electoral period lent support to the strategy that the Social Democrats should join forces with *Det forenede Venstre*:

> [W]hen the worker's representatives suggested economic support for the unemployed, improvement to living conditions, by which productivity would increase, cancellation of poor relief, and protection of spare-time in the holidays, those suggestions encountered resistance from the rich and the representatives of the rich in the upper chamber, while the more democratic group of farmers wanted to support our interests.[25]

In other words, the Social Democratic Party wanted and managed to cooperate with other reform groups and this strategy was received in a positive way. In a pamphlet from 1898, the leader of *Det forenede Venstre*, J. C. Christensen, who would later become Prime Minister, wrote: 'Here [in Denmark, JN], the Social Democratic Party is a parliamentarian party that strives towards its goals through participation in the parliamentary work and not through revolutionary premises.'[26]

However, this pragmatic strategy also drew criticism from within the labour party. In 1889, Gerson Trier and Nicolaj Petersen, both fierce critics of the reformist strategy, founded the newspaper *Arbejderen* (The Worker) that became the primary medium of revolutionary socialism in the following years. Later that same year, social democratic leaders chose to expel the two left-wing opponents who then created a new party, *Det revolutionære socialistiske Arbejderparti*. However, this party was short-

---

24 Callesen & Lahme 1978, 89.
25 Togeby, Lise (1968) *Var de så røde? Tekster og dokumenter til belysning af Social-demokratiets gennembrudsår.* Copenhagen: Fremad, 40: 'naar Arbejdernes Repræsentanter indbragte Forslag om *Understøttelse til Arbejdsløse*, om *Forbedring af Beboelsesforhold*, hvorved det *produktive arbejde forøgedes*, om *Eftergivelse af Fattighjælp* og *Beskyttelse af Fritiden paa Søn- og Helligdage*, da stødte disse Forslag paa *Modstand* netop hos de Rige og netop hos de Riges Repræsentation i Landstinget; medens den mere demokratiske Bondestand dog vilde fremme vore Interesser'.
26 Christensen, J. C. (1898) *Venstrereformpartiet.* Copenhagen: Jul. Gjellerup, 35: 'Hos os er Socialdemokratiet et parlamentarisk Parti, der tilstræber Virkeliggørelsen af sine Formaal gennem Deltagelse i det parlamentariske Arbejde og ikke ved revolutionære Foranstaltninger.'

lived and the newspaper ran into difficulties when Petersen was imprisoned for his political activities.

Interestingly, the word 'democracy' seldom appears in the many debates between the social democratic leaders and their left-wing opposition. There were exceptions, however. In 1906, for instance, Trier mentions that the Social Democratic Party focuses on 'democractic' questions instead of 'social' ones.[27] The overall picture is, nevertheless, that democracy was not on the agenda in the debates between the socialist factions. The few revolutionary socialists never really managed to form a meaningful opposition to the left of the Social Democrats. As for the social democratic leaders, their task was to explain that the pragmatic line was truly socialist and in fact far more revolutionary than the supposedly revolutionary one.

The socialist vision of an absolute democracy

In the formation of the social democratic strategy, the idea of an organic revolution became central. The idea was connected to an important two-fold definition of democracy in which the term was used to describe political democracy, which was representative democracy with universal suffrage, as well as a future society of equality – an absolute democracy. Thus, there was never any doubt that the strategy was a socialist strategy, and if there is any difference between this position and the revisionist tradition within Marxist thought, it is that the Danish Social Democrats did not position themselves as 'revisionists' but instead, as we shall see below, as real revolutionaries since profound change happens slowly.[28] In 1889, for instance, P. Knudsen, the leading theorist in the 1880s and the 1890s, stressed the socialist principle:

> The Social Democratic Party is working for the creation of a totally new foundation of society by claiming that all means of production shall be the property of the society in contrast to the present situation where they belong to one single class [...] The Social Democratic Party will remove the cause of this exploitation and thereby make it impossible. This goal is a revolutionary goal and reaching it will be a revolution.[29]

Here, the most interesting aspect is not the revolutionary rhetoric, but the supplementary idea of an organic revolution, which is quite different from the idea of revolution as a sudden break: 'The reformist movement serves to

---

27 Christensen 1898, 125.

28 For the ideas of evolution and gradual change in early Danish socialist thought cf. Bryld, Claus (2004) 'De klassiske socialdemokratisk grundholdninger'. Bryld, Claus (ed.) *Den socialdemokratiske idéarv*. Roskilde: Roskilde universitetsforlag.

29 Togeby 1968, 47: 'Socialdemokratiet tilstræber at skabe et fuldstændig nyt Grundlag for Samfundsordningen ved at fordre, at alle Arbejdsmidler skal være Samfundsejendom i Modsætning til, at de nu ejes af en enkelt Klasse [...] Socialdemokratiet vil fjærne Aarsagen til Udbytningen og derved umuliggøre denne. Dette Formaal er revolutionært og dets Opnaaelse en Revolution.'

develop and cultivate the workers' understanding of the tasks that lie ahead as well as it prepares them to take over control of society and thereby works towards solving the revolutionary task of the Social Democratic Party: the creation of a new society.'[30]

Thus, as early as the 1880s, a reformist agenda was in place and the double-sided conception of democracy gained a central position in rhetorical strategy.[31] Even writers who were critical of revolutionary rhetoric and preferred 'democracy' to 'socialism', used this binary concept of democracy. In 1895, for instance, an anonymous Social Democrat argued that the Social Democratic Party should position itself more clearly as a party of 'the Democracy' (*Demokratiet*) since this would not mean that one would surrender to the bourgeoisie but would take only the first step on the road that leads to a socialist society:

> Somewhere [...] I have seen the quite misleading explanation that 'the democracy' should feel fully satisfied as soon as it has reached the fulfilment of the consequences of the democratic principle: universal suffrage and totally equality regarding all civic rights. [...] *The consequences of the democratic principle are not just political equalization but also, and mostly, those social changes that become a consequence of the democratic form of rule.*[32]

Thus, the idea was neither that democracy is about equality regarding civic rights, nor that democracy is, as in the writings of Lenin, a bourgeois structure that needs to be transcended. Instead, democracy is conceived of as a principle that once fully acknowledged in a political structure, will automatically lead to a social revolution.

As a matter of fact, this anonymous writer almost prophetically sketched what would become the recipe for a victorious strategy throughout the twentieth century: social equality as the goal and parliamentary legislation as the means. With references to the developments in other countries the author encouraged the Social Democratic Party to whole-heartedly join

---

30 Togeby 1968, 48: 'Den reformatoriske Bevægelse tjener saaledes til at udvikle og modne Arbejdernes Forstaaelse af den Opgave, de har at løse, samt til selv at kunne overtage Ledelsen af Samfundets Anliggender, og den virker derved henimod Løsningen af Socialdemokratiets revolutionære Opgave: Tilvejebringelsen af en ny Samfundsordning.'

31 This idea was not, however, a complete novelty in socialist thought. Long before the revolutionary rhetoric of the early 1870s, Frederik Dreier, for instance, identified democracy as a political principle that would, in time, lead to an organic and peaceful revolution. See Dreier 2003, vol. 1, 75ff.

32 Anonymous (1895) *Demokrati og Socialdemokrati*. Copenhagen, 2: 'Jeg har et Sted – jeg erindrer ikke mere hvor – set fremsat den i hvert Fald noget misvisende Forklaring af Demokratiets Maal, at Demokratiet føler sig fuldt sig fuldt tilfredsstillet, saa snart det har opnaaet Gennemførelsen af det demokratiske Princips politiske Konsekvenser: almindelige Stemmeret og absolut Lighed med Hensyn til alle statsborgerlige Rettigheder [...] *Det demokratiske Princips Konsekvenser er ikke blot politisk Ligestillelse, men ogsaa, og i Særdeleshed, netop de sociale Omformninger, der ville blive en Følge af et demokratisk Styresæt.*'

forces with other progressive groups as long as the common interest also served this strategy:

> [W]hen this first goal is achieved, then no human power can make us not set a new one. [...] What we need is first and foremost that the idea of the people's sovereignty is fully acknowledged. *This* is the first and most important political goal. Regardless of whether they call themselves Left [*Venstre*] or Social Democrats, all good democrats ought to unite around the realisation of this task. When this goal is reached, it is time to find a solution to the big problems.[33]

In his work on *Den socialistiske Fremtidsstat* (The Future Socialist State), Gustav Bang, in 1903, further developed this socialist vision of democracy as a principle of equality that leads first to political democracy and then later to an organic revolution of society. Like his predecessors, Bang pointed out that the Social Democratic Party was in its essence a socialist and revolutionary party:

> The process through which the present capitalist society is transformed into a future socialist society can only be described by one word: revolution. This is a word that can be interpreted in many different ways and be associated with many different visions.[34]

For Bang, there was no doubt that the social revolution of the future should be an organic revolution, the only real type of revolution. According to him, 'absolute democracy will stretch over all parts of public life, most notably over the working life, the most important of all'.[35] In this way, the double-sided vision of democracy was a key concept in the profoundly reformist strategy in early Danish socialist thought: 'For the socialist labour party, democracy is more than just a goal in itself; it is also the means through which its fundamental principle can be realized.'[36]

33 Anonymous 1895, 7–8: 'har vi naaet det første Maal, da kan ingen menneskelig Magt forhindre os i, at vi sætter os et nyt [...] Det, der tiltrænges, er først og fremmest, at *FolkesouveraIniteten* anerkendes fuldt ud og paa alle Omraader. *Det* er Demokratiets første og vigtigste Maal i politisk Henseende. Om denne Opgaves Realisation bør alle gode Demokrater, hvad enten de kalder sig Venstre eller Socialdemokrater, kunne fylke sig til enig kamp. Og først naar dette Maal er naaet, vil Tiden være inde til ogsaa at prøve paa en virkelig Løsning af de store Problemer.'

34 Bang, Gustav (1903) *Den socialistiske Fremtidsstat*. Copenhagen, 4: 'Thi den Proces, hvorigennem der kan bygges Bro fra nutidens Kapitalistiske Samfund til et fremtidigt socialistisk, kan kun betegnes ved det ene Ord Revolution. Det er et Ord, der kan tydes paa forskellige Maade, og hvortil der kan knyttes de mest forskelligartede Forestillinger'.

35 Bang 1903, 70: 'det absolutte Demokrati vil være udstrakt over alle Omraader af det offentlige Liv, og ikke mindst over Arbejdsforholdet, det vigtigste af dem alle'.

36 Bang 1903, 91: 'Demokratiet er for det socialistiske Arbejderparti noget andet og mere end et Maal, det i sig selv er værd at stræbe efter; det er tillige det Middel, ved hvis Hjælp dets Idéer kan føres ud i Livet.'

Hartvig Frisch and the idea of Nordic democracy

The First World War and the revolutions in Russia in many respects mark the wider breakthrough for the concept of democracy. One of the most important causes of this development was the Anglo-American way of identifying democracy as the core idea of the allied powers.[37] Most prominent in this regard was Woodrow Wilson. In several speeches during the war, Wilson put forward the idea of a world safe for democracy, and of democracy as the foundation of the Western world.[38] In addition, the revolutions in Russia had a profound impact on the evolution of social and political language in West-European countries. On the right, many conservative forces began to argue in support of a strong democratic labour party; and on the left, the strengthening of revolutionary agitation and the creation of communist parties forced social democrats to clarify their relationship to democracy, reformism and socialism.[39] In the Danish case, the result was that the Social Democrats sincerely defended 'democracy'. In contrast with the previous period, where 'democracy' in many political circles was identified as something radical or at least something that was going to occur in the future, after the revolutions in Russia and the rise of authoritarian ideologies it was possible to identify 'democracy' as something to defend. Another important development was that the Social Democrats moved very close to government responsibilities. In 1909–10 and again in 1913–1920, the Social Democrats supported the social liberal governments, and in 1916, the Social Democratic leader Thorvald Stauning entered the government.

In this context, 'democracy' was no longer both the means and the end in socialist strategy; now it was primarily a system that needed to be defended.[40] In 1923, for instance, Thorvald Stauning, who the following year became the first social democratic Prime Minister in Denmark, argued that the Danish people had two options: parliamentarianism and dictatorship.[41] A fierce critic of both Soviet communism and Italian fascism, Stauning argued extensively in favour of the existing system of parliamentarian democracy and its continuous development in a democratic direction.[42] Hans Hedtoft

37 See Crick 2002, 75.
38 Some of Wilson's speeches from the war period were translated into Danish in 1918, see Wilson, Woodrow (1918) *Udvalg af Taler og Noter under Verdenskrigen*. Copenhagen: G.E.C. gads forlag. For a use of the concept along the lines mentioned above see, for instance, pages 98 and 144.
39 Ernst Kaper, the mayor of schools and education in Copenhagen, was one of many conservatives who wanted to work together with the Social Democratic Party in order to avoid revolutionary developments in the labour movement. Cf. Kaarsted, Tage (1968) *Påskekrisen 1920*. Aarhus: Skrifter utg. af Jysk selskab for historie, 233.
40 Cf. Lidegaard, Bo (2005) *Kampen om Danmark, 1933–1945*. Copenhagen: Gyldendals bogklubber, 36.
41 Stauning, Thorvald (1923) *Parlamentarisme eller Diktatur? Kan Parlamentslede helbredes?* Copenhagen: Fremad.
42 See Grelle, Henning (2005) *Thorvald Stauning: Demokrati eller kaos*. Copenhagen: Jyllands-Posten. Here it is convincingly argued that this whole-hearted defence of parliamentarian democracy is indeed the key to understand Stauning's political life as a whole. See also Lidegaard 2005, 20ff.

Hansen, the leader of the social democratic youth organization, was so passionate in his defence of democracy against the communists that the common ideological ground almost disappeared.[43]

Although this development was certainly something new in Danish socialist thought it did not mean that the old double-sided vision of democracy totally disappeared. Frederik Borgbjerg was one of many Social Democrats who continued to deploy the idea of democracy as a principle that first leads to a certain parliamentarian system and then to a socialist state of affairs through an organic revolution. In a speech in the parliament just before the general election in 1920, he said:

> The Social Democratic Party has a clear programme [...] Our political programme is the full realisation of democracy. Our social programme: the transmission of democratic thought to the economic realm so the working class will have a totally different position to what it has in capitalist society.[44]

In this way, 'democracy' and 'socialism' were still very closely connected to each other. As it was held, they were based on the same principle: equality.[45] This use of the concept of democracy was also used by members of the younger generation such as Hartvig Frisch who became the leading theorist of the Danish Social Democrats in the interwar period. In the 1930s, he published a number of writings that followed the Kautskyan identification of dictatorship and democracy as counter concepts. His chief publication in this respect was *Pest over Europa* (The Plague over Europe) from 1933 in which 'democracy' was used as a counter concept to the plague that had infiltrated Europe under changing names of bolshevism, fascism, and Nazism. The interesting thing is that Frisch not only identified 'democracy' with a particular form of government, as did Stauning, but that 'democracy' was also given spatial as well as temporal associations. Namely, Frisch argued that democracy was doing best in the Nordic countries where it had taken the shape of *Folkestyre* (the people's rule). Moreover, he made a sharp

---

43 Hansen, Hans (1933) *Kommunisterne Splitter! Et Stridsskrift mod det kommunistiske Splittelsesarbejde indenfor Arbejderorganisationer.* Copenhagen.

44 Togeby 1968, 60–61: 'Socialdemokratiet har et klart Program [...] Vort politiske Program er Demokratiets fulde Gennemførelse. Vort sociale Program: de demokratiske Tankers Overførelse ogsaa paa det økonomiske Omraade, saa Arbejderklassen faar en grundforandret Stilling, en helt anden Stilling, end den har i det kapitalistiske Samfund'.

45 The idea of equality as the founding principle in a democratic form of rule goes all the way back to classical antiquity. It can also be discerned from the idea of a link between a democratic or a republican form of government and the necessity of civic virtues. Sediments of this tradition are visible in Rousseau's famous dictum that only a nation of Gods would govern itself as a pure democracy, see Rousseau, Jean-Jacques (1968) *The Social Contract.* London : Penguin books, 112–114. Montesquieu – and numerous writers on his shoulders – had an even more explicit relation between democracy and equality: 'Love of the republic in a democracy is love of democracy; love of democracy is love of equality.' Montesquieu (1989) *The Spirit of the Laws.* Cambridge: Cambridge University Press, 43.

distinction between 'liberal democracy' and 'social democracy', where the former was the existing parliamentary system, and the second was the future state of affairs, created by the Social Democrats.[46]

With regard to the idea of a distinctly Nordic political culture, Frisch was not alone in his argument. During the 1920s and the 1930s not only social democrats but also many other political groups in Scandinavia increasingly argued in favour of a certain Nordic approach to political as well as economic questions and international relations.[47] Regarding the distinction between the liberal democracy of the past and the social democracy of the future, his language seems at first to be nothing but a repetition of the older figure. Nevertheless, on closer examination, it is possible to notice that Frisch's social democracy was not as utopian as Gustav Bang's vision of an absolute democracy. In fact, Frisch mentioned that the foundation of social democracy was already created in the 'Nordic democracy':

> Now it is time to see if there is marrow and bone in the Nordic democracy. In the Nordic countries, it was the farmers who led parliamentarianism to victory and created political democracy; this is their honour. It is the labour movement who has built upon this foundation and created the pillars of *social democracy*. This building is not yet complete, and there is much hard work for the next generation, but the foundations are done and any Nordic worker or peasant, craftsman or office man, intellectual or artist has reason to defend the work that has been done; to defend it against any attempt to introduce dictatorship or means of violence, whether they come from the East or the South.[48]

---

46 Eg. Frisch, Hartvig (1933) *Pest over Europa: Bolschevisme – Fascisme – Nazisme.* Copenhagen: Henrik Koppels forlag, 16–17: 'Det har været det liberale Demokratis Akilleshæl, at det i sin Kamp for politisk Frihed og mod Stændersamfundets traditionelle Magter – Kongemagten, Kirken, Storgodsbesidderne, Embedshierarkiet og Pengearistokratiet – altid har maattet bruge den almindelige Valgret som Murbrækker. Men den almindelige Valgret betød Stemmesedlen i Arbejdernes Haand, og i samme Øjeblik Arbejderne organiserede sig politisk, maatte det sociale Spørgsmaal om Lighed og Broderskab sættes paa Dagsordenen, thi først dermed vil Stændersamfundet sidste Rester blive sprængt bort […] Vi befinder os med andre Ord paa Overgangen mellem det liberale og det sociale Demokrati.' For discussions of Frisch's book, see also Rasmussen, Anders Holm (1993) *Ideologi og virkelighed hos Hartvig Frisch.* Copenhagen: Museum Tusculanum, and Christiansen, Niels Finn (1993) *Hartvig Frisch: Mennesket og politikeren. En biografi.* Copenhagen: Christian Ejlers' forlag, 151ff.

47 Cf. Janfelt, Monika (2005) *Att leva i den bästa världar: Föreningarna Nordens syn på Norden, 1919–1933.* Stockholm: Carlssons. See also Jussi Kurunmäki's article in this volume.

48 Frisch 1933, 16–17: 'Nu er Lejligheden inde for at vise, at der er Knogler og Marv i det nordiske Demokrati. Det var Bønderne i Norden, der førte Parlamentarismen til Sejr og skabte det politiske Demokrati – den Ære er deres. Det er Arbejderbevægelsen, der har bygget videre paa dette Grundlag og støbt Fundamenterne til *det sociale Demokrati.* Bygningen er ikke rejst endnu, og der er haardt Arbejde nok for den kommende Generation, men Fundamenterne er støbt, og enhver nordisk Arbejder og Bonde, Haandværker og Funktionær, Aandsarbejder og Kunstner har Grund til at værne og forsvare den Indsats, der her er gjort, mod ethvert Forsøg paa at indføre Diktatur og Voldsmetoder, hvad enten de kommer fra Øst eller fra Syd.'

Although still firmly rooted in the socialist tradition, this rhetoric shows a concept of democracy that is not as utopian as earlier. Thus, it is characteristic of the ideological development in social democratic thought during the first decades of the twentieth century that democracy increasingly substituted socialism as the key concept, and the breaking point in this development were the years around the First World War, the revolutions in Russia, the party's rise to power, and not least the actual political context of interwar Europe.

BIBLIOGRAPHY

Anonymous (1895) *Demokrati og Socialdemokrati*. Copenhagen.

Bang, Gustav (1903) *Den socialistiske Fremtidsstat*. Copenhagen.

Bjørn, Claus (1999) *Kampen om Grundloven*. Copenhagen: Fremad.

Bruun, Henry (1938) *Den faglige Arbejderbevægelse i Danmark indtil Aar 1900*. Copenhagen: Kildeskriftselskabet.

Bryld, Claus (1992) *Den demokratiske socialismes gennembrudsår: Studier i udformningen af arbejderbevægelsens politiske ideologi i Danmark 1884–1916 på den nationale og internationale baggrund*. Copenhagen: Selskabet for forskning i arbeiderbevægelsens historie.

Bryld, Claus (2004) 'De klassiske socialdemokratisk grundholdninger'. In Bryld, Claus (ed.) *Den socialdemokratiske idéarv*. Roskilde: Roskilde universitetsforlag.

Callesen, Gerd & Lahme, Hans-Norbert (1978) *Den danske arbejderbevægelses programmatiske dokumenter og love (1871 til 1913)*. Odense: Odense Universitetsforlag.

Christensen, J. C. (1898) *Venstrereformpartiet*. Copenhagen: Jul. Gjellerup.

Christiansen, Niels Finn (1993) *Hartvig Frisch: Mennesket og politikeren. En biografi*. Copenhagen: Christian Ejlers' forlag.

Crick, Bernard (2002) *Democracy: A Very Short Introduction*. Oxford: Oxford University Press.

Dippel, Horst (1986) 'Démocratie, Démocrates'. In Reichardt, Rolf & Schmitt, Eberhard (eds.) *Handbuch politisch-sozialer Grundbegriffe in Frankreich, 1680–1820*. Vol. 6., München: Oldenburg.

Dreier, Frederik (2003) *Samlede skrifter*. vol. 1–5, Copenhagen: C. A. Reitzel.

Engberg, Jens (1979) *Til arbejdet! Liv eller død! Louis Pio og arbejderbevægelsen*. Copenhagen: Gyldendal.

Frisch, Hartvig (1933) *Pest over Europa: Bolschevisme – Fascisme – Nazisme*. Copenhagen: Henrik Koppels forlag.

Grelle, Henning (2005) *Thorvald Stauning: Demokrati eller kaos*. Copenhagen: Jyllands-Posten.

Hansen, Hans (1933) *Kommunisterne Splitter! Et Stridsskrift mod det kommunistiske Splittelsesarbejde indenfor Arbejderorganisationer*. Copenhagen.

Janfelt, Monika (2005) *Att leva i den bästa världar: Föreningarna Nordens syn på Norden, 1919–1933*. Stockholm: Carlssons.

Kaarsted, Tage (1968) *Påskekrisen 1920*. Aarhus: Skrifter utg. af Jysk selskab for historie.

Klein, E. W. (1876) *Socialismen og dens Ledere: En kritisk Belysning*. Copenhagen.

Koselleck, Reinhart (1972) 'Einleitung'. In Brunner, Otto, Conze, Werner & Koselleck, Reinhart (eds.) *Geschichtliche Grundbegriffe*. Vol. 1. Stuttgart: Klett.

Koselleck, Reinhart (2006) *Begriffsgeschichten: Studien zur Semantik und Pragmatik der politischen und sozialen Sprache*. Frankfurt am Main: Suhrkamp.

Lahme, Hans-Norbert (1976) *Det danske Socialdemokratis Gimle-Kongres 1876*. Odense.

Levy, Jette Lundbo & Thing, Morten (1973) *Dansk socialistisk teori, 1850–1900.* Copenhagen: Politisk revy.

Lidegaard, Bo (2005) *Kampen om Danmark, 1933–1945.* Copenhagen: Gyldendals bogklubber.

Meier, Christian et. al. (1972) 'Demokratie'. In *Geschichtliche Grundbegriffe*, vol. 1. Stuttgart: Klett.

Montesquieu (1989) *The Spirit of the Laws.* Cambridge: Cambridge University Press.

Pio, Louis (1974) [1871] *Socialistiske Blade I–II.* Odense: CLIO.

Rasmussen, Anders Holm (1993) *Ideologi og virkelighed hos Hartvig Frisch.* Copenhagen: Museum Tusculanum.

Rosanvallon, Pierre (1995) 'The History of the Word 'Democracy' in France'. *Journal of Democracy*, No. 6/4, 140–154.

Rousseau, Jean-Jacques (1968) *The Social Contract.* London : Penguin books.

Sperber, Jonathan (1991) *Rhineland Radicals: The Democratic Movement and the Revolution of 1848–1849.* Princeton: Princeton University Press.

Stauning, Thorvald (1923) *Parlamentarisme eller Diktatur? Kan Parlamentslede helbredes?.* Copenhagen: Fremad.

Stender-Petersen, Ole (1978) *Kjøbenhavnsposten: Organ for "det extreme Democrati".* Odense: Odense Universitetsforlag.

Tjørnehøj, Henning (1992) *Louis Pio – folkevækkeren.* Copenhagen: Fremad.

Togeby, Lise (1968) *Var de så røde? Tekster og dokumenter til belysning af Socialdemokratiets gennembrudsår.* Copenhagen: Fremad.

Wilson, Woodrow (1918) *Udvalg af Taler og Noter under Verdenskrigen.* Copenhagen: G.E.C. gads forlag.

RUTH HEMSTAD

Scandinavianism, Nordic Co-operation, and 'Nordic Democracy'

A key political concept in nineteenth-century Nordic/Scandinavian countries was 'Scandinavianism'. Part of the vocabulary surrounding it was 'Nordic co-operation', which may be seen as an attempt to re-describe 'Scandinavianism' in the nineteenth and early twentieth centuries. 'Nordic co-operation' was often promoted by historical narratives, that is, by telling the history of the development of Nordic collaboration, which dated to the beginning of the nineteenth century. The history of this co-operation, as told by its protagonists, is commonly presented as a linear and harmonious development. This narrative shies away from controversies and conflicts, and does not discuss how the meaning of 'Nordic co-operation' changes in different historical contexts. To understand the concept and its relation to 'Scandinavianism' and to 'Nordic democracy' it is crucial to open up this field of contingencies, conflicts, controversies and changes, and to acknowledge the contested character of concepts.

This article shows that a particular social democratic notion of Nordic co-operation was entangled with the emergent use of 'Nordic democracy' in the middle of the 1930s. More specifically, the rhetoric of 'labour Scandinavianism' (*arbeiderskandinavisme*) was part of the discursive context that paved the way for the rhetoric of Nordic democracy. 'Labour Scandinavianism', in turn, was a reinterpretation of the Scandinavian movement that emerged in the 1830s. I will therefore discuss and pay special attention to the conceptual history of Scandinavianism and Nordic co-operation – which has remained a relatively untold history – before turning to the 1930s and, finally, to the narratives of Nordic co-operation in the latter half of the twentieth century, as they were presented in two major anthologies on Nordic democracy.[1]

---

1 Lauwerys, Joseph A. (ed.) (1958) *Scandinavian Democracy: Development of Democratic Thought and Institutions in Denmark, Norway and Sweden*. Copenhagen: The Danish Institute (Det Danske Selskab), The Norwegian Office of Cultural Relations & The Swedish Institute; Allardt, Erik et al. (1981) *Nordic Democracy: Ideas, Issues, and Institutions in Politics, Economy, Education, Social and Cultural Affairs of Denmark, Finland, Iceland, Norway, and Sweden*. Copenhagen: Det Danske Selskab.

Scandinavianism

The term 'Scandinavianism' is a neologism from the 1830s, introduced as a concept to describe and stimulate a national and liberal, cultural and political movement in the Scandinavian countries. It was closely related to the concepts of *Norden*, Scandinavia and Scandinavians, which were more frequently used at that time. Scandinavia as well as *Norden* could refer to the same area: Denmark, Norway and Sweden.[2] The more problematic case of Finland, which was an integrated part of Sweden until 1809, but thereafter an autonomous constituent of the Russian Empire, was rarely mentioned. 'Scandinavian' and 'Nordic' were often synonymous, although there was a tendency toward a more frequent use of 'Nordic' in the late nineteenth century in recognition of the higher degree of Finnish participation in the co-operation.[3] Scandinavianism came to signify a movement for fostering closer co-operation and fraternal feelings between the Danes, Swedes and Norwegians. The need for closer collaboration between the Scandinavian peoples was already emphasised in the latter part of the eighteenth century.[4] The movement focused on a common Scandinavian identity and nationality as well as on the strategic political need to stand up to Prussia and Russia.

In the 1830s and 1840s, the idea of a Scandinavian unity spread among students and liberal academics in Sweden and Denmark, and to a certain degree also in Norway. The movement was characterised by social inter-Scandinavian student activities, with several gatherings of students and professors from the universities of Uppsala, Lund, Copenhagen and Christiania (today's Oslo). The intellectual youth advocated liberal and national ideas, and when they met across the Öresund they found, in the words of Åke Holmberg, 'that they were political friends and that the peoples of Denmark and Sweden ought to help each other in the struggle

2 As late as in 1902, the Danish lexicon *Salmonsens Konversationsleksikon* described *Norden* as a 'commonly used name of the three Nordic countries, Denmark, Norway and Sweden' (*hyppig Benævnelse paa de tre nordiske Riger: Danmark, Norge og Sverige*). Copenhagen, b. 13, 462.

3 See Østergård, Uffe (1997) 'The Geopolitics of Nordic Identity: From Composite States to Nation States'. In Øystein Sørensen & Bo Stråth (eds) *The Cultural Construction of Norden*. Oslo: Scandinavian University Press, 31–33; Hemstad, Ruth (2008) *Fra Indian Summer til nordisk vinter. Skandinavisk samarbeid, skandinavisme og unionsoppløsningen.* Oslo: Akademisk Publisering, 20. An example of such a terminological shift is the Scandinavian National Economist Meeting, arranged for the fourth time in 1881, and again in 1888, but now as the fifth Nordic National Economic Meeting. (*Förhandlingar vid det fjerde Skandinaviska nationalekonomiska mötet i Malmö 1881.* Stockholm 1882; *Forhandlingerne paa Det [5.] Nordiske Nationaløkonomiske Møde i Kjøbenhavn 1888.* København 1888).

4 Clausen, Julius (1900) *Skandinavismen historisk fremstillet.* København: Nordiske Forlag, 8–18; Sørensen, Øystein (2001) *Kampen om Norges sjel, 1770–1905. Norsk idéhistorie,* b. III. Oslo: Aschehoug, 228–230; Hemstad, Ruth (2005) 'Proto-skandinavisme og opptakten til skandinavisk samarbeid'. In Sandström, Åke (ed.) (2005) *Formandet av det nya Norden. Om Norden och det nordiska under och efter Napoleonkrigen.* Visby: Högskolan på Gotland, 44–47. An example is the Scandinavian Literary Association (Det Skandinaviske Litteratur-Selskab), established in 1797.

for constitutional rights'.[5] They looked upon themselves as the natural representatives of their nations. It was particularly the nationally-spirited Danes who were the champions of Scandinavianism, for it was meant to support Denmark against German claims on the duchies of Schleswig-Holstein.[6]

As in other national movements, a common history and common or at least kindred languages, together with a common culture, religion and mentality served to underpin the formation of what may be termed as a Scandinavistic ideology. In many ways, the characteristics of the Scandinavian movement tie in with Louis Snyder's definition of a pan-movement, developed in his book on macro-nationalisms. Snyder defines pan-movements as 'politico-cultural movements seeking to enhance and promote the solidarity of peoples bound together by common or kindred languages, cultural similarities, the same historical traditions, and/or geographical proximity. They postulate the nation writ large in the world's community of nations'.[7] These elements alongside a more imperative dimension – the necessity for stronger solidarity and more widespread co-operation – were included in the interpretation of the concept of Scandinavianism to varying degrees.

For the Scandinavianists, the contemporary German and Italian national movements were inspiring examples.[8] The political implications of the concept of Scandinavianism were, however, seldom clearly outspoken, and a common political programme remained both vague and contested. Different political solutions were discussed, ranging from a united kingdom with a common constitution and parliament and based on a common Nordic national identity, to a federation or at least a defensive alliance including the three Scandinavian countries. As a rule, Finland was not, officially at least, mentioned in these speculations.

The Scandinavian movement had its golden days from the 1840s up to the 1860s. The turning point was the war between Denmark and Prussia-Austria in 1864. Danish hopes of securing military assistance from the 'Scandinavian brothers' in the war against the Prussian-Austrian coalition were crushed.[9] After the Danish defeat, contemporary writers as well as later commentators declared Scandinavianism dead as a political project, but it did have a certain effect. It can be argued, according to Kari Palonen, that 'even unrealistic possibilities and mere curiosities are often more important

5 Holmberg, Åke (1946) *Skandinavismen i Sverige vid 1800–talets mitt*. Göteborg: Elanders, 409.

6 Møller, Erik (1948) *Skandinavisk stræben og svensk politik omkring 1860*. København: Gad, 184–192; Sørensen 2001, 231–232.

7 Snyder, Louis (1984) *Macro-Nationalisms: A History of the Pan-Movements*. Contributions in Political Science, no. 112. Global perspectives in history and politics. Westport, Connecticut: Greenwood Press, 5.

8 Møller 1948, 13. For detailed discussions about political Scandinavianism in the mid-nineteenth century, see also Holmberg 1946; Clausen 1900; Lindberg, Folke (1958) *Den svenska utrikespolitikens historia*, III: 4, 1872–1914. Stockholm; Lundh, Hans Lennart (1950) *Från skandinavism till neutralitet. Utrikespolitik och utrikesdebatt i Sverige under Carl XV:s sista år*. Trollhättan [diss.].

9 Møller 1948.

for understanding politics than realized practices taken for granted'.[10] The concept of Scandinavianism, though utterly contested, did survive the catastrophe of 1864. However, the 1864 experience led to a conceptual shift. To avoid the controversies related to the political assumptions, the practical dimensions of Scandinavianism were brought to the fore.

Practical Scandinavian co-operation had developed as a parallel process to the more political Scandinavian movement. The first Scandinavian conference, which later led to regular meetings, was arranged by the natural scientists in Gothenburg in 1839. It was soon to be seen as the first sign of a Scandinavian scholarly unity.[11] A handful of different Scandinavian meetings were held in the 1840s and 1850s in addition to the well-known student meetings. Moreover, the need for a stronger and more widespread co-operation was emphasised on different occasions. After 1864, 'practical Scandinavianism' was coined to underline cultural and civil co-operation, and to mark a distance from a more political Scandinavianism. As a consequence, 'practical Scandinavianism' and 'Scandinavian co-operation' became closely related concepts.

The year 1864 represented a shift in what Koselleck terms 'Erfahrungsraum' and 'Erwartungshorizont'.[12] The political Scandinavianists, organised in new Scandinavian associations established in all the Scandinavian countries in the years following the Danish defeat, still kept their long-term aim of transforming the three Scandinavian nations into one supranational entity, but they had changed their strategy to fulfil this goal. In a new historical context, the meaning of Scandinavianism was thus altered. The activities were directed toward the 'people' of Scandinavia. It was considered necessary to address public opinion in the most general sense, to create a platform for the desired political changes. The significance of this ideological work did not show in political results but rather in social and cultural life through different forms of Nordic co-operation. Although two clearly different issues as such, the Scandinavian movement and idea and the civil co-operation came to be intertwined in different ways.

The main arena for Nordic co-operation in the nineteenth century were the regularly held Nordic meetings, mainly among scholars and different professions. A range of new Nordic meetings emerged in the 1860s and 1870s, including conventions for teachers, lawyers and economists.[13] The Nordic meetings could gather from a handful to up to 7000 participants, as

10 Palonen, Kari (1995) 'Conceptual History as a Perspective to Political Thought'. In Ilkka Lakaniemi, Anna Rotkirch & Henrik Stenius (eds) *Liberalism'. Seminars on Historical and Political Keywords in Northern Europe*. Renvall Institute Publications 7. Helsinki, 8.
11 See Clausen 1900, 43.
12 Koselleck, Reinhart (1979) 'Erfahrungsraum und Erwartungshorizont'. In Koselleck, Reinhart (1979) *Vergangene Zukunft*. Frankfurt am Main: Suhrkamp, 349–375.
13 Hvidt, Kristian (1994) 'Skandinavismens lange linier. Udsigt over et forsømt forsknings-felt'. *Nordisk Tidskrift för vetenskap, konst och industri*, årg.70, nr. 4, 293–304; Møller 1948, 432; Østergård, Uffe (1994) 'Norden – europæisk eller nordisk?'. 'De Nordiske Fællesskaber. Myte og realitet i det nordiske samarbejde'. *Den Jyske historiker*, no. 69–70, 15–18.

was the case with some of the school meetings. In total, at least one hundred different series of meetings took place between 1839 and 1905.[14]

Political Scandinavianism continued to play a certain role up to around 1870. After that time, Scandinavianism as a political programme became irrelevant, as Bo Stråth points out.[15] An alternative programme, although of minor importance, was the republican Scandinavianism of the late nineteenth century, which had one of the leaders of the Scandinavian peace movement Frederik Bajer as a key figure.[16]

With regard to national aspirations, there was something of a paradox in the Scandinavian movement: while they supported nation-building programmes, they also sought a trans-national arrangement. The three Scandinavian nations found themselves in different political situations that forced their national priorities in different directions. This contradictory nature of the movement made Nordic co-operation a contested concept. The controversies and conflicts around Scandinavianism and Scandinavian co-operation were most outspoken in Norway because of the union that the country had formed with Sweden in 1814. In the eyes of the Norwegians, who were increasingly struggling for political independence, Scandinavianism stood for amalgamation and unionism.[17]

There was, however, a renaissance to Scandinavianism and Scandinavian co-operation during the last years before the dissolution of the union between Sweden and Norway in 1905. The number of Scandinavian meetings, conventions, societies and journals grew rapidly. Tensions between Norway and Sweden, Denmark and Germany, and Finland and Russia were part of the new historical context for the emerging Nordic co-operation at the turn of the century. A stronger Scandinavian unity in terms of cultural, economic and possibly also military co-operation gained support to such an extent that it is possible to speak of an 'Indian summer' of the Scandinavian movement.[18] A transformed and reconstructed concept of Scandinavianism, highlighting the practical, cultural and social dimensions, was intensively debated in Swedish and Danish newspapers and periodicals between 1899 and 1905. The Norwegian attitude remained mostly sceptical and negative; the fear of 'amalgamation' was widespread.[19]

The new associations that were established in Denmark, Sweden and Norway were called 'Nordic' and not 'Scandinavian' as had been the case in the 1860s, although no separate Finnish organisations were founded.[20]

---

14 For a detailed overview over Nordic meetings arranged between 1839 and 1929, see Hemstad 2008, 603–620.

15 Stråth, Bo (2005) *Union och demokrati. De Förenade rikena Sverige-Norge 1814–1905. Sverige och Norge under 200 år*, b.1. Nora: Bokförlaget Nya Doxa, 189.

16 On the Scandinavian peace movement, see Mårald, Bert (1974) *Den svenska freds- och neutralitetsrörelsens uppkomst. Ideologi, propaganda och politiska yttringar från Krimkriget till den svensk-norska unionens upplösning*. Studia historica Gothoburgensia 14. Stockholm.

17 Sørensen 2001, 244–252.

18 Hemstad 2008, 87–90.

19 Hemstad 2008, 111–117.

20 'Nordisk förening' was first established in Copenhagen in 1899. A whole range of these associations were soon to spring up in Sweden, but the Norwegian association from 1900 was of less importance. Hemstad 2008, 259–294.

At the time, it was difficult in Finland to participate in Nordic co-operation of this kind. Few Nordic meetings were held in Finland before 1905, partly because of the reluctant Russian attitude toward Finnish participation in Nordic co-operation. The few meetings that were held, such as the Nordic convention for natural scientists in Helsinki in 1902, had to be arranged as common Nordic-Russian meetings. The language conflict in Finland also made Nordic orientation in Finland increasingly controversial from a Finnish-language nationalistic point of view.[21] Generally, though, Finnish participation in the Nordic meetings arranged outside Finland expanded during the latter part of the century.[22]

The new Nordic associations represented a renewed interest in Scandinavian co-operation. The concept of Scandinavianism underwent another re-orientation, which was also made clear in speeches and publications. This was not 'old Scandinavianism'.[23] A new term was therefore introduced: 'Nyskandinavismen'.[24] 'New Scandinavianism' focused explicitly on cultural and practical co-operation, referring to the more widespread co-operation at the time. The political aims, if any, belonged to the future.

The renewed hope for a common Scandinavian future with a stronger sense of solidarity and close co-operation was, however, crushed by the union crisis between Sweden and Norway.[25] Stråth highlights that it was the question of democracy that broke the union.[26] Norway had developed more democratic political institutions than Sweden, especially toward the end of the nineteenth century. The union finally fell in the face of Norwegian claims for more foreign political independence. The question of Norwegian consuls abroad became heavily loaded with nationalistic feelings and served to escalate the national conflict which was driven both by activist Norwegian radical nationalism and Swedish ultraconservative nationalism.[27] The political nationalisms of Norway and Sweden thus put an end to the Scandinavian dream in 1905.

When the union broke up in 1905, the disappointment in Sweden was palpable. The reaction against the way the Norwegians left the union also influenced almost the whole field of civil Nordic co-operation, which was

21 Kaukiainen, Leena (1984) 'From Reluctancy to Activity: Finland's Way to the Nordic Family during 1920's and 1930's'. *Scandinavian Journal of History*, Vol. 9, 201–219.
22 Kaukiainen 1984, 202; Rosenqvist, V. T. (1925) 'De nordiska skolmötena och Finland'. *Nordisk Tidskrift för vetenskap, konst och industri*, 270–278.
23 Hemstad 2008, 92 f.
24 The term was used for the first time in Denmark in 1899. For a detailed discussion of the use of this expression in Denmark, Sweden and Norway in 1899, see Hemstad 2008, 92–104.
25 Lindgren, Raymond E. (1959) *Norway-Sweden: Union, Disunion, and Scandinavian Integration*. Princeton, New Jersey: Princeton University Press, 278; Hemstad 2008 discusses the negative impact of the dissolution of the union on both Scandinavianism and Scandinavian co-operation in detail (297–358).
26 Stråth 2005, 582–590.
27 Stråth 2005, 582–590; Vedung, Evert (1971) *Unionsdebatten 1905. En jämförelse mellan argumenteringen i Sverige och Norge*. Skrifter nr. 57, Statsvetenskapliga föreningen i Uppsala, Acta Universitatis Upsaliensis. Stockholm.

almost abandoned for many years. At least half of the Nordic meetings and congresses held on a regular basis at the turn of the century were cancelled, delayed or boycotted, and Nordic associations wound down. The promising Indian summer turned almost immediately into a cold 'Nordic winter'. In Sweden, the disappointment following the dissolution of the union was directed not only at the Norwegians, but also at the Danes and at the Scandinavian idea in general. Anti-Scandinavianistic tendencies in Sweden after 1905 resulted in a reluctant attitude toward Scandinavian co-operation in general, which was now defined as a form of Scandinavianism. In October 1906, the conservative Swedish newspaper *Svenska Dagbladet* warned against continued co-operation as well as against the concept of 'Scandinavian co-operation' as such.[28]

It is important to note that this period of cool relationships has had little influence on the dominant narrative of Nordic co-operation, which has chosen to stress similarities between the countries instead of national ambiguities. It nevertheless constitutes an important part of the history of Nordic co-operation as well as of the conceptual history of Scandinavianism.[29] The dissolution of the union between Norway and Sweden in 1905 represents a distinct break with – or at least a pause in – this tradition. The experience of 1905 marked a shift in the meaning and interpretations of the concepts of Scandinavianism and Nordic co-operation. As mentioned above, Scandinavianism was proclaimed dead and buried after the Danish defeat in 1864. This was not true. Scandinavianism as a concept and idea survived 1864, but it hardly outlived the events of 1905. There are some exceptions, but the main impression is that the concept of Scandinavianism did not continue to be a mobilising and legitimate idea. It was gradually transformed to a historical category, describing the political Scandinavianism under the period from the 1840s to the 1860s.

Nordic co-operation in the 1920s

The First World War signified a distinct new modification in the history of Nordic co-operation, which put the internal Nordic quarrel into a broader and more dramatic perspective.[30] A symbolic starting point of the new approach was the meeting of the three Scandinavian kings in Malmö in Sweden in December 1914. Different kinds of Nordic meetings came into being – and

---

28 'Skandinaviskt samarbete'. *Svenska Dagbladet*, 16 Oct. 1906.
29 See Hemstad 2008, 605–631.
30 During the First World War the co-operation between the Scandinavian countries has developed to such a degree that it certainly represents a new chapter in their history, wrote the journalist and author L. Th. Arnskov in 1917 in his book Arnskov, L. Th. (1917) *Norden og den ny tid. Det nordiske samarbejde i dets forskjellige former.* København: Nyt Nordisk Forlag. See also Sejersted, Francis (2005) *Sosialdemokratiets tidsalder. Norge og Sverige i det 20. århundre. Norge og Sverige gjennom 200 år*, b. 2. Oslo: Pax, 176–187; Janfelt, Monica (2005) *Att leva i den bästa av världar. Föreningarna Nordens syn på Norden 1919–1933.* Stockholm: Carlssons Bokförlag, 21.

this time not only at the level of the civil society but at a political and official level as well. The number of Nordic meetings and conferences soon rose, reaching a new high. Old meeting traditions were again carried on, and a variety of new meetings were held. In total, around one hundred new series of meetings were arranged between 1905 and 1929, most of them from 1912 onwards.[31]

International developments gave new meaning to the concept of Nordic co-operation, bringing it back from the cold in the 1920s.[32] The term was no longer 'Scandinavian' but 'Nordic' co-operation, including explicitly the now sovereign state of Finland and also Iceland. The new Nordic organisations, the Norden Associations, were founded in 1919 'with the objective of promoting Nordic cooperation in every field of endeavour'.[33] This time, Nordic Associations were founded also in Iceland (1921) and in Finland (1924).

The re-interpreted concept of Nordic co-operation in the 1920s compensated for the loss of the concept of Scandinavianism. Apparently an ordinary expression describing different ways of inter-Nordic transactions, 'Nordic co-operation' also served as a rhetorical figure, as a moral imperative underlining the need and wish for stronger co-operation between the Nordic peoples. However, 'Nordic co-operation' was not unanimously welcomed, especially in Norway and Finland, although it was far less controversial than the concept of Scandinavianism.[34] Finland's conflict with Sweden over the Åland Islands, which were demilitarised and gained local autonomy in 1921, and the language conflict of the 1920s and 1930s increased tension between Finnish-language nationalists and the Swedish-speaking minority, which culminated in the 1930s in the question of language-proportionality in university education. According to Kaukiainen, Finnish linguistic nationalism was directed against Nordicism as part of the attack on the Swedish language.[35] In Norway, the conflict with Denmark over the Greenland question in the 1920s also inflamed anti-Nordic tensions.[36]

Nevertheless, Nils Herlitz, professor in constitutional law and an active member of the Nordic Association in Sweden, maintained that Nordic co-operation aroused sympathy and interest everywhere in the four countries. In his article about Nordic co-operation in the Swedish lexicon *Nordisk Familjebok*, published in 1925, Herlitz underlined in an optimistic manner the vigorous movement toward co-operation and cultural exchange between Denmark, Finland, Norway and Sweden.[37]

31 For an overview, see Hemstad 2008, 614–620.
32 Herlitz, Nils (1959) 'När föreningarna Norden bildades. Minnen från 1918 och 1919'. *Nordisk tidskrift för vetenskap, konst och industri*, 138.
33 Wendt 1981, 656.
34 'Nordiskt samarbete'. In *Nordisk familjebok* (1925), 2nd edn, b. 37 (suppl.), Stockholm, 805–806.
35 Kaukiainen 1984, 204–208; Janfeldt 2005, 170.
36 Blom, Ida (1973) *Kampen om Eirik Raudes land, Pressgruppepolitikk i grønlandsspørsmålet 1921–1931*. Oslo: Gyldendal norsk forlag, 151–152.
37 'Nordiskt samarbete'. In *Nordisk familjebok* (1925), 2nd edn, b. 37 (suppl.), Stockholm, 805–806.

However, the lack of co-operation in the foregoing period was not addressed in the discussion. The lack of references to the experience of intensive Nordic co-operation around the turn of the century and to the experience of 1905 is striking. In the narratives of Nordic co-operation introduced by the Nordic Associations, the point of departure was the First World War.[38] Their first annual report, *Norden 1920*, was published without any historical references.[39] All in all, Scandinavianism and Scandinavian co-operation was only marginally touched upon in the early publications of these associations. Instead, reference was made to Scandinavian solidarity, which, as it was held, had grown strong during the recent years. It was programmatically stated that the need for co-operation was acute and commonly shared.[40] Consequently, while the associations had a great interest in contemporary Nordic co-operation, they carefully avoided drawing attention to such a contested and controversial concept as 'Scandinavianism'.[41] This continued to be an ambivalent concept, primarily in Sweden and Norway. For example, Edvard Hagerup Bull, the first chairman in the Norwegian Nordic Association, claimed in 1928 that political Scandinavianism had even more influence in Norway after its death, as a ghost, or a haunting experience.[42]

Labour Scandinavianism and 'Nordic democracy' in the 1930s

There was, however, one brand of Nordic co-operation that made use of the concept of Scandinavianism. A particular committee of co-operation between the Danish, Finnish, Icelandic and Swedish Social Democratic parties was founded in 1932. The Norwegian Labour Party was excluded from the committee because it was not a member of the Socialist International, participating only as a guest during the first years.[43]

The Scandinavian co-operation committee was initially established in 1913 as a supplement to the regularly held Scandinavian labour congresses and first convened in 1886. Co-operation between the Scandinavian

---

38 See Hansen, Svein Olav (1994) *Drømmen om Norden, Den norske foreningen Norden og det nordiske samarbeidet 1919–1994*. Oslo; Janfelt 2005, 225–231.

39 'Norden'. In Jens Møller, Fredrik Paasche og Nils Herlitz (eds) (1920) *Nordens aarbok 1920*. Stockholm: Norden (Dansk Forening for nordisk Samarbejde, Norsk forening for nordisk samarbeide og Svensk förening för nordiskt samarbete), 1–12.

40 Møller, Paasche, Herlitz 1920, 1.

41 The Nordic Associations (Föreningen Norden) did not employ the concept of Scandinavianism themselves. See also Janfelt 2005, 225–231. Scandinavianism and 'nyskandinavisme' are, however, occasionally used by some groups in Denmark in the 1920s and 1930s; see Andersson, Jan A. (1994) *Nordiskt samarbete: Aktörer, idéer och organisering 1919–1953*. Lund: Lund Political Studies 85, 69–71 and Nielsen, Henning (1938–1939) *Nordens Enhed gennem Tiderne*, b. I–III. København, Oslo, Stockholm: Nord. Bokh.

42 Bull, Edv. Hagerup (1928) 'Det nordiske samarbeide i de siste halvhundrede år. Et tilbakeblik'. *Nordisk tidskrift för vetenskap, konst och industri*, 3.

43 Blidberg, Kersti (1984) *Splittrad gemenskap. Kontakter och samarbete inom nordisk socialdemokratisk arbetarrörelse 1931–1945*. Stockholm: Almqvist & Wiksell International Stockholm, 11; 49.

labour movements broke down in 1918 because of the deep split within the Norwegian labour movement.[44] The committee was re-established as a Nordic Co-operation Committee in 1932 to strengthen the work for international solidarity and to give weight to Nordic international participation by bringing the Norwegian Labour Party back into the fold of international co-operation. [45] As of 1938, the party once again participated in the work of the committee.[46]

Nordic co-operation within the labour movement was intensified during the interwar period through a collaborative network between the different branches of the Nordic labour movement, as Blidberg identifies.[47] She goes on to underline, however, that the co-operation committee did not concentrate on strengthening inter-Nordic co-operation, and Nordicism as an idea did not exert an influence as a mobilising force.[48]

The concept of Scandinavianism did nevertheless play a particular role in the mid-1930s. When the Social Democratic leaders celebrated Nordic democracy in August 1935, they already had an established forum for their Nordic commitment. In February 1935, the Swedish Prime Minister delivered a speech to students of Copenhagen, which was also brought to the people through national broadcasting.[49] Two months earlier, in December 1934 in Copenhagen, the three Scandinavian Social Democratic leaders had given related speeches, published under the heading 'Nordisk samarbejde' (Nordic co-operation).[50] In August that year, the co-operation committee had its meeting in Stockholm together with representatives from the Norwegian Labour Party and labour union. The meeting was a step toward ending the Norwegian isolation from the international labour movement.

The meeting in Copenhagen with the three Scandinavian Social Democratic leaders, Johan Nygårdsvold, president of the Norwegian Parliament, and the Swedish and Danish Prime Ministers, Per Albin Hansson and Thorvald Stauning, was presented as an historical event, in line with the famous student meeting in 1845.[51] In 1934, thousands of people gathered one more time to listen to speeches about Scandinavian solidarity. This time they were not oppositional to the political system: they were listening to the political leaders of their respective countries.[52] But the new political elite

---

44 Blidberg 1984, 32–33.

45 Blidberg 1984, 42.

46 The labour union participated in the committee from 1936.

47 Blidberg, Kersti (1994) 'Ideologi och pragmatism – samarbetet inom nordisk sosial-demokratisk arbetarrörelse 1930–1955'. 'De Nordiske Fællesskaber. Myte og realitet i det nordiske samarbejde'. *Den Jyske historiker*, no. 69–70, 133. See also Sejersted 2005, 182–184.

48 Blidberg 1994, 148.

49 *Nordisk Tidskrift för vetenskap, konst och industri* (1935). Stockholm.

50 *Nordisk samarbejde. Tre taler i Idrætshuset d. 5. december 1934 af Per Albin Hansson, Johan Nygaardsvold, Th. Stauning* (1934). København. The meeting was arranged by the Workers' Reading Society, *Arbeidernes Læseselskab*.

51 See the publisher's preface; Lehmann, Johannes (1934) *Nordisk samarbejde*.

52 Per Albin Hansson became Prime Minister in 1932, Thorvald Stauning was Prime Minister in 1924–1926, and again from 1929, while Johan Nygaardsvold became Prime Minister of Norway in 1935.

were facing massive national and international challenges. By presenting themselves as inheritors of a distinct Nordic historic tradition, they sought to strengthen their legitimacy.

The concept of Scandinavianism was again given attention on this occasion, foremost by Per Albin Hansson. His speech was explicitly about Scandinavianism among the workers, *arbeiderskandinavismen*. This labour Scandinavianism was in fact a new concept, probably introduced in this event.[53] It was most likely not employed at the Scandinavian labour congresses in the nineteenth century, in spite of a range of combinations of words using 'Scandinavianism' as a suffix at that time.[54] In the labour movement, the aim had been to strengthen the labour organisation through Scandinavian co-operation. In Hansson's narrative of Nordic co-operation, however, the order of things was turned the other way around: labour Scandinavianism gave weight to the Scandinavian idea.

Hansson was playing with history. 'Scandinavianism' was at the time primarily a term denoting a historical and bygone epoch. The potential of Scandinavianism as a mobilising concept, as a *'Handlungsbegriff'* in Koselleck's terminology, had dramatically changed after the 1905 experience.[55] The causes lie mostly in the Swedish reaction to the dissolution of the union. Such anti-Scandinavistic feelings were widespread among conservatives and national liberals, but the labour movement did not share them. The Swedish Social Democrats had supported the Norwegian majority in 1905, and the labour congresses carried on as usual. Hansson could therefore emphasise a long tradition of Nordic co-operation within the labour movement. In his speech, 'labour Scandinavianism' was presented as offering new hope for the idea of Scandinavian unity. Scandinavian social democracy, balancing between nationalism and internationalism, was furthermore pictured as the vehicle to realising this dream. Hansson argued against the conservative view of Scandinavianism, which he felt was based on a history of failure and disillusion. What was needed, he stressed, was nothing more than a confident and practical co-operation, as well as respect

---

53 It was taken up the following year by Kaare Fostervoll as a heading in his book about the co-operation between the labour movements (Fostervoll (1935) *Arbeidarskandinavismen i grunnleggingstida*. Skrifter fra Arbeidernes historiske forening. Oslo: Det norske Arbeiderpartis forlag). Hansson explicitly pointed out this task in his speech in 1934 ('Det är en uppgift, som ännu väntar på sin man, att skriva arbetarskandinavismens historia'), *Nordisk samarbejde* 1934, 14. '*Arbetarskandinavismen*' is also used as a heading of an article by Hansson in *Nordens Kalender*, published by the Nordic Associations in 1937.

54 In his study about the labour congresses between 1886 and 1892, Fostervoll employs the concept of labour Scandinavianism only as an analytical and historical category. He explicitly defines labour Scandinavianism as co-operation between the labour movements (Fostervoll 1935, 7; 18). His book has no references to a contemporary use of the concept. In my own studies on early Nordic co-operation, I have not found this concept used in the last part of the nineteenth century or around 1900 in contemporary newspapers or in other sources. Hemstad 2008, 194–195. Neither did labour Scandinavianism as a concept play a role at the meetings in the co-operation committee. Wahlbäck, Krister & Kersti Blidberg (1986) *Samråd i kristid: Protokoll från den Nordiska Arbetarrörelsens Samarbetskommitté 1932–1946*. Stockholm.

55 On '*Handlungsbegriff*', see Koselleck 1979, 113.

for national sovereignty.[56] In this way, Hansson underlined a practical, cultural dimension, breaking away from the more problematic political tradition related to Scandinavianism.

Hansson concluded by summing up the meaning and goal of labour Scandinavianism in one word: democracy. This meant 'democracy within and between the people; social, political, economic, national, Scandinavian and international democracy'.[57] Two months later, in another speech in Copenhagen, it was not about Scandinavian but Nordic democracy. As discussed by Kurunmäki in this volume, one explanation for the change of terms was that Finland was showing increased interest in co-operating with the Scandinavian countries. Accordingly, the Finnish Social Democratic leader joined the next joint social democratic meeting. A common platform for Nordic co-operation was now established on the concept of Nordic democracy.

The Nordic co-operation committee continued to be an important forum for the exchange of ideas and experiences, but plans for a more dedicated political co-operation were not realised. A Nordic defensive alliance was discussed in the latter part of the 1930s, but the rhetoric of Nordic co-operation had its political and national limits.[58]

Narratives of Nordic co-operation

Neither 'Arbeiderskandinavisme' nor any other forms of Scandinavianism in the twentieth century became as important as 'Scandinavianism' had been in the political vocabulary of the nineteenth century. Nordic co-operation, however, continued to be a part of the political language in domestic political debates as well as in different international contexts. Furthermore, Nordic co-operation was institutionalised on the parliamentary level in 1952, when the Nordic Council was founded, and in 1971, when the Nordic Council of Ministry was established.

There is a long tradition of viewing the Nordic countries as one region. The existence and meaning of a common Nordic identity and common Nordic values are probably not quite as obvious as is commonly held. Nevertheless, it has been argued that numerous transnational relations, especially on the civil society level, have no counterparts in other regions.[59] Moreover, the

56 'Vad vi eftersträvat och eftersträva är ingenting annat än ett förtroendefullt och praktiskt samarbete, utan intrång i de olika ländernas självständighet.' *Nordisk samarbejde* 1934, 17.

57 'Skulle man i ett ord sammanfatta arbetarskandinavismens väsen och mål, så gives intet bättre än: *demokrati*, demokrati inom folken, och demokrati mellan folken, social, politisk, ekonomisk, nationell, skandinavisk och internationell demokrati.' *Nordisk samarbejde* 1934, 19.

58 Blidberg 1984, 20–28; Blidberg 1994, 148. The committee is still working under the name of SAMAK (Arbeiderbevegelsens nordiske samarbeidskomité).

59 Stenius, Henrik & Haggrén, Heidi (2005) 'Det nordiska samarbetets vardagspraktiker. Vad vet vi om dessa förutom att de har varit/är viktiga?'. In Häggman, Lars-Erik (ed.) *Finland i Norden, Finland 50 år i Nordiska rådet*. Helsingfors: Pohjola-Norden.

development of Nordic co-operation is often seen as an integrated part of the history of the Nordic countries. This is the case, indeed, in the highly profiled publications *Scandinavian Democracy* from 1958, and *Nordic Democracy* from 1981. These books were updated, enlarged and translated versions of the volume *Nordisk Demokrati* from 1949.[60] And in fact, these very volumes can be viewed as concrete examples of Nordic co-operation.

In both volumes, Nordic co-operation was given a chapter of its own.[61] Franz Wendt, the author of the chapters, was deeply involved in the process of founding the Nordic Council. In his account of Nordic co-operation, he boldly argued that '[o]ne of the most noteworthy aspects of the five Nordic democracies is the close cooperation they have succeeded in creating in a great number of fields. In this respect, the Nordic nations have undoubtedly made greater gains than any other sovereign states'.[62] In Wendt's presentation, the narrative of Nordic co-operation was a story of success. However, alternative narratives could have been told. There was obviously widespread co-operation in the Nordic societies, but there has always been a gap between the most ambiguous plans for Nordic collaboration and the actual results.

Wendt left out the problematic history of Nordic co-operation. He held that an 'unbroken but ever more strongly pronounced course of action and thought has been running through more than one hundred years of pan-Scandinavian endeavours'.[63] He maintained, moreover, that there was continuity from Scandinavianism to 'current Nordic efforts'. Wendt's history writing omits mentioning the neo-Scandinavistic movement around the turn of the century or the effect of the events in 1905. Instead, he draws attention to continuity in putting the 'pan-Nordic idea into practice'. According to him, new and wider groups had hailed the idea since the 1880s. This development, he said, had continued uninterrupted.[64] In this way, Wendt regarded the labour movement as an important bearer of the Scandinavianistic idea, but he did not stress the point. While this is definitely not the whole story, it was a suitable story for a publication about Nordic democracy directed to an international public.

The concepts of Scandinavianism and Nordic co-operation were, like any other key concepts, contested and re-interpreted in differing historical contexts. This shifting historical development has been a central issue in this article. Both concepts constitute the background for the rhetoric of 'Nordic democracy' in the 1930s. The concept of labour Scandinavianism was a crucial mediator in this respect. It converted, so to speak, nineteenth-century Scandinavianism and the emergent co-operation of the 1920s into a partisan conception of co-operation, which was then generalised by the association of 'labour Scandinavianism' with 'Nordic democracy'.

60 Koch, Hal & Ross, Alf (eds) (1949) *Nordisk demokrati*. Oslo: Halvorsen & Larsen.
61 Wendt, Frantz (1958) 'Nordic Cooperation – Past and Present'. In Lauwerys 1958, 370–387; Wendt, Frantz (1981) 'Nordic Cooperation'. In Erik Allardt et al. 1981, 653–676.
62 Wendt 1981, 653.
63 Wendt, 1981, 655.
64 Wendt 1981, 655–656.

BIBLIOGRAPHY

Allardt, Erik et al. (1981) *Nordic Democracy. Ideas, Issues, and Institutions in Politics, Economy, Education, Social and Cultural Affairs of Denmark, Finland, Iceland, Norway, and Sweden.* Copenhagen: Det Danske Selskab.

Andersson, Jan A. (1994) *Nordiskt samarbete: Aktörer, idéer och organisering 1919– 1953.* Lund: Lund Political Studies 85.

Arnskov, L. Th. (1917) *Norden og den ny tid. Det nordiske samarbejde i dets forskjellige former.* København: Nyt Nordisk Forlag.

Blidberg, Kersti (1984) *Splittrad gemenskap. Kontakter och samarbete inom nordisk socialdemokratisk arbetarrörelse 1931–1945.* Acta Universitatis Stockholmiensis, Stockholm Studies in History. Stockholm: Almqvist & Wiksell International Stockholm.

Blidberg, Kersti (1994) 'Ideologi och pragmatism – samarbetet innom nordisk sosial- demokratisk arbetarrörelse 1930–1955'. 'De Nordiske Fællesskaber. Myte og realitet i det nordiske samarbejde'. *Den Jyske historiker* no. 69–70, 132–150.

Blom, Ida (1973) *Kampen om Eirik Raudes land. Pressgruppepolitikk i grønlands- spørsmålet 1921–1931.* Oslo: Gyldendal norsk forlag.

Bull, Edv. Hagerup (1928) 'Det nordiske samarbeide i de siste halvhundrede år. Et tilbakeblik'. *Nordisk tidskrift för vetenskap, konst och industri,* 1–11.

Clausen, Julius (1900) *Skandinavismen historisk fremstillet.* København: Nordiske Forlag.

Fostervoll, Kaare (1935) *Arbeidarskandinavismen i grunnleggingstida.* Skrifter fra Arbeidernes historiske forening. Oslo: Det norske Arbeiderpartis forlag.

Fyra tal om nordisk demokrati (1935). Stockholm: Frihets förlag.

Hansen, Svein Olav (1994) *Drømmen om Norden. Den norske foreningen Norden og det nordiske samarbeidet 1919–1994.* Oslo: Ad notam Gyldendal.

[Hansson, P. A., Nygaarsvold, J., Stauning, Th.] (1934) *Nordisk samarbejde. Tre taler i Idrætshuset d. 5. december 1934 af Per Albin Hansson, Johan Nygaardsvold, Th. Stauning.* København.

Hemstad, Ruth (2008) *Fra Indian Summer til nordisk vinter. Skandinavisk samarbeid, skandinavisme og unionsoppløsningen.* Oslo: Akademisk Publisering.

Herlitz, Nils (1959) 'När föreningarna Norden bildades. Minnen från 1918 och 1919'. *Nordisk tidskrift för vetenskap, konst och industri.*

Holmberg, Åke (1946) *Skandinavismen i Sverige vid 1800–talets mitt.* Göteborg: Elanders.

Hvidt, Kristian (1994) 'Skandinavismens lange linier. Udsigt over et forsømt forskningsfelt'. *Nordisk Tidskrift för vetenskap, konst och industri,* årg. 70, no. 4, 293–304.

Janfelt, Monica (2005) *Att leva i den bästa av världar. Föreningarna Nordens syn på Norden 1919–1933.* Stockholm: Carlssons Bokförlag.

Jorgenson, Theodor (1935) *Norway's Relation to Scandinavian Unionism 1815–1871.* Northfield, Minnesota: St. Olaf College Press.

Kaukiainen, Leena (1984) 'From Reluctancy to Activity. Finland's Way to the Nordic Family during 1920's and 1930's'. *Scandinavian Journal of History,* Vol. 9, 201– 219.

Koch, Hal & Ross, Alf (eds) (1949) *Nordisk demokrati.* Oslo: Halvorsen & Larsen.

Koselleck, Reinhart (1979) *Vergangene Zukunft.* Frankfurt am Main: Suhrkamp

Lauwerys, Joseph A. (ed.) (1958) *Scandinavian Democracy: Development of Democratic Thought and Institutions in Denmark, Norway and Sweden.* Copenhagen: The Danish Institute (Det Danske Selskab), The Norwegian Office of Cultural Relations, The Swedish Institute.

Lindgren, Raymond E. (1959) *Norway-Sweden: Union, Disunion, and Scandinavian Integration.* Princeton, New Jersey: Princeton University Press.

Lundh, Hans Lennart (1950) *Från skandinavism till neutralitet. Utrikespolitik och utrikesdebatt i Sverige under Carl XV:s sista år.* Trollhättan [diss.].

Møller, Erik (1948) *Skandinavisk stræben og svensk politik omkring 1860*. København: Gad.

Møller, Jens, Paasche, Fredrik & Herlitz, Nils (eds) (1920) *Nordens aarbok 1920*. Stockholm: Norden (Dansk Forening for nordisk Samarbejde, Norsk forening for nordisk samarbeide og Svensk förening för nordiskt samarbete).

Mårald, Bert (1974) *Den svenska freds- och neutralitetsrörelsens uppkomst. Ideologi, propaganda och politiska yttringar från Krimkriget till den svensk-norska unionens upplösning*. Studia historica Gothoburgensia 14. Stockholm.

Nielsen, Henning (1938–1939) *Nordens Enhed gennem Tiderne*, b. I–III. København, Oslo, Stockholm: Nord. Bokh.

Palonen, Kari (1995) 'Conceptual History as a Perspective to Political Thought'. In Ilkka Lakaniemi, Anna Rotkirch & Henrik Stenius (eds) *'Liberalism'. Seminars on Historical and Political Keywords in Northern Europe*. Helsinki: Renvall Institute Publications 7, 7–32.

Rosenqvist, V. T. (1925) 'De nordiska skolmötena och Finland'. *Nordisk Tidskrift för vetenskap, konst och industri*, 270–278.

Sandström, Åke (ed.) (2005) *Formandet av det nya Norden. Om Norden och det nordiska under och efter Napoleonkrigen*. Visby: Högskolan på Gotland.

Sejersted, Francis (2005) *Sosialdemokratiets tidsalder. Norge og Sverige i det 20. århundre, Norge og Sverige gjennom 200 år*, b. 2. Oslo: Pax.

Snyder, Louis (1984) *Macro-Nationalisms. A History of the Pan-Movements*. Contributions in Political Science, no. 112. Global perspectives in history and politics. Westport, Connecticut: Greenwood Press.

Stenius, Henrik & Haggrén, Heidi (2005) 'Det nordiska samarbetets vardagspraktiker. Vad vet vi om dessa förutom att de har varit/är viktiga?'. In Häggman, Lars-Erik (ed.) *Finland i Norden, Finland 50 år i Nordiska rådet*. Helsingfors: Pohjola-Norden.

Stråth, Bo (2005) *Union och demokrati. De Förenade rikena Sverige-Norge 1814–1905, Sverige och Norge under 200 år*, b. 1. Nora: Bokförlaget Nya Doxa.

Sørensen, Øystein (2001) *Kampen om Norges sjel, 1770–1905. Norsk idéhistorie*, b. III. Oslo: Aschehoug.

Sørensen, Øystein & Stråth, Bo (1997) *The Cultural Construction of Norden*. Oslo: Scandinavian University Press.

Vedung, Evert (1971) *Unionsdebatten 1905. En jämförelse mellan argumenteringen i Sverige och Norge*. Skrifter nr. 57, Statsvetenskapliga föreningen i Uppsala, Acta Universitatis Upsaliensis. Stockholm.

Wahlbäck, Krister & Blidberg, Kersti (1986) *Samråd i kristid. Protokoll från den Nordiska ArbetarrörelsensSamarbetskommitté 1932–1946*. Kungl. Samfundet för utgivande av handskrifter rörande Skandinaviens historia. Handlingar del 12. Stockholm.

Østergård, Uffe (1994) 'Norden – europæisk eller nordisk?'. 'De Nordiske Fællesskaber. Myte og realitet i det nordiske samarbejde'. *Den Jyske historiker*, no. 69–70, 7–37.

PETER STADIUS

Visiting Nordic Modernity around 1900

Spanish Images

This chapter studies how the Nordic societies were conceived from a Latin European point of view around the turn of the twentieth century. Explorations of Spanish travelogues and diplomatic correspondence show that from the Southern European angle, the Nordic countries appeared as particularly influenced by egalitarian ideas, representing a sphere of modern and calm social and political culture in contrast to the heated and revolutionary politics of the South.[1] While the union crisis between Sweden and Norway led some Spanish observers to deem Swedish political life aristocratic and conservative in contrast to the democratic Norway, the democratic spirit was nevertheless often made into a facet of the whole of Scandinavia, or the Nordic region – *el Norte* – comprising Finland as well. The chapter concludes by recognising that the Spanish picture of the modern egalitarian democracies of the North was strikingly similar to what the American journalist and writer Marquis W. Childs would deliver some thirty years later in his idealised depictions of social democratic Sweden and Scandinavia.

It should be emphasised that the Spanish experiences, representing a Latin European, or southern, image of the North, have a peculiar character, audience and intention. The reports, assessments, images, interpretations and opinions about the Nordic countries are as much comments about Spain and the Latin South as they are about the Nordic conditions. Accordingly, the image of a Nordic modernity presented here is conditioned by specific spatial and temporal dimensions. For the Spanish diplomats and travellers, the North had a special role in their own conception of Spain's relation to Europe and especially to northern Anglo-Saxon, German and Scandinavian Europe. The Nordic countries served as a source of modern industrial perfection. By describing the Nordic conditions, such as universal suffrage,

---

1 I have discussed the travelogue material in my dissertation (in Swedish): Stadius, Peter (2005) *Resan till norr. Spanska Nordenbilder kring sekelskiftet 1900.* Helsingfors: Finska Vetenskaps-Societeten. The diplomatic correspondence, however, was not addressed in that context.

194

the secular education system, women's emancipation, socialism, industrial development and social well-being, the Spaniards brought the world of modernity into the Spanish debates.

Spanish travel descriptions from the Nordic countries were not many, but close to a dozen are nevertheless known from this period.[2] In this article, I will discuss more closely the accounts of Felipe Benicio Navarro from Valencia, his testimony of Scandinavia in general and the wonders of the Stockholm Art and Industrial Exposition of 1897 in particular. Among Navarro's countrymen writing from the north, the author and diplomat Angel Ganivet (1867–1898) is the only one whose production has a place in the Spanish literary canon, whereas the rest are second and third-rate literature with a limited life span (until now). Ganivet's letters from Finland – *Cartas finlandesas* – which he sent to his hometown newspaper *El Defensor de Granada* during his stationing in Helsinki 1896–1898 depicts some of the peculiarities of life in the Finnish capital.[3]

While addressing their topics in accordance with the general conventions of travel literature,[4] Navarro and Ganivet passed differing judgements about the Nordic countries. Ganivet's was clearly a conservative and critical account, while Navarro presented an affirmative and admiring discourse which purposely aimed to show how these northern societies could set a positive example for change back home in Spain. Navarro, the ageing liberal, built his textual strategies around the idea of Scandinavia and the Scandinavian exposition in Stockholm as proof of the viability of modernity and progress. He did it by arguing against a presumed, critical Spanish reader cultivating stereotypes about a barbarian north where culture was never to achieve Latin European standards of refinement and depth. Others, such as the diplomat Antonio de Zayas, had a different agenda when assessing Scandinavian society. In addition to his routine diplomatic work, he published a lengthy essay *Psicología y costumbres del Pueblo escandinavo* (1907), where he set out a respectful but essentially critical view of Swedish society, defending the idea of Latin and Catholic supremacy.[5]

2   Stadius 2005. For an expansive Latin European view, see also Fournier, Vincent (1989) *L'utopie ambiguë. La Suède et la Norvège chez les voyageurs et essayists français (1882–1914)*. Clermont-Ferrand: Adosa; Nencioni, Giuseppe (2008) *Italienare i norr: Reseberättelser från 1400-talet till idag*. Umeå: Johan Nordlander Sällskapet.

3   Ganivet, Angel (1998) *Cartas finlandesas – Hombres del norte*. Madrid: Espasa-Calpe (first edition 1898).

4   In Stadius 2005, I refer also to the works of Odón de Buen, Federico Montaldo, Manuél de Mendívil, Julio de Lazúrtegui, Antonio de Zayas and Angel Púlido. A well-known defender of women's rights, Carmen de Burgos, described the North slightly later. Her depiction of Scandinavia is included in Carmen de Burgos (1915) *Mis viajes por Europa*. Madrid: V. H. de Sanz Calleja. I am grateful to Elena Lindholm Narvaez for this reference.

5   de Zayas, Antonio (1907) *Ensayos de crítica histórica y literaria*. A. Marzo: Madrid. Zayas also published a collection of poems with Swedish themes as *Noches blancas* in 1905 (A. Marzo: Madrid).

Women in politics

In the Spanish diplomats' correspondence, the Nordic countries appeared as the balanced side of world politics otherwise branded by hot nationalism, warfare and social conflicts. Revolutionary movements, anarchism and other radical phenomena were not considered part of the normal political life of the North, but some issues did raise both interest and concern in the foreign observers. The union conflict between Sweden and Norway in 1905 filled pages of diplomatic correspondence, and the advances of radical political groups and the claims for democratic reform were followed and diligently reported back to Spain. In general, such developments were seen to follow prevailing international trends, but there was one theme that was conceived as particularly Nordic, the advancement of women in society and politics.

When Count de la Viñaza, the Spanish ambassador to St. Petersburg, reported on the inaugural session of the new unicameral parliament in the Grand Duchy of Finland on 22 May 1907, he was clearly struck by one aspect: 'this is the first national congress that offers the peculiarity of having various women belonging to the inaugural session of its assembly'.[6] Out of the newly elected 200 national diet members nineteen were women, the first in Europe.[7] According to the ambassador, the women were part of a new 'parliament that will make ultra-radical politics'. One wonders which was worse for the conservative ambassador, the strong socialist presence in the parliament or the presence of women, who were obviously regarded as radicals because they were women. In fact, however, while nine of the nineteen parliamentarians did belong to the left-wing Social Democratic Party, the rest represented less radical agrarian, liberal and right-wing parties.

In addition to the advances of democracy, Viñaza considered women entering politics breaking with the natural order of things. This opinion was expressed also by his colleague Angel Ganivet, who saw the career-minded 'señoras inteligentes' of the North as lacking the will to take on the 'natural' task of maternity. This made the Northern woman 'a man with narrow shoulders and short legs, a social and aesthetic calamity'.[8] In his letters from Finland, Ganivet was quick to refer to the female personages of Henrik Ibsen's plays and readily made known his highly ambivalent feelings about

6 Spanish Ministry of Foreign Affairs Archives, Madrid (SFMA), Caja H2538, no. 65, 13/26 May 1907: '[...] el primer Congreso nacional que ofrece la particularidad de que á él pertenezcan varias señoras que asistían como miembros de la Asamblea á su session inaugural'.

7 The ambassador deemed the case so exceptional that he even mentioned some of the members by name: 'Mrs Gebhard, whose husband also is a Parliament member, Miss Alexandra Gripenberg, known in Europe for her feminist propaganda, Miss Maria Laine, radical socialist, Miss Mina Silliampe [Miina Sillanpää], ex-cleaner and ex-cook, who today leads a socialist daily newspaper, four workers, seven normal primary school teachers, one that has a certificate or title of merchant fleet officer, and some others.' Ibid. See also: *Suomen kansanedustajat 1907 – Finlands folkvalda 1907* (2006). Helsinki: Edita.

8 Ganivet 1998, 107.

the advancement of women in public life. To him, the most problematic and peculiar case was the single adult woman living alone, 'of whom some take a liking for free life and throw off the male yoke: they start by talking badly about men, later they get a bicycle, and finally, they shingle their hair'.[9] This radical and emancipated role model was something that Ganivet, even if he enjoyed the intelligent company of the well-educated Finnish ladies, explicitly wanted to keep out of Spanish society. He was also concerned about the 'mania' of the women in Helsinki to get out on the streets – which they had probably got accustomed to when still single – instead of staying at home. Such things were a threat to the family institution, which to him were the pillar of Spanish society. While Ganivet did admit the advantages of 'an intellectual family union in the Finnish style', this was only possible if the wife 'instruct[ed] herself in discretion; but if she is to educate herself with emancipating or revolutionary ends in mind, it's preferable that she does not leave the kitchen'.[10]

Not only the position of women but also the very names of the Finns made the Finnish society look democratic in Spanish eyes. In his 'Psychological reflections made by the correspondent when reading the address guide of the town of Helsingfors', Ganivet pointed out that Spaniards called themselves in ways that made their individualist and family-related view of society apparent. Famous bullfighters such as Lagartijo and Frascuelo were late representatives of a Hellenic individualism embodied by the singular names of Socrates and Aristotle. The essentially aristocratic Spaniards had names like Rafael del Riego (a famous revolutionary in early nineteenth-century Spain), whereas a Finn might be called T. Riego (but in Finnish of course). Ganivet saw different national psychologies emerge in these different ways of using people's last names:

> In Finland we meet names typical of a democratic and socialist nation, whose ideal individual does not have an own name but is represented by his surname, which is the social label. A nation where people are called Don José, D. Manuel, D. Antonio, can never be socialist; the man of collectivity has to be Fernández, Martínez, Rodríguez, García; this is what they are called here, just with Finnish surnames. There are some miscellaneous aristocrats, but they are an exception. In order to be convinced that this country is democratic, it's sufficient to notice that a vulgar surname like Johansson, Juánez, is being used by all as it would be a most distinguished [label], without seeking any means of differentiation. [...] The Finns are, more than individuals, members of a social organism, and they have as we can see in a thousand details, an outstanding aptness for living freely within those organisations and regulations in which we Spaniards would not even be able to move.[11]

9 Ganivet 1998, 104.
10 Ganivet 1998, 106.
11 Ganivet 1998, 84–85: 'En Finlandia encontramos el nombre típico de una nación democrática y socialista, cuyo individuo ideal no tendría nombre propio, sino el apellido, es decir, el rótulo social. Un pueblo donde se diga D. José, D. Manuel, D. Antonio, no puede ser socialista jamás; el hombre del colectivismo tiene que ser Fernández,

To Ganivet, the social conformer Johansson of Finland was the ultimate democratic and collectivist type, while he ironically sees exactly the opposite take place in Spain: all men are known as hidalgos. The Spanish eagerness to use Don and at least two surnames even for men of no real standing in society marked such aristocratic romanticism. On this occasion Ganivet did not talk about women, but chose instead to exemplify the Finnish democratic spirit with the Scandinavian-sounding name Johansson. Both examples were telling enough of Spanish images of the democratic North.

Mild radicals: the labour movement

For a Spanish observer, the Nordic region was part of a belt where women's emancipation and suffragette movements were felt to be comparatively strong, an area stretching from North America to Russian metropolitan life.[12] In contrast to the emancipation of women, however, the workers' movement was used as an illustration of the moderate rather than radical character of the political life in the North. In 1895, the Spanish minister to Sweden and Denmark, Marquis Prat de Nantuillet concluded that the Labour Day parade in Stockholm was clearly more composed and much better organised than the one in Madrid.[13] Over the years to come he reported on the ascent of socialists and social democrats to the different parliaments in the Nordic countries. The first elected *socialista* to the second chamber of the Swedish Riksdag, Hjalmar Branting, gained a mention[14] as did strikes, lock-outs and demonstrations. In a longer report 'Socialism in Denmark' in 1898, Prat mentioned the evident tendency of the socialist movement to conquer new ground in rural areas.[15] He also noted the newly-founded labour union's strategy of preferring collective bargaining to unilateral regulation and the consensus-seeking nature of labour-market politics in Denmark.[16]

Confronted with situations of tension, Prat found them uncharacteristic of Scandinavian society and political culture. If something radical happened, it was always interpreted against the presumption that calm was the order of the day. Agitation, radical unrest and upheaval were seen as an anomaly to the regular state of affairs. Radicalism could find a place in Scandinavia in an atavistic and purist egalitarian sense but not in a continental revolutionary meaning. Political life was to be conducted by negotiation rather than by

Martínez, Rodriguez, García; y así se llaman aquí, cambiados sus nombres por otros. No faltan aristócratas sueltos, pero son la excepción: para convencerse de que este país es democratic, basta fijarse en que un apellido vulgar, por ejemplo, Johansson, Juánez, es usado por todos como si fuera el más distinguido, sin buscar medios de diferenciación […] Los finlandeses, antes que hombres, son miembros del organismo social, y tienen, como veremos en mil detalles, aptitudes sobresalientes para vivir libres dentro de las organizaciones y reglamentaciones en las que nosotros no podríamos movernos siquiera.'
12 For more on this, see Stadius 2005, 160–162.
13 SFMA, H1752, 2 May 1895.
14 SFMA, H1752, 26 Sep. 1896.
15 SFMA, H1752, 10 Aug. 1898.
16 SFMA, H1752, 3 Sep. 1899.

violent manifestations. Such instances, if they happened, were understood to originate under external influences and were clearly not part of the local predisposition, tradition and custom.

When he reported on the second congress of the national labour organisation in Sweden, *Landsorganisationen* (LO), held in July 1900, Prat drew attention to the 'frankly speaking radical spirit', intransigent proclamations of absolute majority power and other harsh measures on the agenda of the Second International. However, after nine years in Scandinavia, Prat was sure that the Nordic societies would not take the course of the International: it was fortunate that 'such pretentious jumble has not found, nor will it find any echo in this people with more sense than imagination, with more culture than ostentation, [a people] which prefers a small piece rather than its shadow and who know their own rights and respect the rights of others, consider property not a theft, but an ideal for the well-being of the family, striving to accomplish this through assiduous work'.[17]

It was generally held that Scandinavian politics was executed by politicians who genuinely sought the good of the whole society through compromise. This assumption stood in contrast to the idea of Spanish political life as an endless swamp of nepotism and other partisan action. Even a conservative and negatively inclined narrator on the north, such as Antonio de Zayas, admitted that 'in Sweden, politics is not a profession, but a tribute one pays to the state'.[18] Political and social processes were thus seen as planned and implemented for all members of society in a collective fashion. The absence of beggars, high rates of literacy and magnificent public school buildings were regarded as proof of this. The spirit of altruism was stunning, as the medical doctor, senator and propagator of progressive social policies Angel Pulido wrote from Denmark about the different programmes of social relief and philanthropic institutions, all indicating 'this intelligent, wise and loving social action' characteristic of the Danes.[19]

Such a deep-rooted spirit in society was also what Ganivet referred to in defending the Finnish four-estate diet, which was considered backward by liberal nineteenth-century standards. By the same token, Ganivet was critical of the political culture of his own country and wanted to show how the practical spirit and the democratic imperative of the governing elite in Finland had managed to create 'the best governed country I have seen up until today'. Ganivet noted the interest of 'the entire nation' being served and the formally exclusive government working without arbitrary interests.[20]

---

17 SFMA, H1751, dispatch no. 146, 2 Aug. 1900: 'Por fortuna para Suecia tal galimatias pretencioso no ha hallado ni hallará éco en este pueblo con más seso que imaginación, con más cultura que bambolla, que prefiere la tajada á su sombra y que por conocer sus propios derechos respeta los ajenos, considerando la propiedad no como un robo, sino como el ideal del bienestar de la familia al que procura llegar por un trabajo constante'.

18 Zayas 1907, 227: 'En Suecia la política no es una carrera, es un tributo que se paga al Estado.'

19 Pulido, Angel (1911) *Cartas de Escandinavia*. Madrid: El Liberal, 50: 'Esta acción social, inteligente, sabia y amorosa.'

20 Ganivet 1998, 77: '[...] el país mejor gobernado que he visto hasta el día es este de Finlandia, donde todos esos progresos han sido hasta aquí letra muerta'.

Democratic spirit against aristocracy: the union conflict

There was one crucial topic in Scandinavian politics that to some Spanish observers appeared to contradict the harmonious picture of the Nordic region as one political whole. The union conflict between Norway and Sweden drew a distinctive line between the two countries. In this setting, Sweden was described as aristocratic, static and conservative, while Norway was seen to symbolise true democratic spirit. 'The non-conformity of character and temperament is so obvious between the active and enterprise-minded Norwegian and the slow and phlegmatic Swede',[21] Prat said in 1891 already. His early comment was then developed into the much-used metaphor of a marriage doomed to fail. At the same time, it was also felt that the peace-seeking nature of these Northern peoples would make the evident divorce non-violent, dispassionate and strange as in any Ibsen play. A couple of years later, Prat indeed anticipated the separation of the kingdom by drawing on the metaphor of an unsuccessful marriage and by highlighting the distinction between 'democratic' and 'aristocratic':

> If the democratic spirit [el espíritu democrático] reigns supreme in Norway, the dominant opinion about it in the essentially aristocratic Sweden is no less intransigent, calling the Norway, misleadingly named country of brotherhood, and its people rude and violent. There will never be a tie of fraternity between Norway and Sweden, not even a sincere friendship, and Norway has never considered nor will she ever consider herself united and attached to Sweden, and she will work consistently in order to untie the knot. The northern latitude will, however, save this mismatch consortium from a revolution.[22]

At a time when Ibsen's plays were probably the best known images of life and society in Scandinavia outside the Nordic countries, the idea of diverging codes of conjugal life was powerful. For example, Ganivet felt that love in Scandinavia did not mean the same as in Spain, and he explained that 'kärlek' (love) was the combination of 'cher' and 'lek', 'a joke without any serious consequences'.[23] According to him, the Northerners would never be able to feel passion the southern way, but were confined to semi-indifferent conjugal life based on friendship. Many of the Spanish commentators hinted at a certain frivolity of the Nordic women, and some even alluded to the softness and lacking masculinity of the men. For example, the poet

21 SFMA, H1750, 11 Sep. 1891: 'Pero es tan señalada la no conformida de carácter y temperamento entre el noruego activo y emprendedor y el lento y flegmatico sueco.'
22 SFMA, H1751 12 Dec. 1895: 'Si altanerio es el espíritu democrático que en Noruega impéra, no es menos intransigiente la opinion reinante en Suecia, país eminentemente aristocrático, de considerar al mal llamado país hermano, como un pueblo abrupto; nunca habría entre Noruega y Suecia, ni un lazo fraternal, ni aun siquiera una Amistad sincera, Noruega ni se considera, ni se considerará nunca unida y si atada á Suecia, y trabajará sin descanso para deshacer el lazo que á este Reino la liga; la latitude septentrional salva á este conxorcio mal avenida, de una revolución.'
23 Ganivet 1998, 102.

and diplomat Antonio de Zayas recounted one such 'Ibsenian' episode in his critical essay on Scandinavian popular psychology, which, according to him, exemplified both the egoism and hypocrisy typical of all Lutheran societies. Cue a young aristocrat marrying a beautiful young woman of the bourgeoisie, for whom this union is advantageous. After two years of normal life, the wife gets a young lover and starts to fulfil the idea of her 'right to life', a slogan which to Zayas was a Lutheran disguise for self-absorption and giving in to carnal lust. The wife wants a divorce, which the unflappable husband accepts. In fact, he cherishes the noble action of the wife and lover and decides to move to Copenhagen to ease the divorce proceedings.[24]

This story, centred on one key notion about Scandinavian morals in Spain, also suggests that the aristocratic man, or Sweden, cannot keep his bourgeois 'Ibsenian' wife, or Norway, under control. Accordingly, the old elite in these Lutheran societies cannot stop the advancement of radical doctrines, universal suffrage, women's rights, liberal divorce attitudes, etc. The feeble quality, tradition and position of the elite – the male elite – paves the way for the levelling of all things from education to intellectual life.

However, Zayas' critical voice and the diversity of Spanish views on the North do not alter the fact that Scandinavia was chiefly seen as a championing zone of democracy, and the aristocratic image of Sweden is normally highlighted only when talking about the union conflict. For its part, Norway was usually looked upon as *the* champion of democracy among the very democratic Scandinavian kingdoms. Odón de Buen, for example, a natural scientist from a humble family background and of documented socialist symphathies, wrote in 1887 that 'the Norwegian people is essentially democratic'.[25] Many felt in fact that Norway, which had practically no aristocracy and which had been comparatively radical in parliamentary politics for most of the nineteenth century, would opt for a republican state form at its eventual independence. However, Prat took care to point out that 'the Republic of Norway (the only form of government that the Norwegians desire)', would be an unwanted newcomer in the North of Europe, where only monarchies were to be found.[26]

Felipe Benicio Navarro, who also made a train excursion to Norway, had an almost sacral democratic experience in Kristiania when standing in front of the parliament building *Stortinget*, 'whose enviable institution could serve as a model for all continental nations[.]'[27] However, it is worth noting

24 Zayas (1907) *Ensayos de crítica histórica y literaria*, Madrid: A. Marzo, 232.
25 Buen, Odón de (1887) *De Kristiania á Tuggurt. Impresiones de un viaje por Noruega, Suecia, Finlandia, Rusia, Alemania, Holanda, Inglaterra, Francia, Mónaco, Argelia y desierto del Sahara*. Madrid: José Matarredona, 50: 'El pueblo noruego es esencialmente democrático.'
26 SFMA, H1750, 23 Apr. 1894: '[…] la República Noruega (única fórma de gobierno que los noruegos anhelan)'.
27 Navarro, Felipe Benicio (1901) *En la región de las noches blancas (Cartas de un valenciano)*. Madrid: Sucesores de Rivandeyra, 87: '[…] cuyo envidiable organismo bien pudiera servir de modelo á las demás naciones continetales, si en ellas se disfrutara de ls apacibles costumbres públicas y privadas, de la educación moral y social de que gozan estos felices pueblos'.

that in describing the Norwegian political system, Navarro sometimes also wrote about 'these happy nations', that is, in plural, making the generalising image of democratic Scandinavia sound like an axiom.

It should be registered, too, that the late 1890s was an era of deep concern in Spain, not least because of the national contemplations sparked off by the defeat in the Spanish-American War in 1898 and by more general debates on Spanish and Latin decadence. The so-called 'Generation of 1898', a label coined some 15 years later, pondered the causes and in some cases even the possible cures for the appalling state of affairs in the kingdom of Spain. The parliamentary system with its institutionalised so-called pacific alternation – *turno pacífico* – between conservatives and liberals in accordance with a 'positivist system', sacrificed parliamentary democracy in the face of revolutionary threat. There was widespread discontent among liberal intellectuals about the lie of the land, and it is not surprising that for somebody like Navarro, the Norwegian parliament became the positive counter-image to his native Spain.[28]

Order and progress: the Stockholm Exposition in 1897

The Stockholm Exposition of 1897 was officially part of the celebrations of King Oscar II's 25 years of reign. The exhibition was intended to showcase all the progress that the United Kingdom of Sweden and Norway had made during the past decades. Navarro wrote an extensive report of the display, an ode to Scandinavia, which he described as 'an extraordinarily refined civilisation'.[29]

In the fashion of the 1890s, the exposition rested on the two pillars of industrial progress and national romanticism. There was the material comfort and promise of modernity, complemented by the emotional comfort of an identity based on local, rural, traditions. Spectators from abroad would evaluate the quality of each branch. The combination of grand technology and picturesque aesthetics was something Navarro felt the Stockholm Exposition organisers had succeeded with.[30] Such expositions of arts and industry were a vital part of late nineteenth-century *Zeitgeist*, and many saw them as an arena for international competition and comparison. The King of Sweden himself suggested as much in his inaugural speech on 15 May, cultivating a language of metaphors in describing the displays as a

---

28 Such systematic 'guiding' of the parliamentary process from the cabinets had its peculiarities, and allowed in the name of national interest a so-called *caciquismo* in rural areas, the steering of voting by local patrons in order to help alter the election results after universal male suffrage had been introduced in Spain by the liberals in 1890. The logic of the conservative leader and six times Prime Minister Antonio Cánovas built upon the idea of avoiding social and armed conflict and direct civil war, which had been so frequent before the mid-1870s. Election results were thus managed to produce a contained parliamentary process involving the conservative party and an accordingly controlled liberal party.

29 Navarro 1901, 27: '[...] una civilisación extrarefinada'.

30 Navarro 1901, 184.

battle of culture and industry, which shall not, however, 'demand blood nor consume tears'.[31] Fellow Scandinavian neighbour Denmark was invited alongside Norway, and at a late stage Russia, and consequently Finland, too, were welcomed to take part, although Finnish participation remained fairly modest partly as a protest against Russian participation.[32] While people from all parts of European continent and even further were expected to the Swedish capital, the local newspapers were concerned about how other simultaneous expositions, and the World Fair in Brussels in particular, were to affect international popularity.[33]

When he set out on his journey, Felipe Benicio Navarro was convinced of experiencing the Scandinavian wonders of modernity and progress. On his way to the North, Germany gained but few sympathetic remarks, since the *Kaiserreich* was too aggressive politically for his liking. Denmark was already something else, but it was still a semi-continental country, and only when he finally arrived in Sweden did he start enjoying 'the comforts of an extraordinarily refined civilization'.[34] The exposition was then described thoroughly and with much awe. Navarro found the exhibition remarkable in comparison to others because of the high standard of the buildings and the arrangements in general. He saw a special kind of authenticity lacking the vulgarity he had encountered elsewhere. This was a true lesson for other nations which were usually regarded as standing higher in wealth and civilisation, 'as has been seen in all Paris expositions and now this year in Belgium, where the sad spectacle of its disorganised exposition has had to close before time'.[35] The arrangements in Stockholm seemed to prove the almost axiomatic idea of the Northerners as especially well-organised and orderly in their ways. Disorganisation belonged to the continent. In observing and explaining Scandinavian society and democracy around 1900, the erudite Spanish traveller looked to order and calm as ensuring the building of a successful progressive modernity.

Scandinavia had by the 1890s gained a certain place in the minds of the continental audiences and their debates about industrial and political progress. This was an area known for its high rate of literacy and considerable advancement in bringing technical innovations into everyday life for many of its citizens. Inspired by the exposition, Navarro regarded the Swedes as a 'people unceasing in its activity and utilitarian spirit similar to the ant, and with the resistance and perseverance of a healthy and strong race'.[36]

---

31 Quoted in Ekström, Anders (1994) *Stockholmsutställningen 1897 och 1800-talets världs-utställningar*. Stockholm: Nordiska museets förlag, 125.
32 Smeds, Kerstin (1996) *Helsingfors – Paris. Finlands utveckling till nation på världs-utställningarna 1851–1900*. Helsingfors: Svenska litteratursällskapet i Finland, 274.
33 Andrée, S. A. (1891) *Konsten att studera utställningar*. Stockholm: Samson & Wallin, 5. See also Ekström 1994, 117–118.
34 Navarro 1901, 27: 'Con el primer tren sueco comenzamos á disfrutar las comodidades de una civilización extrarefinada.'
35 Navarro 1901, 177.
36 Navarro, 1901, 257: '[...] este pueblo, que tiene la actividad incansable y utilitaria de la hormiga, con la resistencia y constancia de una raza sana y fuerte'.

This 'healthy and strong race' portrayed a special ease for adapting to new technical innovations. The telephone was the most frequently mentioned example, as suitable a symbol for modern innovation as any other electrical gadget. Astonished by the frequent use of telephones in Stockholm, Navarro remarked that there is 'no capital in Europe that would have better or cheaper telephone service'.[37] And it was not only a question of technology as such, but also of public access and affordability in large layers of society.[38] Angel Ganivet was similarly struck: in the Finnish capital of Helsinki,[39] 'the telephone is as common as any kitchen equipment, it's just like one additional person in any conversation'.[40]

Because Spanish diplomatic representation in Scandinavia and Finland was to a large extent motivated by the need to advance the interests of Spanish wine exports, it is no surprise that the Nordic attitude toward alcohol was one of the key topics in diplomatic reports. Laws on import taxes, taxation on selling alcohol, and even worse, possible restrictive laws on alcohol promoted by the strong temperance movements all received high priority when Spanish interests were being defended. The reports noted severe governmental policies concerning alcohol, yet particular attention was paid to the powerful temperance movement in the Nordic countries. There were basically two reasons for such added attention. Firstly, the temperance movement was considered politically influential as it was part of the workers' movement. For example, the Norwegian political field was felt to be influenced by the temperance movement to such an extent that the party field was reported to be played by four groups: the Ministerials, the Socialists, the Democrats and what the Spanish diplomat chose to call *los temperantes*, referring to the temperance movements' political organisation on a local level.[41] Secondly, the temperance movement attracted attention, because it was an odd phenomenon to a Spanish observer. As a movement, it was connected to Protestant revivalism typical of North America and Scandinavia. It was thus not much present in the wine-producing and consuming Southern countries.

The topic of temperance and alcohol consumption merged with diverging ideas of the Nordic level of civilisation. At the turn of the century, the concept and hierarchy of 'cultural areas' focused on the degree and definition of civilisation, and, in conjunction, to the advancement of modernity. It was therefore important to the liberal admirers of Scandinavia to greet high standards of civilisation. Correspondingly, it was equally central in the textual strategy of pro-traditionalists to apply a patronising gaze and

37 Navarro 1901, 131.

38 See also de Buen 1887, 48.

39 In fact, Ganivet only used the Swedish-language name of Helsingfors, which accentuates the Scandinavian atmosphere surrounding him in the capital of the Grand Duchy.

40 Ganivet 1998, 90: 'el teléfono es aquí tan usual como los trastos de cocina; es una persona más en cualqiuer conversación.' For other similar quotes by Spanish travel writers, see Stadius 2005, 183. This early appropriation of the telephone in Finland and Helsinki has been described by Kari Immonen (2002): *Sillat sielujen ja ihmismietteen. Suomalaisen puhelimen kulttuurihistoria keskusneidistä teksitviesteihin.* Helsinki: Edita, p. 13–20.

41 SFMA, H1752, 'No. 183, Copenhagen, 5 Dec. 1907.

objectify the Northern societies and even make them look ridiculous as part of the self-assessment narrative to boost the idea of Spanish and Latin supremacy.[42]

A cemented idea of Nordic inebriation hence conditioned the meeting between Spanish and Nordic society. This was the premise on which Navarro carefully employed his textual strategy in order not to stain his pure image of Scandinavia. He admitted that Sweden in the mid-1800s had been plagued by alcoholism, but he also pointed to the successful efforts to change the situation, and offered a picture of a sunny, well-behaved and civilised society where the dark past of taverns and uncontrolled drinking harmful to society was just a memory. For him, the true essence of this change was exemplified by the Swedish *punsch* liquor, a sweet arrack-scented Scandinavian derivation of rum. Apparently, he saw people drinking *punsch* in such a sophisticated manner at the exposition and its surroundings that it made him go quite far in his analysis about the impact on society of this beverage: 'The *svenska punsch* represents for me, at one and the same time, the sweet and serene Swedish character, in which sobriety and moderation form the two most fundamental elements. The *svenska punsch* is a product, almost a national institution that represents the victory of hygiene and morality over alcohols of various origins that fifty years ago intoxicated and degraded a vast part of the population of the Scandinavian peninsula.'[43] In his narrative, Navarro turned everything, even the issue of alcohol, into a Scandinavian success story. This was far from an easy task taking into account what was being written by some of his compatriots at the same time. For example, Ganivet held that there was no pastime activity, or sport, dearer to the Finns than 'the alcoholic sport'.[44]

Bourgeois welfare societies

Despite the tensions between such positive and negative images of the North, a certain idea of a liberal, modern and democratic society built on

---

42 The image of barbarian Northerners unable to control the consequences of civilisation, that is, food and drink, dates back to antiquity. Tacitus described how men in German tribes would lose their heads with dice games and too much beer. See Tacitus *Germania*, chapter 23. Montesquieu, and many others with him, took it for granted that people in cold climates out of natural reasons would need more alcohol than in warmer climates. For Montesquieu, the heavy drinking in the cold North was just as understandable as the abstaining culture of the Muslims: 'A German drinks through custom and a Spaniard by choice.' See Montesquieu, De l'esprit des lois, 1748/ transl. *The Spirit of Laws*, book XIV, chapters 1 & 10.

43 Navarro 1901, 232: 'El *svenska punsch* representa para mí, en una pieza, el dulce y sereno carácter sueco, en el que la sobriedad y la frugalidad constituyen dos de sus más fundamentales elementos. El *svenska punsch* es un producto, casi una institución nacional que representa la victoria de la higiene y de la moralidad sobre los alcoholes de toda procedencia, con que hace cincuenta años se envenenaba y envilecía una gran parte de la población de la península escandinava.'

44 Ganivet 1998, 179: 'Comparados con el deporte alcohólico, todos los demás deportes o *sports* finlandeses pierden su importancia.'

bourgeois values and technological development is amply recognisable in these letters and reports. Rather than a twentieth-century analysis of mass society, this was a nineteenth-century liberal idea. Consequently, the level of social structure of Scandinavian society was given much attention, but it was seen as perfecting a liberal dream of opportunity for self-fulfilment without class-society obstacles, and not as a result of socialist or Social Democratic policies. In this figure of thought, state intervention was marginalised, and the eyes were apparently fixed on the heavy centralised state bureaucracies of Spain and France as negative models. Further, in this picture, the state and municipalities worked together with private companies to promote a better life for as many as possible in a society which was presented in the positive and utopian image of modern and prosperous Scandinavia. Such an image also apparently embraced the notion of a society much less afflicted by partisanship and corruption. In Navarro's account, for example, the Swedish mining industry, steel works and industrial societies were seen as proof of an individual capacity in a nation which relied rather less on 'absorbing official [state] patronage, without which it seems impossible in other countries to develop anything'.[45]

The perception of a prosperous, progressive, modern and advancing society included most often the entire Scandinavia and quite often Finland, too. It was not an image of social democratic, state-led societies, but rather an idea of active and enterprising societies where the most cruel facets of capitalism had been smoothened by the tradition of social levelling. In this picture, society was marked by mutual responsibility and assistance, and in such a setting, the different interest groups, such as employers and employees, did not confront each other violently but rather resorted to cooperation and compromise.

In fact, Navarro's more or less uncritical praise of the exposition and the Scandinavian society as a whole bears a resemblance to what one Marquis W. Childs wrote in the United States in his apology of Sweden in the emblematic post-depression work *Sweden: The Middle Way* (1936). It is therefore possible to suggest that, when viewed from an outside perspective, there was a kind of bourgeois proto-welfare state in Scandinavia already before the establishment of the political hegemony of the Social Democratic parties.

---

45 Navarro 1901, 259. The mutual understanding between authorities and private enterprise was also in focus for the Basque mining engineer Julio de Lazúrtegui, who visited Sweden the following year, in 1898. See de Lazúrtegui (1898) *Una excursión minero-metalúrgica a Escandinavia*. Bilbao: Imprenta de la Casa de Misercordia.

BIBLIOGRAPHY

Unprinted sources:
Spanish Ministry of Foreign Affairs Archives, Madrid (SFMA): *Correspondecia*: Caja H1750, H1751, H1752, H2538.

Printed sources and literature:
Andrée, S.A. (1891) *Konsten att studera utställningar*. Stockholm: Samson & Wallin.

Buen, Odón de (1887) *De Kristiania á Tuggurt. Impresiones de un viaje por Noruega, Suecia, Finlandia, Rusia, Alemania, Holanda, Inglaterra, Francia, Mónaco, Argelia y desierto del Sahara*. Madrid: José Matarredona.

Burgos, Carmen de (1915) *Mis viajes por Europa*. Madrid: V.H. de Sanz Calleja.

Ekström, Anders (1994) *Stockholmsutställningen 1897 och 1800-talets världsutställningar*. Stockholm: Nordiska museets förlag.

Fournier, Vincent (1989) *L'utopie ambiguë. La Suède et la Norvège chez les voyageurs et essayists français (1882–1914)*. Clermont-Ferrand: Adosa.

Ganivet, Angel (1998) *Cartas finlandesas – Hombres del norte*. Madrid: Espasa-Calpe (first edition 1898).

Immonen, Kari (2002) *Sillat sielujen ja ihmismietteen. Suomalaisen puhelimen kulttuurihistoria keskusneidistä tekstiviesteihin*. Helsinki: Edita.

Lazúrtegui, Julio de (1898) *Una excursión minero-metalúrgica a Escandinavia*. Bilbao: Imprenta de la Casa de Misercordia.

Navarro, Felipe Benicio (1901) *En la región de las noches blancas (Cartas de un valenciano)*. Madrid: Sucesores de Rivandeyra.

Nencioni, Giuseppe (2008) *Italienare i norr: Reseberättelser från 1400-talet till idag*. Umeå: Johan Nordlander Sällskapet.

Pulido, Angel (1911) *Cartas de Escandinavia*. Madrid: El Liberal.

Smeds, Kerstin (1996) *Helsingfors – Paris. Finlands utveckling till nation på världsutställningarna 1851–1900*. Helsingfors: Svenska litteraturällskapet i Finland.

Stadius, Peter (2005) *Resan till norr. Spanska Nordenbilder kring sekelskiftet 1900*. Helsingfors: Finska Vetenskaps-Societeten.

Suomen kansanedustajat 1907 – Finlands folkvalda 1907 (2006). Helsinki: Edita.

Zayas, Antonio de (1907) *Ensayos de crítica histórica y literaria*. A. Marzo: Madrid 1905. – *Noches blancas*, in 1904 (A. Marzo, Madrid).

PETER HALLBERG

The Language of Democracy
in Eighteenth-Century Reformist Thought

The European crisis of the 1930s set in motion a search for alternative security arrangements among the Nordic countries. In addition to elaborating new political and military strategies, the search ventured into the 'soft politics' of values, a notable part of which was the articulation of a common history of social inclusion and democratic governance. While the historical record contained numerous sources for the forging of a renewed collective Nordic identity it however equally contained memories of divergence and violent clashes between the countries that now sought to assert a sphere of political action that went far beyond mere geographical considerations. There was, in other words, plenty of room for selective remembering and forgetting, of interpretation and reevaluation. Beginning in the last quarter of the nineteenth century, one particular political period in Swedish history had become the subject of reevaluation: the Age of Liberty (1719–1772). Initiated as a general critique of conventional academic history writing as overly reliant on a heroic-romantic narrative of monarchical rule, it also focused on the distinctly monarchical interpretation of the Age of Liberty itself, that is interpretations of the period as consumed by violent partisanship that was peacefully put to rest by Gustavus III:s 1771 'revolution'. Against this interpretation, which was carefully designed by Gustavus III himself, as well as by historians and writers hired by him, early twentieth-century re-interpretations described the period 1719–1772 as the golden age of parliamentary rule and, as such, a proto-democratic age wedged in between periods of royal despotism. The landmark study in this critical tradition appeared in 1915, at the time when 'democracy' for the first time emerged as a concept to denote a political order.[1]

The new history was, however, not without its own interpretative problems. Chief among them was perhaps the fact that while the Age of Liberty was a period of extensive parliamentary rule that famously included

---

1 Lagerroth, Fredrik (1915) *Frihetstidens författning*: en studie i den svenska konsti-tutionalismens historia. Stockholm: Bonnier. Lindberg, Bo (2006) *Den antika skevheten. Politiska ord och begrepp i det tidig-moderna Sverige.* Stockholm: Almqvist & Wiksell, 195.

the peasantry in the four-estate Diet, it was also a period of aristocratic dominance, a feature that did not necessarily fit into a neat and progressive genealogy of democracy. Historians who attempted to rehabilitate the Age of Liberty in light of contemporary political developments were of course aware of the problem, first of all, that the meaning and application of the concept of democracy had shifted drastically from the early modern period to the twentieth century. Moreover, they were sensitive to the fact that early modern usages did not conform to meanings expounded in the Classical texts either.

In this chapter, the question of democracy's genealogy will be dealt with in the context of how reformers invoked the past to advance claims to power during a time of intense social conflict during the Age of Liberty itself. The word 'democracy' was not used during the Age of Liberty; neither to denote that era's political system, nor to denote a coherent set of political views.[2] Sweden was not a democracy in the 1770s, and whatever signs of a democratic political culture we may detect, these must be seen as movements in the direction of *democratisation*, the consequences of which were unknown to the actors involved in the movement. Rather than taking a strong position to the effect that democratisation cannot occur without the explicit use of the word democracy on part of its supporters *or* that the political system and culture of the Age of Liberty was a de facto modern democracy, this chapter advances a view according to which it is analytically possible to claim that Sweden during the last years of the Age of Liberty developed in a *democratic direction* even though contemporaries did not use the word 'democracy' to advance their principles and goals. Three ways in which this democratic direction was advanced through historical reflection and writing in the second half of the eighteenth century have been selected for analysis.[3]

Firstly, historical research was advanced on a quite general level as a vehicle for enlightenment and reformist social criticism. Raising the citizens' historical consciousness formed part of a struggle against the kind of ignorance and prejudice that arose from murky knowledge, thus advancing an epistemological *transparency* that extended to political knowledge and practice as well. Secondly, history writing was used to chart the ways in which the state through its bureaucratic expansion had increasingly come to 'colonise' society. Narrating such a history, which was typically framed as a history of corruption, entailed exposing the supposed causes behind the people's loss of liberty, thus effectuating a historicisation of *liberty*. In

---

2   See further Ihalainen, Pasi (2008) 'I vilken mån talades det om folksuveränitet och representativ demokrati på den svenska riksdagen 1771–1772?'. *Historisk Tidskrift för Finland*. Vol. 93, Issue 2, 125–159.

3   The focus on reformist uses of history does not suggest that such a focus was the only, or even most prevalent, one during the period under review. Conservative and monarchical uses of history also flourished. See Hallberg, Peter (2003) *Ages of Liberty. Social Upheaval, History Writing and the New Public Sphere in Sweden, 1740–1792*. Stockholm: Stockholm University and Nurmiainen, Jouko (2009) *Edistys ja yhteinen hyvä vapaudenajan ruotsalaisessa poliittisessa kielessä*. Helsinki: SKS.

this context, one influential writer identified the process of Christianisation and the ensuing Papal rule in the Nordic countries that commenced in the tenth century as a major assault on archaic democratic traditions. The argument was that democratic practices, which were unique to this part of the world, were destroyed by the Catholic Church, thus preparing the way for subsequent corruption by domestic lords. Thirdly, reformists turned to history writing as a way to advance campaigns against noble privilege and inequality. As in the case of the history of bureaucratic corruption, the attraction of history in the fight for *equality* lay in its narrative of decline and oppression. This last aspect of redescribing the past was also central to efforts to forge a new commoner identity.

History, criticism and transparency

In 1770, an anonymous contributor to the newspaper *Dagligt Allehanda* commented on a new development in Swedish historiography. Virtually every important social group save the burghers and the peasantry, he claimed, had recently become the object of historical scholarship. Histories of the nobility, of civil servants, of the clergy, and even of commoners, had recently appeared. Surprisingly, he continued, no one had so far had the 'insight, heart, courage and strength to also depict the fate of our upright burghers or honest peasants'. Such a task, the writer projected, would earn 'a skilful author [...] not only a readership for his work but also the respect and gratitude of every enlightened and reflective upright burgher or honest yeoman'.[4] The title of the supposed commoner history betrayed its content, however. It was not a historical work at all, but the protocol demonstrating prejudices against commoners in the civil service.[5] Other histories he referred had in fact appeared in recent years. A history of the nobility had been published in 1769; histories of civil servants had appeared in 1767 and 1768; and a history of the clergy came out in 1768. Three historical projects will be examined here: Anders Nordencrantz's reflections on history as an aid to political criticism; Eberhardt's history of the nobility; and Carl Brunkman's polemical history of civil servants. As the analysis of this chapter will show, these works had a historical perspective, but they were written as more or less direct interventions in contemporary political debates, specifically in the debates concerning a reform of privileges that was waged between nobles and commoners in the early 1770s.

The notion that the strife between nobles and commoners could be better understood in historical context was widespread among commoner writers. In a new politics of transparency history provided 'proof' of past injustices that could in turn serve as a foundation for social critiques of present practices of representation and justice. Thus, the new historical writing

4   *Dagligt Allehanda* (DA) 28 Aug. 1770.
5   Anon. (1770) *Ofrälsemäns sent omsider, tydeligen förkunnade öde, i anseende til deras befordrings-rättighet, eller Råds- protocoll, som utwisar at de högre ämbeten i riket, endast äro ridderskap och adelen förbehållne.* Stockholm: Carlbohm.

became closely connected to the laws and culture of publicity, which were the conditions of possibility for any genre of foundational critique. The economist and politician Anders Nordencrantz was an early exponent of the culture of publicity. In 1730, he had defended a dissertation that included a chapter that argued for a liberalisation of the print laws.[6] The chapter had to be omitted before the dissertation could be published. He had also translated an article on the same subject from the English periodical *Craftsman*, which was prohibited and had to await publication until the passing of the Ordinance for the Liberty of Printing in 1766.[7] In 1756 he had proposed that the office of the censor should be reformed, making it responsible to the estates rather than to the government, thus ensuring that the people's right to enlightenment was protected by a representative mechanism. The basic tenet of Nordencrantz's social philosophy was that the exercise of free expression was a necessary condition to achieve just and civil government. The suppression of open communication fostered ignorance, which in turn disabled a nation's ability to resist despotism.

An early champion of unencumbered public debate, Nordencrantz conceived of his writings as a corrective to the curse of 'opinion', and it is in this particular context that his view of history as an integral part of political criticism is best understood. It is necessary in this discussion to distinguish between an older and a newer concept of '(public) opinion'. According to the major French dictionaries of the time – Trévoux's and Furetière's – 'opinion' was defined as the opposite of certain knowledge. As for *public* opinion, however, it was described as a true authority.[8] When prejudices, or opinions, were subjected to public scrutiny and intersubjective criticism, they became public opinion, a whole corresponding to a general will. Rousseau may have had this transformation in mind when he in the year 1776 looked back upon the preceding two decades as a period during which conflicting opinions had become one.[9]

6   Nordencrantz, Anders (1730) *Arcana oeconomiae et commercii, eller Handelens och hushåldnings-wärkets hemligheter.* Stockholm: Horrn.

7   von Vegesack, Thomas (2001) *Iakttagelser vid gränsen: när skönlitteraturen möter sina vedersakare.* Stockholm: Natur och kultur, 19, 297 n. 33. The article from *Craftsman*, translated in 1730, was published in 1767 as *Tankar, om friheten i tryck, samt desz nytta och skada; hwilke år 1730 blifwit öfwersatte ifrån den engelska periodiska skriften, kallad Craftsman; men ej kunnat til trycket befordras, förrän riksens högloflige ständer dertil banat wägen: fri, med förordningen af den 2 dec. 1766. Härwid bifogas jämwäl et kort företal, om tryck-frihetens rätta wärde och egenskap.*

8   Ozouf , Mona (1988) '"Public Opinion" at the End of the Old Regime'. *Journal of Modern History*, Vol. 60, Supplement, S1; Baker, Keith Michael (1990) *Inventing the French Revolution: Essays on French Political Culture in the Eighteenth Century.* Cambridge: Cambridge University Press, 167–168. See also Freist, Dagmar (1996) *Governed by Opinion: Politics, Religion and the Dynamics of Communication in Stuart London, 1637–1645.* London: Tauris Academic Studies and Sennefelt, Karin (2003) 'Mellan hemligt och offentligt. Sven Hofman vid riksdagen 1765–1766'. In Skuncke, Marie-Christine and Tandefelt, Henrika (eds.) *Frihetstidens politiska kultur.* Stockholm: Atlantis.

9   'Among the singularities that distinguish the century in which we live from all others', Rousseau wrote, is the spirit of method and consistency that has guided public opinions for the last 20 years. Until now, these opinions have strayed, with no aftermath and no

Adhering to the concept of opinion as synonymous with superstition and prejudice – i.e. the exact opposite of what would later be referred to as 'public opinion' – Nordencrantz defined it as 'a truth or delusion that has insinuated itself into mortal minds without prior scrutiny'. In the present times, Nordencrantz lamented, 'L'opinion est la Reine du Monde.'[10] He did not seem to agree with Condorcet, who in 1776 defined popular opinion in sociological terms as 'that of the stupidest and most miserable section of the population'.[11] Rather, Nordencrantz defined opinion in intellectual terms as a way of thinking that was characterised as impulsive, self-interested and prejudicial. This was a different understanding of the relationship between intellectual and economic capital, one that chastised stupidity but not misery. According to Nordencrantz, opinion was an enemy of liberty. The development of moral sentiments and a genuine concern for the common good necessitated the victory of reason over opinion. Throughout history, opinion had proved to be the preferred tool of tyrants, evidenced at its worst in the 'hatred of reason, knowledge and truth' displayed by the arch villains in Enlightenment rhetoric: the Catholic Church and 'Oriental' despots.[12]

Experience revealed that opinion could be divided into two kinds, universal and particular. The former were the sort of half-truths that enslaved the minds of people everywhere and the latter the sort that had taken root only in some nations.[13] To achieve liberty and preserve peace, men of reason had to combat the universal opinions that enslaved all, as well as the particular ones that enslaved their own country. In the fight against opinion, friends of liberty had one resort only: to spread the spirit of criticism, a quest for truth and enlightenment among the people at large. Just as critique was the only road to scientific and aesthetic progress, it provided the basic condition for the creation and maintenance of free government.[14] According to Nordencrantz, truth was defined as 'a knowledge of the relationship that exists between entities that act upon each other or, if you prefer, an agreement between our concepts of entities and the true characteristics of these entities'.[15]

This definition relies on two important assumptions: that there is an objective and observable relationship between (1) cause and effect and between (2) words and things, or signifier and signified. As opposed to opinion, rational knowledge relayed objective causal relationships and upheld a mirror

    rule, at the whim of men's passions, and these ceaselessly clashing passions made the public drift from one [opinion] to the other with no constant direction.' Quoted in Ozouf 1988, 6.

10   Nordencrantz, Anders (1770) *Undersökning om de rätta orsakerne til den blandning som skedt af lagstiftande och lagskipande, redofordrande och redoskyldige magternes gjöromål, de derpå följde oredor både wid och emellan riksdagarne, så wäl i juridiske som oeconomie: och finance-mål, tillika med förslaget om en säkerhets-act, såsom hjelp deremot, hwilket wid 1769 års riksdag förorsakade så stor miszhällighet emellan riksens högloflige ständer.* Stockholm: Stolpe, preface.

11   Quoted in Farge, Arlette (1995) *Subversive Words: Public Opinion in Eighteenth-Century France.* University Park: Pennsylvania State University Press, 2.

12   Nordencrantz 1770, preface.

13   Nordencrantz 1770, preface.

14   Nordencrantz 1770, 114–115.

15   Nordencrantz 1770, preface.

conception of language and reality, between our knowledge of a thing and that thing's 'true characteristics'. Reason was pragmatically defined as 'truth discovered through experience, studied through reflection and adapted to ordinary life [...]'. The purpose of truth was to help individuals 'discern that which can be of benefit to us: what we should seek and what we should shun'.[16]

Given Nordencrantz's conception of truth and reason it is not surprising that he in his political writings engaged in historical analysis. The general point of his intellectual efforts in this field was, after all, to explain and rectify the nation's present problems. He did so by attempting to tease out causal chains and bestowing upon phenomena their proper names. Nordencrantz was not a positivist in the modern sense. A disciple of Socratic skepticism, he readily admitted that 'the science of history is a history of its transience, and all that we can know with certainty is that all is uncertain'.[17] Nevertheless, he was convinced that historical exegesis remained indispensable to rational public debate. Perfect knowledge of contemporary politics, Nordencrantz argued with the support of David Hume, would ask of us either the ability to prophesise or to extend the search for causes to the beginning of time. While attempts to predict the future would always prove futile, a less demanding variety of a return to the beginning of time was possible. Working within a delimited historical horizon, writers could engage in political criticism.[18]

At a minimum, any sensible account of present problems – specifically the conflation of the legislature and the executive in Swedish political life – would have to take as its starting point the events that, during the minority of Charles XI, paved the way for absolutism in 1680, that is the nobility's self-interested politics that the King eventually punished. Although 'all writers of history and of jurisprudence, yea even the great Montesquieu, have not so observed', Nordencrantz suggested, the history of free states clearly showed that an overzealous ambition to create laws against absolutism had underestimated the need to control those very individuals who had been trusted with making and upholding these laws.[19] Knowledge about the historical causes behind and character of the decline of free states was thus indispensable to rehabilitate, preserve or extend liberties in the present.

In addition to being proficient in legal matters and desiring to serve the common good, Nordencrantz argued that lawmakers in a free state should be versed in 'the history of their own and other peoples, laws, customs, husbandry, interests and the causes of the changes that other free societies had undergone'.[20] Put in the language of history as a teacher of life, Nordencrantz maintained that 'the fate of the ancients [should] serve to

16 Voltaire quoted in Gay, Peter (1954) 'The Enlightenment in the History of Political Theory'. *Political Science Quarterly*, Vol. 69, Issue 3, 377. Nordencrantz 1770, preface.
17 Nordencrantz 1770, preface.
18 Nordencrantz 1770, 138ff.
19 Nordencrantz 1770, 6.
20 Nordencrantz 1770, 13. In his translation of Montesquieu, Nordencrantz complained about 'half-lettered men in politics [who see] each and every action without the context of the chain that links them all to each other'. Nordencrantz 1770, 123.

warn the living'.[21] To a degree, comparative perspectives on politics and history were already central components of modern political thought, but Nordencrantz argued that commentators had failed to take into consideration the complexities of different histories, resulting in a failure to improve laws and political practice.[22] Just as foreign historians had failed to fully appreciate the meaning of the fall of absolutism in Sweden in 1719, Swedish historians would do wisely to tread carefully in their search for wisdom in the revolutions of other nations.[23]

To help combat the forces of opinion and despotism, Nordencrantz encouraged his readers to look into their own nation's past to learn about the dangers of despotism in all its forms.[24] The enlightenment project of avoiding tyranny and realising liberty on earth depended for its success on the ability to spread truth and reason to ordinary men and women. As Fredrik Lagerroth has pointed out, Nordencrantz was a foundationalist in the sense that he wished for a return to the original principles of the 1719/20 Constitution. To overthrow it was, however, far from his intentions.[25] The project was rather to look into the nation's past to identify the root causes of present problems.

Narratives of the colonising state

In the late 1760s and early 1770s, the overshadowing social conflict concerned corporate privileges, specifically as they applied to equal access to offices in the civil service. As the conflict deepened historical works that chartered its origins were conceived and published. One such work was the poet and preacher Carl Brunkman's *Utkast til swenska ämbetsmanna-historien* (1768),[26] which was a response to a work by Carl Johan Strand[27] that tried

---

21 Nordencrantz 1770, 46 n.
22 Nordencrantz 1770, 30.
23 Nordencrantz 1770, 27. The author referred to Edward Wortley Montagu (1759) *Reflections on the Rise and Fall of the Ancient Republicks* and the French translation of the work François René Turpin (1769) *Histoire du gouvernement des anciennes républiques: Où l'on découvre les causes de leur élévation & de leur dépérissement*. A Swedish translation of Montagu's history, *Betraktelser öfwer fordna fria samhällens upkomst och fall, lämpade til Engelands närwarande tilstånd* was published in 1769. The work by Turpin does not appear to have been translated into Swedish.
24 Nordencrantz mentioned the following works as valuable sources, noted here in the titles given by the author: *Hist. des Revol. de Suede* (1695); the English minister to Sweden Robinson's *Etat Present de la Suede* (1695); Volume 2.4 of *Introd. à L'Hist. de L'Europe*; and especially *Lettre au Chevalier Jacob Banks* (1711).
25 Fredrik Lagerroth 1915, 512. Lagerroth considered Nordencrantz the greatest champion of the central ideals of the Age of Liberty: 'liberty, peace and labor' and emphasized his role in politics by noting how he turned the Cap party's program into 'a grand and comprehensive political system'. Lagerroth 1915, 543–534.
26 Trans.: *Outline of a Swedish History of Civil Servants*.
27 Carl Johan Strand was employed in the National Archives and wrote a number of political pamphlets. As opposed to his radical co-worker, Strand belonged to the conservative spectrum of Swedish politics. According to Bring, Samuel E. (1961) *Svenskt boklexikon 1700–1829*. Stockholm/Uppsala: Norstedt/Almqvist & Wiksell, Vol. 2, 80–108, Strand published at least nine political pamphlets in the year 1769 alone.

to rehabilitate the tarnished reputation of civil servants. Another is J. H. Eberhardt's critical history of the Swedish nobility, which was used as a source in the most extensive project for commoner privileges that appeared during the Strife of Estates. In addition a more radical brand of commoner history writing emerged in the radical political press.

In a slim pamphlet entitled *Ämbetsmanna öde i Swerige* (1767),[28] Strand had maintained that he intended to correct the neglect of civil servants in recent historical scholarship. Strand's narrative began with a description of a presocial situation where people 'lived like wild beasts', held cultivation in contempt and used murder to resolve conflicts. The exit from this Hobbesian state of nature did not lead directly to the formation of civil societies, but passed through an equally barbarous society under papism where the stronger, through the apparatus of the state, 'tyrannised the people'.[29] Far from being a Garden of Eden, the state of nature was a dark and dangerous place.

The key event in Strand's account was not the birth of society or the state in general, but the birth of a civilised Swedish nation, which he dated to the middle of the fifteenth century. At this time, he claimed, the Swedish people for the first time became known to other Europeans. However, as long as the vast majority of civil servants were of foreign descent the nation was unable to fully develop. An improved educational system under Queen Christina (1644–54) raised the level of education so that the state could safely recruit nationals to important offices in the civil service. The status of civil servants, Strand continued, improved significantly during the reign of Charles XI (1672–97).[30] Strand explained the contemporary aversions towards civil servants, not least as it was phrased in the political press, as the result of malicious campaigns by 'the unenlightened portion of our citizenry'.[31] Unaware of the history of civil servants, Strand argued, the present generation suffered from political amnesia, which made them susceptible to propaganda. Contemporaries failed to acknowledge how the nation's first Swedish civil servants had in fact liberated the nation from foreign usurpation from within.

In his reply to Strand's history, Carl Brunkman suggested that the work itself was an illustrative example of how the taste for artificial grandeur that afflicted late eighteenth-century society clouded the judgment of its citizens. Strand's narrative and the heroic part he reserved for civil servants, Brunkman suggested, 'is as pleasing to the eye as the Chinese Goldfish on first sight. However it reeks of mud and ooze on closer acquaintance'.[32] The purpose of Brunkman's counter-history was, however, not to critique Strand's obliging account, but to provide an alternative interpretation in line with a deeply anti-aristocratic perspective. Put simply, the bureaucrats

---

28 Trans.: *History of Civil Servants in Sweden.*
29 Strand, Carl Johan (1767) *Ämbetsmanna öde i Swerige.* Uppsala: Edman, 2–4.
30 Strand 1767, 4ff.
31 Strand 1767, 9–10.
32 Brunkman, Carl (1768) *Utkast til swenska ämbetsmanna-historien: Första tidehwarfwet.* Norrköping: Blume, 5.

had abandoned their function to serve the people and instead become their illegitimate masters. In order to popularise his account, Brunkman planned to publish a series of slim and inexpensive booklets for a wide audience. As it turned out, however, the first proved to be the last.

Brunkman immediately directed his readers' attention to a paradox. Through the ages, the nation's servants (i.e. officeholders) had incrementally enslaved the free (i.e. the people). Etymology provided some basic evidence, as the ancient stem for the Swedish word *ämbete* ('public office') was *ambot* and *ambat*, meaning 'bondsman and bondswoman' (*träl och trälinna*). Revealing the true genesis of public office, the etymological analysis supposedly showed that service to the king or the state hardly deserved the status it presently enjoyed. Public office should more correctly be seen as a form of 'servitude' (*trälsyssla*). Ruminating on the character of the highest ranks of civil service, Brunkman suggested that an ambassador – contrary to the popular perception of being a 'Royal equal' (*Konunga-like*) – was simply 'a Royal Servant' (*en Konglig Tjänare*).[33]

True civil servants were, however, not merely the servants of political authority – kings, states or oligarchies – but of ordinary people as well. Brunkman described 'free Societies' (*fria Samhällen*) as divided between two classes of people: 'those who are the Servants and bondsmen of the People or Populace and the Realm' on the one hand and 'honest Citizens' on the other.[34] Free societies could thus be divided into two broad categories or social groups: slaves of the state, on the one hand, and virtuous citizens on the other. Carrying the argument to its logical conclusion, Brunkman argued that the strength of 'Civil Liberty' (*Borgerliga Friheten*) in a nation varied negatively with the number of civil servants it supported. A perfectly free society would be a society without civil servants, populated exclusively with citizens. As Brunkman put it:

> The more liberty [societies] enjoy, the less honor they pay to their Civil servants: and the more respect and honor they accord to its citizens. And where Liberty is most genuine and unbounding, the number of Civil servants is low. But the more Civil Liberties decline, the more they increase. And the more numerous, more powerful and more honored Civil servants become, so much greater is the threat of thralldom.[35]

The general plot of this story about how liberty had been corrupted was that the growth of the early modern bureaucratic state was both ironic and tragic: the servants had enslaved the free. In such societies, Brunkman concluded, 'the People, to whom Power belongs, slave under their own bondsmen and are in consequence unworthy to be ranked as Citizens'.[36]

Although Brunkman's historical account was primarily a polemical treatise that outlined an ideologically charged but empirically vague narrative

33 Brunkman 1768 I, 5.
34 Brunkman 1768 I, 5.
35 Brunkman 1768 I, 5–6.
36 Brunkman 1768 I, 6.

216

of corruption, its central arguments were anchored in the general political histories of the eighteenth century. Narrating the rise of civil servants and the concomitant decline of free republics, or 'Civic bodies', (*Borgerliga kroppar*), he introduced the Roman concept of *Communio*, denoting a form of life 'where all is held in common as in a household'. These ancient communities were known to thrive in families and small republics or, in Brunkman's terminology, 'real' (*ägta*) or 'natural' (*naturliga*) societies. With the rise of large societies, its constituent parts became held together not by the power of love but by the arms of the state.[37] True or natural republics that were ruled by communion and popular self-rule were thus juxtaposed to modern artificial states whose lack of organic roots in popular customs, Brunkman seemed to suggest, would eventually turn them into freaks of nature.[38]

Brunkman's critique of the bureaucratic state was fully compatible with the ideology of labor and ownership that Nordencrantz had discussed by distinguishing between productive and unproductive limbs. Civil servants were the quintessential unproductive limbs of the body politic. Their failure to contribute to the national production inevitably corrupted society. Summarised in a formula according to which 'the soil tilled with my own hands is mine by natural right', and substantiated by the claim that 'wanting to imbibe sustenance from the sweat of others' was immoral, Brunkman described the will to consume without attending to production as an unnatural and hence a base social desire.[39] A profound devaluation of labor was a staple of public debate, expressed earlier in the century as a particular predicament of the Swedish nation: 'poverty assails us from one quarter and pretension from the other. All desire to become great men; the vast majority seeks to serve the crown. Not one wants to work.'[40] Public office was generally seen as the only path leading to higher social status, which explains why the issue of promotions in the civil service was so contested. As a corrective to this recipe for corruption and decline, the 'heads' (*hufwudena*) of 'civic bodies' (*borgerlige kroppar*) should be obliged to engage in work, not merely as a matter of ceremony but in all earnestness, as the Emperors of Japan did.[41]

Brunkman conceded that social stratification had existed since the beginning of time, but argued that as long as every subject or citizen still made a living with their hands, they were all 'free workers' and, because they owned their own labor, they were all noblemen in the true sense of the word.[42] With the advent of a system of taxation and education, he went on to claim, this libertarian tradition was broken and replaced with a spirit

37 Brunkman 1768 I, 6–7, 8.
38 This argument gained influence in European thought towards the end of the eighteenth century, forming the basis of early nationalist thought. See Hallberg, Peter (1999) 'The Nature of Collective Individuals: J.G. Herder's Concept of Community'. *History of European Ideas*, Vol. 25, Issue 6, 301–02.
39 Brunkman 1768 I, 10.
40 Quoted in Edler, Per Jonsson (1915) *Om börd och befordran under frihetstiden*. Stockholm: Carlssons, 107.
41 Brunkman 1768 I, 9.
42 Brunkman 1768 I, 13, 14.

of tyranny, corruption, vanity, and laxity. It was a spirit that Brunkman, with Olof Dalin and many others, believed had reached unparalleled heights in present times. Theirs was a time of material magnificence and spiritual poverty, a view that was voiced among the country's nobility as well.[43]

Brunkman's polemical history was innovative in its attempt to redescribe a number of basic social relationships: between elite and non-elite, between public office and labor, people and nobility. Particularly interesting is the way in which the concept of liberty becomes the lever in these relationships, emerging from what we may call a narrative of corruption, as well as a pessimistic history of mankind in general and of the Swedish nation in particular. By placing a career in the civil service in different moral light, Brunkman prefigured the massive onslaught against the nobility's monopoly on the highest public offices of the realm.

According to Brunkman's narrative of corruption, ancient political traditions had been suspended and a free people had been enslaved by a self-serving aristocracy. The main purpose of Brunkman's history can be described as an attempt to turn the basic master-slave dichotomy into questions with important ideological implications. How can the unfree enslave the free? How can a person that abides by the whim of royal idiosyncrasies pretend to dictate the lives of a free and virtuous people? Pursuing these questions, Brunkman conjured a social paradox that is firmly entrenched in republican political thought: those who rely on the good will of the ruler and on the size of the state treasury are not free and constantly tempted to reap the benefits of corrupting the common good.[44] After all, he concluded, 'like true bondsmen, officeholders always stand on an infirm footing'.[45]

This form of critique was to a large extent directed against the bureaucracy as a corps, disputing its status and supporting claims that justice was administered arbitrarily in eighteenth-century Sweden. It was also likely intended to contribute to critiques of the over-representation of civil servants in the Diet. Finally, the narrative of corruption also reflected poorly on the nobility, from whose cadres the highest officials were recruited. One year after Brunkman's critical history of civil servants was published, a more pronounced critique of the nobility appeared in the bookstores: Johan Hartman Eberhardt's history of the Swedish nobility, which is the subject of the following section.

43 Landahl, Sten (ed.) (1959) *Sveriges ridderskaps och adels riksdagsprotokoll från och med år 1719*. Stockholm: Riksdagens tryckeriexpedition, Vol. 25. Issue 2, 85–99. The attempt to achieve a positive trade balance was recurring during the century. According to von Vegesack, Thomas (1995) *Smak för frihet: opinionsbildningen i Sverige 1755–1830*. Stockholm: Natur och kultur, 42, no less than 58 ordinances to stop the import of unnecessary goods were issued between 1720 and 1794.
44 Skinner, Quentin (1998) *Liberty Before Liberalism*. Cambridge: Cambridge University Press.
45 Brunkman 1768 I, 21.

A history of inequality and oppression

In *Försök til en pragmatisk historia om frälse-ståndet i Swerige* (1769),[46] J. H. Eberhardt[47] set out on a course not unlike Brunkman's. He wanted to 'explain' how a traditionally free people – i.e. commoners – had ended up in a predicament where they were viewed as, and treated like, little more than slaves at the hands of a privileged aristocracy. By which designs and changes in government had commoners been tossed from a state of original liberty to a condition of expected deference towards the first estate? How had the ancient political traditions of Scandinavia been perverted to the point that Adam still toiled, but no longer as a free man but under the whip of a cunning nobleman?

In the preface to the book, Eberhardt described it as the first installment of a projected political history of all four estates. In the end, however, the author only managed to, or only chose to, write a history of the first estate. The work was presented as thoroughly empirical and Eberhardt stated that its primary focus would be to show how noble privileges had evolved in the context of major shifts in political power from antiquity to the present. The author promised to include whatever he believed served the general purpose.[48] As the title states, it was a *pragmatic history*, a genre that the author defined as being contextual and utilitarian. As Eberhardt put it, history could encourage virtue by providing the reader with examples and engaging in moral reflection.[49] The history of the Swedish nobility would accordingly be written in a moralistic vein, allowing the author to either praise or blame the characters and events of the past.

The immediate incentive to Eberhardt's writing the *Försök til en pragmatisk historia* appears to have been a recent disagreement between the clergy and the central bureaucracy over clerical privileges. In 1767, the clergy had requested that their age-old right to collect tithes from noble manors should be reinstated. The right to tithes allowed the clergy to collect one tenth of the national agricultural production. It was a practice with roots in prehistory and, most importantly, in the Bible where the collection of tithes was the practical application of the obligation to render one tenth of the fruits of one's labor to God. Being God's caretakers on earth, the shares went to the clergy.[50] Manors were large country estates that, because of their legal status as *noble* properties, were exempt from taxation. Since the days

---

46 Trans.: *Toward a Pragmatic History of the Noble Estate in Sweden.*
47 Eberhardt was a historian, political writer, church minister and teacher of eloquence at a provincial school.
48 Eberhardt, Johan Hartman (1769) *Försök til en pragmatisk historia om frälse-ståndet i Swerige, ifrån de äldsta til wåra tider.* Stockholm: Stolpe, preface.
49 Eberhardt, Johan Hartman (1766–1781) *Utkast til allmänna historien i äldre och nyare tider.* Stockholm: Hesselberg/Pfeiffer/Ordenstryckeriet, Vol. 1, 3.
50 In Sweden, tithes were institutionalized in the twelfth century where one-third went to the parish minister and two-thirds to the parish church. The latter share was abolished during the reformation, and was transferred to the crown, although some funds were still granted to the church as compensation. *Nationalencykolopedien* (1992) Höganäs: Bra Böcker, 101.

of Eric XIV (1560–68) regular nobles had been exempt from taxation for one manor, barons for two, and counts for three. The clergy's request, which in addition to the purely financial aspect of tax collection involved questions of privilege, was denied.

Eberhardt's history of the Swedish nobility was essentially an attempt to unravel the logic and evolution of antagonistic interests between different social groups, 'classes' or estates, specifically the relationship between two estates, of which one enjoyed more privileges than the other. His chosen strategy was to refrain from writing a history that justified clerical privileges, for example by vindicating the good deeds of the clergy throughout history. Instead, and keeping with the general logic of public discourse at this time, the strategy was to question the legitimacy of *noble* privileges. Although clerical privileges had always set those who preached apart from those who traded or worked, there was no question that the clergy's status was lower than that of the nobility. The fact that the clergy wavered between its standing as a commoner estate and a privileged estate may go some way in explaining why Eberhardt asserted clerical privileges not by arguing for new ones, but by describing ancient ones and, at the same time, painting a sordid picture of how the nobility had gained *its* privileges.

By adopting a language of disinterested historical scholarship, the point could effectively be made without having to employ a language of self-interest that would provoke cries of partisanship. His rhetoric of objectivity aside, Eberhardt's loyalty to the three commoner estates was however apparent. There are few if any signs that the author had anything else in mind but to direct his readers' attention to the way in which the nobility had corrupted what was described as an ancient democratic tradition that upheld liberty and equality for all virtuous citizens. Like other radical writers who adopted the rhetoric of discrimination and social violence, Eberhardt's narrative relied on the dichotomous distinction between nobles on the one hand and that large and variegated group, commoners, on the other.

Eberhardt constructed his basic narrative as a tragedy resulting from a series of ironic historical turns in the relationship between various social groups. His central thesis was that public authority had been illegitimately displaced and that the relationship between the condition of liberty and the exercise of political power had been inversed. From the earliest times, Eberhardt argued, there had been two 'classes' of people: those who were free, and enjoyed political rights, and those who were unfree and enjoyed none.[51] Within the class of free men, some were freer than others, a difference of autonomy that derived from the nature of the relationship that individuals and families had to the ruler and his court. This relationship was dictated by one major circumstance: warfare. The early nobility of the sword, whose social and economic status derived from displays of courage in the battlefield, had to rely on the ruler for their personal and material well being in times of peace. Since they were then governed by the will or benevolence of others, their independence was severely compromised to the point that it

---

51 Eberhardt 1769, 1.

was nullified. Put in a way that draws our attention to the paradox around which Eberhardt's narrative turned, their gain in public power, translated into public office, corresponded to a loss of liberty. Brunkman's idea that those who served the state were de facto unfree was accordingly specified and relayed in a more sophisticated historical narrative, but as we shall see the moral of the story remained the same.

To restore power to commoners, the author attempted to show how the displacement and eventual loss of the nobility's independence implied an erosion of *legitimate power*. According to Eberhardt's concept of autonomy, a person that was someone else's tool was not free and could thus never become the legitimate master of others. If, by some strange design, this nonetheless occurred, the servants would in effect rule the masters. Speculations of this kind are important ingredients in Western political philosophy, especially in neo-Roman and republican thought, according to which the capacity for self-government is the constitutive feature of liberty and just government.[52] With regard to ongoing Swedish political debates, Eberhardt's narrative fit the critiques of corrupted civil servants, their colonisation of the Diet, and the way in which the higher state administration had been turned into the exclusive domain for nobles.

According to Eberhardt, the fact that the early nobility of the sword had relinquished their original liberty for state service meant, that despite the 'resplendent surface' of status attributes, this social group was in fact less free than the nation's earliest freeholding peasants – i.e. the ancient 'yeomen' – whose sole ambition was to manage their property. The liberty of the ancient freeholders was safeguarded and augmented by another provision that was directly related to contemporary political debates: their full and equal participation in politics. Unlike the nobility, whose political role was merely to act as the extended arm of the king, Eberhardt maintained that the ancient freeholders participated in public affairs as equal members in legislative assemblies. The latter institutions were favorably compared to the *Tribuni Plebis* in republican Rome, whose task of representing the plebs provided a popular counterweight to the patrician controlled Senate.[53]

Like their Roman counterparts, the ancient Swedish freeholders and their lawmakers were said to have faithfully represented the interests of the people during the meetings of the estates.[54] In his history of the Swedish people, Eberhardt's adversary Anders af Botin had in fact discussed the phenomenon in similar terms, claiming that supreme power had once been in the hands of 'the Swedish People in general'.[55] Botin had further pointed out that the 'Lawmakers' were 'the leaders of Yeomen and their Spokesmen' and that they were held in high esteem.[56] According to these historians,

---

52 See Skinner 1998.
53 Shelton, Jo-Ann (1998) *As the Romans Did: A Sourcebook in Roman Social History.* Oxford: Oxford University Press, 203–206.
54 Eberhardt 1769, 4.
55 af Botin, Anders (1757) *Utkast till svenska folkets historia.* Stockholm: Salvius, Vol. 1, 124–125.
56 Botin 1757, 126–127.

the legal authorities that represented the Swedish yeomanry were described as discretionary lawmakers that deliberated freely on the foundations and exercise of government. In so doing, they constituted the kind of transparent and uncorrupted parliament that contemporary social critics yearned for in the present.[57]

The particular concept of liberty that arose from the narrative of corruption was further connected in Eberhardt's account to the 'democratic spirit' (*democratiske esprit*) that defined ancient Swedish government. This condition of liberty, he claimed, was destroyed by tenth-century Papism and suppressed during an ensuing aristocratic usurpation that turned politics into a collective means to private ends.[58] The ancient democratic system of government that the Pope's men had stumbled upon in Northern Europe, Eberhardt told his readers, was incongruous to the hierarchical mode of Catholic politics. The Pope accordingly set out to systematically 'undermine *Democracy* in this Realm'. The Church decreed that landholding peasants were not permitted to bear arms during political assemblies, which enabled the king and his court to pass laws against the will of a peasantry unable to defend their rights. Having monopolised violence, the Pope and his backers ended a system that guaranteed a balance of power between the different branches of government. In its place they put a system that conflated the legislative with the judiciary and the executive.[59]

Central to Eberhardt's narrative was that the change of balance of power, which put the bulk of political power in the hands of a Council of the Realm, which was dominated by the 'unfree' nobility of the state, corrupted the traditional concept of autonomous representation by freeholders. Having turned itself into the supreme body of government, the Council of the Realm 'in this found reason to desire to be regarded as the *Representatives* of the Swedish People'.[60] Here was a historical account that was not only a critique of a powerful council admitting only nobles, but also a parallel to Anders Nordencrantz's claim that civil servants wrongly constituted a state within the state, a corrupting conflation of legislative and administrative power. Contrary to ancient Swedish traditions, the Papacy had thus not only suppressed liberty, but also altered the original relationship between a free and an unfree nobility to an extent that the freeholding peasantry lost its political status.

Drawing his readers' attention to the politics of terminology, Eberhardt pointed out that the term *frälse* lost its original meaning of both 'free' and 'noble' in the late thirteenth century. In the same instance as the estate of serfs (*Träldoms-Ståndet*) was abolished in 1295 and the freeholding peasants (*Odal-Allmoge*) were cajoled into paying levies, what had formerly constituted the freest group of an archaic democratic polity now went by the name of *ofrälse*, that is 'un-free'.[61] Moreover, papal usurpation

---

57 See esp. Nordencrantz 1770.
58 Eberhardt 1769, 4.
59 Eberhardt 1769, 5ff.
60 Eberhardt 1769, 5.
61 Eberhardt 1769, 5.

created a new division at the apex of society: between the Roman clergy (the spiritual nobility), and the king's public officials (the worldly nobility). The competition between these two groups for power in turn gave rise to the arrival in Sweden of an '*Aristocracy*, through which the Estate of Nobility for its part gained as much as the Realm in general lost'.[62]

Having invested themselves with political power, the worldly nobility now further entrenched their position in society by advancing the notion of 'rights of estate' (*ståndsrätt*). Their power vis-à-vis the other estates was increased by admitting new members to their own group, which constituted what Eberhardt referred to as a 'new class' (*denna nya class*) of nobles: 'General Noblemen', (*Allmännelige Frälsemän*) which designated freeholders who had agreed to bear arms to defend the nation at war.[63] The new nobility aggressively asserted its elevated status. By introducing public attributes of distinction – such as 'titles, rank, ornaments and rights' – the 'most eminent *class* of the Nobility' – was set apart from other social groups. Their difference was furthermore fortified by inventing a number of public spectacles and displays of decorum, such as 'tournaments that provided the *Stage* on which they demonstrated their skills, gave a reason for the Crests long used by Noble *Families* to set themselves apart from others'.[64]

The power of the new nobility was also displayed in the kind of public yet personal symbols that Habermas discusses in his analysis of what he refers to as the representative public sphere.[65] They wore 'gilt spurs, silver belts, trimmings and frills, in the Council they were close to the Bishops, and outside it close to Councilors of State in *Rank*'. They also began calling their homesteads 'manor houses' and referred to their wives and daughters as 'Mistresses and Misses'.[66] The barrage of social markers that commoners in the 1770s criticised as superficial substitutes for true virtue could accordingly be discussed in historical terms, tracing the representative publicity of the eighteenth-century nobility back to the ascent of the 'new' nobility centuries earlier. In this way, the narrative of corruption was fused with contemporary anti-aristocratic critiques. Transhistorical and contemporary phenomena of corruption and vice could thus be specified and located historically. Put in it simplest possible form, corruption and discrimination had a long history.

Set apart from the rest of society by privileges and outward displays of high status, Eberhardt noted, the three classes which would provide the stratification of the Swedish nobility until 1719 originated with the tri-partite division between 'knights', 'general nobility' and 'yeomen'. Offering a direct comment on contemporary partisanship, the author also concluded that internal competition at court gave rise to the formation of 'two strong parties' that in fits of 'jealousy' competed for power at the expense of the people. In particular, the peasants were subjected to the despotic domination of the

---

62 Eberhardt 1769, 6.
63 Eberhardt 1769, 6–7, 8.
64 Eberhardt 1769, 7.
65 Habermas, Jürgen (1991) *The Structural Transformation of the Public Sphere: An Inquiry into a Category of Bourgeois Society*. Cambridge, Mass.: MIT Press.
66 Eberhardt 1769, 7.

new nobility, as epitomised in the fifteenth-century proverb 'Nobleman the Peasant's King'.[67] During the course of some three hundred years, a social and political revolution had accordingly been completed where the originally free and propertied had been enslaved by the unfree and unpropertied – by men of service and flattery. This notion of a social and political elite whose history revealed an illegitimate revolution was a powerful critique in an age where commoners were increasing their presence in the civil service, thus, as it were, arguing for their right to become unfree as well. Although the group called 'commoners' was composite and consisted of clergy, burghers and peasants, and possibly other groups as well, the critique remained within the imagery of the ancient peasantry. As the following section shows, the idea of specifying the concept of commoners and, in the process, inquiring into a shared history, gained vocal adherents in the Diet and the press during the debates over privileges in the early 1770s.

Conceptual innovation and the problem of identity

Since the ancient lawmakers had to be born peasants, their ownership of land made them independent in the sense that their status derived from properties belonging to the individual person, not from an external power's protection of these properties. As Carl Brunkman had argued in his 1768 history of civil servants, a truly free person relinquished all bonds of authority. Eberhardt offered the following description of ancient Sweden, which he claimed summed up the nation's true or original nobility, i.e. the freeholding peasantry that he preferred to call 'yeomen':

> The earliest householders, who reigned supreme over their children and retainers, occupied the land they had taken and cultivated as their own property and were troubled by nothing other than the customary travail of humankind in nourishing themselves and their dependents through their labor. Their authority as fathers and masters afforded them ascendancy in their homes: disputes among them were settled with their fists and when they finally appointed an arbitrator, distinguished by his age and sagacity, he was given no honors but was foremost among his peers.[68]

This condition was tied to a particular form of ownership: 'allodial' ownership in English.[69] According to a contemporary definition in David

---

67 Eberhardt 1769, 8–9, 10.
68 Eberhardt 1769, 1.
69 The exact term in English for the Swedish 'odal' is 'allodial'. However, in the context of political thought and debate, its closest equivalent is 'yeoman' and its derivatives. Hence, the term 'odal' will be translated as 'yeoman' or, signifying a collectivity, 'yeomanry'. The English word 'commons' as a label for 'common people, the commonalty; the lower order, as distinguished from those of noble or knightly or gentle rank' comes close the way in which both 'commoner' (*ofrälse*) and 'yeoman' (*odalman*) was used in eighteenth-century writings. See *The Compact Edition of the Oxford English Dictionary* (1971) Oxford: Oxford University Press, Vol. 1, 484.

Hume's *History of England* (1761), certain territories of a polity were defined as being 'possessed by an allodial or free title'. Designating not just ownership in general, but aboriginal ownership it carried with it archaic social ideals of traditional forms of sustenance and communal life, stressing the virtues of heritage and honest industry. In the early sixteenth century, villages, sections of land or districts that had venerable roots were accordingly characterised as 'allodial' and used in combination with words like 'village', 'land' and 'field'.[70]

In eighteenth-century political and historical literature, the term *odal* denoted not only the properties of land or other material substances, but also the particular condition of liberty that derived from ownership. Individuals could hence enjoy 'allodial liberty' (*odalfrihet*) or 'allodial right' (*odalrätt*) and could be described as being 'born allodial' in the sense of possessing inherited rights to property. Economic and moral characteristics furthermore converged and gave rise to the designation of a social type – the 'allodial man' (*odalman*) or 'allodial peasant' (*odalbonde*). These uses of the word corresponds to the standard definition of a 'yeoman' in the English language, that is 'a man holding a small landed estate; a freeholder under the rank of a gentleman; hence *vaguely*, a commoner or countryman of respectable standing, esp. one who cultivates his own land'.[71] Collectively such individuals constituted the 'allodial peasantry' (*odalallmoge*).

A good illustration of a wide usage of the term is found in the first volume of Olof Dalin's *Svea rikes historia* (1747), where the author emphasised some of the moral and political aspects pertaining to allodial ownership. Serving as a model of original and free government, Dalin credited ancient Scandinavian political practice with enabling a system of individual self-rule. In these early societies, he wrote, 'order, devotion to the gods, law and justice' were maintained without recourse to an all-powerful sovereign. From Dalin's description one is left with the impression that this social order existed somewhere between two otherwise extreme states of affairs: the state of nature and civil society. The life of the original yeomen was not presocial, since people lived in communities, but prepolitical: laws as a means to regulate social and economic life had not yet been invented.[72] Social life was, in other words, founded on the *spirit* of the law rather than the law itself.

70 Hume, David (1754) *The History of England*. London: Millar, 246, quoted in *The Compact Edition of the Oxford English Dictionary* 1971, Vol. 1, 60. See Pocock, J. G. A. (1999) *Barbarism and Religion*. Cambridge: Cambridge University Press, Vol. 2, 162–257, for an analysis of Hume's historical works.
71 *The Compact Edition of the Oxford English Dictionary* (1971), Vol. 2, 3856; Hulme, Wm. H. (1897) 'Yeoman'. *Modern Language Notes*, Vol. 12, Issue 7, 221–222; Almond, Richard and Pollard, A. J. (2001) 'The Yeomanry of Robin Hood and Social Terminology in Fifteenth-Century England'. *Past & Present*, Issue 170, 52–77, who discusses the linguistic problems surrounding the terminology in England from the fourteenth century onwards.
72 von Dalin, Olof (1747) *Svea rikes historia ifrån des begynnelse til wåra tider*. Stockholm: Salvius, Vol. 1, 197.

The original 'yeomen' (*odalsmän*), Dalin concluded, enjoyed absolute sovereignty over themselves, their land, their household and their work force:

> Each and every householder who had taken possession of a certain area, a certain island, was himself *absolute master* and *judge* over his children and his retainers; few were his subjects but *none ruled him save for God alone*; the earth he inhabited belonged to him *by natural law*, and was inherited by his descendents with the same title: this is the origin of yeomen and of the Swedish nobility.[73]

Although there were different conceptions of the government among the ancients – Anders af Botin, for example, spoke about the existence of 'civil Society' (*borgerligt Samhälle*) during the same period – historians agreed on the existence and natural place of autonomy and ownership.[74] So deeply entrenched was the principle of self-ownership that property owners encouraged superfluous laborers to settle on lands of their own and to assist their master only upon request. This practice accounted for the creation of a more limited form of ownership that Dalin associated with the birth of freeholders.[75] Defined in terms of their capacity for autonomy, the yeomen and the original nobility were identical in ancient Scandinavia and were distinguished from the working peasantry by virtue of their absolute rights to land, answering in legal matters to God alone. Life among the yeomanry was, however, not entirely edenic. Those who were free, Dalin maintained, bought and sold serfs like eighteenth-century people traded horses, and could even kill them if they so desired. This practice was described as an exception in a history of liberty. As Dalin concluded, 'Swedes have from the earliest times been a free people that shunned all forms of thralldom'.[76]

The moral connotations attached to the condition of liberty associated with the yeomanry included positively valorised characteristics, such as tradition, dignity, independence, self-respect, industry and morality. To some, this connotation must have seemed attractive at a time when commerce and luxury were seen as catalysts of moral degeneration and a threat to liberty. The history of the yeomen thus took on contemporary significance, as when Dalin in a pastoral describes how the first settlers sat naked by the communal fire, how they lived contently in their dirt abodes as

73 Dalin 1747, 61, my emphasis. See also 96–97, 113.
74 Botin 1757, 26.
75 Dalin 1747, 61. See also 219–220, where the ancient yeoman is said to correspond to 'each landowning nobleman' and equivalent, in the mid-eighteenth century, to 'counts and barons'. Later on, p. 629, Dalin introduces a different definition, saying that 'all yeomen and the inhabitants of the land' were called 'peasants'. In the second volume he, however, states that 'Sweden's landowners and yeomen' in the period 1300–1500 constituted an aristocracy. von Dalin, Olof (1750) *Svea rikes historia ifrån des begynnelse til wåra tider*. Stockholm: Salvius, Vol. 2, 709.
76 Dalin 1747, 218–219.

if they lived in palaces and referred to the absence in this age of luxurious foods and expensive clothes.[77]

The ancient history of the yeomanry proved useful to the reformers and radicals. History provided them with resources construct a collective identity for a group of people that had little in common, except that they were not noble. Representations of the past also became a central aspect when commoners in the Diet in the early 1770s drafted memorandums and project that called for extending privileges to all estates. Thus, when the burgomaster Alexander Kepplerus in 1771 introduced a project for privileges for the three lower estates, he started with a historical exposé of how ancient rights and liberties had been corrupted under both absolutism and the Age of Liberty. The introduction argued that present-day Sweden had slid into a morass of laws and ordinances that not only hindered economic production and violated individual rights, but also betrayed the country's unique political traditions.[78]

Pursuing this interpretation of Swedish history, Kepplerus made over 40 specific references to legal and constitutional documents and relied on two recent works of history: Ehrensteen's work on noble ownership and Eberhardt's history of the nobility. The latter lent specific support to Kepplerus' claim that the people's right to make their own laws 'has not been and is not merely idealistic, casual or only imagined, but is founded on the ancient rights of the Swedish People'. Ehrensteen, in turn, had shown that this fundamental right had been neither waived nor forcibly abolished and that it should therefore be upheld.[79] In the first paragraph of the actual project for commoner privileges, these rights were dated to the first settlements in Scandinavia. Kepplerus next went on to argue that the nation's commoners' 'rights and liberties' should be upheld

> without interruption, encroachment or amendment, such as they have immemorially pertained to Swedish men or the Peasantry of the Realm as Free-born men since the Realms of Svea and Gothia were settled and provided with Kings.[80]

Paraphrasing Kepplerus' memorandum, a project for commoner privileges that was presented in the estate of peasantry stated that 'all in general and each and every individual should enjoy life, respect and property in total peace and security together with all the benefits, freedoms and liberties,

---

77 Dalin 1747, 278. According to Lamm, Martin (1918) *Upplysningstidens romantik: den mystiskt sentimentala strömningen i svensk litteratur*. Stockholm: Geber, 263, Dalin was ultimately responsible for the amalgamation of Rousseauean naturalist philosophy and a renewed interest in ancient Swedish history.

78 Kepplerus, Alexander (1771) *Borgmästarens och riksdags-fullmägtigens ifrån Lovisa stad, herr And. Keppleri Memorial, rörande privilegier för borgare- och bonde-stånden*. Stockholm: Grefing, 1–12.

79 Kepplerus 1771, 8.

80 Kepplerus 1771, 13.

uninterruptedly and without encroachment, that have since time immemorial pertained to Swedish men and the allodial born Peasantry of the realm'.[81]

Judging from Kepplerus's footnotes, it was Eberhardt that had made him aware of the importance of language and terminology in the struggle for commoner privileges. Citing Eberhardt's account of the trajectory of the word 'un-free' (*ofrälse*) that was discussed in the previous section, Kepplerus wrote:

> When in the ancient Records of the Realm one discovers what the word Commoner means and that from the beginning it was synonymous with Thrall, Unfree, Unprivileged, Expendable Serf, then it seems to me to be very unfitting and contradictory to honor them once privileges are issued. And as the Peasant was formerly called Yeoman, Yeoman farmer, my belief has been that this is more apt an epithet for the free Estates and Inhabitants of this Realm.[82]

In the first paragraph of the actual project for privileges, Kepplerus specified the groups that he had in mind when he spoke about the 'yeomen'. What he called 'rikets Frie eller Odal-Stånd' (*the Free or Yeomen estates of the realm*) included the clergy, burghers and peasants.[83] His definition of 'the Yeoman Estates' (*Odal-Stånden*) was surprisingly inclusive and counted people 'of what condition, age or Sex they may be'.[84] In fact, his discussion of the rights and security of individual property and personal safety applied to the population as a whole, including people at the margins of society, such as farm workers or day laborers. Trying to vindicate the nation's workers, Kepplerus suggested that terms like 'Vagrant' and 'Vagabond' were used to demean and even criminalise the poor. In this context, he added, 'according to the Constitution, the free Swedish People and the workers [...] are like other of their compatriots an equally free People'.[85]

---

81 Landahl, Sten (ed.) (1978) *Bondeståndets riksdagsprotokoll*, Vol. 12. Stockholm: Riksdagens förvaltningskontor, 592–593.
82 Kepplerus 1771, 12.
83 Kepplerus 1771, 13, 20, 28. Lagerroth 1915, 639, suggests that Kepplerus was inspired by Nordencrantz in his selection of social terminology. Nordencrantz did use the term 'odalmän' as a Swedish equivalent to the English 'commons' in a discussion of the English parliament. See Nordencrantz 1770, 39–44. Kepplerus does, however, point to the exact place where Eberhardt discusses the terminology, which suggests that the latter indeed inspired him to change the collective name of 'commoners' (*ofrälse*) to 'yeoman estates' (*odalstånd*). See also Roberts, Michael (1986) *The Age of Liberty: Sweden, 1719–1772*. Cambridge: Cambridge University Press, 195–198.
84 Kepplerus 1771, 14.
85 Kepplerus 1771, 2. Scholars have noted that the combination of humanitarianism, natural law theorizing, individual civil rights, and egalitarianism makes especially Kepplerus' memorandum a striking document that enumerate a number of provisions typically associated with the American Declaration of Independence of 1776 and the French Declaration of the Rights of Man and Citizen in 1789. See Edler 1915, 140 n. 1. Similarities are pointed out by Kjellin, Gunnar (1952) *Rikshistoriografen Anders Schönberg: Studier i riksdagarnas och de politiska tänkesättens historia 1760–1809*. Lund: Ohlssons, 218 and Nordin, Jonas (2000) *Ett fattigt men fritt folk: nationell*

The exclusion of the nobility from the 'yeoman estates' became even more pronounced in the project for privileges that was introduced in the estate of peasantry. According to this project, the three lower estates encompassed 'all those who occupy ecclesiastical, civil and military posts and offices', boldly adding: 'together with every person in the realm who is not noble'.[86] Addressing the internal make-up of these estates, Kepplerus' mention that age, gender and station had no bearing on the matter, the peasantry's project stated that estate *(stånd)* or office *(embete)* was irrelevant as well.[87]

The terminological shift was purposeful but not perfectly executed. Since a number of specific measures in the projects for commoner privileges were more relevant for one estate than another, the collective names 'the Three Yeoman Estates of the Realm' *(Rikets Trenne Odal-Stånd)* or 'the three yeoman estates' *(de trenne odalstånden)* were not always applicable.[88] Accordingly, Kepplerus' frequently reverted to the conventional labels of 'peasants' and 'burghers'. The clergy, who already had privileges and were not properly the subject of the projects, were on the contrary never referred to singularly. Moreover, the estate of peasantry itself, within one single paragraph, used five different names to refer to its own group, including 'non-noble' *(oadel)*.[89] Contemporaries recognised the contradictions of the epithet 'the three allodial estates' *(de trenne odalstånden)* as well. In an anonymous contributor to the newspaper *Dagligt Allehanda*, one writer argued that the proper usage of 'yeoman' was to denote a landowner, which meant that a large portion of nobles were in fact yeomen. By the same token, city burghers were clearly not. Responding to the proliferation of texts on yeomen – in the year 1771 at least eleven texts were published with this word or its derivatives in the title[90] – the notice read:

> For some time now I have seen in divers Pamphlets the desire to introduce a strange interpretation of the word *Yeoman*. It is opposed to *Nobleman*, as if the Nobility were not also Yeomen, like other Citizens of the Realm.[91]

This objection certainly made sense. After all, both Dalin and Eberhardt had noted that the first yeomanry constituted the country's first peasantry *and* its first nobility. Moreover, the latter were obviously landowners, as opposed to burghers. In light of this objection it is clearly the case that Kepplerus did not consider words innocent combinations of letters that simply represented a concrete object or concept. In the terms of modern Saussurean linguistics,

---

och politisk självbild i Sverige från sen stormaktstid till slutet av frihetstiden. Eslöv: Symposion, 197–198. See also Venturi, Franco (1989) *The End of the Old Regime in Europe, 1768–1776: The First Crisis.* Princeton: Princeton University Press.
86   Landahl 1978, 592.
87   Landahl 1978, 593.
88   Kepplerus 1771, 13 and Landahl (1978), 601.
89   Landahl 1978, 598: 'oadel', 'bönder', 'ofälsemän', 'ofrimän' and 'odalman'.
90   Derived from searches in *Svensk Bibliografi 1700–1829* (2000) Online Database: Kungliga Biblioteket.
91   DA, 6 Dec. 1771, quoted in Nordin 2000, 407.

the signifiers (or words) in social and political discourse were arbitrary in that they had no natural, immediate or necessary connection what was signified (or the 'things'). There is a clear sense here that commoners were engaged in what Pierre Bourdieu calls 'the alchemy of representation'. According to Bourdieu, 'the representative creates the group which creates him: the spokesperson endowed with the full power to speak and act on behalf of the group, and first of all to act on the group through the magic of the slogan, is the substitute for the group, which exists solely through this procuration'.[92] The three commoner estates were undoubtedly very different from one another and the change of terminology was introduced to address the problem of difference that had to be overcome to bring about a change in Swedish political culture. The power of the nobility had to be contended with by a unified body of commoners, whatever actual differences persisted due to the fact that the three estates were nonetheless organised into three separate estates.

The dichotomy 'adel-odal' was easily incorporated into the language of radicalism. In the pamphlets and journals that disseminated this language most offensively, history played a part as well. A journal like *Den Swenske upsynings-mannen* celebrated Nordencrantz, who approached present problems from a historical perspective, as a larger-than-life patriot whose mission in life had been to end all injustices.[93] The journal further advertised that 'All Swedish patriots' should consult three new works that presented historical proof of the damage that a self-serving nobility has caused the nation. The journal did not specifically mention Eberhardt's history of the nobility but focused instead on other items, such as documents and works on the Age of Absolutism (1680–1718): a collection concerning the reign of Charles XI (1672–1697), the second volume of Botin's cameral history, and a brand new reissue of Charles XI's 1688 inquisition (or 'reduction') of the aristocracy.[94]

What uses did radical commoner writers have for the history of absolutism? What was, for example, the connection between the 'democratic spirit' that Eberhardt had found in the nation's past and seventeenth-century absolutism? For his part, Kepplerus had argued that remnants of absolutism survived in the form of repressive laws and that these should be changed. There were also indications in the radical pamphlet literature that abusive practices in the military were the result of a failure to root out absolutist principles in the military. By contrast, the editor of *Den Swenske upsynings-mannen* and others referred to the Age of Absolutism not as a Dark Age that affected social and political relations adversely in the Age of Liberty, but as a positive image. Strange as this may seem at first sight, the reason for recovering aspects of absolutism was simple enough: the 1719/20 Constitution was to a large extent the product of a nobility bent on hindering the return of absolutism. Under absolutism, the nobility's privileged position

---

92 Bourdieu, Pierre (1991) *Language and Symbolic Power: The Economy of Linguistic Exchanges.* Cambridge: Polity, 106.
93 *Den Swenske upsynings-mannen* (SUM) March 17. 1772, 77.
94 SUM, 15 Feb. 1772.

had been undercut by the Charles XI, who, in alliance with the commoner estates, had confiscated noble lands and carried out an inquisition against ranking noble public officials. It is the final task of this chapter to investigate this somewhat surprising use of Swedish history in radical publishing.

The uses of absolutism

When absolutism was abolished in 1719, the justification for concentrating power in the Diet had been that an autocratic regime had not only ruined the country but that such government was alien to Swedish political traditions. As Fredrik Lagerroth has suggested, the 'founders' of 1719 were conservative in the sense that they worked to suspend absolutism and restore ancient political traditions.[95] The end of absolutism had entailed a political victory for the estate of nobility, which throughout the seventeenth century had competed for power with the monarchy. Already in the middle of the 1750s, members in the estate of burghers had made a number of positive references to the favorable conditions enjoyed by commoners in the military service under late seventeenth-century absolutism. Commoners tended to be a pawn in the power struggles between the nobility and the court, and during absolutism, royal powers were enabled by alliances between the king and the three lower estates. In his seminal work on the dissolution of the society of estates, Sten Carlsson in fact describes the last decades of that century as 'the first act in the social drama that was to turn a society of estates into a class society'.[96]

In his pragmatic history of the nobility, Eberhardt had also discussed the status of and advances among commoners during the Age of Absolutism. An intimation of this development appears in his treatment of an event from 1660, when a proposition that two new government colleges – the College of Trade and College of Mines – should be populated exclusively with noblemen was defeated. The same year, the commoner estates had managed to include a clause in the Constitution that stated, 'in making appointments *Merits* and *Capacity*, but not descent, were to be considered'.[97] In the context of debates over noble privilege as a prerequisite for higher office, the provision testified to a history of strife and substantiated the notion of a noble reaction against progress among commoners. Eberhardt had further pointed out that in the Testament of Charles XI (1693), this clause had been repeated. Thus, in offices in the military and civil state 'the skill and *merits* of an individual were to be considered, so that nobody be rejected because of humble origins or promoted solely for their noble descent'.[98] The Council of the Realm, however, remained the exclusive preserve of nobles

95   Lagerroth 1915, 254–255.
96   Carlsson, Sten (1973) *Ståndssamhälle och ståndspersoner 1700–1865: studier rörande det svenska ståndssamhällets upplösning.* Lund: Gleerup, 239.
97   Eberhardt 1769, 57–58.
98   Eberhardt 1769, 89.

throughout the Age of Liberty. The social advances made by commoners under absolutism made Charles XI seem a champion of liberty and equality. This, according to Eberhardt, was a king that the commoner estates 'had good reason to revere [...] as a great Ruler in every respect'.[99]

To the radical writers of the early 1770s, the most important aspect of the Age of Absolutism was one of the aspects still associated with the period: Charles XI's inquisition and policy of 'reduction'. Displeased with the way the appointed regency had governed Sweden during his minority, Charles XI eliminated powerful nobles from the government and ordered that land or estates once donated by the Crown to nobles be handed back to or expropriated. The result of these policies, which were carried out with the support of commoners at the Diets of 1680 and 1682, was that about half the estates and land that had been given to nobles had to be returned to the Crown.[100] In the radical media, the policy, which constituted a major assault on noble privilege power but at the same time initiated the Age of Absolutism, was described as having saved ordinary people from economic oppression under the oligarchy of a few powerful families. One writer called it 'equitable' (*rättmätig*) and maintained that Charles XI was the first Swedish king to recognise the virtue of 'natural' (*naturlig*) nobility, that is the meritocratic idea that true noble status is acquired, not inherited. He approvingly quoted the Charles XI's words about how commoners were worthy of privileges.[101]

Even Charles XII – the son of Charles XI who further extended absolutist rule in Sweden – was described as a friend of commoners in the history of social strife and noble corruption. In 1698 he had made merit the sole qualification for appointments in the country's Courts of Appeals; the 1634 Constitution stipulated that half be noble and half commoners. The 1699 abolition of immunities for noblemen in criminal cases resounded in light of the radical campaigns against arbitrary justice: from this year onwards nobles, just like commoners, were to be tried for capital offences by the lower courts, not directly by the Courts of Appeals. Eberhardt had referred to the latter as the nobility's 'privileged forum'.[102] In the radical political press the prejudices of present-day courts had been emphasised and made public through the publication of court protocols.

Positive references to the Age of Absolutism were no doubt a highly radical strategy in an era where denunciation of absolutism formed the backbone of virtually all political and constitutional discussions. Such denunciations referred, however, to the political system under absolutism. As for social relations, absolutism was not logically opposed to principles of

---

99 Eberhardt 1769, 89.
100 See e.g. Dahlgren, Stellan (1993) 'Karl XI: envälde – kameralistisk absolutism?'. In Dahlgren, Stellan, Florén, Anders & Karlsson, Åsa (eds) *Makt och vardag: Hur man styrde, levde och tänkte under svensk stormaktstid*. Stockholm: Atlantis; Rystad, Göran (2001) *Karl XI: en biografi*. Lund: Historiska media.
101 Hallström, Jonas (1770) *Twisten, emellan adel och odal-stånden, om rättigheten til rikets höge tjenster, betraktad på den politiska sidan*. Stockholm: Wennberg & Nordström, 37–38, 29–30.
102 Eberhardt 1769, 91.

equality enshrined in the 1719/20 Constitution, specifically the meritocratic provisions regarding appointments to the civil service. In fact, the great wars during the Age of Absolutism had been beneficial to commoners, as the expansion of the military and civil state required more manpower than the nobility had to offer.[103]

With regard to the relationship between commoners and nobles in the past, the Age of Absolutism was a potentially explosive issue. Under absolutism, the political and economic power of the nobility had abated, something which nobles resented as an infringement of their lawful entitlements and which commoners celebrated as a formula for social leveling. Thus, while writers defending the cause of nobles relentlessly criticised Charles XI's policy of reduction, commoners contributed with annotated translations of a late seventeenth-century work that reevaluated his rule, describing it as favorable to the cause of ordinary people.[104] The reason behind this social inequality, the radical journal *Den Swenske upsynings-mannen* argued, was not least that commoners had failed to, or been cajoled into not challenging the 'Aristocratic or Noble Domination'. What, an anonymous writer asked, had the aristocrats of the seventeenth century actually accomplished beyond being 'Royal Favorites', the automatic reward of being born into 'a supposedly eminent Estate'?[105]

The journal moreover described how the nobility under Charles IX's rule had achieved economic power by engaging in counterfeiting and how the ruler in 1603 had issued an ordinance that castigated such unpatriotic breaches of the law with corporal punishment. Deeply insulted, the nobility, according to the journal, henceforth referred to Charles IX as the 'peasant king' since he, from their point of view, busied himself with protecting the interests of the peasantry, an interest that in the journal's terminology included the rights of the entire productive population.[106]

Judging the policies of Charles XI in the light of the social conflicts of the 1770s, the absolute ruler was in fact described as the polar opposite of one of the most revered kings in Swedish history, Gustavus Adolphus. According to *Den Swenske upsynings-mannen*, the former had safeguarded the rights of peasants, as opposed to the latter, who had merely furthered the ambitions of the nobility. Charles XI had bravely defended the common estates against the 'violence' of the nobility and institutionalised a fair criminal law that punished 'without reference to Person all Malefactors and Perpetrators of Violence'.[107] Evidence of the King's sense of justice was substantiated by publishing a minor tractate where Charles XI sharply

---

103 See Carlsson 1973.
104 Ingman-Manderfelt, Carl (1770) *Owäldug granskning öfwer den oförmodeligen upkomna twisten om frälse- och ofrälse manna rätt til högre ämbeten.* Uppsala: Edman, 13. C.f. von Lichtenstern, Christian Habbaeus and Biörenklou, Mattias (1769) *En swensk mans tankar om desz fädernes-lands tilstånd, år 1675. Öfwersättning ifrån latin, med korta anmärkningar, lämpade til närwarande tid.* Stockholm: Stolpe.
105 SUM, 10 March, 1772, 58.
106 SUM, 17 March, 1772, 65.
107 SUM, 17 March. 1772, 68.

lectured a noble judge who had failed to judge two commoners impartially and by noting his aversion to the tendency among noble military officers to maltreat commoners in general and commoner soldiers in particular.[108]

Concluding remarks

As this chapter has shown, commoners used history as an ideological weapon to criticise noble privileges. The conventional notion of history as a guide to action was thus continued, but this function was put to work not to consolidate and edify the nation in battles against ignorance, delinquency and division. Rather, it was appropriated to forge new images of society and to narrate a hitherto subterranean theme in Swedish political history: the corruption and eventual loss of liberty.

Two major approaches to history have been considered in this chapter. According to Anders Nordencrantz, history could be used to combat prejudicial knowledge. A firm grasp of history could help contemporaries detect inconsistencies in governance and paradoxes in political thought. By unearthing actual causes of present problems, historians could thus assist citizens to achieve just government. The second approach was represented by commoners who in different ways relayed a narrative of corruption, according to which nobles had corrupted political traditions. This narrative was reinforced by two kinds of criticism.

Firstly by the idea that the obvious cause of the betrayal of liberty was the imperfections of the 1719/20 Constitution. When the Age of Liberty replaced the Age of Absolutism the Diet's powers had been extended at the expense of the powers of the king and the Council of the Realm, thus increasing the status of the estates, collectively and individually. The central argument here was that the privileges that had been bestowed upon the nobility and the clergy were to be extended to the two lower estates as well, had the legislators only been allowed by the nobility to do so.

Secondly, the notion of a loss of liberty pointed to more longstanding problems in the nation's history: the tendency of those with power to serve their own narrow interests at the expense of the common good. The Swedish nobility was conceived of as the Other of ancient national political traditions, the historicised version of the rhetoric of social discrimination and anti-aristocratic opinion that flourished around 1770. This story was told in a distinctly pastoral vein that charted how the forces of corruption – first represented by Catholicism and later by nobles – had led to the decline of an ancient society founded on the principles of liberty, property and an early form of parliamentary democracy. Commoner history writing delineated how an originally free people had ended up at the bottom of the social pyramid. In order to legitimate their claims, commoners showed that their demands were fully compatible with ancient political traditions.

108 SUM, 31 March. 1772, 83. See also SUM, 4 April. 1772, 96–100.

In a political discourse that turned to the past for arguments, a history of prejudice and discrimination amplified contemporary complaints about injustices. Such a history also served the important function of forging a collective identity for commoners. A collective history of grievances formed part of an ideological strategy that described eighteenth-century society as existing of two opposing interests or classes. The way in which this image of society was conveyed was at bottom pessimistic. Since successive waves of foreign and domestic corruption, starting with the arrival of the Catholic Church in the Nordic countries in the tenth century, Swedish society had slowly but surely lost institutions that were based on 'a democratic spirit' that benefited the entire population. In its place had emerged a hierarchical society where the first estate reaped their benefits at the expense of the other three: dichotomies such as privileged vs. non-privileged, virtuous vs. vile, nobles vs. commoners captured the essential divisions of late Swedish eighteenth-century society. The conscious introduction of the terms 'yeoman' and 'yeomen estates' was an important and innovative rhetorical move that could only make sense in historical context. The commoner narrative also found its way into the political deliberations in the Diet, where members of the commoner estates referred to ancient rights and liberties and also referred to commoner historians specifically.

While it remains true that the word democracy or Nordic democracy was not used in our modern sense to denote a particular political system, the writers analysed in this chapter in various ways clearly found use in democracy as a rhetorical concept that was closely connected to values like transparency, popular participation, and above all to liberty as non-domination. Moreover, their choice to wage campaigns that tried to gain the citizens' adherence to these values in the public sphere, as opposed to the more regulated arena of parliamentary politics, show these writers to be actively practicing the new politics that they argued was based on an ancient tradition that was unique to the Nordic countries in general and to Sweden in particular.

BIBLIOGRAPHY

Almond, Richard and Pollard, A. J. (2001) 'The Yeomanry of Robin Hood and Social Terminology in Fifteenth-Century England'. *Past & Present*, Issue 170.

Anon. (1770) *Ofrälsemäns sent omsider, tydeligen förkunnade öde, i anseende til deras befordrings-rättighet, eller Råds- protocoll, som utwisar at de högre ämbeten i riket, endast äro ridderskap och adelen förbehållne.* Stockholm: Carlbohm.

Baker, Keith Michael (1990) *Inventing the French Revolution: Essays on French Political Culture in the Eighteenth Century.* Cambridge: Cambridge University Press.

af Botin, Anders (1757) *Utkast till svenska folkets historia.* Stockholm: Salvius, Vol. 1.

Bourdieu, Pierre (1991) *Language and Symbolic Power: The Economy of Linguistic Exchanges.* Cambridge: Polity.

Bring, Samuel E. (1961) *Svenskt boklexikon 1700–1829.* Stockholm/Uppsala: Norstedt/Almqvist & Wiksell, Vol. 2.

Brunkman, Carl (1768) *Utkast til swenska ämbetsmanna-historien: Första tidehwarfwet.* Norrköping: Blume.

Carlsson, Sten (1973) *Ståndssamhälle och ståndspersoner 1700–1865: studier rörande det svenska ståndssamhällets upplösning.* Lund: Gleerup.

The Compact Edition of the Oxford English Dictionary (1971) Oxford: Oxford University Press, Vol. 1 & 2.

Dagligt Allehanda (DA) 28 Aug. 1770.

Dahlgren, Stellan (1993) 'Karl XI: envälde – kameralistisk absolutism?'. In Dahlgren, Stellan, Florén, Anders & Karlsson, Åsa (eds) *Makt och vardag: Hur man styrde, levde och tänkte under svensk stormaktstid*. Stockholm: Atlantis.

von Dalin, Olof (1747) *Svea rikes historia ifrån des begynnelse til wåra tider*. Stockholm: Salvius.

von Dalin, Olof (1750) *Svea rikes historia ifrån des begynnelse til wåra tider*. Stockholm: Salvius, Vol. 2.

Den Swenske upsynings-mannen (SUM).

Eberhardt, Johan Hartman (1766–1781) *Utkast til allmänna historien i äldre och nyare tider*. Stockholm: Hesselberg/Pfeiffer/Ordenstryckeriet, Vol. 1.

Eberhardt, Johan Hartman (1769) *Försök til en pragmatisk historia om frälse-ståndet i Swerige, ifrån de äldsta til wåra tider*. Stockholm: Stolpe.

Edler, Per Jonsson (1915) *Om börd och befordran under frihetstiden*. Stockholm: Carlssons.

Farge, Arlette (1995) *Subversive Words: Public Opinion in Eighteenth-Century France*. University Park: Pennsylvania State University Press.

Freist, Dagmar (1996) *Governed by Opinion: Politics, Religion and the Dynamics of Communication in Stuart London, 1637–1645*. London: Tauris Academic Studies.

Gay, Peter (1954) 'The Enlightenment in the History of Political Theory'. *Political Science Quarterly*, Vol. 69, Issue 3.

Habermas, Jürgen (1991) *The Structural Transformation of the Public Sphere: An Inquiry into a Category of Bourgeois Society*. Cambridge, Mass.: MIT Press.

Hallberg, Peter (1999) 'The Nature of Collective Individuals: J.G. Herder's Concept of Community'. *History of European Ideas*, Vol. 25, Issue 6.

Hallberg, Peter (2003) *Ages of Liberty. Social Upheaval, History Writing and the New Public Sphere in Sweden, 1740–1792*. Stockholm: Stockholm University.

Hallström, Jonas (1770) *Twisten, emellan adel och odal-stånden, om rättigheten til rikets höge tjenster, betraktad på den politiska sidan*. Stockholm: Wennberg & Nordström.

Hulme, Wm. H. (1897) 'Yeoman'. *Modern Language Notes*, Vol. 12, Issue 7.

Hume, David (1754) *The History of England*. London: Millar.

Ihalainen, Pasi (2008) 'I vilken mån talades det om folksuveränitet och representativ demokrati på den svenska riksdagen 1771–1772?'. *Historisk Tidskrift för Finland*. Vol. 93, Issue 2, 125[1]–159.

Ingman-Manderfelt, Carl (1770) *Owäldug granskning öfwer den oförmodeligen upkomna twisten om frälse- och ofrälse manna rätt til högre ämbeten*. Uppsala: Edman.

Kepplerus, Alexander (1771) *Borgmästarens och riksdags-fullmägtigens ifrån Lovisa stad, herr And. Keppleri Memorial, rörande privilegier för borgare- och bonde-stånden*. Stockholm: Grefing.

Kjellin, Gunnar (1952) *Rikshistoriografen Anders Schönberg: Studier i riksdagarnas och de politiska tänkesättens historia 1760–1809*. Lund: Ohlssons.

Lagerroth, Fredrik (1915) *Frihetstidens författning*: en studie i den svenska konstitutio-nalismens historia. Stockholm: Bonnier.

Lamm, Martin (1918) *Upplysningstidens romantik: den mystiskt sentimentala strömningen i svensk litteratur*. Stockholm: Geber.

Landahl, Sten (ed.) (1959) *Sveriges ridderskaps och adels riksdagsprotokoll från och med år 1719*. Stockholm: Riksdagens tryckeriexpedition, Vol. 25. Issue 2.

Landahl, Sten (ed.) (1978) *Bondeståndets riksdagsprotokoll*, Vol. 12. Stockholm: Riksdagens förvaltningskontor.

von Lichtenstern, Christian Habbaeus and Biörenklou, Mattias (1769) *En swensk mans tankar om desz fädernes-lands tilstånd, år 1675. Öfwersättning ifrån latin, med korta anmärkningar, lämpade til närwarande tid*. Stockholm: Stolpe.

Lindberg, Bo (2006) *Den antika skevheten. Politiska ord och begrepp i det tidig-moderna Sverige*. Stockholm: Almqvist & Wiksell.

Nationalencykolopedien (1992) Höganäs: Bra Böcker.

Nordencrantz, Anders (1730) *Arcana oeconomiae et commercii, eller Handelens och hushåldnings-wärkets hemligheter.* Stockholm: Horrn.

Nordencrantz, Anders (1770) *Undersökning om de rätta orsakerne til den blandning som skedt af lagstiftande och lagskipande, redofordrande och redoskyldige magternes gjöromål, de derpå följde oredor både wid och emellan riksdagarne, så wäl i juridiske som oeconomie: och finance-mål, tillika med förslaget om en säkerhets-act, såsom hjelp deremot, hwilket wid 1769 års riksdag förorsakade så stor miszhällighet emellan riksens högloflige ständer.* Stockholm: Stolpe.

Nordin, Jonas (2000) *Ett fattigt men fritt folk: nationell och politisk självbild i Sverige från sen stormaktstid till slutet av frihetstiden.* Eslöv: Symposion.

Nurmiainen, Jouko (2009) *Edistys ja yhteinen hyvä vapaudenajan ruotsalaisessa poliittisessa kielessä.* Helsinki: SKS.

Ozouf , Mona (1988) '"Public Opinion" at the End of the Old Regime'. *Journal of Modern History*, Vol. 60, Supplement.

Pocock, J. G. A. (1999) *Barbarism and Religion.* Cambridge: Cambridge University Press, Vol. 2.

Roberts, Michael (1986) *The Age of Liberty: Sweden, 1719–1772.* Cambridge: Cambridge University Press.

Rystad, Göran (2001) *Karl XI: en biografi.* Lund: Historiska media.

Sennefelt, Karin (2003) 'Mellan hemligt och offentligt. Sven Hofman vid riksdagen 1765–1766'. In Skuncke, Marie-Christine and Tandefelt, Henrika (eds.) *Frihetstidens politiska kultur.* Stockholm: Atlantis.

Shelton, Jo-Ann (1998) *As the Romans Did: A Sourcebook in Roman Social History.* Oxford: Oxford University Press.

Skinner, Quentin (1998) *Liberty Before Liberalism.* Cambridge: Cambridge University Press.

Strand, Carl Johan (1767) *Ämbetsmanna öde i Swerige.* Uppsala: Edman.

Svensk Bibliografi 1700–1829 (2000), Online Database: Kungliga Biblioteket.

von Vegesack, Thomas (1995) *Smak för frihet: opinionsbildningen i Sverige 1755–1830.* Stockholm: Natur och kultur.

von Vegesack, Thomas (2001) *Iakttagelser vid gränsen: när skönlitteraturen möter sina vedersakare.* Stockholm: Natur och kultur.

Venturi, Franco (1989) *The End of the Old Regime in Europe, 1768–1776: The First Crisis.* Princeton: Princeton University Press.

PETRI KOIKKALAINEN

From Agrarian Republicanism
to the Politics of Neutrality

Urho Kekkonen and 'Nordic Democracy'
in Finnish Cold War Politics

The period following Joseph Stalin's death in 1953 in the Soviet Union was perceived abroad as an era of liberalisation and modernisation. Nikita Khrushchev, who became First Secretary of the Soviet Communist Party in September 1953, was renowned for his claims to be able to raise the economic output of the Soviet Union and the standard of living of its citizens to meet or exceed the leading Western countries within a decade or two. At this same time, influential Western commentators argued that the extremely competitive international situation would ultimately force all countries, East and West, to apply the same fundamental laws of management, economy and strategy. As a result, the socialist and capitalist systems of politics, administration and economy would gradually converge.

This situation opened up a substantial new field of interest for Finnish politicians and intellectuals. By the early 1960s, they started to think that their country might be at the forefront of historical evolution instead of at its periphery. Urho Kekkonen (1900–1986), the long-standing president of Finland (1956–1981), who also was prime minister between 1950–1953 and 1954–1956, was a leading exponent of this idea. The country's geographical position between the blocs, as well as its cultural heritage and economy, appeared to offer it unique capabilities to work as a 'bridge-builder'. Combined with an active international politics of neutrality, this contributed in a substantial way to the meanings that the term 'Nordic Democracy' gained in Finland during the 1960s and 1970s. For Kekkonen, 'Nordic democracy' symbolised not merely a bridge between the Cold War blocs, but it was also the very base that enabled Finland to stand against the blocs and, in particular, communism. In 1960, when the Soviet government leader Nikita Khrushchev visited Helsinki, Urho Kekkonen famously argued that even if the rest of Europe was to turn to communism, Finland would 'remain a traditional Nordic democracy' if the majority of the Finnish people so wished, which he believed they would.[1]

---

1 Kekkonen, Urho (1973) [1960] 'Finland Sticks to Her Traditional Democracy'. In *Neutrality: The Finnish Position*, 2nd exp. ed., London: Heinemann, 83–86, at 84. In this translation, the wording was 'Scandinavian democracy', but the original Finnish-language version reads 'Nordic democracy'. See Kekkonen, Urho (1967[1960]) 'Suomi

238

In order to truly understand what Kekkonen could have meant when he said these words, and in order to put this rhetorical statement into a broader context, this article explores the emergence of a modernist vocabulary associated with concepts such as neutrality, conflict-regulation and ideological convergence in Finland during the 1960s. The case is assessed against the backdrop of an older political discourse that had its roots in the newly independent republic of the 1920s and 1930s. The developments strongly affected what came to be regarded as the 'Nordic' element in Finland's political existence. Central to the discussion will be the transformation of the Finnish agrarian republican tradition of thought, represented by the Agrarian League as a political movement, towards a more modernist version of neutrality and internationalism.

Finnish political traditions during the Cold War

In the aftermath of the Second World War, the political identity of the Republic of Finland was a contested issue. During the late 1940s, the goals of the Finnish extreme left were frequently described with reference to the slogan 'Czechoslovakia's way is also our way', allegedly coined by the communist parliamentarian and minister Hertta Kuusinen after the coup in Czechoslovakia in 1948.[2] The non-communist parties from the Social Democratic Party (SDP) to the conservative National Coalition strived to secure the future of Finland 'on a national basis', thus trying to minimise the political influence and the risk of intervention by the Soviet Union. During the 1940s and 1950s, the rhetoric of the anti-communist camp in the war of words emphasised the 'democratic'[3] form of government understood as the right of Finns to decide about their own issues, political independence, national liberty and unity, and also the traditional conservative themes of home, religion and fatherland.[4]

pysyy perinteellisen kansanvallan pohjalla'. In *Puheita ja kirjoituksia, vol. 2: Puheita presidenttikaudelta 1956–1967*. Helsinki: Weilin + Göös, 117–119, at 118.

2   Kuusinen's party was The Finnish People's Democratic League, FPDL (Suomen Kansan Demokraattinen Liitto, SKDL), which consisted of multiple sub-associations, of which only one was the Communist Party of Finland. Nevertheless the FPDL was considered by the other parties, as well as by the non-communist media, to be an umbrella organisation controlled by the Communists, and its members and supporters were referred to simply as Communists. Alhtough still frequently attributed to Kuusinen, it is likely that she never uttered these words. The slogan appears to have been written by an enthusiastic journalist reporting for the Communist newspaper *Vapaa sana* ('Free speech') on a party meeting at which minister Kuusinen had given a speech on Czechoslovakia's situation. See Larmola, Heikki (1994) 'Miksi Tsekkoslovakian tie ei ollut Suomen tie. Tsekkoslovakia ja Suomi Neuvostoliiton sodanjälkeisessä valtapiirissä'. *Historiallinen aikakauskirja*, Vol. 92, No. 3, 212–228.

3   The Finnish compound word 'kansanvaltainen' (democratic) is an almost direct equivalent of the original Greek term consisting of an element denoting 'the people' and an element denoting 'rule' or 'power'. See also Kurunmäki's article in this volume.

4   See the revised party programmes of the National Coalition (1945), the Agrarian League (later the Centre Party) (1946), and the Social Democratic Party (1952), which also contain examples of the aforementioned use of 'democratic'.

In general, the party-political discourse in Finland during the immediate post-war era on issues such as independence and national unity represented a continuation from the themes of the 1920s and 1930s rather than a decisive break with them. In the case of the non-socialist parties, this meant reliance on themes such as the building of the young nation, healing the wounds of the civil war, and the importance of a self-standing national political culture. For the Social Democrats, who had adopted a more affirmative attitude than before the war towards 'political independence, national defence and the international efforts for peace [through multilateral organisations respecting international law]',[5] the implication was to participate in the international workers' movement, but to find a nationally suitable application of its goals.

In the post-war context, the Agrarian League specifically wanted to defend 'the form of our society, founded on the Nordic liberty of peasants'.[6] There is no doubt that the explicit notion of the Nordic character of this liberty was well suited to the post-war situation, in which the victorious Soviet Union had put its mark on Finland's international position and in which the wartime collaboration with Germany had raised questions about the country's Western image. However, the references to Nordic peasant freedom can also be viewed in the light of the agrarian republican ideology that emanated from the pre-war era, as well as against the background of the challenge from right-wing extremism in the early 1930s. Although distinctly anti-socialist and anti-Scandinavian,[7] the party had allowed for governmental cooperation with the Social Democratic Party in 1937 and largely abandoned its language-based anti-Scandinavian prejudices. As a consequence, the Social Democrats' relationship with the non-socialist parties and with the Agrarian League in particular improved by the end of the 1930s. Thus, it became possible to emphasise the need to negotiate in industrial conflicts, which at the time were seen as a major source of political tension.

In the early 1960s, however, significant parts of the political vocabulary that derived from the so-called First Republic (1919–44) appeared either seriously obsolete or inappropriate. With regard to the legacy of agrarian republicanism, this had a lot to do with socio-economic change that had begun to decrease the number of small farms and peasants and thus

---

5 SDP (1952) The Social Democratic Party of Finland [Suomen sosialidemokraattinen puolue], 'Suomen sosialidemokraattisen puolueen periaateohjelma (perusteluineen)' (The Programme of the Principles of the Social Democratic Party of Finland (with supporting arguments)). All translations from Finnish sources are by the author, unless otherwise indicated.

6 AL (1946) The Agrarian League [Maalaisliitto], 'Maalaisliiton puolueohjelma' (The Party Programme of the Agrarian League).

7 Kekkonen was no exception in this, and as late as in 1935 he wrote under the pseudonym 'Mies Suomalainen' ('Finnish Man') as follows: 'We do know that Nordic co-operation, as it is carried out by the Nordic Association, is clearly hostile to the active promotion of the Finnish agenda, and the sort of friendship with Finnish culture that it frequently trumpets is rather problematic.' Kekkonen, Urho (1935) 'Suomalaisuuden rintamalta: Suomalaisuuskysymys on ratkaistava demokraattisin keinoin' (From the Front of the Finnish Cause: the Finnish Question must be Solved by Democratic Means). Letter to the editor, under pseydonym, *Suomalainen Suomi*, 1935, No. 2.

weakened the countryside as a reliable base for electoral support as well as for political imagery. In addition, perceptions about the world ideologies had changed: in the capitalist West, governments were now extending their social policies and creating new welfare services, and in the socialist East, following Stalin's death in 1953, official communist ideology was being interpreted in an increasingly pragmatic way by Nikita Khrushchev. In such circumstances, new opportunities arose for Finnish political leaders to optimise their choices within the ideological *spielraum* that was available for a small country geographically located between powerful ideological blocs. During the 1960s, Finnish international politics turned from a mere balancing of its existence between the East and the West to a more active policy, seeking alternatives to either Western Capitalism or Soviet-style Communism.

From the 1920s to the 1930s, the National Progressive Party (Kansallinen edistyspuolue) and the Social Democratic Party had been the most 'international' – or least nationalistic – of the Finnish political parties. While the latter portrayed itself as part of the international socialist movement in terms developed by German socialists during the late nineteenth century, the former was closest of all Finnish parties to European or Anglo-American liberalism with its stress on the rights of the individual, property rights and the need to strengthen the country's fledgling independence by effectively responding to the demands dictated by international economic competition. It might then seem natural to assume that either the liberal or the social democratic tradition would have served as the main basis for the eventual internationalisation of Finnish politics after the Second World War. The obvious model for the Social Democrats could then have been Sweden, whose politics of neutrality came to be associated with social democratic politicians such as Östen Unden, Tage Erlander and Olof Palme. But Finland's case was different, and Finnish social democrats were not in a position comparable to those in Sweden. A major reason for this was the anti-communist and anti-Russian 'brothers-in-arms-axis' that was formed by right-wing social democratic war veterans with the conservative National Coalition in Finland. The axis was particularly powerful in the local politics of the bigger cities, and it ensured the rightwing reputation of the whole Social Democratic Party. From the perspective of Communists and their supporters in the Soviet Union, Social Democrats emerged as their main ideological rival. The Liberals' electoral support had decreased steadily since the 1920s, and in 1951 remaining members of the National Progressive Party reformed to become a new Finnish People's Party (Suomen Kansanpuolue, 1951–1964), a minor middle-class interest party with a substantial emphasis on national and Christian values.

Immediately after the war, the conservative National Coalition struggled to preserve 'what our people has inherited from the previous generations, such as its love of liberty with the will to defend the country, the people's religion, national culture, morally healthy family-life, vibrant peasant-farming and frugality'.[8] The Liberals were in decline, and the majority of

8 NC (1945) The National Coalition [Kansallinen kokoomus], 'Kansallisen kokoomus-puolueen ohjelma' (The Programme of the National Coalition Party).

Social Democrats were, until the mid-1960s, in rigid opposition against the Finnish Communists and the Soviet Union. This situation opened up significant room for political manoeuvre for the Agrarian League. From the early 1940s onwards, some new political initiatives had already started to change the party's traditional rural and nationalistic image. In 1943, Urho Kekkonen became part of a group of politicians who had grown pessimistic about Finland's chances in the war against the Soviet Union, and who demanded measures that would ensure peaceful and confident relations with Russians after the war. Johannes Virolainen (1914–2000), one of the party's young hopefuls, worked to remodel the party's image towards a more modernist political centrism during the late 1940s. He was inspired in particular by the German-Swiss third way economist and social philosopher Wilhelm Röpke (1899–1966), who rejected planned economy but tried to circumvent the excesses of capitalism by developing 'economic humanism' which involved the decentralisation of political power and property ownership. The point of the 'third way', as Virolainen used the term, was to get beyond the restrictions that were immanent in both the socialist and the capitalist ways of thinking.[9] Although the party's official programme still said almost nothing about industrialisation, Kekkonen gained popularity in 1952 by publishing the pamphlet *Onko maallamme malttia vaurastua?* (Does our Country Have the Patience to Get Wealthy?), which advocated rapid modernisation of Northern Finland by the government-assisted expansion of heavy industry and the harnessing of the natural resources of the North, especially its forests and big rivers.[10]

However, it would be a mistake to assume that the politics of the Agrarian League went simply from being 'agrarian' to being 'modern'. The party's celebrated ideological heritage, which centred on the figure of the free peasant, was simply too important to be rejected outright. Despite the trend towards urbanisation, the majority of people still lived in the countryside during the 1950s. In addition, the ideological non-adherence of Finnish agrarian republicanism to both socialism and capitalism was also potentially highly useful as an ideological basis under the new circumstances.

The end of ideology in the Finnish context

During the 1940s and 1950s, all Finnish discussion on politics was intricately linked to questions regarding communism. The rift between the Communists and the non-communists was conceived as a deeply ideological one. During the wars against the Soviet Union, the enemy had often been portrayed as representing a completely different world-view,[11] Finland

9 Hokkanen, Kari (1996) *Maalaisliitto sodan ja vaaran vuosina 1939–1950: Maalaisliitto-Keskustan historia 3*. Helsinki: Otava, 378–386.

10 Kekkonen, Urho (1952a) *Onko maallamme malttia vaurastua?* Helsinki: Otava.

11 The appropriate Finnish word in this context is 'maailmankatsomus', which is close to 'world-view' or the German word *Weltanschauung*. From it was derived the adjective 'katsomuksellinen' (the German equivalent would be *anschauunglich*), which was frequently used as a prefix to describe the nature of the difference between Finland and the Soviet Union.

being the easternmost guardian of the western way of life. The Finnish Communist Party was legalised in 1944, and as a part of the Finnish People's Democratic League (FPDL), it participated in three post-war cabinets during 1944–48. The last of these, however, led to very strained relations between the Communists and the other parties, most notably because of a brief communist take-over of the security police. While the Communists came to be regarded by all the other parties as ineligible for cabinet, the electoral support of this otherwise ostracised group rose steadily after 1948. In 1958, they gained 23.2 per cent of the vote and became the largest parliamentary group with 50 out of 200 representatives. In the eyes of the political and academic elite, an interesting and problematic aspect of this development was that the increase of communist support was greatest in the northern and eastern peripheries of Finland, where the party could even reach absolute majorities. On the political map of Finland, it appeared as if vast areas of the territory had turned red, and that the colour was expanding rapidly. In this sense, Finland appeared to be almost an antithesis of the continental European and Anglo-American diagnoses made during the mid-1950s and early 1960s of an 'end of ideology'.[12]

However, many experts on social and economic policy had started to shift their attention from ideology to issues such as economic growth and population-level welfare indicators. As Pekka Kuusi, a social politician close to the Social Democratic Party, put it in his highly influential book *60-luvun sosiaalipolitiikka* (Social Policy of the 60s), '[t]here is no return to the woods. Not even a chance to stay where we now are. If we want to continue our life amidst Sweden and the Soviet Union, two nations conscious of the need to grow and able to grow, we are doomed to grow'.[13] The cumulative effect of these new trends could now be detected in party programmes in which the modernist, economist and social scientific parlance had started to dominate. A model example of this was the *Agrarian League's Goals for the 1960s*, published in 1962, with all-new emphases on comprehensive 'national planning', the holistic and interdependent nature of the socio-economic system, and the need to efficiently utilise the resources of all parts of the country.[14] Party programmes also started to resemble each other

12 On the general thesis, see Bell, Daniel (1960) *The End of Ideology: On the Exhaustion of Political Ideas in the Fifties.* Cambridge, MA: Harvard University Press; on the Swedish situation where the 'actual words "socialism" and "liberalism" are tending to become mere honorifics, useful in connection with elections and political festivities', Tingsten, Herbert (1955) 'Stability and Vitality in Swedish Democracy'. *Political Quarterly,* Vol. 2, 140–151, at 145; on Finnish social science on the spread of communism, Nousiainen, Jaakko (1969) *Research on the Finnish Communism.* Reprint Series B 5, University of Turku: Institute of Political Science.

13 Kuusi, Pekka (1961) *60-luvun sosiaalipolitiikka.* Porvoo: WSOY (4th reprint, 1963), 34. The book is often mentioned as the blueprint of Finland's social policy during the 1960s, and parts of it were rather directly adopted into the programmes of the Social Democratic Party. According to Kuusi, the suitable 'ideology' for the 1960s was not capitalism or communism, but 'kansantuloajattelu', literally 'national income thinking', in which 'most essential is to understand the economic activity of the people as a single entity'. (Kuusi 1961, 33).

14 AL (1962) The Agrarian League [Maalaisliitto], 'Maalaisliiton tavoitteet 1960-luvulla' (The Agrarian League's Goals for the 1960s), party programme.

more than ever before. Social scientists slowly but surely recognised the importance of this fact and started to speak about the 'integration of world-views'[15], which could well be interpreted as a Finnish variant of the end-of-ideology thesis. By the mid-1960s it was already perceivable that one of its most significant elements would be 'the gradual liberalisation and adaptation to rules of the game of the parliamentary democratic system'.[16]

The social scientists were not, however, merely passive registrars of events. As early as 1949, Jussi Teljo, a former collaborator of Kekkonen's in the 1930s and the new professor of Political Science at the University of Helsinki, launched a full attack against the normative and historicist *Allgemeine Staatslehre* tradition of the pre-war era. Such 'metaphysics' he deemed to be purely 'verbal exercises', which could not lead to the 'discovery of any real knowledge'.[17] Teljo's comment reflected a more profound change in attitudes, where a new empiricist and often behaviouralist epistemology replaced the old functions of philosophy and social science as providers of political principles and comprehensive world-views. According to the new approach, the task of scientists and philosophers was no longer to take principled stands in the battle between *Weltanschauungen*, but it was to provide empirical clarity to the activity of politics (often defined as the 'political behaviour' of a population or some of its sub-groups) and also to offer preventive or therapeutic measures that could help dealing with 'radical', 'authoritarian' or otherwise 'deviant' forms of behaviour.

In Finland, a paradigm case of 1950s behaviouralism was the set of studies undertaken on northern and eastern 'backwoods communism'. The studies sought to explain the presence of the red colour on the Finnish map, i.e., why an unexpected amount of radicalism had arisen in parts of the country that had no proletariat in the traditional sense, and no communist organisational traditions comparable to the industrial centres of southern Finland.[18] Implicit in these studies was a notion of political normalcy that included social democrats and the major non-socialist parties, but excluded communists. This national divide corresponded with the wartime presumptions of political loyalty, but the basis of 'explaining communism' was now socio-economical and even social psychological rather than purely ideological. Factors such as poverty, inadequate education, social

---

15 'Katsomuksellinen integraatio'; the German translation 'anschauungliche Integration' would be more literal.

16 Borg, Olavi (1965) 'Ideologisia virtauksia Suomen poliittisessa elämässä'. *Sosiologia*, Vol. 2, No. 4, 162–170, at 169.

17 Teljo, Jussi (1950) 'Valtio-opin tehtävät ja menetelmät', an inaugural lecture, *Suomalainen Suomi*, 1950, No. 1, 14–18, at 16.

18 See, e.g., Nousiainen, Jaakko (1956) *Kommunismi Kuopion läänissä. Ekologinen tutki-mus kommunismin joukkokannatukseen vaikuttavista tekijöistä Pohjois-Savossa ja Poh-jois-Karjalassa*. Joensuu: Pohjois-Karjalan kirjapaino Oy; Nousiainen 1969; Allardt, Erik (1956) *Social struktur och politisk aktivitet: en studie av väljaraktiviteten vid riksdagsvalen i Finland 1945–54*. Helsinki: Söderström; Allardt, Erik (1964a) 'Social Sources of Finnish Communism: Traditional and Emerging Radicalism'. *International Journal of Comparative Sociology*, Vol. 5, No. 1, 49–72; Littunen, Yrjö (1960) 'Aktiivisuus ja radikalismi'. *Politiikka*, Vol. 2, No. 4, 151–185.

exclusion, and traumatic parental relationships were identified as factors causing communist behaviour.

According to the international relations theory of the early 1960s, the possibility for a dynamic ideological change was dealt with using such concepts as convergence, interdependence, and linkage politics.[19] These concepts were associated with post-war economic and technological progress, which had allegedly had a globally homogenising influence on areas of life such as the consumption culture, industrial relations and the general direction of the economy. According to the American scholars Brzezinski and Huntington, it was widely believed that the 'laws of physics, of strategy, of engineering, and even of industrial management and economics are universally true and eventually must be respected as such by all modern societies. Hence ideological and political claims must be limited'. The pressures for convergence created by modern modes of production and the increased affluence of citizens, increasingly so even in the Soviet Union, were amplified by 'the unprecedented impact of international affairs and new, rapid means of communications'.[20]

Perhaps the most significant impetus for these considerations was the period of Soviet liberalisation following Stalin's death in 1953. By the early 1960s, the Soviet Union had become to be widely regarded as a dynamic and rather pragmatically governed society, thanks largely to the internationally visible role of Nikita Khrushchev.[21] Before this (temporary) period of doctrinal relaxation and even self-critique, Western political scientists and politicians had regularly characterised the Soviet Union as a 'totalitarian' system that fundamentally lacked 'freedom' and 'democracy'; in other words, that there was a categorical and qualitative difference between the politics of the East and the West.[22]

19 See, e.g., Brzezinski, Zbigniew and Samuel P. Huntington (1964) *Political Power: USA/ USSR.* New York: Viking; Rosenau, James N. (1969, ed.) *Linkage Politics. Essays on the Convergence of National and International Systems.* New York: The Free Press.
20 Brzezinski and Huntington 1964, 11 and 428; see also Rosenau, James N. (1969) 'Introduction: Political Science in a Shrinking World'. In Rosenau 1969 (ed.), 1–17, at 2.
21 For example, Kuusi was highly impressed with Khrushchev's economic prognoses, even describing them as a challenge 'engraved in the books of the Gods of History'. Kuusi 1961, 28. In Khruschchev's own words (27 January 1959, on launching a new seven-year-plan): 'If calculations are based on production per capita, around five years may be required in addition to the present seven-year-plan to catch up with and surpass the United States in industrial production [it would be 1971]. By then, or maybe earlier, the Soviet Union will be in the world's first place in terms of both absolute amount of production and production per capita. It will be a world-historical victory of socialism over capitalism in a peaceful competition in the international arena. [...] The political system that gives people more material goods, which gives people limitless possibilities for mental growth, that system is the most progressive and controls the future.' Quoted in Kuusi 1961, 27–28.
22 Brzezinski and Huntington presented a memorable image: 'Slavery and freedom; dictatorship and democracy; communism and capitalism; collectivism and individualism; the totalitarian state and the constitutional one: how easy and appropriate it is to pin one label on the United States and its opposite on the Soviet Union. The human mind craves simple distinctions; and Russians, Americans, and Europeans all have their own motives for embracing the "black-and-white" approach.' Brzezinski and Huntington 1964, 7.

Now, however, there was a move away from this purely black and white view to one comprising shades of grey. In many western interpretations, convergence most commonly meant that the Soviet Union would gradually transform itself, moving towards becoming a pluralist political democracy.[23] However, while Brzezinski and Huntington acknowledged that the western countries might adopt some ideas from the planned or socialist modes of production and distribution during the process, they also argued that the link between economy and politics was not so great that such measures would override their fundamentally liberal, democratic and constitutional *political* values, at least in countries in which a long history of them existed. Nevertheless, it was more likely that there would be a process of 'evolution', whereby both the United States and the Soviet Union would develop their policies and institutions based on their very own distinctive values and histories.[24]

The Finnish diplomat Max Jakobson[25] has argued that from the late 1950s onwards, president Urho Kekkonen's thinking can most precisely be described in terms of the 'so-called convergence theory, according to which communism and capitalism gradually "grow together": in the market economies, the public sector will expand and level out the injustices of the system, and in the communist systems, the freedoms of the individual will expand with the increase of material welfare'.[26] With the rise of the new left in Europe and America in particular, it had become possible to question whether the western concepts of freedom and democracy were the only valid ones or whether there also existed a version of freedom and democracy in the Soviet Union, which was not necessarily worse than the western model, but simply represented a different paradigm.[27] In addition, the terms of comparison between different political systems changed: instead of detecting the presence of an essentially defined freedom or democracy as absolute demarcating criteria, new forms of measurement were developed which allowed comparisons all over the ideological spectrum. These were typically socio-economic and quantitative in kind: gross national income per capita

---

23 According to Brzezinski and Huntington (1963, 13), the notion of convergence served almost everyone's needs: 'To Americans and western Europeans it offers what appears to be the only way out of a hopeless and endless conflict. To neutralists it provides the historical sanction for their position. To the Titoists it justifies their isolation from the rest of the communist community. To the Chinese it explains why they, in contrast to the Soviets, remain uncorrupted orthodox Marxist-Leninists. The theory of convergence is not only an abstract intellectual position but also a source of optimism for many and justification for all.'

24 Brzezinski and Huntington 1964, 429ff, see also Rosenau 1969.

25 Originally a journalist, he served in senior positions in the Ministry for Foreign Affairs during the 1960s. He was Kekkonen's close advisor regarding foreign policy. He was also Finland's candidate for the General Secretary of the United Nations, but narrowly lost the race against the Austrian Kurt Waldheim in 1971.

26 Jakobson, Max (1981) *Veteen piirretty viiva: Havaintoja ja merkintöjä vuosilta 1953–1965*. Otava: Helsinki, 170–171.

27 See Kekkonen, Urho (1976) [1963] Private letter to Dr. Matti Luoma, Vaasa, January 14th, 1963. In Kekkonen, *Kirjeitä myllystäni 1*, 154–156; Eskola, Antti (1969) *Vasen laita lavea*. Helsinki: Kirjayhtymä.

and its annual growth, average life expectancy, number of medical doctors per 1 000 inhabitants, or the percentage of women in professional careers.[28] The crises in Berlin in 1961 and Cuba in 1962 tested the credibility of the convergence theory, but Finnish foreign policy responded by emphasising the 'defensive' and pragmatic character of Soviet foreign policy: if the fundamental issues were the needs for security and the balance of military power, then it was not necessary to interpret the events through ideological lenses.[29]

It should be noted that Kekkonen's use of the term freedom was not without contradiction. On one side, he clearly had sympathy for the modernist theory of convergence, according to which economic and social evolution would gradually also transform the meanings of the traditional ideological concepts. On the other side, and more pertinently with regard to the theme of Nordic democracy, he repeatedly presented 'the Nordic concept of liberty' (*det nordiska frihetsbegreppet*), with its traditional links to parliamentarianism and local self-government, as the common ground that united the Nordic countries despite their differences in foreign and economic policy, including the NATO membership of Denmark, Norway and Iceland.[30] This 'traditional' meaning is also how Kekkonen's assurance to Khrushchev of Finland's sticking to its Nordic form of democracy was presented in Finland and marketed abroad.[31]

Kekkonen also favoured the German sociologist Ralf Dahrendorf's conflict regulation theory, which demanded full political recognition to even the radical (communist) parties and compromise between legitimate political interests. Here was another possible source of contradiction: whereas the convergence theory predicted the dilution of ideology, the conflict regulation theory advised that existing ideologies should be taken for granted. But the latter theory also implied that the process of regulation itself would level out at least the most excessive ideological differences, thus making the views at least partly compatible. Dahrendorf's model broadened the range of participants and the number of potential issues in parliamentary politics, but it also demanded an initial ideological move from the radicals, who should publicly commit themselves to the 'rules of the game', i.e. to 'such procedural norms as are binding for the contestants without prejudicing the outcome of the contest'. According to Dahrendorf,

---

28 E.g. Kuusi 1961; Niitamo, Olavi (1966) 'Ennakointi ja ohjelmointi'. In Pentti Viita (ed.) *Suomi 1975: ennusteita, analyyseja, näköaloja*. Helsinki: Tammi, 144–161.

29 Jakobson, Max (1968) *Finnish Neutrality: A Study of Finnish Foreign Policy Since the Second World War*. London: Hugh Evelyn, 69ff.

30 Kekkonen, Urho (1949) 'Finland och Norden: Det nordiska frihetsbegreppet' (Finland and the Nordic Countries: The Nordic Concept of Freedom). Speech to the representatives of the Nordic Parliamentary Union in Helsinki, 16 June, 1949; Kekkonen, Urho (1957) 'Itsenäinen Suomi 40-vuotias' (Independent Finland 40 Years). Independence Day speech, Helsinki, December 6th, 1957; Kekkonen, Urho (1961a) Address of the President of Finland to the General Assembly of the United Nations, October 19th, 1961; Kekkonen, Urho (1980) 'Suomesta pohjoismaana' (On Finland as a Nordic Country). In Kekkonen, *Tamminiemi*. Helsinki: Weilin + Göös, chapter 4.

31 Kekkonen 1973 [1960], 84.

the institutions of the liberal democratic state were 'very nearly the model of effective conflict regulation'.[32] In Finnish politics, the model would give promise to all ideological camps. For the radical left, it contained the possibility of 'sliding towards socialism' by means of gradual parliamentary reform. For the bourgeois parties, the model promised greater systemic stability and predictability and a 'tamed' communist party. By allowing the extreme left the possibility of holding power, they however had to accept the long-term potential for the transformation of policy, values and institutions. Initially, Dahrendorf's ideas had visible supporters in Finland both among the social liberals[33] and the radical left.[34] Indeed, another change in culture had occurred: while the fifties' modernists in academia and literature did not make much noise about their political allegiances (if they had any, they were usually liberal centrist or social democratic), it became rather commonplace during the 1960s for young academics, civil servants and artists to profess radically leftist views.

Social science, conflict regulation and the Communists

By the mid-1960s, modernist, empiricist and 'ideologically fluid' language had permeated the mainstream of Finnish social science. This process went very much hand in hand with the transformation of mainstream political discourse, where for example the Social Democratic Party had already in the 1950s abandoned its traditional demands of extensive socialisation of property, and the Agrarian League was making its vocabulary more attractive to the middle-class and to urban and suburban industrial workers. As for the extreme left, it now became possible to regard the umbrella organisation, the FPDL, as not just being 'communists', but as noted by the political scientist Olavi Borg, as having 'its own rather modern programme that distinguishes if from the Communist Party, and makes little mention about socialism'.[35]

The Agrarian League was now in a favourable position. Some agrarian politicians such as Kekkonen had argued for peace in 1943–44; there had been coalition cabinets including both the Agrarian League and the FPDL during 1944–48; the FPDL had supported Kekkonen in the decisive votes of the 1956 presidential election. Such facts had already established at least an image of a political connection between these two parties. One of the main accusations against Kekkonen before and during his presidential campaigns had been that he was too close to the Communists, or indeed a communist

32 Dahrendorf, Ralf (1959) *Class and Class Conflict in Industrial Society.* London: Routledge & Kegan Paul, 226 and 308.

33 Allardt, Erik (1964b) *Yhteiskunnan rakenne ja sosiaalinen paine.* Porvoo: WSOY; Allardt, Erik (1964c) 'Suomalaisen yhteiskunnan perusvastakohtaisuudet'. In *Kansalaisajattelun seminaari 8 – 13.6. 1964. Alustukset, yleiskeskustelun puheenvuorit ja työryhmien tiivistelmät.* Helsinki: Henkisen maanpuolustuksen suunnittelukunta.

34 Eskola, Antti (1965) 'Poliittisten ristiriitojen säätely ja kommunismi'. *Sosiologia,* Vol. 2, No. 2, 62–68.

35 Borg, Olavi (1970) 'Eduskunta ja puolueet', in Olavi Borg (ed.) *Mitä puoluetta äänestäisin.* Helsinki: Otava, 23–42, at 34.

in disguise. Kekkonen's standard reply was that the Agrarian League was the only political force that could effectively compete with the Communists, especially in the relatively poor and politically unpredictable northern and eastern regions.[36] Kekkonen consolidated his domestic political power after a crisis that resulted from the Soviet Union's protests in 1958 against K. A. Fagerholm's majority coalition which included the Social Democrats. Fagerholm's government resigned, and his party (SDP) did not enter the government again until 1966. As a result of Kekkonen's instrumental role in the appointment of a new cabinet, he substantially strengthened his position with regard to the composition of future coalition governments. The fact that cabinets were no longer appointed without at least the president's tacit consent gave him a unique possibility to regulate the overall political and ideological climate of the country.[37]

As opposed to the rather diffuse concepts of international interdependence and ideological convergence, the introduction of the conflict regulation model in Finnish politics is easier to trace. The term was coined by the German industrial and political sociologist Ralf Dahrendorf in his *Soziale Klassen und Klassenkonflikt in der industriellen Gesellschaft* in 1957.[38] In Finland, the value and applicability of Dahrendorf's work was realised by Allardt, who during the 1950s had become known as a promising young sociologist working on political values and attitudes. His arguably most influential book *Yhteiskunnan rakenne ja sosiaalinen paine* (The structure of society and social pressure)[39] contained an application of Dahrendorf's theory, which in Allardt's own work marked a transition from empirical value research to theoretical sociology that focused on the general dynamics of the social and political system.

Against the stances of all the non-communist parties, Allardt demanded that the FPDL be readmitted into the cabinet. According to Allardt, 'regulated' conflicts were beneficial to societal development, but 'non-regulated' conflicts were dangerous. In Finland, the division between communists and non-communists was strongly characteristic of the latter type of conflict.[40] 'As long as the other parties exclude the Communists from government responsibilities', Allardt argued, 'they apply entirely different rules to the people's democrats than to the other parties', which meant that 'the poorest

36 E.g., Kekkonen, Urho (1952b) 'Toimeentulevaiset ja toimeentulemattomat' (The Haves and the Have-Nots). *Kyntäjä*, 1952, No. 12. When the communist support started to decrease in these areas after 1958, the voters moved towards the Agrarian League rather than to the Social Democratic Party.

37 Suomi, Juhani (1992) *Kriisien aika: Urho Kekkonen 1956–1962*. Helsinki: Otava, 131–220; Hokkanen 1996, 445–453. According to some opposition politicians and constitutional lawyers, this practice was unparliamentary and unconstitutional (see, e.g. Merikoski, Veli [1978] *Presidentinvalta vai parlamentarismi*. Helsinki: Weilin + Göös). The debate ultimately led to constitutional reforms during the 1980s after Kekkonen resigned from office in 1981.

38 Its English translation *Class and Class Conflict in Industrial Society* was published in 1959

39 Allardt 1964b.

40 Allardt 1964b, 54.

and socially most disadvantaged part of the population is kept politically out in the cold'.[41]

In the parliamentary elections of 1966, the parties of the left were the winners: the SDP gained 55 and the FPDL 49 out of 200 seats. The FPDL got its first ministerial posts in almost twenty years with the active support of Kekkonen, who was known to be interested in modern sociology and 'ideas relating to the social whole'.[42] Part of the political package was to rehabilitate the SDP, the majority of whose members had now distanced themselves from the brothers-in-arms-axis of the post-war years, and started to emphasise the importance of friendly relations with the Soviet Union. In a famous speech to the Pohjois-Pohjalainen (North-Ostrobothnian) Student Nation of the University of Helsinki, Kekkonen interpreted this political shift with a reference to Allardt's sociology and used it to illustrate a story taken from his personal experience. As a student leader in the 1920s, he had been involved in attempts to 'unite' the Finnish people, 'not in co-operation with the Left, but by handing them [our view of] unity'. It was only later that he began to realise the futility of this attempt and the need to 'recognise that the Left had the right to keep its own ideals just as we kept our own. We should have recognised that diversity comes first, and after debate, compromise and co-operation between the diversities comes the whole. *To agree to disagree.*'[43]

Kekkonen was thus not envisioning an ideologically harmonised life between capitalism and socialism, but 'a pluralist society' created by 'economic and technological progress and the continuous growth of education'. Such a society, according to Kekkonen, could be strong enough to endure ideological competition even from the direction of the Communists, who as a political force after all represented a large part of the electorate. Kekkonen described the reasons for the Communist participation in government with a lengthy paraphrase of Allardt's recent article.[44] Even if it is hard to determine the degree to which the rehabilitation of communists was a result of the sociologists' argumentation or the more general political tendencies favouring the Left, or just a part of Kekkonen's power politics, this process can even now be described as the great political *tour de force* of Finnish sociological thinking.

41 Allardt 1964c, 10–11. He also outlined an aspect of national security in the issue: 'If my presumptions are correct, the situation is really serious from the point of view of a person observing social structure. To continue with the present policy would mean that over 20 per cent of the population are kept politically out in the cold for a very long time. All results achieved so far demonstrate that such a situation really can lead to explosive eruptions if a favourable opportunity should occur.' (Allardt 1964c, 11.)

42 Paakkunainen, Kari (1985) *Demokratia, tiede, kansanvalistus: Valtiotieteellisen yhdistyksen intellektuaalihistoria 1935–1985*. Helsinki: Finnish Political Science Association, 283.

43 Kekkonen, Urho (1967) 'Yhdenmukaisuudesta erilaisuuteen' (From Unity to Diversity). Speech at the annual celebration of the North-Ostrobothnian Student Nation, February 4th. The last sentence was originally in English in an otherwise Finnish speech (emphasis added).

44 Kekkonen 1967, the article paraphrased by him was Allardt, Erik (1966) 'Sosiaalisia ongelmia ja ristiriitoja', in Pentti Viita (ed.), *Suomi 1975: ennusteita, analyyseja, näköaloja*, Helsinki: Tammi, 162–183.

Finnish neutrality and the Scandinavian outlook

The 1960s were a period of unforeseen activity in Finnish foreign politics, the main achievements of which included Finland's auxiliary membership of EFTA in 1961 (Finn-EFTA), membership of the OECD in 1969, the early preparations for the CSCE conferences, and the Finnish membership of the United Nations Security Council during 1969–70.[45] President Kekkonen's visits to the United States, Canada, United Kingdom and France during the early 1960s were significant in framing the contents of the Finnish politics of neutrality and seeking international recognition for it.

According to the president's chief foreign policy advisor, western leaders eagerly asked Kekkonen about the significance of communism, but he consistently attempted to downplay the importance of ideology, and emphasised the Soviets' pragmatic interest in economic development and security; in other words, issues that could be shared by any country.[46] Speaking to the General Assembly of the UN, he declared the Finns' interest to observe world politics 'in the role of a doctor rather than a judge',[47] and his reply to Kennedy's query in 1961 concerning the viability of western democracy in a small country that was neighboured by a communist giant is equally revealing:

> Maybe after thirty years from now, the capitalist system will have evolved by way of economic regulation and social legislation, and the communist system will have liberalised to the extent that it will be difficult to find cause for an argument. If this is held as too optimistic an estimation pertaining to time, we may add a couple of decades.[48]

This world-historical horizon was clearly a novelty in the Finnish politics of neutrality, which had so far consisted of attempts to keep the Soviet influence as low as possible in domestic politics, and to remain non-committed to either side of ideological and military conflicts in international politics. Previously, the cautiousness of Finland's foreign policy had been greatly heightened by the Soviet Union's suspiciousness of Western multilateral organizations, including the Nordic Council. A telling example of this was the Soviet government newspaper *Izvestia*'s declaration in January 1955 that Finland's potential membership of the Nordic Council was an 'unfriendly act', resulting from the policy of 'warmongers'.[49] Admittedly,

---

45 Regarding regional co-operation before Kekkonen's presidency, Finland had become a member of the Nordic Council in 1955 and was a member of the Nordic passport union. His predecessor J. K. Paasikivi had made frequent official visits to the Soviet Union, but Kekkonen was the first president of Finland to pay visits to the leading Western countries.

46 Jakobson 1981, 230–232 et passim.

47 Kekkonen, Urho (1961a) Address of the President of Finland to the General Assembly of the United Nations, October 19th, 1961.

48 Jakobson 1981, 236.

49 Quoted in Kekkonen, Urho (1955a) Speech to the co-operative committee of Nordic agrarian parties, January 26th, 1955.

three of the existing four member-states of the Council were also founding members of NATO. A memorandum later released by Kekkonen about an informal discussion with the Soviet leadership in Moscow only months later (September 1955) strongly suggested that the Soviets' sudden reversal of position regarding Finland's membership in the Nordic Council was the result of prime minister Kekkonen's personal assurances that the course of Finland's policy would not change. According to the memorandum, Kekkonen's position had been that the Finns' motivation to join the Council did not spring from contemporary foreign policy issues, but from the 'deep historical traditions and the very close interaction in all fields of life with the Nordic peoples'.[50]

If Finland's geopolitical position was previously perceived as a handicap, by the early 1960s it was even possible for it to be seen as an advantage. If it was to be the case that the ideological blocs were approaching each other and that economic systems across the globe were transforming into a mixed model – as was widely believed by a range of Finnish and international commentators – Finland might suddenly be at the very centre of development instead of being at its periphery. Also the modernised versions of the agrarian political tradition, irreducible to either Anglo-American Capitalism or Soviet Communism and historically rooted in the Nordic figure of the free peasant, could now be the basis of some promising scenarios. Taken together, Finland could even provide the ideal circumstances for the evolution of advanced political and socio-economic models. It is plausible to assume that such a horizon of expectations, or Kekkonen's 'working hypothesis' of ideological evolution towards a global synthesis, was the basis of Kekkonen's optimism regarding Finland's international position.

The ambitious 'Kekkonen plan' of a Nordic nuclear-free zone introduced in 1963 can also be understood against the background of ideological convergence. The purpose of the plan, from Kekkonen's perspective, was to reduce the ideological and military tensions in the Nordic region, and also ultimately to reduce the importance of the whole issue of ideology in the Nordic countries. Kekkonen repeatedly argued that Soviet interest in Scandinavia was defensive and centred on security, and not aggressive and centred on ideology.[51] However, when viewed from the perspective of the other Nordic countries, Kekkonen's politics were understandably often seen as serving Soviet interests in the cold war groupings. It is no secret, for example, that the Swedish and Norwegian governments found it difficult to applaud Kekkonen's initiative, although it was possible to see some merits in its keeping the Soviet Union satisfied and, eventually, the position of the Nordic countries intact and calm.[52]

---

50 Kekkonen 1980.
51 See Jakobson 1968, 95–101.
52 See Andrén, Nils with Gylfi Þ. Gíslason (1981) 'The Nordic Countries between East and West'. In Erik Allardt et al. (eds): *Nordic Democracy. Ideas, Issues, and Institutions in Politics, Economy, Education, Social and Cultural Affairs of Denmark, Finland, Iceland, Norway, and Sweden*. Copenhagen: Det danske selskab, 677–690, at 688–689.

Whereas it had been possible to explain the Berlin crisis of 1961 and its consequences for Finnish politics[53] as examples of the Soviets' overriding but ultimately pragmatic (i.e. non-ideological) concern for security, the Warsaw Pact's intervention in Czechoslovakia in August 1968 was a clear turning point for the worse. The severity of Kekkonen's disappointment provides corroboration for this interpretation. 'It feels like all the work that I have done in political institutions since the late 1940s has been in vain', wrote the depressed president in his private diary one day after the invasion, and he contemplated leaving his post to younger hands.[54] Preceded by the replacement of Khrushchev by Leonid Brezhnev who took the title General Secretary of the Communist Party (previously held only by Stalin) in 1966, the events in Czechoslovakia were widely interpreted as signs of the Soviet Union returning to a more dogmatic form of communism, even neo-Stalinism. As a result, speculation about Soviet liberalisation and the ensuing convergence of ideologies rapidly lost its acuteness, and at least as an immediate reaction, Kekkonen felt the intervention was almost a terminal blow to his long-term expectations.

Also at this time, the domestic political aspirations which were based on the assumption of the fluidity of ideologies had begun to fade. A good example of this was the debate concerning conflict regulation theory. By the end of the decade, the ensuing struggle between the 'rightist' and 'leftist' interpretations of the theory – in other words, whether the need to accept the parliamentarian 'rules of the game' would tame the radical communists, or whether communist participation in government would be a start of radical socialist reforms – appears to have ended in victory of the more rightist hopes. 'Finland will probably never move to socialism slowly and peacefully sliding', complained the left-wing ideologist and social psychologist Antti Eskola.[55] His comments reflected a deep disappointment in both the achievements of the FPDL in government since 1966 and the theoretical ideas that he had personally supported during the early and mid-1960s.

---

53 Following the Berlin crisis, the Soviet Union issued a diplomatic note to Finland in October 1961 proposing 'military consultations' based on the Finnish–Soviet Treaty of 1948. Kekkonen travelled to Novosibirsk, and his personal negotiations with Khrushchev cancelled the threat of consultations. According to Jakobson, the Finns' negotiating position was based on the assumption that the Soviet interest in military co-operation with Finland was defensive and pragmatic, not ideological, and probably an overreaction against the threat of a militarising Germany. See Jakobson 1968, 1981. The 'note crisis' has been a fiercely debated issue among Finnish historians. Some have given great credit to Kekkonen's leadership and negotiating skills in solving the threatening situation. See Suomi 1992, 475–520. Others have suggested that Kekkonen had more or less directly ordered the note from Moscow to ensure his re-election as president in 1962. See Rautkallio, Hannu (1992) *Novosibirskin lavastus. Noottikriisi 1961.* Helsinki: Tammi. It is now quite widely agreed that the Soviet Union wanted to influence the presidential election of 1962, but the degree of Kekkonen's or other Finnish politicians' involvement in the events remains open to debate.

54 Kekkonen, Urho 2002 [1968] Entries in private diary on August 21st, August 22nd, and August 23rd, 1968. In Juhani Suomi (ed.) *Urho Kekkosen päiväkirjat 2: 1963–68.* Helsinki: Otava, 2002, 409–411, at 411.

55 Eskola 1969, 105.

Now, he viewed the whole conflict regulation theory as a 'bourgeois dirty trick' that was only designed to lend support to 'bourgeois democracy'.[56]

Nevertheless, even if the world historical perspective of ideological synthesis was now emptied of its greatest promises, the Finnish diplomats, who chiefly oriented themselves westwards, still had something to boast about. Throughout the political and ideological turmoil of the preceding half a century, Finland had after all been able to preserve its democratic constitution (at least formally) intact. Between 1955 and 1962, Finland had obtained recognition for its politics of neutrality not only from the Soviet Union, but also from the leading western countries. At the same time, it had substantially strengthened its connections with multilateral organisations, such as the Nordic Council, the United Nations and EFTA. A flagship item of Finland's foreign policy was its regular participation with the UN peacekeeping troops, which started during the Suez crisis in 1956 and was substantial both in terms of personnel and money invested.[57] As early as 1961, Kekkonen portrayed Finnish foreign policy in a well-received speech in Washington as exemplifying 'a particular Nordic view on international affairs, which is independent of differences in foreign policy [e.g., the NATO membership of some Nordic countries]'.[58] These achievements and more were listed in Max Jakobson's *Finnish Neutrality*, a semi-official outline document and defence of Finland's foreign policy that was aimed at the international audience. In the book Jakobson provided a quintessential account of the particular 'Scandinavian' character of the foreign policy of Finland and its Nordic neighbours:

> There is, one might say, a common Scandinavian outlook on international affairs that transcends differences of national policy – a rational, moderate, pragmatic approach well suited to the role of mediation so often assigned to Scandinavians. It could not very well be otherwise, for the Scandinavian nations have indeed every advantage: they are politically stable, socially advanced, economically prosperous; they have no major international claims to press or to counter; no present or recent colonial record, and no racial problems. In short, they have no good reason to behave in a fanatical, neurotic or irrational manner.[59]

For Jakobson, this cool, reasonable and pathology-free style was also a reflection of the Finnish national character, which tended to be 'the opposite of flamboyant, distrustful of rhetoric, interested in practical things rather

---

56 Eskola 1969, 79–83.
57 Contributors of military personnel in the Suez operation were Brazil, Canada, Colombia, Denmark, Finland, India, Indonesia, Norway, Sweden and Yugoslavia; countries whose positions in the coming decades would often resemble those of Finland's in forums such as the United Nations.
58 Kekkonen, Urho (1961b) 'Suomen asema kansainvälisessä politiikassa' [Finland's Position in International Politics]. Speech at the National Press Club, Washington, D.C., October 17th, 1961.
59 Jakobson 1968, 107–108.

than theory', albeit also 'inclined to be withdrawn, even self-effacing, at worst isolationist and suspicious and intolerant of other, different peoples'. An obvious purpose of this remark was to respond to the criticisms that were levelled at what Jakobson called Finland's 'mercifully modest [...] contribution to the output of words in the United Nations, for instance'.[60] The inevitable point of comparison was with Swedish foreign policy, which then and especially during Olof Palme's social democratic government in 1969–76 was active in condemning the actions of the great powers, and which had visible results in the form of temporary freezes in the diplomatic relations between the United States and Sweden. Based on Jakobson's writings, one gets the impression that the Finnish senior diplomats regarded Sweden as a more 'flamboyantly' oriented member of the Scandinavian family, against the Finns' careful, logical and balanced neutrality in all directions. Jakobson has more than once made biting remarks about the moralising or uninhibited nature of the Swedish critique of the great powers, motivated primarily by a domestic need to maintain a distinct national self-image. 'Because of their country's favourable geopolitical position', he has said, 'the Swedish political leaders have afforded to feed their citizens with the caviar of moralising foreign politics, whereas the Finns have had to be content with the oatmeal porridge of realpolitik'.[61]

Nordic, but still Northern

After the successes in the international arena and the modernization of the economy, one might suppose that president Kekkonen or the Centre Party no longer needed to adhere in their rhetoric to the agrarian figure of the peasant. This, however, turned out not to be the case, and instead during the period from the 1950s to the 1970s, there was a curious transformation of the agrarian imagery, strongly connected to presidential politics.

The archetypal peasant that was the centrepiece of pre-war Agrarian politics most probably lived in the (north)western region of Ostrobothnia or in the eastern regions of the country, particularly Karelia. These were the party's electoral strongholds, and also areas where the image of freeholder farming most closely corresponded to the local conditions. After the war, the party also started to campaign more actively in the northern and north-eastern regions of Lapland and Kainuu. The population of these remote areas was on the increase due to reallocation of land to war veterans and refugees, and to the establishment of thousands of new small farms. As well as being the main ideological battleground against 'backwoods communism', these regions were also target areas for big national investments.[62]

60 Jakobson 1968, 108; see also Norbert Götz in this volume.
61 Jakobson, Max (1983) *38. Kerros: Havaintoja ja muistiinpanoja vuosilta 1965–1971.* Helsinki: Otava, 80.
62 Partly by coincidence, Kekkonen joined the ideological move northwards, since part of the land from a farm that he had acquired in South Karelia in 1938 was lost to the Soviet Union in the interim peace of 1940. He bought a new farm in Kainuu, where he had attended

From Kekkonen's extensive post-war campaigning tours of the north, a new figure had entered his political vocabulary. This was the modest but resilient lumberjack or small farmer, often a war veteran, who became the embodiment of the deepest national virtues. Maybe the purest example of this character was Matti Pyykkönen from Kainuu, who Kekkonen mentioned in several texts. Pyykkönen, aged 33 when Kekkonen met him in the mid-1950s, was a veteran who had spent four years in wars, a lumberjack, a husband, and a father of five. The family lived in a miserable cabin, and unlike many others, had not received land or a farm of their own, despite some vague promises made during the war by some unnamed authorities. 'Should all people like Pyykkönen now move after money into the southern cities', Kekkonen asked, and replied: 'Finland needs these lumberjacks. If there were no loggers, green gold would not come for anyone to use. If wood processing mills were not running and bringing about wealth and currency, there would be no building of factories, no schools, no hospitals, no import of cars, no tractors, no silks nor perfumes. These Matti Pyykkönens are indispensable.'[63]

Kekkonen's personal reputation, which had been tarnished by his extensive participation in the capital's political intrigues since the 1930s, was a constant worry in his campaigns for the presidential elections of 1950 and 1956. His relationship with the Russians, which many considered to be too intimate, could be especially harmful. Rumours about his alleged opportunism, alcoholism and adultery were circulated in the political press. In such circumstances, Kekkonen's close connection with the ordinary citizens of the countryside was established as a central campaign weapon. The target audience was identified as the small farmers of the countryside, because they still made up a large part of the population and were often politically undecided between the Agrarian League and the FPDL. Kekkonen's close friend and political ally, folklorist Kustaa Vilkuna, was a key figure in producing the campaign materials, which included a history of the Kekkonen family. To professor Vilkuna's initial disappointment, he could not find any free peasants but only farm labourers among Kekkonen's forefathers; however, he was able to interpret their mobile lifestyle as a sign of their inborn courageousness and shrewdness.[64]

During Kekkonen's presidency, agrarian imagery was used extensively. The president frequently travelled to the north, where he met his friends and acquaintances who were often small farmers, reindeer herders, frontier guards and Sámi people. As proof of his ability to survive and his skills, Kekkonen and his entourage were often photographed, filmed and interviewed while skiing long distances in the wilderness of Lapland, or while visiting local people in the villages. The exceptional president was

school, and was elected to parliament in 1945 as a representative of that northeastern region. Suomi, Juhani (1986) *Urho Kekkonen 1936–1944: Myrrysmies.* Helsinki: Otava 247–250.

63 Kekkonen, Urho (1955b) 'Ent. Rintamamies Matti Pyykkönen Kylmäjoen kämpältä' (Former Front-Line Soldier Matti Pyykkönen from the Kylmäjoki Cottage). *Suomen Kuvalehti*, 1955, No. 5, January 28th.

64 Herlin, Ilkka (1993) *Kivijalasta kurkihirteen: Kustaa Vilkunan yhteiskunnallinen ajattelu ja toiminta.* Helsinki: Otava, 316–319.

also noticed abroad: *Paris Match* published a lengthy reportage titled 'Un skieur dans le Grand Nord: M. Finlande, 63 ans', which included impressive colour photographs of the president skiing, ice-fishing and relaxing with a big cigar.[65] The role of the 'peasant' in such descriptions – no longer the archetypal freeholder of the agrarian rhetoric of the 1920s and 1930s, but rather a natural survivor of the harsh northern conditions – was to provide evidence of the president's close connection with the people. Kekkonen's long commitment to the Agrarian League, as well as the folklorist Vilkuna's use of rural symbols and themes in promoting the president's public image, strongly suggest that Kekkonen's public relationship with the 'ordinary citizens' was a modification of the peasant imagery that had a long history in the Finnish tradition of agrarian republicanism.

However, there are several ironies and contrasts in this modification of the peasant imagery and political narratives attached to it. The figure of the peasant, the bedrock of the Agrarian League's democratic agrarian republicanism, was now being used by Kekkonen, who like many other agrarian politicians had been a staunch defender of parliamentarianism in his youth, to legitimise what became his almost monarchical position in Finnish politics during the 1960s and 1970s. The message conveyed by various photographs, films and literary sources was that the head of state had an intimate and trustful relationship with the common citizens, but that a mediating layer consisting of politicians, businessmen and journalists was partly problematic. Even if Kekkonen did not present the case as a city versus countryside issue, it could be concluded from his writings that the embodiments of Finnish common sense and resilience were much more likely to be found in the peripheries than in the urban elites. This view was particularly evident in a collection of the president's private letters that was published in 1976 in two books under the title *Kirjeitä myllystäni* (Letters from my Mill).[66] There, highly critical or even hostile letters to politicians, senior civil servants and newspaper editors were accompanied by friendly messages to the people of the north, often praising their prudence and acknowledging the reasonability of their wishes. The collection stayed in the national bestseller list for months, and as a fine example of *divide et impera*, it revealed a line between Kekkonen's circle of friends and allies and those whose views, often about foreign policy, relegated them almost permanently into secondary positions.

Whereas the pre-war agrarian republicans had used the figure of the peasant in order to legitimise their non-socialist and non-capitalist version of Nordic democracy, Kekkonen now utilised a modified version of this symbolism to reinforce his own position and also to consolidate his foreign policy. Therefore, the figure of the peasant was again in the service of a Nordic model, but this time in defence of the politics of neutrality that was

65 *Paris Match* (1963) 'Un skieur dans le Grand Nord: M. Finlande, 63 ans'. Reportage with photographs, 8 June, 1963.
66 Kekkonen, Urho (1976) *Kirjeitä myllystäni 1: 1956–1967; 2: 1968–1975*. Helsinki: Otava. Kekkonen named the collection after Alphonse Daudet's collection of short stories (1869).

257

controlled almost solely by the president of the republic.[67] Kekkonen's revised use of political narratives including the free Nordic peasant was no longer intended as a legitimisation of a form of government based on the peasants' economic autonomy, local self-governance and parliamentarianism, but as a rhetorical device that helped the Finnish audience understand the necessity of Kekkonen's form of rule and the correctness of his foreign policy. The free Nordic peasant had become an obedient and humble figure that endured even the most difficult of challenges.

It was certain that all this still meant Nordic democracy for Kekkonen. Not everyone agreed. In 1976, when Kekkonen's political power was at its peak, Georg C. Ehrnrooth, the chairman of the small right-wing Constitutional People's Party (Perustuslaillinen kansanpuolue), was celebrated on his 50th birthday by an anthology written by a group of well-known political opponents of Kekkonen. They chose to give the book the name *Pohjoismaisen kansanvallan asialla*, 'Advocating Nordic Democracy'.[68]

Conclusions

The ideological makeup of Finnish politics changed rapidly during the 1960s. This was partly due to expectations that were based on the warming international climate, and partly due to domestic pressures against the narratives of national unity that had dominated Finnish politics since the 1920s. The overall framework of thinking that was relevant to politicians and experts of the decade can be elucidated with reference to such theoretical concepts as ideological convergence and conflict regulation. While such doctrines were not always directly applied to Finnish politics, they are helpful in enabling us to grasp the general preconditions for political agendas of that time. If we accept Jakobson's account, substantiated by Kekkonen's remarks, the president of Finland was a believer in ideological convergence. For him it opened a new, dynamic horizon for Finnish foreign policy. Instead of being a peripheral country, Finland could now benefit from its position between the East and the West. It could even be the ideal base for the evolution of mixed political and economic models.

Similar trends influenced the domestic politics of the 1960s. The ostracised communists were admitted into the government based on reasoning that was substantially aided by Finnish sociologists. Also other forms of social scientific expertise became increasingly relevant because of the building-up of welfare services and the acceptance of modernist economic and administrative planning by almost all the political parties. The smallness of Finland

67 In the preface to the first volume of the letter collection, Kekkonen indeed wrote: 'I have been asked, why I bring my private correspondence into the public arena while still being alive, and while many of those persons whom I treat more or less gently in my letters are also alive. My answer is: I publish my correspondence in order to strengthen our official foreign policy.' Kekkonen 1976, I, 5.

68 Ehrnrooth, Georg C. & Eskelinen, Heikki (eds) (1976) *Pohjoismaisen kansanvallan asialla: [Georg C. Ehrnroothille 27.7.1976] = För nordiskt folkstyre: [till Georg C. Ehrnrooth 27.7.1976]*. Helsinki: Oy Libertas Ab.

and the proximity of its political and academic elites during those years, sometimes even recalled as the golden age of Finnish social science, may help explain the relevance of the academic discourse to the decision-makers.

The ideological realignment aided by social science however contained two potentially conflicting lines of argument. The first was the rationalist, 'de-ideologising' tendency to concentrate on such 'commonly shared' issues as gross national product, welfare indicators and security. Such highly pragmatic themes were prominent in the increasingly expert-led social policy as well as in Finland's foreign policy. This way of thinking was in contrast to the social liberal or pluralist argument of 'agreeing to disagree', which stressed the need to recognise the diversity of values held by various social and political groups, and the necessity of conflict when such interests entered the political arena. While the first viewpoint was consensual and spoke about the uniformity of national (and international) goals, the second emphasised conflict and the necessity of political negotiation between diverse groups. While in hindsight the arguments seem to be to some extent incompatible, this appears not to have been perceived as problematic during the 1960s. Even a single person, such as president Kekkonen, could perfectly well be an advocate for both of them.

In contrast to Sweden, an agrarian party played a substantial and often more significant role than the Social Democrats in changing Finland's ideological and international position. This was partly because of the SDP's problematic relationship with the Soviet Union after the war. The Agrarian League's traditional position also enabled mediation between capitalism and communism. More than that, the most visible Finnish politician of the latter half of the century rose from their ranks.

BIBLIOGRAPHY

Note on the sources: Party programmes (AL, NC, SDP) are retrieved from the Finnish Social Science Data Archive's Pohtiva database, http://www.fsd.uta.fi/Pohtiva/. Many of the speeches and writings of Urho Kekkonen are retrieved from the National Library of Finland's Doria database (UKK-aineisto): Published writings of President Urho Kekkonen (1900–1986), https://oa.doria.fi/handle/10024/7353.

AL (1946) The Agrarian League [Maalaisliitto], 'Maalaisliiton puolueohjelma'. (Source: Pohtiva.)
AL (1962) The Agrarian League [Maalaisliitto], 'Maalaisliiton tavoitteet 1960-luvulla', party programme (Source: Pohtiva).
Allardt, Erik (1956) *Social struktur och politisk aktivitet: en studie av väljaraktiviteten vid riksdagsvalen i Finland 1945–54*. Helsinki: Söderström.
Allardt, Erik (1964a) 'Social Sources of Finnish Communism: Traditional and Emerging Radicalism'. *International Journal of Comparative Sociology*, Vol. 5, No. 1, 49–72.
Allardt, Erik (1964b) *Yhteiskunnan rakenne ja sosiaalinen paine*. Porvoo: WSOY.
Allardt, Erik (1964c) 'Suomalaisen yhteiskunnan perusvastakohtaisuudet'. In *Kansalais-ajattelun seminaari 8 – 13.6. 1964. Alustukset, yleiskeskustelun puheenvuorit ja työryhmien tiivistelmät*. Helsinki: Henkisen maanpuolustuksen suunnittelukunta.
Allardt, Erik (1966) 'Sosiaalisia ongelmia ja ristiriitoja', in Pentti Viita (ed.), *Suomi 1975: ennusteita, analyyseja, näköaloja*, Helsinki: Tammi, 162–183.
Andrén, Nils with Gylfi Þ. Gíslason (1981) 'The Nordic Countries between East and

West'. In Erik Allardt et al. (eds): *Nordic Democracy. Ideas, Issues, and Institutions in Politics, Economy, Education, Social and Cultural Affairs of Denmark, Finland, Iceland, Norway, and Sweden.* Copenhagen: Det danske selskab, 677–690.

Bell, Daniel (1960) *The End of Ideology: On the Exhaustion of Political Ideas in the Fifties.* Cambridge, MA: Harvard University Press.

Borg, Olavi (1965) 'Ideologisia virtauksia Suomen poliittisessa elämässä'. *Sosiologia*, Vol. 2, No. 4, 162–170.

Borg, Olavi (1970) 'Eduskunta ja puolueet', in Olavi Borg (ed.), *Mitä puoluetta äänestäisin.* Helsinki: Otava, 23–42.

Brzezinski, Zbigniew and Samuel P. Huntington (1964) *Political Power: USA/USSR.* New York: Viking.

Dahrendorf, Ralf (1959) *Class and Class Conflict in Industrial Society.* London: Routledge & Kegan Paul.

Ehrnrooth, Georg C. & Eskelinen, Heikki (eds) (1976) *Pohjoismaisen kansanvallan asialla: [Georg C. Ehrnroothille 27.7.1976] = För nordiskt folkstyre : [till Georg C. Ehrnrooth 27.7.1976].* Helsinki: Oy Libertas Ab.

Eskola, Antti (1965) 'Poliittisten ristiriitojen säätely ja kommunismi'. *Sosiologia*, Vol. 2, No. 2, 62–68.

Eskola, Antti (1969) *Vasen laita lavea.* Helsinki: Kirjayhtymä.

Herlin, Ilkka (1993) *Kivijalasta kurkihirteen: Kustaa Vilkunan yhteiskunnallinen ajattelu ja toiminta.* Helsinki: Otava.

Hokkanen, Kari (1996) *Maalaisliitto sodan ja vaaran vuosina 1939–1950: Maalaisliitto–Keskustan historia 3.* Helsinki: Otava.

Hokkanen, Kari (2002) *Kekkosen maalaisliitto 1950–1962: Maalaisliitto–Keskustan historia 4.* Helsinki: Otava.

Jakobson, Max (1968) *Finnish Neutrality: A Study of Finnish Foreign Policy Since the Second World War.* London: Hugh Evelyn.

Jakobson, Max (1981) *Veteen piirretty viiva: Havaintoja ja merkintöjä vuosilta 1953–1965.* Otava: Helsinki.

Jakobson, Max (1983) *38. Kerros: Havaintoja ja muistiinpanoja vuosilta 1965–1971.* Helsinki: Otava.

Kekkonen, Urho (1935) 'Suomalaisuuden rintamalta: Suomalaisuuskysymys on ratkaistava demokraattisin keinoin'. Letter to the editor, *Suomalainen Suomi*, 1935, No. 2, published under the pseudonym *Mies Suomalainen* (Source: Doria/UKK.)

Kekkonen, Urho (1949) 'Finland och Norden: Det nordiska frihetsbegreppet'. Speech to the representatives of the Nordic Parliamentary Union in Helsinki, 16 June, 1949. (Source: Doria/UKK.)

Kekkonen, Urho (1952a) *Onko maallamme malttia vaurastua?* Helsinki: Otava.

Kekkonen, Urho (1952b) 'Toimeentulevaiset ja toimeentulemattomat'. *Kyntäjä*, 1952, No. 12. (Source: Doria/UKK.)

Kekkonen, Urho (1955a) Speech to the co-operative committee of Nordic agrarian parties, January 26th, 1955. (Source: Doria/UKK.)

Kekkonen, Urho (1955b) 'Ent. Rintamamies Matti Pyykkönen Kylmäjoen kämpältä'. *Suomen Kuvalehti*, 1955, January 28th, No. 5. (Source: Doria/UKK.)

Kekkonen, Urho (1957) 'Itsenäinen Suomi 40-vuotias'. Independence Day speech, Helsinki, December 6th, 1957. (Source: Doria/UKK.)

Kekkonen, Urho (1960) Speech at a lunch offered by N. S. Khrushchev on his visit to Finland, September 9th. (Source: Doria/UKK.)

Kekkonen, Urho (1961a) Address of the President of Finland to the General Assembly of the United Nations, October 19th, 1961 (in Finnish). (Source: Doria/UKK.)

Kekkonen, Urho (1961b) 'Suomen asema kansainvälisessä politiikassa'. Speech at the National Press Club, Washington, D.C., October 17th, 1961 (in Finnish). (Source: Doria/UKK.)

Kekkonen, Urho (1967) 'Yhdenmukaisuudesta erilaisuuteen'. Speech at the annual celebration of the North-Ostrobothnian Student Nation, February 4th. (Source: Doria/UKK.)

Kekkonen, Urho (1973/1960) 'Finland Sticks to Her Traditional Democracy'. An English translation of the lunch speech to Khrushchev, in *Neutrality: The Finnish Position*, 2nd exp. ed., London: Heinemann, 83–86.

Kekkonen, Urho (1976) *Kirjeitä myllystäni 1: 1956–1967; 2: 1968–1975*. Helsinki: Otava.

Kekkonen, Urho (1976) [1960] Private letter to Jussi Saukkonen, December 19th, 1963. In Kekkonen *Kirjeitä myllystäni 1*, 102–105.

Kekkonen, Urho (1976) [1963] Private letter to Dr. Matti Luoma, Vaasa, January 14th, 1963. In Kekkonen *Kirjeitä myllystäni 1*, 154–156.

Kekkonen, Urho (1980) 'Suomesta pohjoismaana'. In Kekkonen *Tamminiemi*. Helsinki: Weilin + Göös, chapter 4 (Source: Doria/UKK.)

Kekkonen, Urho (2002) [1968] Entries in private diary on August 21st, August 22nd, and August 23rd, 1968. In Juhani Suomi (ed.) *Urho Kekkosen päiväkirjat 2: 1963–68*. Helsinki: Otava, 2002, 409–411.

Kettunen, Pauli (1999) 'A Return to the Figure of the Free Nordic Peasant'. *Acta Sociologica*, Vol. 42, No. 3, 259–269.

Kuusi, Pekka (1961) *60-luvun sosiaalipolitiikka*. Porvoo: WSOY (4th reprint, 1963).

Larmola, Heikki (1994) 'Miksi Tsekkoslovakian tie ei ollut Suomen tie. Tsekkoslovakia ja Suomi Neuvostoliiton sodanjälkeisessä valtapiirissä'. *Historiallinen aikakauskirja*, Vol. 92, No. 3, 212–228.

Littunen, Yrjö (1960) 'Aktiivisuus ja radikalismi'. *Politiikka*, Vol. 2, No. 4, 151–185.

Merikoski, Veli (1978) *Presidentinvalta vai parlamentarismi*. Helsinki: Weilin + Göös.

NC (1945) The National Coalition [Kansallinen kokoomus], 'Kansallisen kokoomuspuolueen ohjelma'. (Source: Pohtiva.)

Niitamo, Olavi (1966) 'Ennakointi ja ohjelmointi'. In Pentti Viita (ed.) *Suomi 1975: ennusteita, analyyseja, näköaloja*. Helsinki: Tammi, 144–161.

Nousiainen, Jaakko (1956) *Kommunismi Kuopion läänissä. Ekologinen tutkimus kommunismin joukkokannatukseen vaikuttavista tekijöistä Pohjois-Savossa ja Pohjois-Karjalassa*. Joensuu: Pohjois-Karjalan kirjapaino Oy.

Nousiainen, Jaakko (1969) *Research on the Finnish Communism*. Reprint Series B 5, University of Turku: Institute of Political Science.

Paakkunainen, Kari (1985) *Demokratia, tiede, kansanvalistus: Valtiotieteellisen yhdistyksen intellektuaalihistoria 1935–1985*. Helsinki: Finnish Political Science Association.

Paris Match (1963) 'Un skieur dans le Grand Nord: M. Finlande, 63 ans'. Report with photographs, 8 June, 1963.

Rautkallio, Hannu (1992) *Novosibirskin lavastus. Noottikriisi 1961*. Helsinki: Tammi.

Rosenau, James N. (1969) 'Introduction: Political Science in a Shrinking World'. In Rosenau (ed.) *Linkage Politics. Essays on the Convergence of National and International Systems*. New York: The Free Press, 1–17.

Rosenau, James N. (1969, ed.) *Linkage Politics. Essays on the Convergence of National and International Systems*. New York: The Free Press.

SDP (1952) The Social Democratic Party of Finland [Suomen sosialidemokraattinen puolue], 'Suomen sosialidemokraattisen puolueen periaateohjelma (perusteluineen)'. (Source: POHTIVA.)

Suomi, Juhani (1986) *Urho Kekkonen 1936–1944: Myrrysmies*. Helsinki: Otava.

Suomi, Juhani (1992) *Kriisien aika: Urho Kekkonen 1956–1962*. Helsinki: Otava.

Tingsten, Herbert (1955) 'Stability and Vitality in Swedish Democracy'. *Political Quarterly*, Vol. 2, 140–151.

Teljo, Jussi (1950) 'Valtio-opin tehtävät ja menetelmät', an inaugural lecture, *Suomalainen Suomi*, 1950, No. 1, 14–18.

NORBERT GÖTZ

Parliamentarian Democracy Going Global

The Fading Nordic Model

The twentieth century may well be known as the 'age of extremes', but it was also one of parliamentarisation, democratisation, and globalisation. These processes have had a profound impact on the world scale, and yet 'the Parliament of man, the Federation of the world' as once envisioned by Victorian poet Alfred Tennyson (1842)[1] has been conspicuous by its absence.[2] The League of Nations and the United Nations have frequently been mistaken for the ideal and much sought-after world parliament. In reality these organisations have been and, indeed, have only set out to be intergovernmental instruments: their work is a far cry from substantial parliamentary involvement – let alone parliamentary power.

The ever-quickening pace of globalisation forces parliamentarians to devote increased attention to transnational issues; at the same time parliamentarians have become increasingly desired partners in global governance. Their access to broader constituencies and their unparalleled capability to provide bottom-up democratic legitimisation make them attractive showpieces. This tendency was observed a few years ago by a committee of the Swedish parliament, which noted: 'every self-respecting international organization (even purely governmental organizations, such as the World Bank or WTO) is now, in various ways, trying to relate to parliaments and parliamentarians'.[3] The attempt to lend a parliamentary dimension to the United Nations can be regarded as a long-standing feature of the democratic Nordic profile there, one that has gained new momentum in today's favourable environment of globalisation

The most prominent document to call for parliamentarians to have a heightened role in international policy-making was the so-called Cardoso

1 Tennyson, A. (1842) 'Locksley Hall'. *Poems, vol. 1.* London: Moxon (available at <http://eir.library.utoronto.ca/rpo/display/poem2161.html>).
2 A history of the idea of a world parliament is provided by Kissling, C. (2005) 'Repräsentativ-parlamentarische Entwürfe globaler Demokratiegestaltung im Laufe der Zeit: Eine rechtspolitische Ideengeschichte'. *Forum historiae iuris* 9, <http://www.forhistiur.de/zitat/0502kissling.htm>.
3 *Riksdagens protokoll* UMJU1, (2002/2003) 'Johannesburg – FN:s världstoppmöte om hållbar utveckling: Sammansatta utrikes-, miljö- och jordbruksutskottets betänkande.'

Report, presented in June 2004 by an eminent panel summoned at the initiative of UN Secretary-General Kofi Annan. The experts took the view that addressing the democracy deficit in global governance requires a more structural linkage of parliamentarians with international intergovernmental processes. They also asked governments to more regularly 'include members of parliament in their delegations to major United Nations meetings, while taking care to avoid compromising their independence'.[4] Similarly, the Parliamentary Assembly of the Council of Europe, in a resolution adopted on 28 April 2004, called on the governments of its member and observer states to 'include parliamentarians in their national delegation and endow them with the possibility of participating actively' in the work of the UN General Assembly.[5] A subsequent resolution, adopted by the Parliamentary Assembly on 23 January 2006, described the inclusion of parliamentarians in national delegations as a first step toward achieving a thorough parliamentarisation of the General Assembly.[6]

How the second step in this development might look is indicated in a resolution adopted by the European Parliament on 9 June 2005. Although it did not pointedly request parliamentarians to be included in government delegations, the European Parliament called for the establishment of an independent 'United Nations Parliamentary Assembly (UNPA) within the UN system, which would increase the democratic profile and internal democratic process of the organisation and allow civil society on the world scale to be directly associated in the decision-making process'.[7] Currently, there is an ongoing international campaign for the establishment of a Parliamentary Assembly at the United Nations, initiated by the private Committee for a Democratic UN.[8] Cooperation between the United Nations and the Inter-parliamentary Union (IPU) has become increasingly close over the last decade and a half. That said, still open to debate is whether this development represents steps toward a parliamentary dimension of the United Nations or rather serves as a fig leaf and a noncommittal substitute for the development of a genuine parliamentary dimension *within* the United Nations system.[9]

---

4 [Cardoso-Report] (2004) We the Peoples: Civil Society, the United Nations and Global Governance: Report of the Panel of Eminent Persons on United Nations-Civil Society Relations. A/58/817. New York: United Nations, 48.

5 Parliamentary Assembly (2004) 'Resolution 1373 (2004): Strengthening of the United Nations'. Strasbourg: Council of Europe. <http://assembly.coe.int/Documents/ AdoptedText/ta04/ERES1373.htm>.

6 Parliamentary Assembly (2006) 'Resolution 1476: Parliamentary Dimension of the United Nations'. Strasbourg: Parliamentary Assembly of the Council of Europe. <http://assembly. coe.int/Main.asp?link=/Documents/AdoptedText/ta06/ERES1476.htm>

7 European Parliament (2005) 'Resolution P6_TA-PROV(2005)0237: Reform of the UN', Strasbourg. <http://www2.europarl.eu.int/omk/sipade2?PUBREF=-//EP//TEXT+TA+P6- TA-2005-0237+0+DOC+XML+V0//EN&L=EN&LEVEL=3&NAV=S&LSTDOC=Y>.

8 For the campaign website see <http://unpacampaign.org>. Accessed 9 August 2010.

9 Götz, N. (2007) 'Sechzig Jahre und kein bisschen weise: Die Vereinten Nationen in der postnationalen Konstellation'. *Neue Politische Literatur* 52/1: 37–55, at 52.

The current discourse on global governance and the democracy deficit brought about by the domestic impact of globalisation, as well as the quest for a parliamentarisation of the United Nations, suggest the need to take stock of earlier parliamentary involvement in the work of the United Nations. A study of the Nordic countries in this context is a particularly substantive case in point for a number of reasons. First, these countries are among the few states to regularly include a broad range of legislators in their national delegations to the General Assembly. Second, they have a unique record of having done so more or less continuously since the preparatory work for the drafting of the Covenant of the League of Nations. And third, their representatives have been actively engaged in the parliamentarisation of world assemblies at different points in time. As we shall see, the Nordic countries have understood the inclusion of parliamentarians in intergovernmental delegations as a characteristic trait of 'Nordic democracy' and consider themselves a model for the world.

This chapter starts with an overview of parliamentarian patterns at world assemblies in general, and continues with a description of the Nordic practice of sending parliamentary party representatives to the Assembly of the League of Nations and, later, to the General Assembly of the United Nations. It then goes on to sketch the discourse on democracy that accompanies this practice. Finally, this chapter examines the Scandinavian self-understanding of having pioneered the parliamentarisation of international affairs. The concluding remarks will put the ambivalent findings of this article into a more general perspective.

'Parliamentary diplomacy' at world assemblies

Why is the United Nations General Assembly often compared to a 'parliament of mankind' despite the fact that it is institutionally defined as – and for all practical purposes indeed acts as – a recurring conference of the governments of the world? There are two principal reasons for this conjecture, or wishful thinking: one related to the working methods of the General Assembly, the other to the staffing of the delegations of some countries.

Technically speaking, the structure and methods of government cooperation in multilateral diplomacy employ a system typical for legislatures. In international relations and international law the term 'parliamentary diplomacy' has been established as a concept to denote multilateral negotiations characterised by institutionalisation, rules of procedure, public debate and the vote on draft resolutions.[10] The assemblies of the League of Nations and of the United Nations are prototypes of parliamentary diplomacy, not least because their multi-purpose function and the vast range of issues discussed is comparable to that of national assemblies. What is more, the group formation and 'bloc voting' that occurs in negotiations in such fora

10 Rusk, D. (1955) 'Parliamentary Diplomacy: Debate vs. Negotiation'. *World Affairs Interpreter* 26: 121–138, at 121–122.

has implicitly or explicitly been understood as parallel to parliamentary caucusing and has even been described as an 'embryonic party system'.[11] However, the reference 'parliamentary' in this context is solely an analogy of methods to legislative bodies and does not imply an involvement of these bodies.

The founding countries of the League of Nations and of the United Nations were war-time alliances whose victories enabled them to establish new world orders representing the power structure of the day. These alliances took advantage of and were to a degree influenced by and depended on the idealist aspirations of larger publics that had a World Federalist appeal, which would lend legitimacy to the construction of world organisations. In the pre-history of both organisations, key actors such as Woodrow Wilson, the U.S. Department of State and participants of the 1945 United Nations Conference on International Organization envisioned the benefits of wider national representation not limited to governments. However, the principle of national sovereignty was not called into question, and the composition of national delegations remained a matter left to the domestic discretion of the individual countries. In a report, adopted by the first League Assembly and later analogously applied at the United Nations, it was made clear that:

> The Assembly has no right to interfere with the choice which a Member of the League may make of persons to represent it, nor to prevent a Representative from saying what he pleases; but it is essential that it should be thoroughly understood that, when a Representative votes, the vote is that of the Member which he represents.[12]

As states are the only entities eligible for membership in international organisations like the League of Nations and the United Nations, the varying backgrounds of individual members of a delegation are thus levelled out by the principle of *one* common and binding national vote. The only international organisation to practise formal multi-partite representation is the International Labour Organisation (ILO), with governments, national trade unions and national employers' federations commanding votes independently from one another.[13]

Whereas governments always determine the composition and official position of their delegations, the selection of delegates is occasionally done in agreement with the broader aspirations of international organisation mentioned above. Thus, the selection of national delegates to the Assembly of the League of Nations and the General Assembly of the United Nations has not been confined to diplomats and cabinet members. From the outset, a number of governments have chosen to arrange delegations consisting of

---

11 Bailey, S. D. (1964) *The General Assembly of the United Nations: A Study of Procedure and Practice*. Rev. edn. New York: Praeger, 21.

12 Assembly 1920, 320

13 Kettunen, P. (2009) 'The Nordic Model and International Labour Organisation'. In N. Götz and H. Haggrén (eds) *Regional Cooperation and International Organisations: The Nordic Model in Transnational*. London: Routledge, 67–68.

parliament members (sometimes opposition party members), representatives of non-governmental organisations, or simply public personalities to represent their nations alongside professional diplomats. While many member states have occasionally featured un-conventional delegates here and there, only few have made including a spectrum of political and/or societal representation within their delegations a matter of principle. In the days of the League of Nations Denmark and Switzerland were the only states to include parliamentarians at all regular sessions of the Assembly. Other countries with consistent participation of legislators were Sweden, Norway, France, Italy (before and after the Fascist regime); the Benelux countries were also noteworthy in this regard, though to a lesser degree.

As members of the United Nations, the states mentioned above generally continued their tradition, and the United States became another prominent member to include bipartite congressional representation in all delegations to the UN General Assembly, with the exception of the third and fourth sessions. A more systematic assessment of individual member states' practises is beyond the scope of this chapter. Here, let it suffice that the Scandinavian countries stand out in the company of Western members for two reasons. First, as mentioned, they are unique in their regard to the concerted continuity with which they include a strong representation of parliamentary parties, both from the government and the opposition, frequently on nomination of these parties. Second, the high formal status regularly assigned to Scandinavian legislators within delegations is unusual. Based on these traditions the Scandinavian countries can, indeed, be regarded as 'a special case in the U.N.'[14] The following excerpt from a report by a Danish youth delegate to the General Assembly illustrates how this 'Nordic model' of democratic governance was perceived in national terms:

> I think it is in agreement with something of the best in the democratic tradition of Danish people's rule [folkstyre] that not only those in power, but also the political opposition as well as popular movements and organisations and different sections of the population are drawn into collaboration in societal matters. The composition of the Danish UN delegation reflects this tradition [...].[15]

An earlier study showed the low overall correlation between parliamentary representation in delegations to the General Assembly and the countries' respective political regime or geographic location.[16] Although the study did not correctly account for the Scandinavian situation, it can nonetheless be established that while a tradition of parliamentary representation is practised in numerous countries, particularly the Western countries mentioned above,

14 Winther, C. (1965) 'Vier et særtilfælde i FN'. *Information* (4 May).
15 Report by youth delegate Uffe Torm, 19 April 1971, National Archives, Copenhagen, Foreign Ministry 1946–72, 119.H.2.a.1971.
16 Goormaghtigh, J. (1979) Parliaments and the United Nations: Dissemination of Information to Parliamentarians. New York: UNITAR, 64.

there is also considerable fluctuation from one session to the next. Despite increased membership in the United Nations, the number of countries that send parliamentary representatives to New York has decreased in the past forty years. At the sixty-fourth session of the General Assembly in Autumn 2009, twenty-seven countries included parliamentarians. The countries with three or more parliamentary delegates in attendance at the Autumn 2009 session were Denmark, France, India, Italy, Kenya, Malaysia, Norway, and South Africa. Countries with one or two legislators included, among others, Australia, Ethiopia, Nigeria, Pakistan, the Philippines, Russia, Tanzania, and the United States.[17]

Sending Nordic legislators to world assemblies

Political scientist Erling Bjøl has shown that the memoirs of long-time Danish Foreign Minister Peter Munch falsely recall Munch as having criticised the composition of his country's delegation to the second congress in The Hague in 1907 for not having included a representative from parliament or peace organisations. It was not until the 1910s, when the Danish government arranged its delegation to the third congress in The Hague, that parliamentary representatives were seriously considered and, in fact, designated.[18] As it turned out, the congress was cancelled due to the ongoing First World War, leaving Denmark's landmark decision in wait for another day. Nevertheless, the war opened a watershed in international relations, clearing the way for democratic and parliamentary thought. The unprecedented destruction brought on by the war was viewed by contemporaries as a moral breakdown of the old system of international relations, a system based on secret bilateral diplomacy and opposing alliances of great powers. *Democracy* was the catchword of the day – to be realised both in domestic politics with regard to the organs in charge of foreign affairs, as well as in the multilateral operation of international relations – a concept promising a peaceful world order and a cure for the ill-conducted planet.

At the Peace Conference convened in Paris in January 1919 some national delegations already included representatives of parliament and/or of the opposition. Although Scandinavian representatives and other neutrals were not granted official status, they were invited to an unofficial hearing of a sub-committee of the commission drafting the Covenant of the League of Nations in March 1919. At this hearing the representative of Norway acted as vanguard, leading the parliamentarisation of the League, proposing

---

17 United Nations 2009. Legislators from the United States are not identifiable from this list. Cabinet members who are also members of parliament have not been considered. For the 1960s, cf. Baehr, P. R. (1970) *The Role of a National Delegation in the General Assembly.* Occasional Paper 9. New York: Carnegie Endowment for International Peace, 86; for the 1970s, cf. Goormaghtigh 1979, 61–4.

18 Bjøl, E. (1983) *Hvem bestemmer? Studier i den udenrigspolitiske beslutningsproces.* Skrifter fra Dansk Udenrigspolitisk Institut 9. Copenhagen: Jurist- og Økonomforbundet, 111, 189, 241.

that deliberations of the Assembly be made public, and calling for annual meetings of the Assembly and an increase in the maximum number of delegates from three delegates per country to five.[19] One of the motives behind Norway's proposed enlargement of delegations was an attempt to allow for the inclusion of representatives from each of the major political parties.[20] At a later stage, it was another initiative by Norway that obligated the League and later the United Nations to reimburse travel expenses incurred by the principal delegates of member states. The idea was to enable small or distant countries to actively participate in the sessions, not least by sending members of government or parliament from the home country in addition to the professional diplomats residing nearby.[21]

Following the precedent set by Danish–Icelandic negotiations in the summer of 1918, the Danish delegation to the Paris peace conference was the second instance in Nordic foreign affairs in which parliamentarians participated in government delegations alongside officials from the executive branch of government. The Danish delegation was already on site in Paris for discussions on the border issue regarding the Schleswig region. The governments of Sweden and Norway, who also appointed parliamentary delegates, were forced to send their delegations to the Paris meeting at short notice; the legislators did not arrive in time and, thus, both countries were solely represented by their respective ministers to Paris.[22] Although the practice of parliamentary representation in international negotiations corresponded with the democratisation of foreign policy *Zeitgeist*, as well as with the former commission work and parliament claims for representation in the delegation, there were also more immediate political reasons for who was appointed to the delegation. It was significant for the Danish government to include a representative of one of the opposition parties in order to pacify political forces at home and to integrate them in its own restrained strategy in the Schleswig question. As revealed in Peter Munch's diary, 'the present political conditions and the difficulty, which was steadily brought about by claims against the government as pro-German'[23] helped establish a tradition of parliamentary or party delegation.

By sending high-ranking figures to Geneva already for the first Assembly of the League of Nations, the Scandinavian governments established a practice that helped root a general culture of prominent visits and made a noticeable impact on other countries.[24] While high-profile participants from Denmark and Sweden were often members of parliament in Denmark

19 Miller, D. H. (1928) *The Drafting of the Covenant*, vol. 2. New York: Putnam's Sons, 633.
20 Jones, S. S. (1969) *The Scandinavian States and the League of Nations*. Reprint. New York: Greenwood, 60.
21 Hambro, C. J. (1931) *Folkeforbundet og dets arbeide*. Oslo: Aschehoug, 59.
22 Bjøl 1983, 114, 161; Munch, P. (1923) 'Les États neutres et le Pacte de la Société des Nations'. In Munch, P., (ed.) *Les origines et l'œuvre de la Société des Nations*, vol. 1. Copenhagen: Gyldendal, 162.
23 Munch, P. (1963) Erindringer, vol. 4: 1918–1924: Freden, Genforeningen og de første Efterkrigsaar. København: Busck, 61.
24 Jones 1969, 96–9.

and Sweden, it was Norway that initially put a higher value on a potential delegate's international reputation. In a unique twist, the world-renowned explorer Fridtjof Nansen was made chairman of the Norwegian delegation and given a formally superior status over even Prime Minister Otto Blehr, who chose to participate as a regular delegate at the second and third sessions of the Assembly. Not before the second half of the 1920s did newly-elected *Storting* president Carl J. Hambro succeed in extending parliamentary influence over the Norwegian delegation. The other modification to the multi-party representation in Norway came in 1935: Until that time the Labour Party was not represented in the delegations because it opposed Norway's membership in the League of Nations.[25]

Overall, the elements of popular representation found their way to Scandinavian delegations despite acceptance of the League's principle that independent states represented by their governments constitute the relevant agents in international relations. In the Scandinavian countries, the basic principle from the beginning had been to send representatives of the major parliamentary parties; usually these representatives were nominated by the parties and also served as acting members of parliament. These representatives were authorised to speak in the name of the government and were thereby obliged to adhere to previously discussed government instructions. In this way the political opposition was given a chance to participate in policy formulation and implementation, but was also constrained by shared responsibility. Both tendencies made parliamentary ratification of decisions taken in Geneva more likely, especially in cases of minority governments. The strive for non-partisan foreign policy, in general, and the Scandinavian political culture of consensus, in particular, contributed to the establishment of this tradition.

At the same time, the broad composition of delegations fostered their very continuity by reducing the risk of disruption from political changes in the home country. For example, the delegation to the Assembly of the League was left virtually untouched when Sweden underwent a change of government in September 1936. Both the former Minister of Foreign Affairs and his successor simply continued their participation in the delegation – the only alteration being a shuffling of the chairmanship.[26] For Denmark it has been noted that roughly the same parliamentarians who served as their parties' foreign policy experts were also delegated to the meetings of the League year after year, leading to a comparison with 'Tordenskjolds soldiers' – a small group that lives on the continuous re-launch of its individual members.[27] In practice, they functioned as a substitute foreign policy committee accompanying the foreign minister, who nearly always participated throughout the entire session of the Assembly.[28] The same tendencies can be observed of the other Scandinavian countries.

25 Colban, E. (1961) *Stortinget og utenrikspolitikken*. Oslo: Universitetsforlaget, 159.
26 Assembly (1936) Records of the Seventeenth Ordinary Session of the Assembly. Geneva: League of Nations, 27.
27 Bjøl 1983, 119.
28 Winther, 1965.

While the sessions of the League Assembly lasted for about three weeks, the UN General Assembly convenes for a period of roughly three months, meaning a posting in a delegation to the UN would require a significantly longer time commitment than that which had been necessary for delegations to the League; thus, it is not a given that the principle of delegation member continuity was upheld in regard to parliamentary representation in Scandinavian delegations until the mid-1960s. Whereas it was obviously impossible for foreign ministers to attend the General Assembly for more than a few weeks at most, the Scandinavian commitment to continuing the practice of keeping parliamentary representation throughout each session demonstrates the ideological significance those countries attributed to the United Nations at the time. The precedent established in Geneva played a role, as did the fact that travel opportunities were scarce, making delegation postings and the generous daily allowances that accompanied them, seem all the more attractive. Moreover, the foreign services of the Scandinavian countries were small in size during that earlier phase, and therefore in urgent need of outside senior expertise in order to guarantee adequate representation in the diverse committees of the General Assembly. Furthermore, the continuous representation of parliamentary groups was secured, to a degree, by delegating the task of representation to non-legislators who were experts in their respective fields. This type of delegate was not dependent on maintaining voter support and, obviously, did not have the worry of weakening the respective parliamentary group due to regular and long periods of absence. Tellingly, the principle that parliamentary groups should be represented by parliamentarians was adhered to much more closely once the quest for continuity of individual delegates was abandoned.

Norway, represented by the exile government residing in London, was the only Scandinavian country originally admitted to the United Nations Conference on International Organization, which drafted the UN Charter in San Francisco in the spring and early summer of 1945. Not only did the Norwegian delegation to this conference include representatives of all major political parties, it also included a representative of the home front at the request of the resistance movement fighting the German occupants in Norway. Although inclusion of the Home Front representative was a non-recurring instance, the tradition of party representation and civil society representation was continued at the General Assembly.

In contrast to Norway, Denmark's status as an Allied nation during World War Two was doubtful and contested. Following the liberation on 5 May 1945, an interim government was formed between the main political parties and the resistance movement. Although the former were discredited by their pragmatic collaboration with the Nazi occupants, the interim government nevertheless possessed the political legitimacy of groups with democratically-elected representatives. The latter had moral capital and normative democratic credibility despite being self-acting and politically heterogenous, including a significant Communist element. This temporary, post-war domestic balance of power was reinstituted when a delegation was sent to the San Francisco Conference; the delegation was comprised of a representative of the four cooperating democratic parties in the person of social democrat and League of Nations veteran Hartvig Frisch, and a representative of the resistance movement in the person of medical professor Erik Husfeldt. The delegation entailed institutional and moral aspects of democratic authority, explicitly allocating roles 'in such a way that both the period before and after 29 August 1943 appeared in a favourable light'.[29] The leader of the delegation was Minister to Washington and Cabinet Minister without Portfolio Henrik Kauffmann, who had been the driving force behind Denmark's formal admittance to the Allied camp.

Like the Norwegian example, the San Francisco Conference was the only instance in Danish history in which democratic representation in a national delegation was understood to imply the inclusion of the resistance movement of World War Two. Yet, all subsequent Danish delegations to the General Assembly of the United Nations included legislators and representatives of civil society. Like their Scandinavian colleagues, the Danish parliamentarians always enjoyed a high formal status within their delegations, that is, they were designated to the numerically-limited categories of 'representatives' or 'alternate representatives' (in accordance with the rules of procedure of the General Assembly), not to the unrestricted subordinate category of advisers. The only exception to this rule in Denmark occured in 1966, when the parliamentary delegates were merely designated as advisers. However, the ambition of establishing a new symbolic order with a stronger position of the executive was crushed. Parliamentary delegates felt de-classified and were already able to improve their status at the following session; even so, they only moved up to 'alternate representative' status, which they have maintained ever since.[30]

The 1966 lapse in status for Danish parliamentarians was an institutional consequence of a development common to all Scandinavian countries: In the first two decades of the post-war era, a limited number of well-known parliamentarians or politicians designated by parliamentary groups attended the whole session of the General Assembly year after year and exercised substantial influence on their countries' policies. For a number of reasons, this pattern changed in the mid-1960s. The professionalisation of national parliamentary politics, the staff development of the foreign service, and the diminishing authority of the United Nations are probably among the most important factors.[31] A large number of back-benchers filled the parliamentary slots on the delegations, not only alternating from one year to the next, but also replacing each other mid-session. In this way, parliamentary delegation to the United Nations was transformed from being a principled cooperation of powers in the realm of the executive into what can be viewed primarily as a learning experience and monitoring function for the legislators concerned. However, this is not to say they lost their

29 Frisch, H. (1945) 'Rapport over De forenede Nationers Konference i San Francisco'. In H. Frisch & E. Husfeldt (eds) *Rapporter fra de delegerede ved Forenede Nationers konference i San Francisco.* Copenhagen: Schultz, 3.
30 See National Archives, Copenhagen, Foreign Ministry 1946–72, 119.H.2.a.1966, 119.H.2.a.1967.
31 Cf. Bjøl 1983, 122.

political function altogether. In Denmark's case it remained a particular responsibility of the U.N. ambassador 'at an early stage to involve the parliamentary delegation in his considerations'.[32] The Danish government – despite difficulties in coordinating internal meetings with the consultation mechanism of the European Communities after the membership decision in 1972 – declared it of utmost importance to continue 'to receive advice and guidance from the parliamentary representatives at the U.N.-mission in New York'.[33] However, in the past two decades the presence of parliamentarians has been curtailed on all Nordic delegations, and it no longer covers the whole period of the General Assembly. When interviewed, only a minority of Danish, Norwegian and Swedish parliamentary delegates to the sixty-first session of the General Assembly in 2006 viewed their role on the delegation as political involvement.[34]

Under the conditions described above, lending parliamentary members 'adviser' or 'observer' status would have more accurately described their actual position within the delegations. Yet, a substantial change in their nominal status was not realised to the effect that the Scandinavians had to introduce a unique system of footnotes in their delegation lists to describe a complex system of replacements in the numerically restricted categories of representatives and alternate representatives to the General Assembly. The reason for this discrepancy between role and nominal status can only be understood in terms of political culture. Crucial were the strong parliamentary traditions in the Scandinavian countries, the symbolic reference to the sovereign and his or her elected representatives, and satisfaction regarding the display of a particular, non-conventional profile in world affairs, with connotations of democracy and enlightened consensus.

The second exception to the high nominal status of parliamentarians in Scandinavian delegations is Sweden's practice, which has been in place since the fifty-seventh session of the General Assembly. Sweden was among the first newcomers to the United Nations in Autumn 1946. With two exceptions, Sweden has always sent legislators to the General Assembly[35] and has afforded them high status, listing them under the categories of 'representatives' or 'alternate representatives'. However, since 2002, parliamentary members of the Swedish delegation have been pooled in the category 'special advisers'.[36] The parliamentarians' re-categorisation was accompanied by a formal redefinition of their role, shifting them from

---

32 *Folketingstidende* 1974/75, 968.
33 *Folketingstidende* 1945–76, 3964–5; cf. 3987, 4055.
34 Interviews conducted by the author in Copenhagen, Oslo and Stockholm in January 2007.
35 The two exceptions to this rule are the session of admission (to which the country was invited at a late stage and in which it was eager to keep a particularly low profile), and the session of 2009 (when the extra work load occasioned by the Swedish presidency of the European Union caused the foreign ministry to ask parliament not to send legislators to that session, offering instead participation in the commission work of the United Nations in Spring 2010).
36 United Nations (2002) *List of Delegations to the Fifty-seventh Session of the General Assembly*. ST/SG/SER.C/L.597. New York: United Nations. 114.

'participating' to 'observing' members of the delegation. At the same time they were made subject to a particular instruction programme on United Nations issues. As maintained by the former head of the foreign ministry's Department of Global Security, Hans Lundborg, the reason for the change was Sweden's participation in the European Union's continuous coordination, also conducted in New York, which according to him, left no space for parliamentarians.[37] The comment deserves to be taken with a grain of salt: Given the ever-increasing observer-like role of parliamentarians on the delegation since the 1970s, the European Union, a well-known scapegoat for all kinds of changes – if it had any effect at all – would most appropriately have to be seen as the catalyst uncovering the mature life-lies of the Scandinavian delegation practice.

Denmark and in particular Norway, the state to assign the highest status to parliamentary United Nations delegates, keep closer to the traditional Scandinavian profile. Parliamentary representatives to the United Nations can also be found in the delegations of Iceland and Finland. As personnel and financial resources are scarce in Iceland, the size and composition of delegations has been object to considerable fluctuation over the years.

From the very beginning, Finland aspired to the same method of parliamentary delegation as that practiced by the Scandinavian countries. In the bill authorizing the start of Finland's application process to membership in the League of Nations, the right to instruct the delegation on how to vote was reserved for the government. At the same time, the bill allowed for the possibility that 'representatives of one and the same country present and defend different views'. When this possibility for contradiction was discussed in the parliamentary Committee for Foreign Affairs, a substantial minority suggested mandatory Parliament participation in the selection of Finnish delegates. However, the majority of the committee agreed on the ambiguous stipulation that the government should take into account the confidence enjoyed by selectees in Parliament.[38] In practice, the majority of Finnish delegations to the League in the 1920s included a legislator. This tradition was revived in the course of closer collaboration between the three Scandinavian countries beginning in the year 1935.

Also, once their first delegation was sent to the United Nations in 1956, the Finnish government included legislators. The background of this decision was the intention of distinguishing Finland as a member of the Nordic group.[39] While Finland's parallel admission to the Nordic Council, a body of legislators, might have made the delegation of parliamentarians seem like a natural choice, the early 1960s saw a new system emerge to correspond with Finland's foreign policy during the Cold War. The chosen policy line aimed for presidential control and far-reaching de-politicisation in order to avoid confrontation with the Soviet neighbour. This policy was

37 Interview.
38 Eduskunta (1920) *Riksdagen, Handlingar* (Prop. 17, including Utskottets för utrikesärenden betänkande N:o 2 [= U.B.]), 1–2.
39 Cf. Jakobson, M. (1982) *Den finländska paradoxen: Linjer i Finlands utrikespolitik 1953– 1965*. Helsinki: Schildt, 84.

not always popular with the domestic public and, thus, not something particularly attractive for parliamentarians to be associated with, either. Soon enough another system emerged and, although not always applied in a consistent manner, it foresaw the designation of delegates who themselves were not members of parliament but had been proposed by parliamentary party groups.[40] Frequently, such non-parliament member delegates were journalists, employees of the party administration, civil society activists, or scholars. On the strength of their appointment by the major parties, these types of representative are called 'political delegates', or sometimes 'polegates'. They constitute a distinct group within the delegation, and in many respects they resemble the category of predominantly parliamentarian political delegates of the Scandinavian countries. They also have the capacity to demand a revision of instructions on particular issues, but as one parliamentarian once remarked, 'the faster one learns to cope with the role of an observer or apprentice, the better for oneself and one's reputation'.[41] The Swedish People's Party of Finland was the only party to continue proposing parliamentary representatives to Finnish delegations to the General Assembly until the mid-1970s. Records in the party archive clearly show the promotion of Scandinavian or Nordic political culture as part of the party's perceived mission in Finnish politics.[42]

Despite not otherwise sending parliamentarians, the Finnish government sent a full-scale parliamentary delegation to the twenty-fifth session of the General Assembly. While the legislators did not stay longer than two weeks, their attendance did demonstrate at least a ceremonial appreciation of the United Nations. A rather bizarre proof of the Scandinavian delegation model's normative power in Finland is provided by the white book on Finnish participation in the fiftieth session of the General Assembly. In this document all political delegates are identified by party affiliation and at the same time titled *kansanedustaja*, literally meaning 'people's representative', the Finnish term for 'member of parliament'. In actual fact none of these representatives occupied a seat in parliament, nor had they ever. Thus, the term *kansanedustaja* was stretched to function as a denomination for 'representative *for* parliament' or 'people's representative' in an extended sense, a tribute to the defining institution of political delegation and the population behind it on the occasion of the half-centennial anniversary of the United Nations.[43] It was also a symbolic demonstration of commitment to the cause of the world organisation concurrent with that demonstrated twenty-five years earlier. However, the foreign ministry's orchestration of

---

40 Götz, N. (2009) 'Government and Multipartisan Representation: The Finnish Composition of Delegations to the General Assembly of the United Nations'. In B. Wegner et al., (eds) *Finnland und Deutschland: Studien zur Geschichte im 19. und 20. Jahrhundert*. Hamburg: Kovac.

41 Zilliacus, J. (1978) *En bit av det stora äpplet*. Helsinki: Söderström, 9; cf. Törnudd, K. (1982) 'Kunskap om utrikespolitik'. In *Ord och handling: Utrikespolitiska uppsatser*. Helsinki: Schildt, 120–121.

42 Swedish Central Archives, Helsinki, Minutes of the meetings of the Swedish parliamentary group.

43 Foreign Ministry (1995) *Yhdistyneiden kansakuntien yleiskokous* 50, 5.

a parade of Potemkin villagers in New York in the autumn of 1995 suffered from a lack of even the most elementary substance – a remarkable blunder for a representative of the Nordic group of countries, especially considering this group's frequent criticism of the declaratory character seen in much United Nations politics and its disdain for the misuse of the UN as a theatre for plots staged to satisfy domestic audiences, adding to the unrealistic aura surrounding the world organisation.

Democracy and representation in government delegations

When Carl J. Hambro conducted his campaign to bolster *Storting*-influence on the Norwegian delegation policy in the 1920s, he started by demanding that 'delegations sent to Geneva develop in the most organic way possible to represent the national assemblies and the will of the people, manifest in the national assemblies'.[44] Indeed, the practice of parliamentary representation in Nordic delegations to the world organisation has been explained in such a way: 'The starting point is that it is in our democracy's and political community's interest that the Riksdag is fully represented, not just by the governing party'.[45]

These quotes and the general problem under discussion here might raise expectations that words like 'democracy', 'people's rule', and so on are frequently coupled with the practice of sending parliamentarians to world assemblies. This is not the case. To the contrary, such occasions are rare, and explicit reference to the concept of 'democracy' tended to be made in situations where the delegation practice appeared precarious in one way or another. Ultimately, the most trenchant observation on the practises of involving parliamentarians in diplomatic relations discussed in this chapter might be that of international lawyer Max Sørensen, in which he expressed his dissatisfaction with Danish parties for not appointing the most skilled representatives to UN delegations: 'Nordic democracy has not always been up to its task'.[46]

The most critical moments in the history of Nordic delegations were two Swedish and two Finnish cases of exclusion in the 1950s and 1960s. In these cases, delegates put forth by parliamentary parties were rejected by the government, based on the justification that the maintenance of a credible policy of neutrality made consensus on defense issues a prerequisite. In other words, in these cases the instrument of parliamentary representation in government delegations was used for disciplining the opposition, which in turn criticised the measure as undemocratic.[47] Interestingly, the concept of 'Nordic democracy' or 'Nordic democracies' was used in this connection

---

44 *Stortingstidende* 1920, 3632.
45 Swedish politician Yngve Möller, according to Karlsson, A. (1965) 'Parlamentarikerna i den svenska FN-delegationen'. Student paper, Stockholm: University, 31.
46 Pedersen, A. B. (1954) 'Nordisk Fredsforbunds kongres'. *Freds-Bladet* 63: 59–61, at 59.
47 Cf. Jernström, F. (1994) *Sju liv*. Esbo: Schildt, 96; Bjereld, U. (1997) *Hjalmarsonaffären: Ett politiskt drama i tre akter*. Stockholm: Nerenius & Santérus.

as a means to defend the government position. Thus, after Conservative party leader Jarl Hjalmarson had been banned from the Swedish delegation, Prime Minister Tage Erlander contrasted the hot spots of the Cold War with the tranquil situation in Scandinavia, which he attributed to 'the domestic firmness and cohesion of the Nordic democracies'.[48] Endorsing the exclusion of Hjalmarson and the Finnish social democrat Väinö Leskinen in 1959, the left-wing Finnish news daily *Päivän Sanomat* wrote – in an ironic twist – of those who now 'scatter ashes on the ruins of Nordic democracy'.[49]

From a Finnish point of view, the inclusion of legislators in government delegations seemed problematic in the Cold War era, with ordinary connotations of democratic governance in mind. According to the memoirs of Finnish parliament member Albin Wickman, not only was 'democratic spirit' lacking in the Finnish delegation to the General Assembly, but he had also never in the thirty years of his political career 'taken part in any event, in which an equally pronounced "der Führer"-regime prevailed'. Starting from the proposition that the United Nations are and should be 'the highest form of people's rule' and having this appalling experience in mind, he called for 'a thorough reform with regard to our delegates' right to feel in the U.N. that they represent a democratic nation and a government that is not headed by a dictator'.[50] Although this frustrated politician addressed the problem in general terms and did not formally address the specific situation of legislators, his intervention, explicitly based on words like 'democratic' and 'people's rule', arises from a context of parliamentary representation in Scandinavian delegations to the General Assembly. Commenting on the general state of matters of the era, historian R. Michael Berry, at the time when the Cold War was still a reality, ascribed to Finland an 'authoritarian form of political democracy [...] deviating from the norms of Nordic parliamentarianism'.[51] It is also worth noting that in a joint declaration on Nordic cooperation made in the early 1930s by the respective foreign ministers with the aim of increasing awareness about the League of Nations, the Finnish side precluded the concept of democratic statehood from being mentioned as the basis of Nordic cooperation.[52]

Other examples highly representative of the implicit Scandinavian attitude toward the inclusion of legislators in UN delegations underline the democratic merits of this principle, rather than pointing at shortcomings of a specific practice. After the elections of 1960 the newly-created *Socialistisk Folkeparti* achieved representation in Denmark's parliamentary foreign affairs committee and thus also gained the opportunity to put forth a representative delegation member. In this connection the designated delegate, Kai Moltke, announced: 'Of course I consider it both a good

---

48 'Statsminister Erlanders tal på Konserthuset den 17 september 1959', National Library Stockholm, Östen Unden's Archive, vol. 20.

49 *Päivän Sanomat*, 12 September 1959.

50 Wickman, A. (1967) *Frihet är det bästa ting*. Helsinki: Söderström, 232–233.

51 Berry, R. M. (1987) *American Foreign Policy and the Finnish Exception: Ideological Preferences and Wartime Realities*. Helsinki: SHS, 440.

52 Degerman 1957, 39

and *democratic* order, that not only representatives of government, experts and officials – but also representatives for the parties of the Folketing participate in the delegation to the U.N.'.[53] A similar case can be recorded for Norway when the Socialist Electoral League entered Parliament and the UN delegation in 1973. Socialist delegation member Berit Ås, who had made unprecedented use of the freedom to express reservations regarding the Norwegian policy in New York, later lauded the Norwegian system of multi-party representation as 'both democratic and fruitful'.[54]

Despite their different content, the statements of Moltke and Ås had one basic thing in common with the complaint by Finnish legislator Wickman: They were written from a defensive position. The words 'democracy' and 'democratic' fell when newcomers who pointedly did not partake in the foreign policy consensus of the other parties came into the picture and, confronted with critical comments, had to vindicate themselves for enjoying a position in the delegation. Moltke did this by first bringing to mind the principle of democratic participation, and then followed up by advocating innovation, namely a more clear-cut and modern division of labour than had prevailed to date. He suggested that, in order to avoid conflicts of interest, a more appropriate definition of a party representative's role should be outlined to address the dual task of acting as observer for a given party and as a discussant at internal delegation meetings. At the same time he argued for relieving party representatives from the inopportune duty of functioning as civil servants for the government in the committee work of the General Assembly. Although exceptions were tolerated both before and after, the Scandinavian party representatives' role was redefined in the 1960s in the way suggested by Moltke. This change was not the outcome of a crumbling foreign policy consensus, but rather a consequence of the structural change described in the previous section: Instead of designating the same political United Nations experts every year, frequently-substituted party representatives would be sent to postings akin to a study trip to New York.

There are cases that reflect the supposition expressed by Danish historian and diplomat Troels Fink, in which he found that U.N. delegations of 'democratic states reflect domestic political antagonisms, but act as national units'.[55] However, as a rule, when the issue of party representatives in Scandinavian delegations to the United Nations is taken up, references are limited to operational aspects of the practice like those addressed in the second part of Moltke's argument. The issue of party representatives is rarely discussed as linked to the concept of democracy, although the practical aspects only make sense in virtue of their embeddedness in democratic political culture. Thus, the actual discourse is largely limited to underlining or, at times, questioning the relevance of having parliamentary disseminators and discussants at hand, and to giving a share of the non-partisan national conduct of foreign affairs to relevant political agents.

53 Moltke, K. (1961) 'Om partier, F.N. delegation, overbevisning og afstemning'. *Information* (10 August).

54 *Stortingstidende* 1973/74, 3681.

55 Fink, T. (1961/1962) 'Danmark og FN', *Folketingstidende, Tillæg B* 113: col. 720–726, at 720.

'Consensus' and 'unity' are the key concepts in this connection, comprising two relevant dimensions: the maintenance and rebuilding of a community of values on the one hand, and its expressive manifestation on the other. Thus, the political element in delegations has had practical and symbolic value in ensuring that Scandinavian policies have been raised above party politics.[56] Not least, there was an external dimension to such a national consensual approach. As expressed by Danish Foreign Minister Poul Hartling in Spring 1968, if there were 'any hope to be heard out in the world and to gain influence on the course of events, we have to provide for other countries to also have confidence that our policies are realistic and representative of our society'.[57] In view of the observation that use of words such as 'democracy' in practice signals problems rather than achievements, their general absence might be interpreted as an indicator of satisfactory functioning of the Scandinavian delegation system from a contemporary parliamentarian – and national – point of view.

This is not to say the word 'democracy' necessarily indicated domestic problems or was absent in more general contexts of Nordic self-understanding within the League of Nations and the United Nations. For example, in a foreign policy debate in Autumn 1945 Swedish parliamentarian Edgar Sjödahl referred to the Atlantic Charter, the first sketch of the idea of the United Nations in 1941, and the hope it had brought to small 'democracies of Western or, as I prefer to call it, Nordic character'.[58]

From the early days of the League, representatives from Scandinavia not only expressed particularly democratic self-images of their countries and of their regional group in the international context, but also thought of shared democratic values as the essential idea behind Nordic liaison. Examples of this shared belief can be found in the parliamentary debate on Norwegian United Nations policy in January 1948. Parliamentary delegation member Terje Wold underlined that there was a common understanding in the Nordic countries that they were 'true democracies'.[59] Foreign Minister Halvard Lange pointed to a specific democratic culture and shared meaning of words and concepts as the basis for Nordic cooperation.[60] In a manuscript, probably written in Summer 1947, Lange had even explicitly described the common basis for Nordic cooperation in the United Nations as 'Nordic culture [...] and Nordic democracy'.[61] At about the same time, pointing out that it was probably regarded as natural that 'the three Nordic democracies each have their own woman at the UN', the Swedish delegate Ulla Lindström highlighted a specific element of this culture, namely state feminism.[62] The

56 Hambro, E. (1965) 'Høyre: Utenrikspolitikk byggt på respekt for rett og rettferdighet'. In Heradstveit, P. Ø. (ed.) *Partiene og utenrikspolitikken*. Oslo: Aschehoug, 28.
57 *Folketingstidende* 1967/68, 2076–2077.
58 *Riksdagens protokoll, Första Kammaren*, Nr. 32, 37, (1945).
59 *Stortingstidende* 1948, 32.
60 *Stortingstidende* 1948, 43.
61 Lange, Halvard (1947) 'Internasjonalt samarbeid mellom nasjonene'. Foreign Ministry, Oslo, Halvard Lange's archive, vol. 15.
62 Lindström, Ulla (1947) 'Kvinnor i FN'. National Archives, Stockholm, Ulla Lindström's archive, vol. 7.

Fig. 1: 'Sitting next to each other: Sweden got Saudi Arabia and Syria as neighbours at the UN'

plural of the term 'Nordic democracy' decouples its constituents. That said, Nordic specifics might have been addressed at times even when the plural form was employed, as exampled in the quote above.

The issue of democracy was sometimes also raised in contexts that were problematic not because they essentially constituted a claim for democratic participation, but because they made democracy an argument of cultural chauvinism. Swedish Foreign Minister Östen Undén caused a minor scandal in Autumn 1947 when he publicly commented that in the United Nations 'all shades were represented, from the age-old democracy Iceland to the patriarchically reigned Yemen, where slave trade is still allowed and where thieves get their left hand chopped off'.[63] A caricature and poem, published in the social democratic newspaper *Ny Tid* after Sweden had taken her seat in the General Assembly in November 1946, might be seen as a congenial

63 Grafström, S. (1989) *Anteckningar 1945–1954*. Handlingar 15. Stockholm: Kungl. Samfundet för utgivande av handskrifter rörande Skandinaviens historia, 841.

specification of Undén's statement with regard to the operational mode of democracy.

The text of the poem contrasts cool and sober-minded Swedish delegates with hot-tempered oriental delegates and states: 'While Nordic man is inclined / to adjust, weigh up pros and cons / the middle way is rarely chosen / on the Eastern part of our globe.'[64] Undén had presented his maiden speech at the General Assembly three days before the publication of this remarkable piece of artwork. In this speech he had recalled that Sweden was often referred to as 'the land of the middle way' in the United States, and that this metaphor connoted 'methods [...] for the solution of domestic problems, especially in the social field', which also defined Sweden's attitude to the resolution of international problems.[65] The approach of multipartite parliamentary representation in delegations to the General Assembly clearly reified this self-image of progressiveness and rational corporatist choice at the national level in an international context and provided a welcome differentiation toward the outside world. Thus, in a Danish memorandum on the composition of the delegation to the third session of the General Assembly in Autumn 1948, the logic of distinction was explicitly applied in assessing that, for example, 'in the Latin American countries, one is undoubtedly not quite as advanced as to also let opposition parties participate in the delegations'.[66]

The Nordic model of parliamentary representation

In 2000, in a motion regarding Sweden's United Nations policy, deputies from the Left Party claimed that 'the standpoint of the Swedish government to broad compose Swedish U.N. delegations including parliamentarians, interest organisations, and popular movements is an example for many other countries'.[67] Indeed, at least one case can be reconstructed from among the archives of the foreign ministry in which a foreign (Japanese) diplomat was instructed in 1963 to gather information about the Swedish delegation practice.[68] And as yet, the recent lowering of parliamentarians' status within Swedish delegations to the General Assembly has not left traces in accessible documents of the Riksdag.

While the student of Nordic politics will find it unsurprising that self-applauding of this kind is found, there have also been some more unexpected initiatives aimed at the outside world, made in attempt to change this world for the better. And conversely, the world often seems to have been inclined

---

64 *Ny Tid* 22 November, 1946 ('Bänkkamrater'). Interestingly, the caricature associates artificial Hebrew letters with an Arab from Syria.

65 General Assembly 1946, 969.

66 J. Rechendorff's memorandum of 16 April 1948, National Archives, Copenhagen, Foreign Ministry 1946–72, 119.D.9.a.

67 *Riksdagens protokoll, Motioner* (U 21), (1999/2000).

68 Wachtmeister, Wilhelm, Memorandum 7 August 1963, Foreign Ministry Archive, Stockholm, HP 48 DD, vol. 6.

to admire the Nordic model. As Edvard Hambro, in another self-praising sequence, once reported from the League of Nations:

> One can often hear grand words on the role Norway might play. With great insistence it is maintained that small states have an important task in Geneva, and that a sheer mystical power is inherent in those words just expressed by one of the Nordic representatives. A few regard them as a sort of international noblemen [adelsmennesker], which cannot be praised loudly enough for their courage and their independence.[69]

Some twenty-five years later, a Norwegian parliamentary delegation member expressed a similar observation somewhat more soberly: He noticed with delight the high esteem Norway and the other Scandinavian countries enjoyed in the United Nations, something he believed was derived from an internationally shared 'substantial respect for our democracy'.[70]

At the League of Nations, Denmark seems to have been the only country to actually let different political parties formally appoint delegates as government representatives. Denmark was therefore internationally discussed as a model of democratic delegation.[71] As mentioned earlier, the other Scandinavian countries included a particularly high proportion of parliamentarians in their delegations, too. Hence, as implied in the words of Christian L. Lange, long-time Secretary-General of the Inter-Parliamentary Union and member of the Norwegian delegation to the League, the Nordic countries started to view themselves as champions of the parliamentarisation of international relations:

> More and more the Nordic example [of sending legislators] is followed, so that the Assembly subsequently has a predominantly political-parliamentary character, and this again has influenced the debates, which have become more lively and realistic than what is usual in exclusively 'diplomatic' conferences. [72]

In hindsight this statement seems a tad over-enthusiastic, not only in regard to the characterisation of the League, which in the 1930s gave the impression of being increasingly out of touch with reality, but also concerning the overall parliamentary element in national delegations, which was never impressive. As a matter of fact, Norwegian representatives to the Assembly became agitated by what were predominantly diplomatic delegations sent by other countries, pointing out that 'The League of Nations cannot become the organ it should be, the Council cannot become the organ it should be, if

69 Hambro 1938, 34.
70 *Morgenbladet*, 26 April 1961.
71 Schücking, W. & Wehberg, H. (1924) *Die Satzung des Völkerbundes*. 2nd rev. edn. Berlin: Vahlen, 284; Knoll, G. (1931) *Der deutsche Regierungsentwurf zu einer Völkerbundssatzung vom April 1919: Zugleich Betrachtungen zur Völkerbundsverfassung und zu ihrer Reform*. Leipzig: Weicher, 83.
72 Lange 1937, 24.

a onesided and predominantly diplomatic element meets in the Council and in the delegations'.[73] As conceded by the author of this proposition, Carl J. Hambro, president not only of the Norwegian *Storting,* but also of the League's last assemblies (in 1939 and 1946), the idea that the League had to be strengthened through a general parliamentarisation and that the task of the Assembly was to exercise 'what one could call parliamentary control' was a personal project rather than anything acknowledged by the bulk of actors.[74] Although the parliamentarisation project never advanced particularly far, Edvard Hambro, son of the former, who himself was to become a president of the General Assembly of the United Nations, concluded in 1938 that

> the parliamentary culture we have brought with us from our own *Storting*, our respect for constitutional forms and dignity, which we have also tried to introduce in the League of Nations, have only been of benefit to our reputation and helped the League to advance on a better track.[75]

Essentially, people from the Nordic countries have tended to view themselves as representing the vanguard of the parliamentarisation of world assemblies, both in form and in substance, and occasionally, they have advocated their model and quite bluntly requested a following. At the meeting of the Inter-Parliamentary Union in Vienna in 1954, for instance, the Danish Social Democrat Alsing Andersen asked permission to ride one of his 'hobby-horses – the question of the composition of the delegations to the U.N.'. As no protest was voiced, Andersen declared it 'regrettable that in most cases they consist almost exclusively of officials' and, in view of the political character of the issues discussed at the United Nations, that it seemed 'a serious mistake to include so few Members of Parliament among the delegates'. He concluded his plea by referring to the Scandinavian example, by observing that many countries had not yet included any legislators in their delegations, and by underlining parliamentarians' significance 'for the establishment of the right kind of contact between the various peoples and for the right understanding of the U.N.'s work'.[76]

More fundamentally, during the General Assembly debate on the cooperation between the United Nations and the Inter-Parliamentary Union of November 2000, the Norwegian Deputy Permanent Representative to the United Nations, Arne B. Hønningstad, proclaimed the following in regard to the texture of democracy:

> the world needs a United Nations where citizens feel that they are genuinely represented in their political diversity. The United Nations must have a parliamentary dimension. The Nordic countries have chosen to include parliamentarians representing different parties in

73 Hambro, C.J. (1931) *Folkeforbundet og dets arbeide*. Oslo: Aschehoug, 60.
74 Hambro, 1931, 12.
75 Hambro 1938, 80–81.
76 Andersen, A. (1954) 'A Danish Socialist View on a Revision of the U.N. Charter', *Socialist International Information* 4, 722.

their delegations to the General Assembly and to special conferences. I would recommend this as a general model, as one element in building a parliamentary dimension. The United Nations would also benefit from drawing more heavily on the political expertise of these parliamentarians in connection with the General Assembly and other meetings.[77]

Apart from in the context of development assistance, it is not common diplomatic practice for Nordic government representatives to give advice of this kind to sovereign fellow-nations – advice not only on how to design institutions, which by convention are not the business of other states, but at the same time advice that runs the risk of appearing conceited and self-indulgent. It is well-known that Sweden and Norway, in particular, are sometimes held up to ridicule for their tendency to give the impression of 'moral superpowers', and it is not by accident that Nordic peoples are inclined to assert that it is others, not they themselves who tend to view Norden as a model. This would, indeed, be a remarkable observation if the asserted modesty were not belied by the fact that the adoption of and preoccupation with others' perceptions appears to be a favourite Nordic hobby. Be this as it may, it is conspicuous how frankly a Norwegian delegate advocated the Nordic model of parliamentary representation in delegations to international conferences in order to attain a better representation of citizens in their political diversity. By some irony, the statement might have been weightier as it had been delivered by a diplomat, not by a parliamentarian who would have appeared to have championed his own cause.

Concluding remarks

When Egil Aarvik, chairman of the Norwegian Nobel Committee, delivered his presentation speech for the laureate of the Nobel Peace Prize 1982, he said that winner Alva Myrdal belonged to the world community while at the same time being 'ideologically firmly rooted in Nordic constitutional principles and in our democratic ideals'. In the same vein, he added that these were the ideals that had motivated her when heading the Swedish delegation at the Geneva disarmament negotiations.[78] According to a prominent strand of discourse, Nordic values are the most appropriate blueprint for an emerging universal political culture. The Swedes have gone so far as to send to the General Assembly an 'NGO ambassador' tasked with representing global civil society on the Swedish delegation and to use the latter as a channel for transnational 'non-governmental' viewpoints.[79]

77 General Assembly 2000, 3–4.
78 Aarvik, E. (1982) [Presentation Speech on the occasion of the awarding of the Nobel Peace Prize for 1982, Oslo, December 10, 1982]. <http://nobelprize.org/nobel_prizes/peace/laureates/1982/press.html>.
79 Götz, N. (2008) 'Corporatism and Universalism in Foreign Affairs: The Case of Civil Society Inclusion in Swedish Delegations to the General Assembly of the United Nations'. In W. Rothholz and S. Berglund (eds) *Vom Symbol zur Realität: Studien zur politischen Kultur des Ostseeraums und des östlichen Europas.* Berlin: Wissenschafts-Verlag, 76–78.

Unsurprisingly, 'Nordic democracy' has not usually been delimited as aggressively as in some of the cases described in the two previous sections, neither in contrast to less developed Arab or South American nations, nor as a model to follow. Usually, Scandinavian governments simply chose to demonstrate that they took the League of Nations and the United Nations seriously and sent delegations that included representative parliamentary elements, accordingly. They were also otherwise exemplary. For instance, at the first Assembly of the League of Nations Denmark, Norway and Sweden were the only countries to include women in their delegations in positions higher than secretaries; and they continued to send female delegates to an environment that for a long time remained almost completely dominated by men. Generally speaking, the Scandinavian governments collaborated closely with each other and benefited from their shared image of progressive and reasonable Scandinavia, which they were able to advance by applying elements of their countries' political culture in the context of the League of Nations and, later, in that of the United Nations. In particular, this culture refers to a reliance on law, to a pragmatic and constructive approach in day-to-day work, and to the desire to strive for compromise and consensus. As summarised in 1936 by the Swedish liberal politician Kerstin Hesselgren, in Geneva the Scandinavian countries were called *'the serious nations – sometimes with a touch of derision, because we are so faithful to law clauses, but also with respect for the sobriety that lies at the bottom of it'.*[80] Mutual Scandinavian collaboration provided in itself a marketable example, and there is after all a grain of truth to Lord Cecil's prediction in early 1919, in which he said that were the Scandinavian countries to get together, they would resemble a great power.[81] Their reputation also benefited from the fact that they provided major items on the credit side of the League's balance sheet, namely peaceful resolution of the Åland and Greenland crises. Their close cooperation caused Denmark, Norway, and Sweden to be perceived in the League of Nations as an 'Entente of the Northern States.[82] Similarly, in the United Nation, these countries plus Iceland and, eventually, Finland, have been identified as the 'Scandinavian bloc' or the 'Scandinavian group', with a manifest approach of constructively mediating between East and West, and North and South, thereby displaying a distinct voting behaviour. Recently, Swedish and Finnish membership in the European Union and the development of the common European foreign and security policy have left the Scandinavian group in the United Nations largely obsolete.[83] That said, the brand name 'Scandinavia' lives on, synonymous for 'best practice', and

---

80 Hesselgren, Kerstin (1936) 'Sverige och Nationernas Förbund.' Speech held in Göteborg, September 1936. Gothenburg University Library, Women's History Collections A 14: Kerstin Hesselgren IIIc:5. The italicised phrase is English in the original.

81 Munch 1963, 68–69.

82 Zimmern, S. A. (1939) *The League of Nations and the Rule of Law 1818–1935*. 2nd rev. edn. London: Macmillan, 506.

83 Laatikainen, K. V. (2003) 'Norden's Eclipse: The Impact of the European Union's Common Foreign and Security Policy on the Nordic Group in the United Nations'. *Cooperation and Conflict* 38, 409–441.

Norway and Iceland perceive themselves in the role of preservers of the Nordic profile.[84]

One important element that distinguished the Scandinavian group in the League of Nations as well as in the United Nations and thereby contributed to its profile is what I call the parliamentarisation project. This project entailed a procedural dimension and a personal one: The procedural dimension required competences and working methods to be established at the assemblies, which resembled domestic parliamentary structures; the personal dimension involved the inclusion of parliamentarians or party representatives in the work of the organisation. The driving force for this approach, though ill-documented and largely left on an implicit level, was the desire to enhance legality and democracy in global governance, not only because these principles imply a favourable environment for small states, but also because they are fundamental ends in themselves.

Although people from the Nordic countries usually have understood and accepted the fact that the two principal world assemblies of the twentieth century were not world parliaments, but essentially intergovernmental diplomatic conferences, they do have a long record of engagement in the parliamentarisation of these bodies. The idea of a world parliament is clearly a source of inspiration for the piecemeal approach of strengthening and eventually transforming the United Nations into a more parliamentary structure, which is a central theme of the Nordic countries' practical work and physical presence in this organisation. Obviously, any parliamentarisation that renounces the involvement of parliamentary actors must remain incomplete.

Even so, the inclusion of parliamentarians in delegations to the General Assembly is only one possible answer to the question of how to increase democratic input and feedback with regard to the conduct of international affairs. If a United Nations Parliamentary Assembly is indeed established, as has been demanded by the European Parliament among others, an essential issue will be how to incorporate this institution into the overall framework of the United Nations. Although the issue of democratising international affairs ranks high on the agenda, the main thrust of the debate seems to be directed at the involvement of civil society actors. A recent example of this emphasis can be spotted in the United Nations advertising campaign in connection with the 2005 world summit, 'Everyone's a Delegate'. While the goal of stepping up civil society involvement in world affairs is, indeed, worth all support, one thing should not be forgotten: Anyone who wants to strengthen the position of the people in international relations needs to be aware of the fact that self-appointed actors, even if dedicated, can only under exceptional circumstances count on legitimacy comparable to that of elected representatives of broader constituencies.

In view of the current discourses on democracy deficit in international relations and cosmopolitan democracy, the observation that the involvement

---

84 Eliassen, K. (1998) 'Kjell Eliassen'. In Uecker, H. (ed.) *Die Zukunft der nordischen Zusammenarbeit: Bonner Botschaftervorträge*. Bonn: Bouvier, 34.

of Nordic parliamentarians in delegations to the United Nations has declined over the past four decades is clearly counter-intuitive. This development might be interpreted as a consequence of the fading of a specific type of Nordic democracy. More fundamentally, the decline illustrates Harold Nicolson's classical conclusion that 'democratic diplomacy has not as yet discovered its own formula'.[85] This review of parliamentarian participation in Nordic delegations to the General Assembly makes it safe to conclude that not even Nordic democracy provides the magical formula for democratic diplomacy. However, what 'Nordic democracy' in this context does demonstrate is a persistent effort on behalf of these member states to connect representatives of the people with the major institutions of global governance.

BIBLIOGRAPHY

Aarvik, E. (1982) [Presentation Speech on the occasion of the awarding of the Nobel Peace Prize for 1982, Oslo, December 10, 1982]. <http://nobelprize.org/nobel_prizes/peace/laureates/1982/press.html>.

Andersen, A. (1954) 'A Danish Socialist View on a Revision of the U.N. Charter', *Socialist International Information* 4, 719–22.

Assembly (1920) 'Report on the Relations between, and Respective Competence of, the Council and the Assembly: Amended and Adopted by the Assembly on December 7th, 1920'. *The Records of the First Assembly: Plenary Meetings*. Geneva: League of Nations.

Assembly (1936) *Records of the Seventeenth Ordinary Session of the Assembly*. Geneva: League of Nations.

Baehr, P. R. (1970) *The Role of a National Delegation in the General Assembly*. Occasional Paper 9. New York: Carnegie Endowment for International Peace.

Bailey, S. D. (1964) *The General Assembly of the United Nations: A Study of Procedure and Practice*. Rev. edn. New York: Praeger.

Berry, R. M. (1987) *American Foreign Policy and the Finnish Exception: Ideological Preferences and Wartime Realities*. Helsinki: SHS.

Bjereld, U. (1997) *Hjalmarsonaffären: Ett politiskt drama i tre akter*. Stockholm: Nerenius & Santérus.

Bjøl, E. (1983) *Hvem bestemmer? Studier i den udenrigspolitiske beslutningsproces*. Skrifter fra Dansk Udenrigspolitisk Institut 9. Copenhagen: Jurist- og Økonomforbundet.

[Cardoso-Report] (2004) *We the Peoples: Civil Society, the United Nations and Global Governance: Report of the Panel of Eminent Persons on United Nations-Civil Society Relations*. A/58/817. New York: United Nations.

Colban, E. (1961) *Stortinget og utenrikspolitikken*. Oslo: Universitetsforlaget.

Eduskunta. (1920) *Riksdagen, Handlingar* (Prop. 17, including Utskottets för utrikesärenden betänkande N:o 2 [= U.B.]).

Eliassen, K. (1998) 'Kjell Eliassen'. In Uecker, H. (ed) *Die Zukunft der nordischen Zusammenarbeit: Bonner Botschaftervorträge*. Bonn: Bouvier.

European Parliament (2005) 'Resolution P6_TA-PROV(2005)0237: Reform of the UN', Strasbourg. <http://www2.europarl.eu.int/omk/sipade2?PUBREF=-//EP//TEXT+TA+P6-TA-2005-0237+0+DOC+XML+V0//EN&L=EN&LEVEL=3&NAV=S&LSTDOC=Y>.

85 Nicolson, H. (1939) *Diplomacy*. London: Thornton Butterworth, 101.

Fink, T. (1961/1962) 'Danmark og FN', *Folketingstidende, Tillæg B* 113: col. 720–726.

Folketingstidende 1967/68 vol. 119.

Folketingstidende 1974/75 vol. 126.

Folketingstidende 1975/76 vol. 127.

Foreign Ministry (1995) *Yhdistyneiden kansakuntien yleiskokous* 50.

Frisch, H. (1945) 'Rapport over De forenede Nationers Konference i San Francisco'. in Frisch, H. & Husfeldt, E. (eds), *Rapporter fra de delegerede ved Forenede Nationers konference i San Francisco*. Copenhagen: Schultz.

General Assembly (1946) *Official Records* 1.

General Assembly (2000) *Official Records* 55 (55).

Goormaghtigh, J. (1979) *Parliaments and the United Nations: Dissemination of Information to Parliamentarians*. New York: UNITAR.

Götz, N.(2007) 'Sechzig Jahre und kein bisschen weise: Die Vereinten Nationen in der postnationalen Konstellation'. *Neue Politische Literatur* 52/1, 37–55.

Götz, N. (2008) 'Corporatism and Universalism in Foreign Affairs: The Case of Civil Society Inclusion in Swedish Delegations to the General Assembly of the United Nations'. In W. Rothholz and S. Berglund (eds) *Vom Symbol zur Realität: Studien zur politischen Kultur des Ostseeraums und des östlichen Europas*. Berlin: Wissenschafts-Verlag.

Götz, N. (2009) 'Government and Multipartisan Representation: The Finnish Composition of Delegations to the General Assembly of the United Nations'. In B. Wegner et al. (eds) *Finnland und Deutschland: Studien zur Geschichte im 19. und 20. Jahrhundert*. Hamburg: Kovac.

Grafström, S. (1989) *Anteckningar 1945–1954*. Handlingar 15. Stockholm: Kungl. Samfundet för utgivande av handskrifter rörande Skandinaviens historia.

Hambro, C.J. (1931) *Folkeforbundet og dets arbeide*. Oslo: Aschehoug.

Hambro, E. (1938) *Norge og Folkeforbundet*. Oslo: Tanum.

Hambro, E. (1965) 'Høyre: Utenrikspolitikk byggt på respekt for rett og rettferdighet'. In Heradstveit, P. Ø. (ed.) *Partiene og utenrikspolitikken*. Oslo: Aschehoug.

Hesselgren, Kerstin (1936) 'Sverige och Nationernas Förbund.' Speech held in Göteborg, September 1936. Gothenburg University Library, Women's History Collections A 14: Kerstin Hesselgren IIIc:5.

International Institute of Administrative Sciences and Unesco (1951) *National Administration and International Organization: A Comparative Survey of Fourteen Countries*. Brussels.

Jacobsen, K. & Mykletun, J. (1973) *FN – Norden – Norge*. Oslo: PRIO.

Jakobson, M. (1982) *Den finländska paradoxen: Linjer i Finlands utrikespolitik 1953–1965*. Helsinki: Schildt.

Jernström, F. (1994) *Sju liv*. Esbo: Schildt.

Johnsson, A. B. (2004) 'Statement by Mr. Anders B. Johnsson, Secretary General'. Geneva: Inter-parliamentary Union. <http://www.ipu.org/Un-e/sp-unga041004.pdf>.

Jones, S. S. (1969) *The Scandinavian States and the League of Nations*. Reprint. New York: Greenwood.

Karlsson, A. (1965) 'Parlamentarikerna i den svenska FN-delegationen'. Student paper, Stockholm: University.

Kettunen, P. (2009) 'The Nordic Model and International Labour Organisation'. In N. Götz and H. Haggrén (eds) *Regional Cooperation and International Organisations: The Nordic Model in Transnational*. London: Routledge.

Kissling, C. (2005) 'Repräsentativ-parlamentarische Entwürfe globaler Demokratie-gestaltung im Laufe der Zeit: Eine rechtspolitische Ideengeschichte'. *Forum historiae iuris* 9, <http://www.forhistiur.de/zitat/0502kissling.htm>.

Knoll, G. (1931) *Der deutsche Regierungsentwurf zu einer Völkerbundsatzung vom April 1919: Zugleich Betrachtungen zur Völkerbundsverfassung und zu ihrer Reform*. Leipzig: Weicher.

Laatikainen, K. V. (2003) 'Norden's Eclipse: The Impact of the European Union's

Common Foreign and Security Policy on the Nordic Group in the United Nations'. *Cooperation and Conflict* 38, 409–441.

Lange, C. L. (1937) 'De nordiske land i det internasjonale politiske samarbeid'. *Nordens kalender* 8 (1937), 20–36.

Lange, Halvard (1947) 'Internasjonalt samarbeid mellom nasjonene'. Foreign Ministry, Oslo, Halvard Lange's archive, vol. 15.

Larsen, K. (1976) *Forsvar og Folkeforbund: En studie i Venstres og Det Konservative Folkepartis forsvarspolitiske meningsdannelse 1918–1922.* Jysk Selskab for Historie, Skrifter 31. Århus: Universitetsforlaget.

Lindström, Ulla (1947) 'Kvinnor i FN'. National Archives, Stockholm, Ulla Lindström's archive, vol. 7.

Miller, D. H. (1928) *The Drafting of the Covenant*, vol. 2. New York: Putnam's Sons.

Moltke, K. (1961). 'Om partier, F.N. delegation, overbevisning og afstemning'. *Information* (10 August).

Morgenbladet, 26 April 1961.

Munch, P. (1923) 'Les États neutres et le Pacte de la Société des Nations'. In Munch, P. (ed.) *Les origines et l'œuvre de la Société des Nations*, vol. 1. Copenhagen: Gyldendal.

Munch, P. (1963) *Erindringer*, vol. 4: *1918–1924: Freden, Genforeningen og de første Efterkrigsaar.* København: Busck.

Nicolson, H. (1939) *Diplomacy.* London: Thornton Butterworth.

Ny Tid 22 November 1946.

Parliamentary Assembly (2004) 'Resolution 1373 (2004): Strengthening of the United Nations'. Strasbourg: Council of Europe. <http://assembly.coe.int/Documents/AdoptedText/ta04/ERES1373.htm>.

Parliamentary Assembly (2006) 'Resolution 1476: Parliamentary Dimension of the United Nations'. Strasbourg: Parliamentary Assembly of the Council of Europe. <http://assembly.coe.int/Main.asp?link=/Documents/AdoptedText/ta06/ERES1476.htm>

Pedersen, A. B. (1954) 'Nordisk Fredsforbunds kongres'. *Freds-Bladet* 63, 59–61.

Päivän Sanomat, 12 September 1959.

Rechendorff, J (1948) Memorandum of 16 April 1948, National Archives, Copenhagen, Foreign Ministry 1946–72, 119.D.9.a.

Riksdagens protokoll, Första Kammaren, Nr. 32, (1945).

Riksdagens protokoll, Motioner (U 21), (1999/2000).

Riksdagens protokoll UMJU1, (2002/2003) 'Johannesburg – FN:s världstoppmöte om hållbar utveckling: Sammansatta utrikes-, miljö- och jordbruksutskottets betänkande.'

Rusk, D. (1955) 'Parliamentary Diplomacy: Debate vs. Negotiation'. *World Affairs Interpreter* 26, 121–138.

Schücking, W. & Wehberg, H. (1924) *Die Satzung des Völkerbundes.* 2nd rev. edn. Berlin: Vahlen.

Stortingstidende 1920.

Stortingstidende 1948.

Stortingstidende 1973/1974.

Tennyson, A. (1842) 'Locksley Hall'. *Poems, vol. 1.* London: Moxon (available at <http://eir.library.utoronto.ca/rpo/display/poem2161.html>).

Three Commissions (1920) 'Draft of a Convention Respecting an International Juridical Organization: Drawn up by the Three Commissions Appointed by the Governments of Sweden, Denmark and Norway, with an Explanatory Statement Extracted from the Report of the Swedish Commission'. In Advisory Committee of Jurists (ed.) *Documents Presented to the Committee Relating to Existing Plans for the Establishment of a Permanent Court of International Justice.* Harrow: Permanent Court of International Justice.

Törnudd, K. (1982) 'Kunskap om utrikespolitik'. *Ord och handling: Utrikespolitiska uppsatser.* Helsinki: Schildt.

United Nations (2002) *List of Delegations to the Fifty-seventh Session of the General Assembly*. ST/SG/SER.C/L.597. New York: United Nations.

United Nations (2009) *List of Delegations to the Sixty-fourth Session of the General Assembly*. ST/SG/SER.C/L.618. New York: United Nations.

Wachtmeister, Wilhelm (1963) Memorandum 7 August 1963, Foreign Ministry Archive, Stockholm, HP 48 DD, vol. 6.

Wickman, A. (1967) *Frihet är det bästa ting*. Helsinki: Söderström.

Winther, C. (1965) 'Vi er et særtilfælde i FN'. *Information* (4 May).

Winther, C. (1966) 'Hvis vor FN-politik skal være effektiv: Ambassadøren bør beklæde formandsposten'. *Berlingske Tidende* (10 June).

Zilliacus, J. (1978) *En bit av det stora äpplet*. Helsinki: Söderström.

Zimmern, S. A. (1939) *The League of Nations and the Rule of Law 1818–1935*. 2nd rev. edn. London: Macmillan.

Zulueta, T. d. (2004) 'Strengthening of the United Nations'. Strasbourg: Council of Europe, Parliamentary Assembly, Political Affairs Committee. <http://assembly.coe.int/Documents/WorkingDocs/doc04/EDOC10120.htm>.

Zulueta, T. d. (2005) 'Parliamentary Dimension of the United Nations.' Document 10771. Strasbourg: Council of Europe, Parliamentary Assembly, Political Affairs Committee. < http://assembly.coe.int//Main.asp?link=http://assembly.coe.int/Documents/WorkingDocs/Doc05/EDOC10771.htm>.

Contributors

Norbert Götz is Professor at the Institute of Contemporary History, Södertörn University, Sweden. His wide range of research interests includes political culture, international relations, democracy, welfare state, nationalism, peace and conceptual history.

Peter Hallberg is Assistant Professor in the Department of Political Science at Stockholm University and Eva Österberg Pro Futura Fellow at the Swedish Collegium for Advanced Study.

Jan Hecker-Stampehl has been working as a research assistant and lecturer in Nordic history at the Department for Northern European Studies at Humboldt University Berlin since 2005. He took his PhD in Modern History at the same university in 2009 with a thesis on debates about integration and Nordic identity in Northern Europe during the Second World War.

Ruth Hemstad, PhD, is Head of Section in the Department of Scholarship and Collections at the National Library of Norway in Oslo. Her PhD-thesis (2008) concerned Nordic cooperation, Scandinavianism, and the dissolution of the Swedish-Norwegian union in 1905.

Petri Koikkalainen is University Lecturer of Political Science at the University of Lapland, Finland. His research interests include political theory, philosophy, conceptual history and the history of political thought.

Jussi Kurunmäki is Assistant Professor in the Department of Political Science at Stockholm University. His main fields of research include parliamentary democratization, nationalism, theories of democracy, history of ideas, political rhetoric, and conceptual history.

Carl Marklund is Assistant Professor at the Department of Political Science and Contemporary History at AGH-University of Technology and Science, Krakow, and a post-doctoral researcher at the Network for European Studies, University of Helsinki.

Jeppe Nevers is Assistant Professor of History at the University of Southern Denmark. His field of research and teaching is modern Danish and European history, with an emphasis on politics and ideas.

Peter Stadius holds a PhD (2005) in history from the University of Helsinki. Since 2006 he is the acting University Lecturer in Nordic Studies at the same university. His research interests include the historical images and the outside stereotypes of the Nordic region.

Johan Strang recieved his PhD in philosophy from the University of Helsinki in the spring of 2010 on a dissertation on the legacy of the Uppsala School in philosophy. He works as a researcher at the Centre for Nordic Studies at the University of Helsinki.

Index

STUDIA FENNICA ETHNOLOGICA

Making and Breaking of Borders
Ethnological Interpretations,
Presentations, Representations
Edited by Teppo Korhonen,
Helena Ruotsala & Eeva Uusitalo
Studia Fennica Ethnologica 7
2003

Memories of My Town
The Identities of Town Dwellers and
Their Places in Three Finnish Towns
Edited by Anna-Maria Åström,
Pirjo Korkiakangas & Pia Olsson
Studia Fennica Ethnologica 8
2004

Passages Westward
Edited by Maria Lähteenmäki
& Hanna Snellman
Studia Fennica Ethnologica 9
2006

Defining Self
Essays on emergent identities in Russia
Seventeenth to Nineteenth Centuries
Edited by Michael Branch
Studia Fennica Ethnologica 10
2009

Touching Things
Ethnological Aspects of Modern
Material Culture
Edited by Pirjo Korkiakangas,
Tiina-Riitta Lappi & Heli Niskanen
Studia Fennica Ethnologica 11
2009

Gendered Rural Spaces
Edited by Pia Olsson & Helena
Ruotsala
Studia Fennica Ethnologica 12
2009

STUDIA FENNICA FOLKLORISTICA

Creating Diversities
Folklore, Religion and the Politics
of Heritage
Edited by Anna-Leena Siikala,
Barbro Klein & Stein R. Mathisen
Studia Fennica Folkloristica 14
2004

Pertti J. Anttonen
Tradition through Modernity
Postmodernism and the Nation-State
in Folklore Scholarship
Studia Fennica Folkloristica 15
2005

Narrating, Doing, Experiencing
Nordic Folkloristic Perspectives
Edited by Annikki Kaivola-Bregenhøj,
Barbro Klein & Ulf Palmenfelt
Studia Fennica Folkloristica 16
2006

Mícheál Briody
The Irish Folklore Commission
1935–1970
History, ideology, methodology
Studia Fennica Folkloristica 17
2007

STUDIA FENNICA HISTORICA

Medieval History Writing and Crusading
Ideology
Edited by Tuomas M. S. Lehtonen
& Kurt Villads Jensen with Janne
Malkki and Katja Ritari
Studia Fennica Historica 9
2005

Moving in the USSR
Western anomalies and Northern
wilderness
Edited by Pekka Hakamies
Studia Fennica Historica 10
2005

Derek Fewster
Visions of Past Glory
Nationalism and the Construction
of Early Finnish History
Studia Fennica Historica 11
2006

Modernisation in Russia since 1900
Edited by Markku Kangaspuro
& Jeremy Smith
Studia Fennica Historica 12
2006

Seija-Riitta Laakso
Across the Oceans
Development of Overseas Business
Information Transmission 1815–1875
Studia Fennica Historica 13
2007

Industry and Modernism
Companies, Architecture and Identity
in the Nordic and Baltic Countries
during the High-Industrial Period
Edited by Anja Kervanto Nevanlinna
Studia Fennica Historica 14
2007

Charlotta Wolff
Noble conceptions of politics in
eighteenth-century Sweden
(ca 1740–1790)
Studia Fennica Historica 15
2008

Sport, Recreation and Green Space
in the European City
Edited by Peter Clark, Marjaana Niemi
& Jari Niemelä
Studia Fennica Historica 16
2009

Rhetorics of Nordic Democracy
Edited by Jussi Kurunmäki
& Johan Strang
Studia Fennica Historica 17
2010

STUDIA FENNICA LINGUISTICA

Minna Saarelma-Maunumaa
Edhina Ekogidho – Names as Links
The Encounter between African and
European Anthroponymic Systems
among the Ambo People in Namibia
Studia Fennica Linguistica 11
2003

Minimal reference
The use of pronouns in Finnish
and Estonian discourse
Edited by Ritva Laury
Studia Fennica Linguistica 12
2005

Antti Leino
On Toponymic Constructions
as an Alternative to Naming Patterns
in Describing Finnish Lake Names
Studia Fennica Linguistica 13
2007

Talk in interaction
Comparative dimensions
Edited by Markku Haakana,
Minna Laakso & Jan Lindström
Studia Fennica Linguistica 14
2009

Planning a new standard language
Finnic minority languages meet
the new millennium
Edited by Helena Sulkala
& Harri Mantila
Studia Fennica Linguistica 15
2010

STUDIA FENNICA LITTERARIA

Changing Scenes
Encounters between European
and Finnish Fin de Siècle
Edited by Pirjo Lyytikäinen
Studia Fennica Litteraria 1
2003

Women's Voices
Female Authors and Feminist Criticism
in the Finnish Literary Tradition
Edited by Lea Rojola & Päivi
Lappalainen
Studia Fennica Litteraria 2
2007

Metaliterary Layers in Finnish Literature
Edited by Samuli Hägg, Erkki Sevänen
& Risto Turunen
Studia Fennica Litteraria 3
2009

STUDIA FENNICA ANTHROPOLOGICA

On Foreign Ground
Moving between Countries and
Categories
Edited by Minna Ruckenstein
& Marie-Louise Karttunen
Studia Fennica Anthropologica 1
2007

Beyond the Horizon
Essays on Myth, History, Travel and
Society
Edited by Clifford Sather & Timo
Kaartinen
Studia Fennica Anthropologica 2
2008

www.ingramcontent.com/pod-product-compliance
Lightning Source LLC
Chambersburg PA
CBHW081736270326
41932CB00020B/3295